SCIENCE IN GITA VED AND PURAN

Hidden Science in Ved, Puran

DR. B.G. MATAPURKAR

INDIA • SINGAPORE • MALAYSIA

ISBN 979-8-89498-859-7

विज्ञानम् ब्रम्हेति व्यजानात् । विज्ञानात् खलु इमानि भूतानि जायन्ते ।
विज्ञानेन जातानि जीवन्ति। विज्ञानम् प्रयन्त्यभिविशन्तीति ॥ (तैत्तरीयोपं भृगु **3-1-5).**

Vidnyanam brahmeti vyajanat I vidnyanat khalu Imani jayante I
Vidnyanen jatani jivanti I vidnyanam prayantyabhivishantiti II
Taittariya Upanishad Bhrigu. 3-1-5.

The prime objective of the RIGVEDA is the subject of science.

First VEDA

World's Oldest written Scientific treatise in

Obscure and symbolic Rhymes

CREATORS' CREATIVITY IS THE CREATION OF NATURE

MORTALS ARE THE BYPRODUCT OF THE CREATION

ANY MORTAL WHEN SUCCESSFUL IN CREATIVITY

HE ACHIEVES A PLACE WITH THE CREATOR

"RIGVED "

(See RIBHU RISHI'S achievements in the book)

SHORT SUMMARY OF SANSKRIT LITERATURE

1. Ved 2. Smriti 3. Darshan 4. Puran 5. Gita

1. Ved: Rigved, Yajurved, Atharv Ved, Samved.

3. Darshan: Nyaya Shastra, Uttar Mimansa, Poorva Mimansa, Vaisheshik Shastra, Sankhya, Yog shastra.Puran

4. 18-Puran

Ved. Vedang and Upved.

Vedang: Vyakran, Jyotish, Nirukt, Chhand, Kalpsutra.

Upved: Arth-ved, Dhanur-ved, Gandharv-ved, aayur-ved

HIGHLIGHTS OF RIGVEDA

Sanskrit was not taught to Ignorant in India, that without the Proper knowledge of the creation, it will be interpreted in wrong direction, like in modern times, comparing the vast ocean of knowledge with religious faith.

Rigveda is the oldest literary monument of human civilization; UNESCO has included it in the World Heritage list.
Rigved believes in Yadnya i.e. hard purposeful actions or Yadnya-karma.
What a wonderful concept of Rigved on this subject:

अधारयन्त वहनयोस्भजन्त सुकृ त्यया भागंदेवेशु यज्ञियम्
Adharyant vahanayosmjant sukru tyaya Bhagdeveshu yadniyam II8II
Rigveda. 1-20-8

Those who perform yajnas (**यज्ञ**) duty with honesty and expertise enjoy their share of happiness and **rejoice among the divinities**. To emphasize this an example of Rishi Ribhu is quoted:

Rigveda believed in the highest estimation for research and development – YADNYA KARMA. (A mortal Rishi, named 'Ribhu' became immortal as he divided one Chamas Patra (A live Container) into four CHAMAS patra, for Yadnya (**Research** and development). He developed cows and horse from this live container. Hence came to the level of Devata).

This science was utilised during MAHABHARAT era by Rishi Ved Vyas in creating 100 sons for Gandhari wife of Dhritarashtra, from aborted embryo. Because of this knowledge and regular use of such technique he confidently left for his work informing that do not open the containers for two years. (see birth of **Kauravas** in Aadiparv of Mahabharat)

About Rishi Ribhu and his two brothers Vibhvan and Vaj in Ved:

शमी तरणित्वेन वाघतो मर्तासः सन्तो अमृतत्वमानशुः। सौधन्वना ऋभवः सूरचक्षसः संवत्सरे समपृच्यन्त धीतिभिः

Shami taranitvena vaghato martasah santoamrutatvamanshuh I Sodhanvana ribhava soorchakshasah samvatsare sampruchyanta The oldest civilization on Earth dwell on Bharatiya Subcontinent, which was nick named later by invaders to their advantage. The civilization developed independently from the world with the vast ocean of Sanskrit Literature, written during different eras of oldest literary monument of human civilization. Whatever initiates in Cosmos perishes someday. So was the fate of the Sanskrit civilization. Everything repeats in cycles; hence it will certainly surface again.dhitibhih || 4 II Rigveda 1-110-4

During Rigvedic era, a female named Sudhanva had three children, Ṛibhukṣan, Vibhvan and Vāja. These three persons form the Ṛibhus as mentioned in Rigveda, 1st Maṇḍala, 16th Anuvāka, 111th Sūkta. The Ṛubhus, brilliant as the Sun, became connected with the ceremonies.

इदाह्नः पीतिमुत वो मदं धुर्न ऋते श्रान्तस्य सख्याय देवाः। ते नूनमस्मे ऋभवो वसूनि तृतीये अस्मिन्त्सवने दधात

Idanhah pitimut vo madam dhurna rute shrantasya sakhyay devah I te nunamasme rubhava vasooni tritiye asmintsavanedadhat ||११||

Rigveda.4-33-11

Those who perform timely challenging work, become rich others remain poor. Rishi Rubhus, creators, the holy men bring you soma drink to celebrate and enjoy. **The divines extend**

a hand of friendship after being evaluated for hard work and sacrifice. May the Rubhus bring us, in truth, wealth in the third session of yajna. (Yajna word be taken in its true meaning – **Yajna = यज्ञ,** as Research and development see authors work elsewhere).

AUTHORS PUBLICATIONS

श्रीमद्भागवतगीता
एक वैज्ञानिक
सार
बाळकृष्ण मातापुरकर
Exploration of Science in
SHRI MADBHAGWAT GITA
DR. B. G. MATAPURKAR
SCIENCE IN GITA
SONG OF
SCIENCE
SHRIMAD BHAGWAT GITA
DR. B.G. MATAPURKAR
SCIENTIFIC PERSPECTIVE
OF UNIVERSAL ETERNAL
DHARM & RELIGION
ANALYTICAL THOUGHT BY
DR. B.G. MATAPURKAR
स्वातंत्रता
सम्राज्ञी

The poem mentioned here is relevant from the 'religion' point of view which divides Humans in sects, faith, group, etc. This poem is written immediately after the assassination of Prime Minister Indira Gandhi. It was followed by the mass killing of peoples of a community. It is reproduced here. The author feels it is relevant in the perspective of Rigvedic science.

HUMANITY

Rise O' Human above religion,

Controlling thy passion,

For the Nation.

That made your stance possible,

Every Cell you possess with Pride,

Is made of National Soil in stride,

Thence control your emotions for a while.

If any call of a different function,

like different religions,

behaves Challenging your existence as a Human,

Rise o' Human above religion,

As Cells make you Human,

Controlling the passion,

The religions too, make Nation,

And survive for the Nation!!!

These maps are from Avantiputra7 - Own work by Avantiputra7. Timings are approximate. Time calculated is different by different authors.

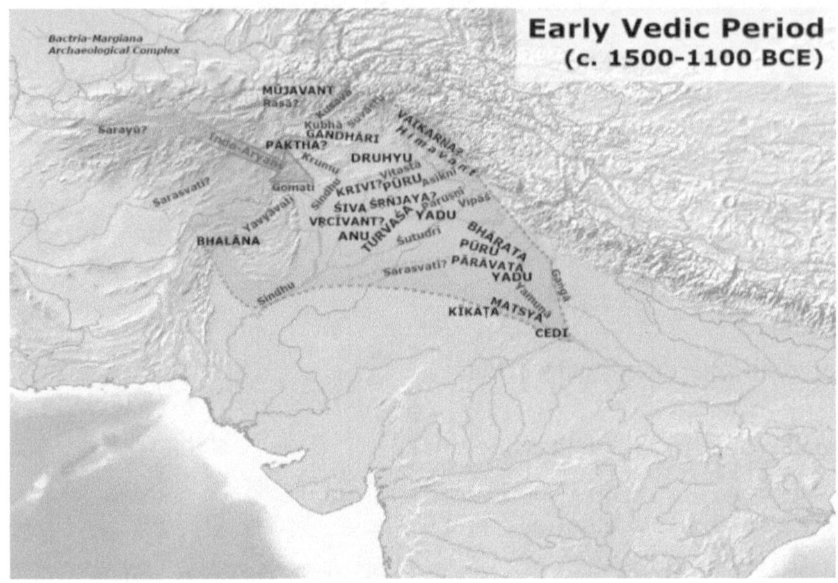

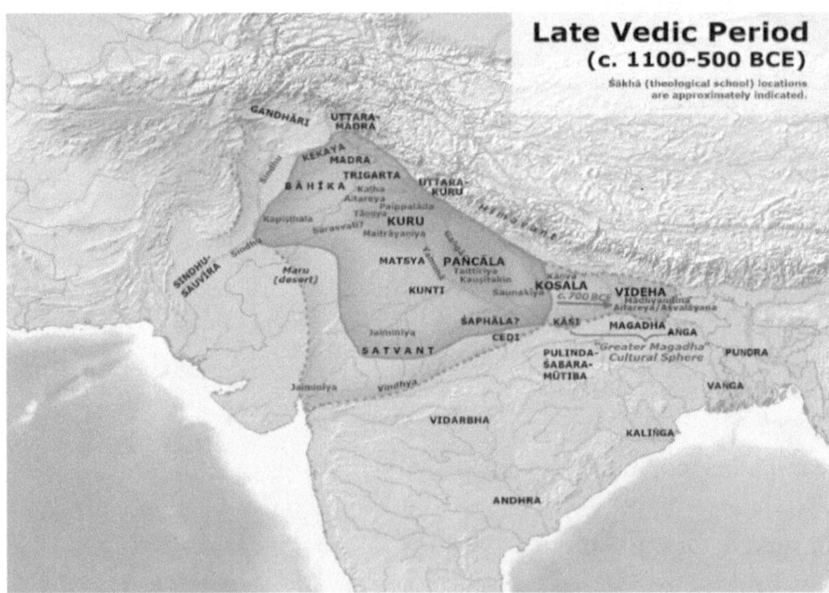

Timings during Vedic period

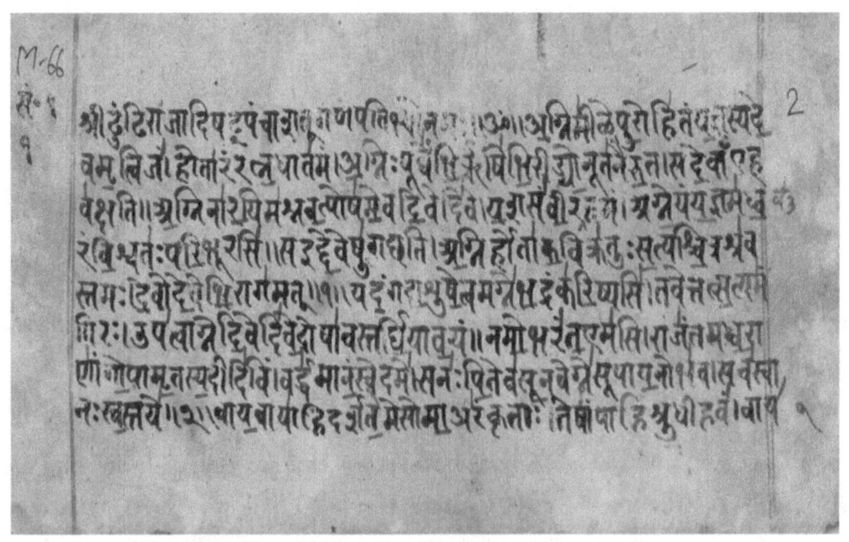

Source of above images is from Wikipedia.

AIMS AND OBJECTIVES

After the renaissance in the west, the discovery of Sanskrit literature and the history of culture of Sanskrit speaking civilization, was discovered in the latter part of the eighteenth century, after invasion of country of Bharat varsha. Only after that Sanskrit was exposed to western society. Rigveda is the oldest knowledge in the history of the modern world. When science was unknown in the west the Sanskrit Speaking civilization was highly developed. The science is scripted in Veda and Purana literature. **In the opinion of Ella Wheeler Wilcox, India is the land of VEDAS. It contains the idea of the perfect life, Scientific achievements like Electricity, Electronics, and Airship, all known to seers of Vedic India.**

In this book, an attempt is made to explore only the Scientific achievements of Sanskrit Speaking Civilization scripted in Rigveda, and the same is brought to light with authentication by appropriate VED Richas (ऋचा) or Vedic stanzas. Therefore, the book reading gets partially interrupted. Even though the Rigveda and Sanskrit **literature stresses rituality and liberation (Moksha- मोक्ष), which is the primary aim of living beings, there is obscure, hidden, and enigmatic revelation of science in** the Sanskrit Vedic literature. The same is brought to light, especially for the younger generation of the entire humanity. Many scientific achievements were much more advanced. All need to be investigated for human benefits. The fact of such science must be researched. It is equally true that the Moksha is spiritual but essential for the incarnation as human. It has been scientifically analysed and stressed in the book.

Unfortunately, the hidden, symbolic, enigmatic, and obscure science of Vedic literature, is understood when modern science steps on and reveals that science to the materially engrossed modern civilization. Vidnyan (विशेष

ज्ञान विज्ञान, - special knowledge) or science was an integral part of Sanskrit civilization. It was much more advanced than modern science. Basically, "Spirituality" is a gift of Sanskrit Speaking civilization to the entire humanity. It is PARA Science. Modern science is still investigating it and will be successful shortly.

The author would like to provide some excerpts from Vedas that provide clues to deep scientific concepts hidden within the Vedic Richas - ऋचा. This is only possible when one shuns the idea that the Vedas are religious and unscientific. The obscurity of statements in Mantras which are enigmatic too, is responsible for the belief and twisting of meaning of such Mantras by western scholars and dittoed by modern Indian authors. The author on analysing the fact that in Mahabharat 5 sons were born through two females while 101 children born from single mother. (Kunti and Madari gave birth to 5 Pandavas while 100 sons-Kauravas, were born to one female Gandhari, wife of blind king Dhritarashtra). How this is scientifically possible? On exploration it was detected that the scientific description exists in the Bhagwatam - न इति, by Rishi Vyas. Details are published in author's previous publications. Hundred and one children were developed in an artificial uterus from the cells of aborted embryo of Gandhari. The time involved in the process was total four years (2 years for arrested pregnancy and 2 years for initiation of germination and developmental growth of foetuses in the artificial devices. All needs a scientific explanation which is provided in the book. The scientific explanation needs authentication, which is provided by the appropriate Richas - ऋचा, from the literature of Vedas and puranas. The authentication must be scientifically analysed and compared with the modern science. The same has been attempted in the book.

The subject of science is continuously undergoing evolution and hence the scientific achievements also are subject to change. Like shape of Earth was flat but later shape of Earth became round. The Sun used to rotate around the Earth later with scientific establishment of truth Earth rotating around the Sun. All these changes faced the wrath of custodians of religion. But such modern truths were known to Vedic Rishis and Sages thousands of years back. But no researcher ever faced the wrath. Rishis believed that the scientific achievements are never perfect and not reached to ultimate success. They are subject to change. Hence Rishis always used the word NETI i.e., NA ITI. This means it is not the end, and the ultimate end has still not been achieved. Future generations must investigate and research out the facts more appropriately. What a wonderful concept! The authentication must be with the appropriate Richas. All this was a great research and analytical challenge for the author. It was a herculean task and needed challenging work attempts.

The Sanskrit literature summarily translated and described, is full of spirituality, religion, and para-science in mind. Most translations available are with religious tinge. It needs to be rectified. Gradually, modern science has started believing and accepting the subject of para science. In the past, this was considered as absurd and unbelievable, because of the unavailability of scientific proof. Sanskrit-speaking civilizations always believed in spirituality. Several scientific explorations have been achieved by Rishis and Sages of the past. Author feels this is due to the Yogic practices and silent dynamism of meditation practices. How the meditation technique developed has been explained in the book.

CONTENTS

AUTHOR'S OPINION

Rigveda is the oldest written literature on earth. The knowledge is preserved for many, many years. Unfortunately, in the recent past, it is opined to be the useless poetic disposition of religious nature. It is meaningless literature just for "time-pass and is written by unscholarly people. If one feels there is a deep meaning in every stanza of Rigveda, then only one may feel to explore it with a purpose. Otherwise, no one would like to look at it. Interestingly, Rigveda discusses the manifestation of Nature. It explores the manifestation of Stars, and the Sun but in an obscure manner. Rigveda has discussed the cause of the manifestation of the cosmos (Brahmanda – ब्रम्हांड). Readers must explore this book and read 'RICHAS'- (ऋचा) Mantras of Rigveda provided for the authentication and truthfulness of derivations in an analytical manner. I feel privileged and fortunate to write such a deep meaning scientific and the oldest literature available on earth.

Vedic literature is obscure, symbolic, enigmatic, and camouflaged but the scientific matter is deep-rooted and hidden in stanzas. Rigveda is massively scripted. It has 1028 SUKTA and Mantra or stanzas are 10552. My interest was awakened when I published books in Marathi and English language on the Scientific exploration of the Shrimad Bhagwadgita. At the same time after my success in research on adult Autogenous tissue Stem cells. This research establishes the regeneration of tissues and organs in the body using the body's own tissue stem cells, which are normally responsible for the repair and healing of tissues injured during normal wear and tear during health and disease. It is based on my hypothesis, registered copyright 1994. Adult stem cell research work received an international patent from the U.S. A. in 2002 and 2003, in the name of Maulana Azad Medical College, New Delhi, under Delhi University. In the Mahabharat epic, one female named Gandhari gave birth to 101 children – i.e., 100 sons, KAURAV. But in the same epic, five "Pandavas" were born from two females named 'Kunti' and 'Madri'. Obviously, my curiosity forced me to explore if any scientific explanation exists in the said epic. To my surprise, a great scientific explanation in detail is present in the in Aadi-Parva chapter of the epic. Scientific descriptions as per modern science, about the birth of 101 children to one female, exists in my scientific research articles in peer-reviewed journals and in the book "Exploration Science in Bhagwadgita", Mahi Publication. (Exploration of science in Shrimad Bhagvadgita, analytical study by Dr. B.G.Matapurkar,1st Ed, 2020, Mahi publication, Ahemdabad).

I presented the scientific details about the birth of 101 children in one of the international conferences, on Stem cells. It became a Press Trust of India (PTI) news that spread all over the world. This encouraged me to explore science in RIGVED too. Thus, this book is in your hand. The reader may refer to the book "Song of science Shrimad Bhagwadgita" Notion Press, India, Singapore, Malaysia. 2020, 1st edition, 2020.

Rigveda discusses the place KURUKSHETRA.

इळआयास् त्वा पदे वयं नाभा पृथिव्या अधिजातवेदो नि धीमह्य् अग्ने हव्याय वोळ्हवे||

Iirluayas tva pade vayam Nabha prithivya adhijatavedo ni dhimahya agre havyaya volruhave II Rigveda. 3-29-4.

Oh! Agni, we place you down to shine, in the best place (नाभा पृथिव्या) a central place on earth, (PRITHVI) in the region made by Gods (देवनिर्मितं), of ILAVRAT, on an auspicious day. This place has rivers called DRISHADVATI (दृशद्वत्ा), APAYA, and SARASWATI (See map, page 9 and 10).

Manu smriti mantra endorse this as follows:

सरस्वतीदृशद्वत्योर्देवनद्योर्यदन्तरम् । तं देवनिर्मितं देशं ब्रह्मावर्तं प्रचक्षते ॥ १७ ॥
sarasvatīdṛśadvatyordevanadyoryadantaram |
taṃ devanirmitaṃ deśaṃ brahmāvartaṃ pracakṣate || 17 || -

The region lies between the divine rivers Sarasvati and Dṛaṣhadvatī- दृशद्वत्यो - (सरस्वती दृशद्वत्योर्देवनद्यो). Sanctioned by Gods (देवनिर्मितं). The place is called 'Brahmāvarta' II17II Manusmriti, 2- 17.

ILA VRATA is a region of the SARASWATI and DRISHADWATI rivers. Later, the place was named as KHANDAVA and KURUKSHETRA. It is the best and most principal place on earth. It is the place of King BHARAT (India derives its name as "Bharatvarsha" form the name Bharat -king. Varsha means region or country).

स तु वस्त्राण्यध पेशनानि वसानो अग्निर्नाभाप्रथिव्याः |अरुषो जातः पद इळायाः पुरोहितो राजन्यक्षीह देवान

Sa tu aavastranyadha peshanani vasano agnirnabhapraiyhivyah I arusho jatah pada ilayah purohito rajanyakshih devan || Rigveda. 10- 1- 6.

AGNI with golden hue and brightness, establish yourself at the naval/umbilical region of earth (र्नाभाप्थिव्याः).

य इमे रोदसी उभे अहमिन्द्रमतुष्टवम | विश्वामित्रस्यरक्षति बरह्मेदं भारतं जनम

Ya ime rodasi ubhe ahamindramtushtavam I vishavamitrasya rakshti brahmedam bharatam Janam II12II Rigveda. 3- 53-12.

It is surprising to note that humans have not composed the Vedas. The composition is APOURUSHEYA (अपौरुषेय). How can the Veda be APOURUSHEYA i.e., not written by humans? On analysis of Sanskrit literature following facts are worth the pondering: -

Rigveda very clearly indicates that the Ved is POURUSHEYA i.e., humanly composed. The following Mantra is from Rigveda 1, 71, 3

यज्ञेन वाचः पदावीयमायन तामन्वविन्दन्निषुप्रविष्टाम I तामाभ्रत्या वयदधुः पुरुत्रा तां सप्तरेभा अभि सं नवन्ते II3II Rigveda 1-71-3.

Yadnyena vachah padaviymayan tamanvavindanishrashu pravishatam I tamabhratya vayadadhuh purutra tam saptarebha abhi sam navante ||3|| Rigveda 1-71-3.

With YADNYA- KARMA or hard work and research, a person gets Knowledge, GYAN (DNYAN). A higher state of knowledge (PADVI) is bestowed. All Vedas, Gayatri, etc. are composed and distributed. Spiritually elevated, realized RISHIS are responsible for such a composition.

It is interesting to note the following Suktas, where Rishis and Sages are depicted with each Sukta of various Mandals of Rigveda: -

The Samhitā of the Rig Veda, the Rig-Vedic Compilation, is in ten Books or Mandals. It has in all 1028 Hymns or Sūktas with 10552 verses or Richās. The classification in terms of Mandalas is based on assigning Mandalas to a single Rishi or family of Rishis. The second Mandala goes by Gritsamada, the third Vishwāmitra, fourth Vāmadeva, fifth by the house of Atri, the sixth Bharadwāj, seventh Vashishtha. The first, eighth and tenth Mandalas are collections of Sūktas by various Rishis. The ninth Book devoted to a single God, Soma, and the hymns authored by different Rishis. The Sūktas addressed to Agni in each of these Mandalas.

Why is such an allotment assigned? Do they indicate the contribution of such Rishis questioning the Apourusheya origin of Veda?

The VEDIC knowledge is research-based. It is in UPANISHADs:

तस्माव्दा एतस्मादात्मन आकाश संभूतः I आकाशाद्वायुः I वायोरग्निः I अग्नेरापः I अद्भ्य पृथ्विः I पृथिव्या औषधयः I औषधिभ्यो S अन्नम् I अन्नाद् पुरूषः

Tasmadva etasmadatman Aakash sambhutah I Aakashadvayuh I vayoragnih I agnerapah I adabhya prithvih I Prithivya Aushadhayah I

Aushadibhyo annam I Annad purushah II (Taittariya Upnishad Brahmanandavalli, Anuvak 1 Mantra 2).

The mantra explains the sequence of manifestation of Nature and living beings including humans. This is after research and hard work (YADNYA-KARMA). Obviously, this is possible by human beings only. In fact, RISHIS, Sages, and MUNIS of Sanskrit Speaking Civilization were comparable to modern-day scientists. They composed the knowledge in rhyme in Mantra form. **The written book knowledge indicates one more fact, that the knowledge must be there before the script of the Rigvedic era. Hence, later included in the composition.**

There are Vedic prayers and Shanti Mantras available in Veda and Purana. These indicate that the tradition was for the Teacher and the disciple (or GURU and SHISHYA) must study together and develop knowledge, both and all be knowledgeable. VIZ:

ओम सहनाववतु । सहनोभुनक्तु। सहवीर्यं करवा वहै । तेजस्विनाव धीतमस्तु । मा विद्विषावहै। ओम शान्तिः शान्तिः शान्तिः

Om sahanavvatu I sahanobhunaktu I sahaveeryaam karava vahe I tejasvinav dhitamastu I maa vidvishavhei I om shantihih shantihi shantihi II TAITTARIYA Upanishad, Brahmananda Valli, Anuvak 1, Mantra 1.

All these narrations in Veda and Purana indicate that the VEDA is not APOURUSHEYA or is in fact written by Sages, composed by RISHIS, and Saints i.e., the Scientists, and analysts of Sanskrit Speaking Civilization.

Before each SUKTA the information about the Rishi's name, involved in the written knowledge in different mandals. Every Sukta has the following details attached Rishi, Subject, Chhanda, and Swara: (See table above) for example, Rigveda 1-1-1 see the detail:

Ṛṣi (sage/seer): Vaiśvāmitraḥ; **विश्वामित्र.**

Devatā (deity/subject-matter): agniḥ; **अग्नि.**

Chandas (meter): gāyatrī; गायित्रि.

Svara (tone/note): Swar; स्वर.

This indicates the Veda are composed by Sages and Rishis, hence not APOURUSHEYA.

Rigveda has 10 Mandals. The following table explains various Suktas and Mantras in different Mandals: -

*Mandal - 1 (Total Sukta 191 - Total Mantra 2006). Rishi Vishva mitra.

Mandal - 2 (Total Sukta 43 - Total Mantra 429), Rishi Gritsamada

Mandal - 3 (Total Sukta 62 - Total Mantra 617) Rishi Vishvamitra.

Mandal - 4 (Total Sukta 58 - Total Mantra 589). Rishi Vamdeva.

Mandal - 5 (Total Sukta 87 - Total Mantra 727). Rishi Atri.

Mandal - 6 (Total Sukta 75 - Total Mantra 765). Rishi Angirasa

Mandal - 7 (Total Sukta 104 - Total Mantra 841). Rishi Vasishtha

*Mandal - 8 (Total Sukta 103 - Total Mantra 1716). Rishi Kanva

Mandal - 9 (Total Sukta 114 - Total Mantra 1108). Rishi Kashyap.

*Mandal - 10 (Total Sukta 191 - Total Mantra 1754).

** The first, eighth, and tenth Mandalas are collections of Sūktas by various Rishis. Hence rishi name is not in 10th Sukta, presented in this table.

Rigveda is an established identity of Sanskrit Speaking civilization. It is the oldest written evidence of human knowledge. Fortunately, it was categorized, as useless, orthodox, and religious hence probably, not destroyed and has reached us. Otherwise, it could have been destroyed too, by greedy invaders into India – The "Bharat Varsh". All types of knowledge (VIDYA) are in Veda. Vidya primarily means "**correct knowledge**" in any field of science, learning, philosophy, or any factual knowledge that is beyond dispute. Veda is a poetic presentation, and sacred scripture. It is considered second to none. It is for the whole humanity of the world. Basic concepts about the manifestation of the universe or multiverse. Mahabharat **(Shrimad Bhagwat),** mentions "Ek ev pura Vedah Pranavah Sarva vangmayah".

एक इव पुरा वेदाः प्रणवः सर्व वांग्मयः

Ek eiva pura vedah pranavah sarva vangnayah I (Shrimad Bhagwat).

In the beginning, Rigveda was the only one out of all Vedas. Later established three more Vedas.

It is interesting to note that the main subject of Rigveda is Science. It is clearly indicated in Taittariya Upanishad, Briguvalli, 3-5: -

विज्ञानं ब्रह्मेति व्यजानात् । विज्ञानाद्ध्येव खल्विमानिभूतानि जायन्ते । विज्ञानेन जातानि जीवन्ति । विज्ञानं प्रयन्त्यभिसंविशन्तीति । तद्विज्ञाय । पुनरेव वरुणं पितरमुपससार । अधीहि भगवो ब्रह्मेति । त >\होवाच । तपसा ब्रह्म विजिज्ञासस्व । तपो ब्रह्मेति । स तपोऽतप्यत । स तपस्तप्त्वा ॥ १॥ इति पञ्चमोऽनुवाकः ॥

Vidnyanam brahmeti vyjanat I vidnyanatdhyev khalvimanibhutani jayante Ividnyanenjatani jivanti Ividnyanam prayantyasamvishantiti I tatvidnyay I punareva varunam pitaramupassar I adhihi bhagvo brahmeti I tahovacha I tapasa brahma vijidnyasasva I tapo brahmeti I sa tapotapyat I sa tapastatva I 1 I iti panchamonuvakah II Taittariya Upanishad, Briguvalli, 3-5.

Rishi Bhrigu understood that Intelligence is Brahman – Brahma - the Consciousness; because it is from Intelligence, that all these living beings are born; having been born from it, they live by it, and (in the end) on departing they enter Intelligence and become one with it. Having known that he approached his father again saying: 'Revered Sir, instruct me about Brahman.' Varuna told him: 'Desire to know Brahman by Tapas. (Or hard work). He performed Tapas (hard work and penance) and realized that the Mind – **मन,** is not an organ or tissue of the body but is superior to the body, as it has a control over the body and not the vice versa. Mind is

Vidnyan – a special knowledge called Pradnya the (see chapter of nomenclature used in Rigveda).

Rishi Badarayan has classified Veda into 4 different Vedas. Subjects are different in different Vedas. The subjects are: -

The subject of Rigveda is Science, Yajurveda is purposeful actions or Yadnya Karma, Samaveda is music, and Atharvaveda is the revelation of Brahma or Brahma- Sakshatkar (ब्रम्ह साक्षात्कार).

It will not be out of context to mention here that all Vedas have prayer Mantras. These mantras have deities who are praiseworthy. Deities are devata or are Gods. Hence the Vedas are categorized as religious. In fact, these Vedas are highly scientific and analytical may it be Music, Veda Karma, Yadnya karma etc. The supernatural or essential elements in nature, are recognized as Devatas. The prayers are directed towards these devatas in different Vedas. Viz: - Akhand-Jyoti-Swaroop- uninterrupted light and energy are provided by Surya- Sun, hence Sun-God. Manifest nature and life on earth. All are due to Sun. Surya controls everything on earth. Hence termed SAMRAT or the Emperor, who controls the dynasty. Rigveda 10-88-4, 11,12.

मिंथुनावभूंताुमादित्प्रापंश्यन्भुवंनानि विश्वां ॥11॥

Mithunav bhutamaditprapshyanbhuvanani Vishva II 11 IIrigved 10–88-11

The Gods, who established AGNI, are worth the prayer. SUN is son of Aditi (Energy). The SUN in SWARGA, started roaming in Antariksha (Veda describes 7 abodes in swarga – Bhu, Bhuvah, Swah, Maha, Jana, Tapa, Satya. Out of these the Swah is Swarga or Antariksha). All abodes observed by living beings on earth (See chapter Space travel). These are clear indications of the fact that humans have written Vedic literature.

विश्वंस्मा अुग्निं भुवंनाय देुवा वैंश्वानुरं केुतुमह्नांमकृण्वन् । आ यस्तुतानोुषसों विभाुतीरपों ऊर्णोंति तमों अुर्चिषाु यन् ॥12 ॥ rigved 10-88-12

Vishvasma agnim bhuvanay deva veishvanaram ketumnham krunvan I aa yastatanoshso vibhatirpo urnoti tamo archsha yan II 12 II Rigved 10-88-12

Universal fire (विश्वंस्मा अग्निं) i.e., Super TEJAHPUNJAH, manifests SUN (वैश्वानुरं), which in turn illuminates the ignorance or darkness (तमो).

मित्रो जनान्यातयति ब्रुवाणो मित्रो दाधार पृथिवीमुत द्याम्। मित्रः कृष्टीरनिमिषाभि चष्टे मित्राय हव्यं घृतवज्जुहोत॥ ऋग्वेद - मण्डल » 3; सूक्त » 59; मन्त्र » 1

Mitro jananyatyati bruvano mitro dadhar prithvimut dyam I mitrah krushtiranimishabhi chashte mitraya havyam ghritvajjyuhot II Rigved. 3-59-1.

Those who preach TRUTH, spread knowledge about truth, maintain friendship and respect the supreme soul who sustains and nurture the whole universe and the living beings, are real friend (मित्र) to all II 1 II. Rigveda. 3-59-1

This indicates the highest respect to supernatural absolute truth. Hence protection, avoiding misuse, and disrespect to nature becomes mandatory. Anything man worships will automatically protected. Therefore, the manifest nature and elements are Devatas. Prayer and praise extended to all Devatas. In fact, this protection goes to useful plants or Vanaspati Devata. Plants that are scientifically important and provide Oxygen or Ozone in the atmosphere. Plants provide food for living beings. Hence, are worshiped by Sanskrit Speaking Civilization, for example - plants known as TULSI or Basil, the ASHWATHA tree (has a mention in Shrimad Bhagwadgita also) Peepal or (अश्वत्थ – ASHVATHA tree) Ficus Religiosa, and Banyan or Ficus Benghalensis tree, all these trees are worshiped and protected. These trees also have medicinal value as well (See ayurveda). Such trees must not be used for fuel purposes. Human psychology is whatever we worship will not be damaged. Similarly, the supernatural elements get protection and prayed for human benefits. It is interesting to note that in Astrology – the Jyotish Shastra, to curtail the harmful effects of planets on persons, is obviated by prayers and JAPAH (counting mantra 108 times. There is science involved in 108 counts, see elsewhere).

(In summary "According to Vedic cosmology, 108 is the basis of creation, represents the universe and all our existence. In Astrology "There are 12 zodiacs and 9 planets and when multiplied, we get 108. Additionally, there are 27 lunar mansions, and they are divided into 4 quarters. When 27 is multiplied by 4, the result is 108).

A word about DHARMA meaning in Vedic literature. Dharma is the virtue of an element to recognize it, it is an ethical and moral duty, a religious duty performed by a living being. Whatever sustains is dharma.

Manusmriti 8.15, Mahabharat 13.145.2, It is also mentioned in Mahabharat 3.30.8 In Mahabharata 3.312 and 313.128

धर्म एव हतो हन्ति धर्मो रक्षति रक्षितः तस्माद्धर्मो न हन्तव्यो मा नो धर्मो हतोऽवधीत् II

Dharma eva hato hanti dharmo rakshati raksitah tasmad dharmo na hantavyo ma no dharmo hato vadheet II Manusmriti 8.15, Mahabharat 13.145.2, It is also mentioned in Mahabharat 3.30.8 In Mahabharata 3.312 and 313.128 sacrifices of virtue destroy who sacrifices. Preserver himself is blessed and preserved. Hence do not sacrifice virtue, and if destroyed, it will destroy us.

In Sanskrit, it is defined as DHARAYATE ITI DHARMA-धारयते इति धर्म (Rishi Kanaada-कणाद). In ATHARVA VEDA (12-1-17) it is पृथ्विंम् धर्मणा धृति. PRITHVIM DHARMANA DHRITI or the world is sustained by the dharma of cosmos. Similar truth is reiterated in ATHARVA VEDA (12-1-17) it is पृथ्विंम् धर्मणा धृति. **In short, it propagates the idea that which sustains us and all manifestations thence it is ATMA or spirit and the divine self in all living beings as well as non-living manifestations.**

विश्वस्वम् मातर्मोषिधिनां ध्रुवां भूमिं **पृथिविं धर्मणा धृताम्** | शिवां स्योनामनु चरेम विश्वहा ||17|| **ATHARVA VEDA (12-1-17).**

Vishavasvam matarmoshidhinam dhruvam bhumim prithivim dharmana dhritam I shivam syonamanu charem vishvaha II Atharva ved. 12-1-17.

In summary, Veda is the outcome of the wisdom of Vedic Rishi and Muni who were the scientist of the Vedic period. There are highly analytical scientific derivations in the literature of Sanskrit-speaking civilizations. All this stimulated me to draft the present book. Hence, I am pleased to bring this book to your hand. I am sure readers will appreciate the challenging work involved in writing the book.

One more interesting event worth the mention is, Rigveda is the oldest literature in the world. Mahabharat era is a later development, written by Rishi Vyas. During Rigveda period, scientist Ribhu or Ribhu Rishi created cows and horses after dividing the "CHAMAS PATRA". The division of Cell (or the cell with a covering membrane becomes container or PATRA-पात्र). Later, human cloning by Rishi Dvepayana-द्वैपायन, during the Mahabharat era (101 children from embryonic stem cells, developed outside the human body, in an (स्वनुगुप्तेषु देशेषु, स्व-self + अनु-Disciplined + गुप्त- special, secret, and protected, hidden, + देश- place, device) self-regulated, auto-operated device), is as per the research and development during the era. It is very much the same as modern science. The knowledge and development of the Rigveda era carried forward to the Mahabharat era and human development was possible, after success in animal experiments during the Rigveda era.

There have been instances when the inference was difficult to be interpreted, and author took refuge to the meditation techniques to solve the problem. Meditation has rewarded author with reasonable solutions. Such problems I have faced in research also. When I could regenerate Ureter and Uterus in - vivo, smooth muscle regeneration was essential. But the Medical Textbooks declare that the Smooth muscles do not regenerate, and Cardiac muscles never regenerate. But on the contrary, it revealed in healing and regeneration, that the healthy Granulation tissue in a healing wound has a red pulsatile granular surface. This red pulsatile tissue is due to newly growing capillary blood vessels. This pulsatile feature is due to the smooth muscles grown in the blood capillaries. That means the smooth muscles do grow in our body. This clarified the age-old problem of smooth muscle does not grow and as mentioned in medical textbooks. Such experiences helped me in authoring this book.

In modern era of scientific awakening, there is religious marketing. Hidden political agenda in democratic societies. These modern religions basically, are sects, groupism, and belief that their religions are only rightful and therefore force to embrace what they believe is the final message of God. The Vedas are religious scripts, that have been propagated to believe that during invasion of Vedic land in the past few centuries. This stigma must be removed by the new generation of Vedic descendants. This is only possible if one believes that Vedas are analytical and scientific. I have authenticated the scientific facts by providing the Sanskrit Mantra from Rigveda itself. I feel the attempt is preliminary and just the beginning of an exploration of science in Veda and Purana. I have attempted to discover the science in Rigveda to the maximum extent, but it is not complete. Further research on the science of Rigveda is essential.

– Balkrishna Matapurkar.

FOREWORD

World's first Ved, the Rigveda a scientific perspective is one of the series pf publications of the author. It is basically a research work searching hidden science in a voluminous literature in a language which is not in common use. It makes an interesting reading because of thoughtful and analytical presentation with authentication.

The author learned Veda during childhood from his uncle and Guruji Shri Govind Ramchandra Matapurkar (He was commonly recognized as "Takle Guruji" - टकले गुरुजी).

Overall understanding about Religion is that it is faith, spiritual, and superstitious. Vedic sages and rishis believed that religion – spirituality, and VIDNYAN (विज्ञान= विशेष-ज्ञान) or the science are protagonists to each other. DHARMA (धर्म, गुणधर्म) is the virtue of the element or matter (it applies equally to all living and non-living) by which it can be recognized. Both indulge in experimentation, observation, result, and inferences. **Both are seekers of truth**. One searching for absolute truth and the other is for scientific truth, more analytically.

In Rigveda, the oldest written evidence in the world, presentation is enigmatic, obscure, objective, and symbolic. It is difficult to understand. It is not the fault of the seeker. It is about understanding a language, if the language is known, everything gets revealed otherwise all is obscure. This book tries to unravel the mysterious presentation and unearth the hidden scientific facts of Rigveda, which is in the Sanskrit language, now not in common use.

The Vedas are in the form of MANTRAs or hymns, Brahmanas, and Aranyaka which include the UPANISHADS. Therefore, the stanzas of the Upanishad presented in support and for authentication of inferences. The author of this book is experienced in original, innovative research on Adult Stem Cells in regenerating organs in the body using the body's own tissue stem cells, which participate in normal healing of the body. His research has received international patents from the U.S. Patent Office. The scientific work has been published in peer-reviewed scientific journals of repute. The publications include the scientific basis for the birth of 101 children from one female. This encouraged him to explore hidden science in Gita and Upanishads.

Rigvedic literature and its Upanishads discuss about the pre-embryonic development of a living being. What is responsible for ovum and sperm formation. The riddle, why the human foetus survival delivered before seven months of gestation. Why at seven months and after the foetus survives has been discussed by the Vedic Rishis and sages? Such analytical scientific thought existed thousands of years before, is amazing and thought provoking.

The author has utilized his research experience in searching hidden science facts in Sanskrit literature. The comparison of science facts with available scientific knowledge of modern science with references, is par excellent. The authentication by Sanskrit stanzas of Sanskrit literature makes it easy to understand the subject and verification by knowledgeable reader is easy. Explanation by providing flow charts and diagrams of manifestation of nature which makes understanding the subject comfortably.

Finally, the Rigveda has been repeatedly translated and explained with religious angle. Scientific explanations are rare. The author's research is commendable. It is for the first time that the scientific angle has been explored, in detail. Reader will certainly appreciate the hard work and research analytical efforts of the author. This book will certainly be a reference book for the academic purpose in future.

CHAPTER 1

VEDIC PRAYERS

An ever-pondering question is, after all, why one must indulge in prayers? Obviously, it is for solace. How is it answered and fulfilled? It is by the deity's blessings bestowed upon the person praying. What are the scientific aspects in such prayers? It is auto-suggestion. It is for preparing oneself to proceed with an action in that direction. It is for the self or the ATMA. A prayer is a form of a request to the deity. How can be the response possible from a non-perceivable and invisible being, as a deity? Veda believes that the whole manifestation in 'Brahmanda - ब्रम्हाण्ड, is a living entity, it is emphatically stressed in Rigveda that whatever is in BRAHMANDA is in living bodies- (यथा ब्रम्हांडे तथा पिन्डे or अहम् ब्रम्हास्मिन्). Request or prayer is answered by another living entity. The living entity is a fraction of the ultimate absolute truth परमसत्य, which is ATMATATTVA-आत्म तत्व. This is present in every living being. Therefore, the prayer becomes an autosuggestion. The fractionalized super soul – the SELF, as Aatma-Spirit, present in bodies, gets blessed in return. The fractionalized truth or soul, of the ultimate absolute truth the super soul – PARAMATMA, is invigorated and energized for the action in the direction of action and the result bestowed afterward.

Scientifically speaking, the frequency (the number of vibrations per second) generated from the recitation matches the frequency of the object of recitation the sound is enhanced (Tuning fork experiment).

Mantras are not just words but sound waves and vibrations with frequency. The absolute truth or Param "Atma tattva" is pulsatile and vibrating creating a slow intense humming sound - Vedic Ohm. The whole universe is nothing but vibration. If one considers scientifically atomic electrons, protons and neutrons are only energies in vibration. The entire universe is made up of energy, and this energy in different states of vibration makes up and manifests the objects of the universe. The persons or people have 'thought vibrations." In fact, our mind in different states of thinking, has different vibrations. Sometimes happy or sometimes people's mind is in a different state or in diseased state of vibration. When the tuning fork vibrates at the same frequency, the frequency of sound merge with each other, and enhance the sound volume. Similarly, there is the chanting vibrations of Gayatri. This is well explained by YOGA Shastra by Patanjali. It can be explained by tuning fork experiment.

Hence the prayers are of utmost importance. Some Rigvedic prayers are given below: -

'ॐ भूर्भuवः स्वः तत्सवितुर्वरेण्यं भर्गो देवस्य धीमहि धियो यो नः प्रचोदयात्। (Rigveda 3 – 62 -10).

Om Bhurbhuvah svah tatsavitur varenyam bhargo devasya Dhimahi dhiyo yonah prachodayat I Rigved. 3-62-10.

The Absolute ruth in all manifest world the Earth, Antariksha, and space - Bhu Loka, Bhuvar Loka, Swar Loka, is creator of all, and which is the most adorable, and is worth meditating on, is prayed to awaken our Intelligence.

What is religious in this prayer? The religious mental attitude needs to be avoided.

An interesting factor to be noted in this prayer is, only three abodes or lokas, are used i.e., Bhuh BHUVAH, SWAH. Other four are discovered, in the later period when space travel was advanced. The 4 abodes are MAH, JANAH, TAPAH, and SATYAM. This indicates the development of science was gradual and with scientific proof.

For interested reader Commentary on above mantra, by Sāyaṇa: Ṛgveda-bhāṣya is given below: -

Yajus. 3.35; Prachodayāt (प्रचोदयात्) = who may animate, or enlighten our intellect; Savitā = the soul, as one with the soul of the world, Brahma; when we meditate on the light which is one with Brahma, his own light, which, from its consuming influences on ignorance and its consequences, is termed Bhargas (भर्गो), and is that which is desirable, from its being to be known or worshiped by all (vareṇyam -वंरेण्यं) the property of the supreme being, (parameśvara), the creator of the world, and the animator, impeller or urger (savitā), through the internally abiding spirit (antaryām) of all creatures; yaḥ, although masculine, may be relative to the neuter noun bhargas, that light which animates all (dhiyaḥ) acts (karmāṇi), or illumes all understanding (buddhiḥ); again, devasya savituḥ may mean, of the bright or radiant sun, as the progenitor of all, sarvasya prasavitur, and bhargas may be understood as the sphere or orb of light, the consumer of sins, pāpānām tāpakam tejo maṇḍalam; bhargas may also mean food, and the prayer may only implore the sun to provide sustenance, tasya prasādād annādi lakṣaṇam phalam dhīmahi tasya ādhārabhūta bhavema, we anticipate from his favour the reward that is characterized by food and the like, that is, may we be supported by him.

In the same context of Gayatri Mantra, the following Rigveda Richas (1ca) are worth analysing:

आपो हि ष्ठा मयोभुवस्था न ऊर्जे दधातन ।महे रणाथ चक्षसे॥१॥ Rigveda10-9-1.

Aapo hi shtha mayobhuvastha n urje dadhatan I mahe ranath chakshseII 1 II. Rigved. 10-9-1.

Savitur is main body element - the liquid element. Liquid element the soul element, (one out of the 5 basic elements), which provides us vigour and strength, we pray you to gladden us by your essence.

क्षेत्रस्य पते मधुमन्तमूर्मिं धेनुरिव पयो अस्मासु धुक्ष्व।मधुश्चुतं घृतमिवसुपूतमृतस्य नः पतयोमृळयन्तु ॥२॥ Rigveda. 4-57-2.

Kshetrasya pate madhumantamurmi dhenuriv payo asmasu dhukshva I madhushchutam ghritamivasuputmrita Sya nah patayomrulyantu II 2 II. Rigved. 4-57-2.

The field or mother nature, you bless us with yield abundant Harvest as per the Nature's Divine Law, we pray you to bestow your Grace on us, like flow of Clarified Butter (घृतमिव).

The Sun provider of food or vegetation on earth, hence the grace of the Sun is prayed for. This is SANATAN DHARMA where the prayer is also scientific. All is based on scientific derivations. Is it justified to compare this Dharma with religion influenced by groups and divisive forces as faith and sect, with ulterior motives. Sanatan Dharma is eternal, perpetual, and everlasting. It is not propagated by single divine agents like Buddha, Mahaveer, Mohammad, Christ and so on. Some of these faiths are the bifurcation of Sanatan Dharma. It is left for the reader to decide, what is eternal.

(According to Bhavishya Puran, Prati Sarga Bhavishya Puran: Prati Sarg: Part III 3.3.5-27. (Photo clip of page given below). Mohammad name is transformed version of name MAHAMAD - महामद. He is supposed to be re-incarnation of Tripurasura who established Mlechh Dharma. His Guru was Shukracharya (Guru of Demons).

Bhavishya Puran: Prati Sarg, Part III: 3, 3 5-27

एतस्मिन्नन्तरे म्लेच्छ आचार्येण समन्वितः ।
महामद इति ख्यातः शिष्यशाखासमन्वितः ॥ ५ ॥ Mahamada
नृपश्चैव महादेवं मरुस्थलनिवासिनम् ।
गङ्गाजलैश्च संस्नाप्य पञ्चगव्यसमन्वितैः ।
चन्दनादिभिरभ्यर्च्य तुष्टाव मनसा हरम् ॥ ६ ॥
भोजराज उवाच—नमस्ते गिरिजानाथ मरुस्थलनिवासिने ।
त्रिपुरासुरनाशाय बहुमायाप्रवर्तिने ॥ ७ ॥ Tripurasura
म्लेच्छैर्गुप्ताय शुद्धाय सच्चिदानन्दरूपिणे ।
त्वं मां हि किंकरं विद्धि शरणार्थमुपागतम् ॥ ८ ॥
सूत उवाच--इति श्रुत्वा स्तवं देवः शब्दमाह नृपाय तम् ।
गन्तव्यं भोजराजेन महाकालेश्वरस्थले ॥ ९ ॥
म्लेच्छैस्सुदूषिता भूमिर्वाहीका नाम विश्रुता ।
आर्यधर्मो हि नैवात्र वाहीके देशदारुणे ॥ १० ॥
बभूवात्र महामायी योऽसौ दग्धो मया पुरा ।
त्रिपुरो बलिदैत्येन प्रेषितः पुनरागतः ॥ ११ ॥ Tripuro
अयोनिः स वरो मत्तः प्राप्तवान्दैत्यवर्द्धनः ।
महामद इति ख्यातः पैशाचकृतितत्परः ॥ १२ ॥
नागन्तव्यं त्वया भूप पैशाचे देशधूर्तके ।
मत्प्रसादेन भूपाल तव शुद्धिः प्रजायते ॥ १३ ॥
इति श्रुत्वा नृपश्चैव स्वदेशान्पुनरागमत् ।
महामदश्च तैः सार्द्धं सिन्धुतीरमुपाययौ ॥ १४ ॥
उवाच भूपतिं प्रेम्णा मायामदविशारदः ।
तव देवो महाराज मम दासत्वमागतः ॥ १५ ॥
ममोच्छिष्टं स भुञ्जीयाद्यथा तत्पश्य भो नृप ।
इति श्रुत्वा तथा दृष्ट्वा परं विस्मयमागतः ॥ १६ ॥
म्लेच्छधर्मे मतिश्चासीत्तस्य भूपस्य दारुणे ॥ १७ ॥
तच्छ्रुत्वा कालिदासस्तु रुषा प्राह महामदम् ।
माया ते निर्मिता धूर्त नृपमोहनहेतवे ॥ १८ ॥
हनिष्यामि दुराचारं वाहीकं पुरुषाधमम् ।
इत्युक्त्वा स द्विजः श्रीमान्नवार्णजपतत्परः ॥ १९ ॥
जप्त्वा दशसहस्रं च तद्दशांशं जुहाव सः ।
भस्म भूत्वा स मायावी म्लेच्छदेवत्वमागतः ॥ २० ॥
भयभीतास्तु तच्छिष्या देशं वाहीकमाययुः ।
गृहीत्वा स्वगुरोर्भस्म मदहीनत्वमागतम् ॥ २१ ॥
स्थापितं तैश्च भूमध्ये तत्रोषुर्मदतत्पराः ।
मदहीनं पुरं जातं तेषां तीर्थं समं स्मृतम् ॥ २२ ॥
रात्रौ स देवरूपश्च बहुमायाविशारदः ।
पैशाचं देहमास्थाय भोजराजं हि सोऽब्रवीत् ॥ २३ ॥
आर्यधर्मो हि ते राजन्सर्वधर्मोत्तमः स्मृतः ।
ईशाज्ञया करिष्यामि पैशाचं धर्मदारुणम् ॥ २४ ॥ Paisachya dharama (demoniac religion)
लिङ्गच्छेदी शिखाहीनः श्मश्रुधारी स दूषकः ।
उच्चालापी सर्वभक्षी भविष्यति जनो मम ॥ २५ ॥
विना कौलं च पशवस्तेषां भक्ष्या मता मम ।
मुसलेनैव संस्कारः कुशैरिव भविष्यति ॥ २६ ॥
तस्मान्मुसलवन्तो हि जातयो धर्मदूषकाः । dharma dhushika (Polluter of righteousness)
इति पैशाचधर्मश्च भविष्यति मया कृतः ॥ २७ ॥

Bhavishya Puran: Muhammad: Reincarnation of Tripurasur (C/O Shiv Puran)

Mahamrityunjaya Mantra

महामृत्युन्जय मंत्र

ॐ त्र्यम्बकं यजामहेसुगन्धिं पुष्टिवर्धनम् ।उर्वारुकमिव बन्धनान्मृत्योर्मुक्षीय मामृतात् ॥ Rig Veda 7.59.12.

Om tryambakam yajamahe sugandhim pushtivardhanamI urvaruka miva bandhananmrityormikashiya mamrutat IRigved. 7-59-12.

We worship the Three-Eyed deity, who is fragrant and provide nourishment, free us from all bondages of mortal world, the birth-death cycle, and detach us from perishable things of manifest world, and not separated from the absolute truth, an Immortal Essence which is omniscient and omnipresent. It is like the ripened cucumber (खरबूजा) fruit gets detached from the main vine, on ripening and spreading fragrance in surroundings.

Commentary by Sāyaṇa: Ṛgveda-bhāṣya is as follows: -

Tryambaka: the father, ambuka of the three deities, Brahma, Viṣṇu and Rudra; also identified with mahatva (Ṛgvidhāna); whose fame is fragrant: sugandhim = prasāritapuṇya kīrtim, whose fame of virtue is spread; in like manner as the fragrance of a tree full in flower sheds sweetness, so spreads the fragrance of holy actions; the augmenter of increase: puṣṭi vardhanam, the augmenter of nutrition, jagad-vījam, the seed of the world; or, the multiplier of good things subservient to objects of bodily enjoyment, wealh, śarīradhanādiviṣayān vardhayati yaḥ; may I be liberated: mṛityor mokṣiya = may I be liberated from the world, or the revolutions of life and death; may I attain mokṣa;

प्र तद्विष्णुः स्तवते वीर्येण मृगो न भीमः कुचरो गिरिष्ठाः । यस्योरुषु त्रिषुविक्रमणेष्वधिक्षियन्ति भुवनानि विश्वा ॥

Pra tad Vishnuh stavate viryen mrigo n bhimah kucharo girishtha I yasyorushu trishuvikramaneshvadhikshiyanti bhuvanani Vishva II

There is an interesting story about Vishnu. In the form of microcosm as Vamana murti, Vishnu covers the entire cosmos with his three steps. It is symbolic but envelopes highest scientific facts in the symbolic story. The Vishnu is depicted as sleeping human figure which means dormant phase of manifest cosmos. With his three steps he covers entire cosmos. This means the entire cosmos is from gas, liquid, solid. This capacity is in Vishnu in a dormant phase. The primordial gasses as Vishnu interact with `each other to form Aap or liquid, this in turn after interaction of virtues of different liquids form solid. This has been explained with example elsewhere in this book. The third step is on the head of King Bali. Vishnu pushes King Bali into earth. The solid is pushed deep under earth so thsst the solids get converted into various elements like Gold, Silver, Copper,etc."Viṣṇu is therefore glorified, that by his prowess he is like a fearful, ravenous, and mountain-haunting wild beast, and because of that in his three paces all worlds abide." See diagram on page- 43. Change as per final book page----

सहस्रशीर्षा पुरुषः सहस्राक्षः सहस्रपात् । स भूमिं विश्वतो वृत्वात्यतिष्ठद्दशाङ्गुलम् ॥१॥ Rigveda10-90-1.

Sahastrashirkhah purushah sahastrakshah sahastrapat I sa bhumim vishvato vritvatyatishthaddshangulam II1II Rigved 10-90-1

The absolute truth having omnipresence, pervades each part of the Creation has Thousand Heads, Thousand Eyes and Thousand Feet, extends beyond 10 directions (ऋए दिशा), representing 10 fingers-toes included.

Making the presence of Universal Wisdom read this mantra: -

महो अर्णः सरस्वती प्र चेतयति केतुना ।धियो विश्वा वि राजति ॥१॥. Rigveda.3.12.

Maho arnah Saravati prachetayati ketuna I dhiyo Vishva virajati II 1 II Rigveda 3-12-1.

Saraswati, (A symbolic image) deity awakens Intellect and provides Universal Wisdom and is embodiment of Universal Wisdom in conducting Yadnya-karma ||Rigveda. 1.3.10, 11, and 12||.

A noteworthy intention is all prayers are for the welfare of Mankind in general. These are not for any faith, cult, religion, or group. This suggests magnanimity of Rishis of the Sanskrit Speaking Civilization.

There are many Vedic prayers and Shanti Mantras available at the beginning of Veda and Purana. These indicate that the tradition was for Teacher and the disciple or GURU and SHISHYA must study together and develop knowledge, both and all be knowledgeable. VIZ, see mantra below:

ओम सहनाववतु । सहनोभुनक्तु। सहवीर्यं करवा वहै ।तेजस्विनाव धीतमस्तु । मा विदविषावहै। ओम शान्तिः शान्तिः शान्तिः II **TAITTARIYA Upanishad, Brahmananda Valli, Anuvak 1, Mantra 1.**

Om sahanavavatu I Sahanobhunaktu I sahaveeryam karavavahe I tejasvinavdhitamastu I ma vidvishavahe I Om Shanti Shanti sahnti II1 II Taittariya Upanishad. Brahmanandvalli, 1-1.

The SHANTI MANTRA in RIGVD: `

स्वस्ति न इन्द्रो वृध्दश्रवाः । स्वस्ति नः पूषा विश्ववेदाः । स्वस्ति नः स्तार्क्षो अरिष्ट नेमिः स्वस्तिनो बृहस्पतिर्दधातु II 6 II **(Rigved 1- 89- 6 to 8)**

Svasti na indro vridhashravah I Svasti nah pusha Vishva vedah I Svasti nahr starksho Arishta nemih Svastino brihaspatirdadhatu II 6 II Rigved. 1-89-6 to 8.

May Indra, who listens to much praise, guard our welfare; may Pūṣhan, who knows all things, guard our welfare; may Tārkṣya (Garud – Vishnu vahan), with unblemished weapons, guard our welfare."

Listening and gaining knowledge with age, INDRA is full of wisdom, knower of the whole universe, the PUSHNA – Nitrogen cycle- which is for vegetation, which is responsible for the manifest body. The body is an instrument for VED or DNYAN. All auspicious and end of all inauspicious, the TARKSHYA- the GARUD, along with BRIHASPATI – the GURU, help humans to get pleasure and satisfaction in life. All this is for the welfare of living beings.

In this prayer stanza, the 4 deities are worshipped, and prayers are extended to these 4 deities. These are:

Here there are 4 DEVTAS that may grant everything good, and pleasant, as per moral standards and welfare to all humans. The 4 Gods are Indra, Pusha, Garud, and Guru (– the Brihaspati or planet Jupiter).

Indra – the sphere of electromagnetic rays and vibrations, sound waves, radiation, etc. from all the celestial elements. Infusion of energy in clouds is possible from this layer – the Indra. This is responsible for rain hence called Rain – God. This is the scientific explanation for Indra as rain God as per modern science.

Pushna – Nitrogen element in the atmosphere. This provides vegetation on earth (see pushn-chakra- Rigveda 6-54-3.

पूष्णश्चक्रं न रिष्यति न कोशोऽवं पद्यते। नो अस्य व्यथते पविः ॥३॥

Pushnashchakram na rishyati na koshova padyate I no Asya Vythate pavih II 3 II Rigved. 6-54-3

As per modern science the Nitrogen in atmosphere never exhausts nor the stock diminishes, its efficiency never diminishes. The seed formation in plants the SOMA or the moon is equally essential. Further in Rigveda the common effect of moon and Pushna compared with each other in Rigveda 9 – 69- 5.

सोमः पवते जनिता मतीनां जनिता दिवो जनिता पर्थिव्याः । जनिताग्नेर्जनिता सूर्यस्य जनितेन्द्रस्य जनितोत विष्णोः ॥ 5 ॥

Somah pavatejanita matinam janita divo janita prithivyah I janitagnerjanita Suryasyta janitendrasya janito Vishnoh II 5 II Rigved. 9-69-5.

Both (Moon=सोम and Nitrogen-पूष्ण) work synergistically and essential to produce seeds in plants and vegetations. In short it is live and let live.

All such derivations and inferences indicate only one thing and the scientific bend of Sages, Rishis of the Sanskrit era, and development of Veda knowledge. In Nitrogen cycle, as per modern science, the stock of nitrogen remains steady. How was this known to Vedic civilization?

About Tarakshya:

Tarkshya – Garuda is a celestial element – in English it is a star - AQUILA), It looks like Garuda (see figure below). Related to summer and winter solstice of Sun. It decides Spring and Rainy seasons. Southern Solstice of Sun invites rain on the earth hemisphere.

(**Aquila** is a constellation on the celestial equator. Its name is Latin for 'eagle' and it represents the bird that carried Zeus/Jupiter's thunderbolts in Greek-Roman mythology.

Its brightest star, Altair, is one vertex of the Summer Triangle asterism. The constellation is best seen in the northern hemisphere during summer, as it is located along the Milky Way. Because of this location, many clusters and nebulae are found within its borders, but they are dim). The following figure is adopted from Google search. Above description is from Wikipedia. Figure below simulates Garuda – eagle. This indicates how deep was the research and knowledge acquired by Sanskrit Speaking Civilization?

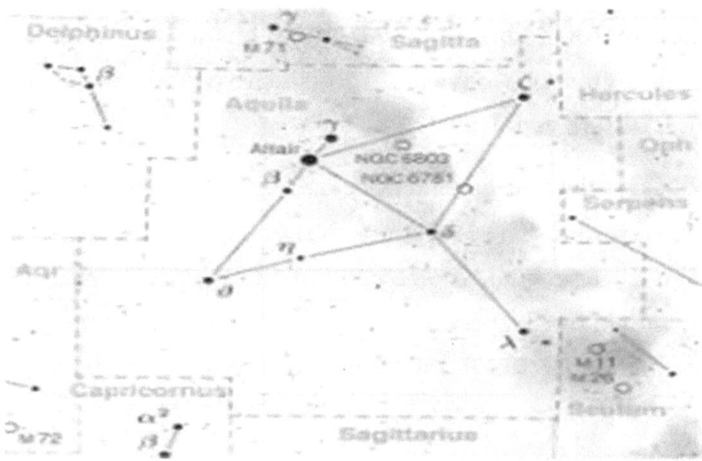

Tarksha is Garuda and in English is Eagle. Rigveda description is exactly matches Greek assumption. Rigveda is considered the oldest ever written document. It is unfortunate that the Rishi culture is ignored, and due credit is missing to the Vedic knowledge. This may be a purpose full attempt to emphasize that the knowledge of cosmos is from western civilization to slave country population of east. Rectification is only possible by awareness of young generation and establish due credit to actual researchers. It is unfortunate that the young generation believes it, because they are taught for generations the same thing. One must shed off the mind-set that the science is from the west.

Guru – Brihaspati is Devata for Mind and intellect. The intellect is mindful thinking. Let it be for the welfare of the living beings on the whole earth.

Rain, Energy, Air, Aakash, Prithvi (5 basic elements- the Panchmahabhut) is life for the earthlings. Hence prayers and Yadnya-Karma (purposeful actions), were directed towards fetching benefits, from such supernatural elements and termed as DEVATAS or God and prayers directed towards such Gods.

पृषदश्वा मुरुतुसूरंचक्षसो विश्वें :पृश्निंमातरः शुभंयावांनो विुदथेंषु जग्मंयः । अुग्निजिह्वा मनंवु :
नो देुवा अवुसा गंमन्निह ॥ ७ ॥ Rigved. 1-89-7

Prushashva marutah prishnimatarah Shubham ya vano vidatheshu jagmayah I Agnijivha manavah soorchkshaso vishve no deva avasa gamannih II 7 II Rigved. 1-89-7.

Moher of Marut the Speed element is Prishni (पृश्निमातरः) or beam of rays, radiations, waves etc. The Marut are the sons of Pṛiśhni **पृश्नणी**, generated from beams (details could not be found in Rigveda Richas) gracefully-frequently moving with speed on tongues of Agni (Sun radiations) equally radiant as the Sun (सूरचक्षसो विश्वे), all over the world, may all the Devtas-Gods (Super-natural elements) come hither (गमन्निह) for our preservation. (see 7th Mantra above)"

In the presence of learned and full of wisdom, men listen and see which is pious, worship and praise God, with healthy body and mind.

भद्रं कर्णेभिः शृणुयाम देवा भद्रं पश्येमाक्षभिर्यजत्राः । स्थिरैरङ्गैस्तुष्टुवांसस्तनूभिर्व्यशेम देवहितं यदायुः ॥८॥ (Rigved 1- 89- 6 to 8), This Richa is also in (Yajurveda 25- 21) and Samveda 1874.

Bhadram karnebhih shrunuyam deva bhadram pashyemakshabhiryajatrah I sthirerangeistunsastunoo bhirvakshema devahitam yadayuh II 8 II Rigved. 1-89- 6 to 8. In Yajurved. 25-21, and Samved. 1874.

Om, listen with ears which is good and pious. One must see which is good and pious, and with healthy body we praise the Gods. Whatever life destined by Super soul let us live that. Provider of intellect the Jupiter -the Guru, grant such mind-set to us.II 8 II

The same is in SAMVEDA: 2.9.3(1849-187) उत्तरार्चिकः/ नवमप्रपाठकःतृतीयोऽर्द्धः/ the complete Mantra is:

ओम भद्रम कर्णेभिः श्रुणुयाम देवा भद्रम् पश्येमाक्षभिर्यजत्राः । स्थिरेरंगैस्तुष्टुवासस्तनूभिर्व्यशेमहि देवहितं यदायुः ॥2॥ स्वस्ति न इन्द्रो वृध्दश्रवाः स्वस्ति नः पूषा विश्ववेदाः । स्वस्ति नस्ताक्ष्र्यो अरिष्टनेमिः स्वस्तिनो बृहस्पतिर्दधातु ॥3॥ **Rigveda » Mandal:1» Sukta:89» Mantra:6 - 8**

Listen only pious statements, Vision be looking for pious sights, Praise Super soul and super natural elements, with healthy mind and soul, at the same time the God who provides mind and intellect the Brihaspati provide us such a mind set. (Rigved 1- 89-8).

For detailed reading see Appendix 1. at the end of the book.

Oh! the supernatural elements! While meditating on such elements, let us hear and see what is auspicious and with healthy mind and body, let us pray Gods at the same time let us live the destined lifespan bestowed to us by the Almighty.

Another SHANTI Mantra, like above is:

शं नो'मित्रः शं वरुंण शं नो विष्णुंरुरुक्रमः :शं नो'भवत्वर्यमा । शं न इन्द्रो बृहस्पति :II ९ II (Rigved 1- 90 – 9).

Sham no mitrah sham Varunah sham no bhavatvaryama I sham no Indro brihaspatih sham no vishnururukramah II 9 II Rigved, 1-90- 9.

मित्र वरुण अर्यमा (Related to eyes- netra-chakshu) **इन्द्र बृहस्पति और विष्णू** (Vishnu covered entire world in three steps.) (९)

In this mantra the deities are 6. Mitra, Varun, Aryama, Indra, Brihaspati, Vishnu. Mitra-Varun indicates rainy season. Water is lifeline for the living beings on earth. Interestingly all deities are related to NAKSHTRA or constellations. Hence prayer (for these Gods) is for the ultimate welfare of the living beings.

Mitra governs DAY, (Mitra- **one of the gods in the category of Aditya's, sovereign principles of the universe**. He represents friendship, integrity, harmony, and all else that is important in the successful maintenance of order in human existence).

Varun governs night, grant us pleasure.

(Aryama is the third son of Aditi (Prakriti the Nature), mother of the twelve Adityas. After creating Prajapati, Sun divides itself into twelve forms each representing a month of the year. Aryama represents the Vaishakha month and is the ruler of Uttara Phalguni nakshatra in Vedic Astrology). Scientifically, **Indra the sphere of electromagnetic rays and vibrations, sound waves, radiation, etc. from all the celestial elements. Infusion of energy in clouds is possible from this layer – the Indra. Hence prayer is for bestowing boon of rain.**

Brihaspati (The Jupiter) is related to intellect. Prayer is for providing intellect for honourable deeds and understanding tahe proper action to be performed.

Vishnu's vehicle is Garuda, which is in the previous stanza. In this current stanza, the Vishnu name has appeared. Vishnu is the protector of the Bramhanda.

प्र तद्विष्णुः स्तवते वीर्येण मृगो न भीमः कुचरो गिरिष्ठाः । यस्योरुषु त्रिषु विक्रमणेष्वधिक्षियन्ति भुवनानि विश्वा ॥

Pra tadvishnuh stavate viryena mrigo na bhimah kucharo garishthah I yasyurushu trishu vikramaneshvadhikshiyanti bhuvanani Vishva II

The Vishnu is depicted as sleeping human figure which means dormant phase of manifest cosmos. With his three steps he covers entire cosmos. This means the entire cosmos is from gas, liquid, solid (Trigunatmaka-त्रिगुणात्मक). This capacity is in Vishnu in a dormant phase as "micro-cosm" – as Vaman Avtar. The primordial gasses as Vishnu interact with each other to form Aap - आप or liquid, this in turn after interaction of virtues of different liquids, and temperature-ताप, form solid. The third leg is on the head of king "Bali" and pushed him under the earth. That is remaining is pushed under earth. This is for conversion of the rest into another form like Gold, Silver, Iron Copper, Diamond, platinum. The process is going on and on for more development in nature. This has been explained with example elsewhere in this book. "Viṣṇu is therefore glorified, that by his prowess (विक्रमणेष्वधि) in his three paces all worlds abide." See diagram below:

Diagram: Manifestation of Universe

(Artists presentation)

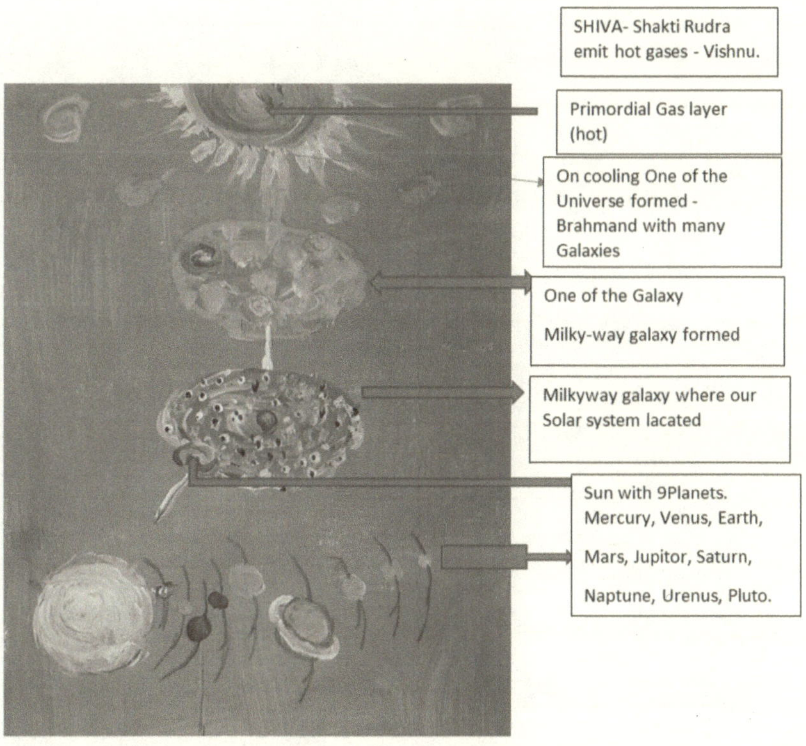

Chart to explain Manifestation and Annihilation of Cosmos.

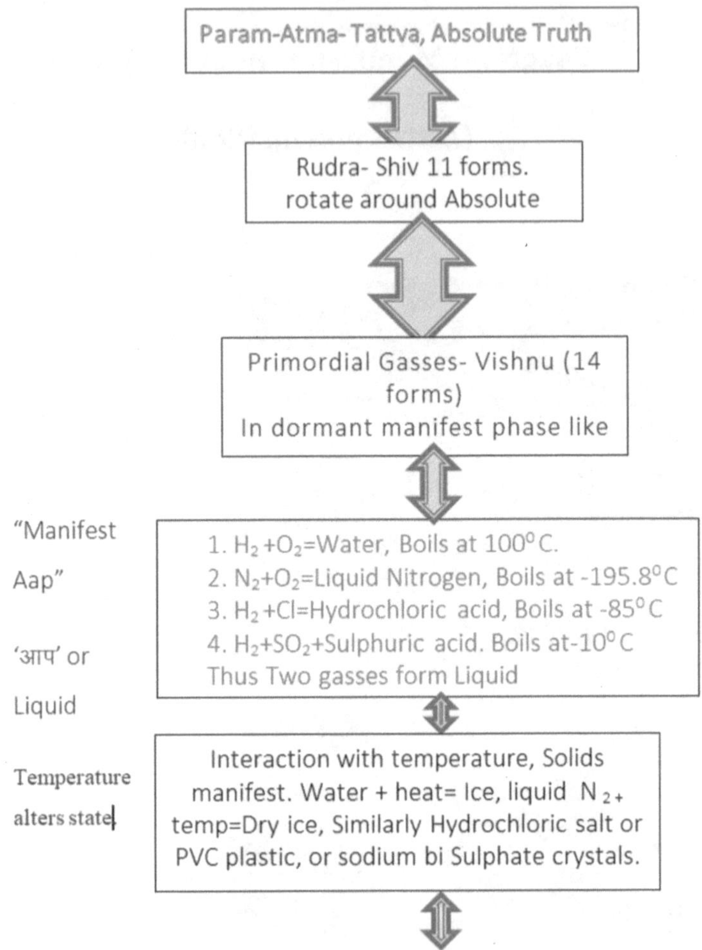

Rigveda maintains here that the manifestation process is in reverse order when Annihilation times arrives Thus the cosmos is oft repeated.

पुनरावर्तिनो जगत (Gita). AS per Vedic concept

Natural powers are considered as deities and divinities, hence are prayed for human welfare. All living beings must live in harmony and peace, is expressed in prayers. The deities included are Sky, Space, Antariksh, universe, earth, Aap-liquid - Water, vegetation-Vanaspati etc. This is basically a co-ordination in all natural powers. This expresses the view that the everything is interdependent. This is also the knowledge about environment. It expresses the cosmos and the co-ordination between the basic elements in cosmos- the Earth, Aap, Fire, Vayu, Nabha. All are responsible for manifestation in Nature. Therefore, the Prayer is: -

ओम द्यौः शान्तिरन्तरिक्षं शान्तिः पृथ्वि शान्तिरापः शन्तिरोषधयः शान्ति । वनस्पतयः शान्तिर्विश्वेदेवाः शान्तिर्ब्रम्ह शान्तिः सर्वं शान्तिः शान्तिरेव शान्तिः सा मा शान्तिरेधि ॥ ओम शान्तिः शान्तिः शान्तिः

Om Dyauh Shaantir-Antarikssam Shaantih Prthivii Shaantir-Aapah Shaantir-Ossadhayah Shaantih | Vanaspatayah Shaantir-Vishvedevaah Shaantir-Brahma ShaantihSarvam Shaantih Shaantir-Eva Shaantih SaaMaa Shaantir-Edhi |Om Shaantih Shaantih Shaantih ..

Meaning of each word: 1: Om, Peace is in Sky; Peace is in Space (between Earth and Sky); 2: Peace on Earth; Peace is in Water; Peace is in Plants; 3: Peace is in Trees; Peace is in Gods (energy which is presiding over the various elements of manifest Nature); Peace is in Uni and Multiverses Brahman (Absolute Consciousness – Param Chaitanya – the absolute truth); 4: Peace is invading everywhere; Peace alone (which is outside) is in Peace (which is inside); May you be (established in) that Peace (and make your life fulfilled);5: Om, Peace, Peace, Peace.

In summary, one must preserve Nature (Prakriti- **प्रकृति**) and Nature will preserve all living beings. The preserved nature in return will preserve all moving and non-moving (**चराचर**) beings.

CHAPTER 2

GAYATRI

Veda and Sanskrit literature consider Gayatri mantra as the mother of Veda. Bhagwadgita says it as VED MATARAM (**वेद मातरम्**), and Chhanda Samaham – **छंदसामहम्**.

बृहत्साम तथा साम्नां गायत्री छन्दसामहम् |मासानां मार्गशीर्षोऽहमृतूनां कुसुमाकर :|| 35||
Gita 10- 35

Brihatsam tatha samnam gayatri chhandasamaham I masanam margashirsho hamrutunam kusumakarah II 35 II Gita 10-35.

Margashirsha Panchami is Vasant Panchami. Fifth day of the month Margasheersha. It is Hemant Ritu. It is the beginning of flowering season. The Devi Gayatri, the Rudra Gayatri, the Brahma Gayatri, the Param Hansa Gayatri, and several other Gayatri mantras are also found in the Vedas. Its importance can be estimated by the fact that the Veda has devoted voluminous 2449 RICHAS (**ऋचा**) or mantra for Gayatri. Doesn't it need a truth full research / discovery on the subject?

Gayatri Mantra 10, is in 3rd mandal of Rigveda, Sukta 62, a mantra before this is 9, which preconditions readers for the value described in 10th mantra.

यो विश्वाभि विपश्यंति भुवंना सं च पश्यंति। स नः पूषाविता भुंवत्॥9II Rigveda 3-62-9.

Yo vishvabhi vipashyati bhuvana sam cha pashyati I sa nah pushavita bhuvat II 9 II. *Rigved.* 3-62-9.

One who is creator and controller of world)विश्व(, all abodes)भुवना(and looks after, equally)सम्, पश्यति(and provides protection and nourishment by supplying Nitrogen (पूषा पुष्टिकर्त्ता (for food and vegetation for us)यः, सः, नः(so as, we achieve growth.

Therefore, one must care and extend prayers to creator. See stanza next:

GAYATRI mantra also known as the **Sāvitri Mantra. The mantra is** dedicated to the Vedic deity Savitr. Savitra – सवित्र, is the 10th name of Surya-the Sun.

ॐ भूर्भुव स्सुवः तत्सं वितुर्वरेण्यं भर्गो देवस्यं धीमहि धियो यो नः प्रचोदयात् ॥ 10 II Rigveda 3-62-10.

Om Bhurbhvassuvah tatsa viturvarenyam bhargo devasta Dhimahi dhiyo yo nah prachodayat II 10 II Rigved. 3-62-10.

All humans')यः नःधियः(stimulate intellect with best virtues, efforts, and nature. Adopt)धीमहि (the effect)प्रचोदयात् (of the deity who manifested cosmos and Nature,)सवितुः (who is provider of prosperity, heat, light (Prakash – knowledge, enlightenment), who is omniscient and omnipresent, who is knower of everything,) देवस्य(is destroyer of miseries)भर्गः (must extend prayers. ॥१०॥

There are 33 devata /deities described in Rigveda. The worship of absolute truth inspires mind and intellect. Repeated chanting of mantra helps in acquiring health of body and mind, success, peace, prosperity as well as spiritual enlightenment. This mantra enjoys the greatest place amongst all Veda mantras. One can firmly establish and stabilize the mind. It is an appreciation, to both the nurturing sun and the absolute truth. It is an important Veda mantra even in Shrimad Bhagwadgita Shri Krishna praises this, Gayatri Mantra. It is an oldest mantra, therefore, often referred to as "the mother of the Vedas". In the **Bhagavad Gita,** Lord Krishna revealed to Arjuna – "Among all the mantras, I am the Gayatri". Why all this praise? It is worth understanding that the acceptance or non-acceptance of "Absolute truth" the routine of Nature is not going to change. Nature, cosmos or Bramhanda – ब्रम्हांड, will not be disturbed. It will follow the natural laws as per the guidelines of omnipresent and omniscient absolute energy. One may get SOLACE by accepting absolute truth. Otherwise, life may be berserk and far from peace and tranquillity. Every grain of this nature is pervaded by the absolute truth. All char -Achar -moving or non-moving is the result of the ultimate energy and absolute truth. (A word of caution here is that there is nothing in this nature and cosmos which is not moving. Everything in manifest world is moving. Certain things seemed relatively non-moving. But these are moving, only relatively appear non-moving). Fractionalized absolute truth is pervaded in everything in nature. Everything has birth, growth, lifespan, and death. Everything is living. Everything is oft repeated Punaravartino Jagat – पुनरावर्तिनो जगत (Gita).

The 11th mantra further stresses that:

देवस्य सवितुर्वयं वाजयन्तः पुरंध्या। भगस्य रातिमीमहे ॥11 II

Devasya saviturvayam vajayantah purandhya I bhagasya ratimimahe II 11 II Rigveda 3-62-11.

With the intellect)पुरन्ध्या (one enhances understanding and mental aptitude)वाजयन्तः(, so the one who provides stimulus and prosperity)भगस्य (to us, hence one must pray for such help from the absolute truth)देवस्य(. ॥११॥

In other word, the Vedas illustrate that the cosmos in which we live is the reality itself-but camouflaged. What seen is illusion. Kaal Chakra the cycles of the day and night, the different seasons, birth and death, planting and harvesting, all are the displays of the reality. Just as a first view of the ocean awakens a sense of wonder at the apparent limitlessness of the earth's waters, so with every dawn and dusk, every birth and death, the mind overflows momentarily with wonder at the unseen whole. Thus, it is said:

त्रिपादूर्ध्व उदैत्पुरुषः पादोऽस्येहाभवत्पुनः । ततो विष्वङ्व्यक्रामत्साशनानशने अभि ॥

Tripad urdhva odeitprushah pado syehabhvtpunah I tato vishvangavyakramatsashananshane Abhi II

"Three-fourths of Purușha ascended; the other fourth that remained in this world proceeds repeatedly, and, diversified in various forms, went to all animate and inanimate creation." On this subject the **Commentary by Sāyaṇacharya who considers this as a cosmic ritual. Ṛgveda-bhāṣya indicates that Aadi-purush** proceeds repeatedly: either in individuals by death and birth, or in the world by its temporary dissolution and renovation; It is the Cosmic Ritual. A finely tuned mind can know this reality, but such a mind must be able to see intuitively and go beyond the outward forms of things or illusion – MAYA. When this has been accomplished through TAPA – तप, and self-discipline, the seer can present everyday experience to others as a kind of doorway into the in depth meaning of life. The Vedas are just such a doorway a revelation of the infinite reality as it appears in the cosmos. But the Vedas do not oversimplify, nor did the Rishis and sages of the Vedas underestimate the complexity of things. They recognized that the symbols of reality are ever shifting and may overlap. During the day, for example, light is the product of Aditya (the sun), while at night it is product of agni (fire). So, Aditya and agni are described as brothers. Similarly, the power of illumination is symbolized both by light in the cosmos and intelligence within the human personality. So, the "light" means brightness of SUN, or BUDDHI the intelligence or both. **Thus, the highest reality is not limited to a particular symbol or personified by any single force of nature. It is not the Sun god, the moon god, or the god of lightning that are eulogized in the Vedas. These are only the "priests" of a cosmic ritual, an ongoing ceremony that takes place directly before our eyes in the form of the universal rhythms of life.** We are all, (gods and man), part of this ritual; each has a role to play.

In the following verse, the Vedas describe the Sun's role in that cosmic ceremony:

Rig Veda 6.71.1.

उदु ष्य देवः सविता हिरण्ययां बाहू अयंस्त सवनाय सुक्रतुः। घृतेन पाणी अभि प्रुष्णुते मखो युवा सुदक्षो रजसो विधर्मणि **II 1 II** Rigveda. 6-71-1

Udushya devah Savita hiranyaya bahu ayansta savanay sukratuh I ghriten pani abhi prashnute makho yuva sudaksho rajaso vidhrmani II 1 II Rigved. 6-71-1.

With golden arms divine deity Sun – SAVITRA, provide water for various useful purposes, in the various services of the world. Sun lets the melted ghee drip from his hands onto space.

Scientific analysis:

In fact, what modern science recognizes as NUCLEUS in every cell, is the acceptance of spiritualism by which it is recognized that the Absolute truth which is omniscient and omnipresent in everything (Manifest – Unmanifest, moving – Non-moving etc.) in cosmos is KSHETRADNYA - क्षेत्रज्ञ). Nucleus state retains Nature and Individuality. If Nucleus tempered it ceases to exist. But gives rise to new one It is called as transmutation and disintegration of elements. This is the astonishing and amazing power of Nucleus. This is due to electrons in the nucleus. The NUCLEUS by Atomic Physicists, is described as:

What is a Nucleus? The most integral component of the cell is the nucleus (plural: nuclei).

Nucleus Definition: A nucleus is defined as a double-membraned eukaryotic **cell organelle** that contains the genetic material. What is a Nucleus? The most integral component of the cell is the nucleus (plural: nuclei). Structure Of Nucleus: Typically, it is the most evident organelle in the cell. The nucleus is completely bound by membranes. It is engirdled by a structure referred to as the nuclear envelope. (This is the CHAMAS PATRA of RIBHUS which was divided by the Rishis) The membrane distinguishes the cytoplasm from the contents of the nucleus The cell's chromosomes are also confined within it. DNA is present in the Chromosomes (Gunavidhi), and they provide the genetic information required for the creation of different cell components in addition to the reproduction of life.

Vedic knowledge expresses that the SPIRIT by crystallization transforms into matter and vice varsa.

तन्मित्रस्य वरुणस्याभिचक्षे सूर्यो रूपं कृणुते द्योरुपस्थे । अनन्तमन्यद्रुशदस्य पाजः कृष्णमन्यद्धरितः सं भरन्ति II 5 II Rigveda. 1-115-5.

Tanmitrasya varunasyaabhichakshe Suryo rupam krunute dyorupasthe I Anantamanyadrushsya pajah krishnamanyadharitah sam bharanti II 5 II Rigved. 1-115-5

"The Sun, is the sight (eyes - वरुणस्याभिचक्षे) of Mitra and Varuṇa, displays his form (of brightness) in the heavens, and his rays extend, on one hand, his infinite and brilliant power, or, on the other by hiding from our sight, bring on the darkness during night."

Commentary by Sāyaṇa: Ṛgveda-bhāṣya: Mitra and Varuna, an indirect representation referred to the world. His rays: haritaḥ, may also mean his horses. SAVITRA manifest from MITRA-VARUNA, in Antariksha spread light, heat, and brightness.

Scientific explanation. All living beings two-legged or 4 legged are blessed by Sun God - Savitra dev. The Sun is the chief source for heat, light, and energy for all. In modern times, the science has replaced the belief from elements as matter and consider all as energy wave, this achievement of modern science is in 20th Century, on the contrary, Vedic Rishi have narrated matter as energy thousands of years back in symbolic, obscure, and enigmatic way. See Rigveda 5-81-2:

विश्वा॑ रू॒पाणि॒ प्रति॑ मुञ्चते क॒विः प्रासा॑वीद्भ॒द्रं द्वि॒पदे॒ चतु॑ष्पदे । वि नाक॑मख्यत्सवि॒ता वरे॒ण्योऽनु॑ प्र॒याण॑मु॒षसो॒ वि रा॑जति ॥ Rigveda 5-81-2

Vishva rupani prati munchate kavih prasavid bhadram dvipade chatushpade I vinakamkhyatsavita varenyonu prayanamushaso virajati II 2 II Rigved. 5-81-2.

The Savitā in all forms has invigorated all living beings (multiped, biped and quadruped); and the Savitā has enlightened the heaven as well.

चित्र देवानाम् उद्गावनीकं चक्षुमित्रस्य वरुण स्यग्नेः । आ प्राद्यावपृथिवी अंतरिक्ष सूर्य आत्माजगतस्तस्युषश्च ॥

chitra devanam udgavnikam Chakshu mitrasya varunasyagne I Aa pradyava Prithvi Antariksha surya Atma jagatastasyushachya II

SUN, is the eyes of Mitra and Varun. It enlightens and invigorate earth and Antariksa. As it is being the soul of world or all Jagat.

Now the question is Gayatri Mantra or the narration which highlight the purpose behind the framing of mantra is important. This has been wonderfully analysed in Chhandogya Upanishad.

गायत्री वा ईदं सर्वं भूतं यदिदं किं च वाग्वै गायत्री वाग्वा इदं सर्वं भूतं गायति च त्रायते च ॥ छांदोग्योपनिशद. 3-12-1.

Gayatri va idam sarvam bhutam yadadi kim cha vagvei gayatri vagva idam sarva bhutam gayati cha trayate cha II Chhandogyopnishad 3-12-1.

The importance of the gāyatrī is emphasized. Gāyatrī is poetry, leads to Brahmanda – whole cosmos and all CHARACHAR i.e. moving and non-moving existing in it. It is vāk, word, (Shabda-शब्द, च वाग्वै). It identifies everything that exists. Vāk or SHABDA that gives a name/sign, a status. All BHUT in cosmos is VAK, which eliminates all fear in minds.

The gāyati cha trāyate cha (गायति च त्रायते च) —that sings to things and protection. It also means gāyantam trāyate—that is, he who repeats the gāyatrī is saved. (Ga means singing, and tra means saving or protecting.)

या वै सा गायत्रीयं वाव सा येयं पृथिव्यस्या ँ हीदँ सर्वं भूतं प्रतिष्ठितमेतामेव नातिशीय ते || 2 || छांदोगयोपनिषद. **3-12-2.**

Ya vei sa gayatriyam vav sa yeyam priyhivyasya hid sarvam bhutam pratishthit metameva natishiya te II Chhandogya Upanishad. 3-12-2.

That which is this gāyatrī is that which is this earth. For all things [moving or non-moving] are attached to this earth and cannot get away from it.

Yā vai sā gāyatrī, that which is this gāyatrī; iyam vāva sā, it is that; yā iyam pṛthivī, which is this earth; hi, for; asyām, to this [earth]; sarvam bhūtam, all things [moving or non-moving]; pratiṣṭhitam, are attached; etām eva na atiśīyate, cannot get away from it.

As Gayatri related to living beings by singing so it is related to Earth or related to the BHUTA. Atma and Pran are synonymous. Because the living beings are fractionalised Atma, Panchmahabhuta, and Pran. All are born from earth, nourished by earth and get back to earth after death.

वै सा पृथिवीयं वाव सा यदिदमस्मिन्पुरुषे शरीरमस्मिन्हीमे प्राणाः प्रतिष्ठिता एतदेव नातिशीयन्ते ॥३॥ छान्दोग्योपनिषद ३.१२.3.

Vei sa prithiviyam vav sa yadidmsminpurushe shariram sminhime pranah pratishthita etadeva natishiyante II 3 II Chandogya Upanishad. 3-12-3

Body is basically transformed earth. Or it is form of earth and Gayatri as well. ANTAHPURUSH in body is soul. Hence it is gayatri. SHRUTI of Veda are great efforts of Rishis and Sages. Brahman hood in brahmins is due to gayatri. See below:

यद्वै तत्पुरुषे शरीरमिदं वाव तद्यदिदमस्मिन्नन्तः पुरुषे हृदयमस्मिन्हीमे प्राणाः प्रतिष्ठिता देव नातिशीयन्ते ॥ ४॥ 7aNdoGyopin8d 3-12-4

Yadvei tatpurusha sharir midam vav tadyadidamsminnantah purusha hridayam smiNhime pranah pratishthita dev natishiyante II 4 II. Chhandogyopnishad 3-12-4.

This mantra relates to the hard efforts of Brahmins (Knower of BRAHMA). This brahman hood manifests Gayatri. In the form of body as Gayatri, in which soul resides, Heart denotes soul hence the Gayatri, therefore, prayer is advocated.

In short Gayatri is gratitude, respect, and prayer of the creator and in return his blessings. What science involved in this Gayatri Mantra?

Let us understand that the Rigvedic mantra was offered for recitation to child before going to Brahmacharyashram (ब्रह्मचर्याश्रम) or to student hood i.e. after the thread ceremony or Monjivrat function (मौंजी व्रत = उपनयन संस्कार). It is for the student going to Gurukul for learning. This was for all the students of the society desirous for learning. Recitation daily improves intellect and sharpens the brain and mind-set of the student. During modern times a lot of research efforts have been made on this topic.

[1. Harshananda S. 3rd ed. Chennai: Ramkrishna Math; 2010. Upanayana, Sandhya Vandana and Gayatri Mantra Japa.

2. Bhatta KV. 4th ed. South Canara: Kaitanje Prakashan; 2004. Shri Gayatri Mantra Rahasya. [PubMed].

3. Bernardi L, Sleight P, Bandinelli G, Cencetti S, Fattorini L, Wdowczyc-Szulc J, Lagi A. Effect of prayer and yoga mantras on autonomic cardiovascular rhythms: comparative study. BMJ. 2001 Dec 22-29;323(7327):1446-9. [PubMed]. 4. Effect of Gayatri mantra chanting on cognitive functions in school children

DOI: https://doi.org/10.17511/ijpr.2018.i03.02].

Chanting by student or any person, improves learning power, concentration, eternal power, peace of mind, and improves quality of life.

Scientific studies have reported that brain areas such as frontal lobe of brain (concerned with association of brain function), anterior cingulate, (decision-making skills, see figure) Para hippocampal gyri (The Para hippocampal gyrus plays an important role in memory.), thalami (plays a role in wakefulness, consciousness, learning and 67ummemory.), and hippocampus activity significantly decreased both sides followed by chanting mantras. **Not only this but the Vedic Sanskrit word chanting improves the vocabulary, clarity of pronunciation of the individual. It increases the attention by activating the cells in the brain.** It decreases the stress by calming the thought process. Thereby increase the performance. Thus improves the capability of learning. Reduces anxiety and calms down the active memory cells because of rhythmic sound waves produced by recitation. Due to recitation sound the memory and attention are influenced because of influence on both brain hemispheres.

The following photos are to indicate the anatomical parts of brain. The terms used in above paragraph are parts of Brain. Reader will have clarity about the variety of brain part.

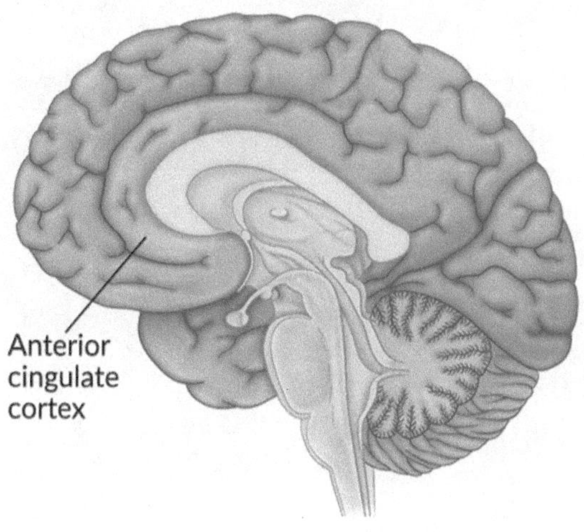

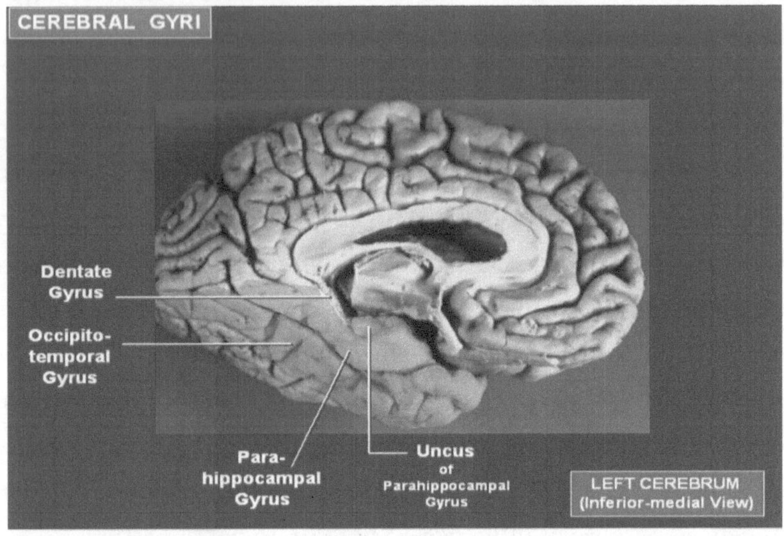

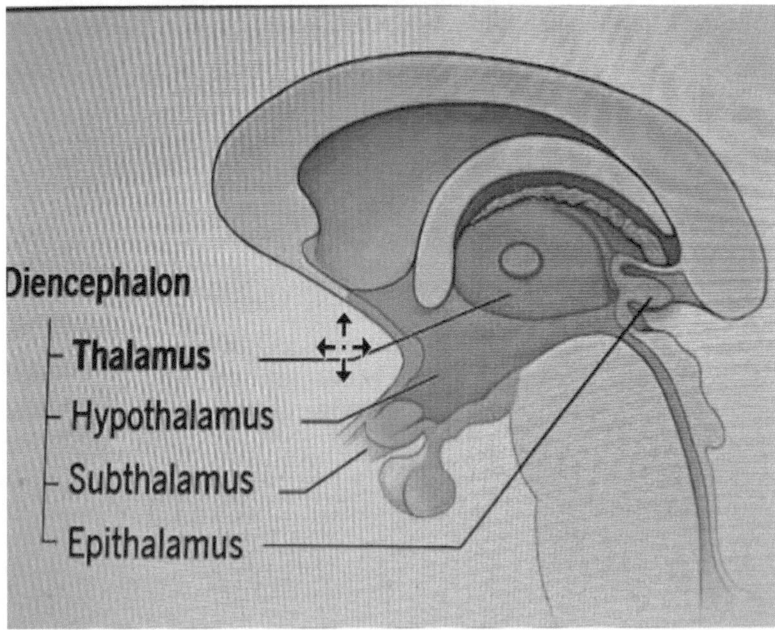

The effect of chanting of Vedic Mantra has been explained in 1st Chapter.

CHAPTER 3

MITRA-VARUN

In Rigveda these two words Mitra and Varuna (मित्र, वरुण) are frequently used together. The following explanation is worth the reading:

ता माता विश्ववेदसासुर्याय प्रमहसा । मही जजानादितिॠतावरी ॥3॥ Rigveda 8-25-3.

Ta mata Vishva ved sa suryaya pramhasa I mahi jajaana diti rytavari II 3 II Rigved. 8-25- 3

Mother Aditi (Nature) manifested all-knowing bright and righteous MITRA-VARUNA, for vanquishing / killing asuras. Asuras (असुर) are Demons or Evil minded.

Specific virtues of Varun and supportive association of Mitra, both are incorporated in water. These both are having opposite nature but in combination control and regulate the manifest world.

संसृष्टं धनमुभयं समाकृतमस्मभ्यं दत्तां वरुणश्च मन्युः । भियं दधाना हृदयेषु शत्रवः पराजितासो अप नि लयन्ताम् ॥7॥ Rigveda. १०.०८४.०७ (मन्युसूक्तं).

Samsrushtham dhanam ubhayam samakrutam asmabhyam dattam varunascya manyu I bhiyam dadhana hridayeshu shatravah parajitaso ap ni layantam II Rigved. 10-84-

Both (मुभयं = उभय.) these elements (*samakṛtam* - "mix; saṃsṛj; combine; accompany) Mitra and Varun are of opposite nature and behaviour, one is + ive while the other is – ive, One easily burns (Inflammable). **(Dattam Varunasya= ignite;; fuel). दत्तां वरुणस्च्य),** Energy of both is helpful to refrain enemies. The other is helpful in burning is friend or helpful (Mitra). Modern science explains it as Hydrogen and oxygen forming water – Aap. See text below.

धीरा त्वस्य महिना जनूंषि वि यस्तस्तम्भ रोदसी चिदुर्वी । प्र नाकमृष्वं नुनुदे बृहन्तं द्विता नक्षत्रं पप्रथच्च भूम ॥1॥ Rigveda 7-86-1.

Dhira Tvasya mahina janushi vi yastastambha rodasi chidurvi I pra nakamrushavam nanude brihanta davita nakshtram paprathchcha bhum. II 1 II Rigved. 7-86-1

Omnipresent Varun's birth (जनूंषि) and its presence is important. This Varun has stabilized Earth and Celestial sphere / Antariksha, in place and helped in the propagation of earth and celestial bodies (*rodasī* = "heaven and earth). At the same time Sun and Constellations are also helped by Varun. The Varun has expanded nature -prakriti on earth (भूम).

On analysis the description fits into Hydrogen and Oxygen. Presence of Hydrogen is important for the manifest Nature (Prakriti- प्रकृति) on earth floor, is known to modern scientists.

नीचीनबारं वरुण :कवन्धं प्र ससर्ज रोदसी अन्तरिक्षम् । तेन विश्वस्य भुवनस्य राजा यवं न वृष्टिर्व्युनत्ति भूम ॥3॥ Rigveda 5-85-3.

Nichinabaram varuna kavandham pra sasrja rodasi Antariksham I ten vishvasya bhuvanasya **raja** yavam na Vrishtirvyunatti bhum. II 3 II Rigved. 5-85-3.

Varuṇa is responsible for rain or downward fall by opening cloud for the (benefit of the) heaven, the earth, and the firmament, thence is king (RAJA - विश्वस्य भुवनस्य राजा) of all the world, watering the soil (भूम), as the rain on barleycorn (यवंम्). Manifestation of clouds having down pouring capacity (नीचीनबारं वरूण) is by Varun.

What is the scientific explanation of all this statement?

The qualities and the actions of Varuna as described in Sanskrit literature (Rigveda. 5-85-3, 7-86-1, 7-35-13, 10-84-7, 8-25-3, and 1-25-20) are: -

1. It has control over Earth and DYU lok (Antariksha-अन्तरिक्ष),

2. Stabilises both and provides energy to move,
3. Provide energy to Nakshatra to move in speed,
4. Provide speed to Sun and Nakshatra,
5. Expands Earth floor – Bhum भूम,
6. Creates clouds.
7. Atomic number is one – Aja ekpad – अज एकपादयो

If one considers Varun as Hydrogen the properties of Varun are explainable. Hydrogen is inflammable (Rigveda 10-84-7, अस्मभ्यं दत्तां वरुणश्च मन्यु (word meaning dattam ="give; add; perform; put; administer; fill into; give; **ignite; put on; offer; use; fuel; pour; grant).** The Mitra. or supportive element is Oxygen then the support for burning is Oxygen. Hydrogen and Oxygen make water. Both Mitra and Varun are in water. Why water-Emperor (JALA-Samrat) Varun created Clouds? (See mantra above Rigveda. 10-84-7 मन्युसूक्त).

Varun has extra intellectual power and possess knowledge about the whole world. Celestial space and the earth is enlightened by Varun. Accede the request and bless the devotees. Everything manifests due to Varun. Hence it is called "AJAEKPAD" (**अ॒ज एक॑पाद्दे॒वो**), Creator of all the elements. Atomic number is one. (See Rigveda. 7-35-13):

शं नौ अ॒ज एक॑पाद्दे॒वो अ॑स्तु शं नोऽहिर्बु॒ध्न्य :शं स॑मु॒द्रः । शं नौ अ॒पां नपा॑त्पे॒रुर॑स्तु शं न॒ : पृश्नि॑र्भवतु दे॒वगौपा ||13II Rigveda 7-35-13.

Sham nou aja ekpad devo astu sham nohirbudhnyah sham samudrah I sham no apam napatpe rurstu sham nah prishnirbhavatu dev gopa II 13 II Rigved. 7-35-13

The scientific meaning of the word "AJAEKPAD" (**अ॒ज एक॑पाद्दे॒वो**) will be clear after knowing modern chemistry of Hydrogen. (See below).

[Chemistry details about Hydrogen: Hydrogen. symbol is H, is a highly flammable gas (Formula is H_2) and the most common component of the universe. It is the lightest element ever and is colourless, odourless, and tasteless. It's also in most organic compounds. Hydrogen is non-metallic element **with the atomic number 1**, and it is also roughly 75% of the universe's mass. It's also the most abundant chemical element on the periodic table. Hydrogen(H) is a gas and is the first element on the periodic table. It is highly flammable. It is an elemental gas present in a trace amount in earth's atmosphere. Hydrogen is somewhat reactive because of its flammability. It is used as a component in fertilizer and fossil fuels. Hydrogen is one of the most important elements on our planet earth. Hydrogen can make a very essential molecule called water once the hydrogen has a covalent bond with oxygen. Hydrogen is the first element on the periodic table. It is also the most abundant element in the universe; stars in the main sequence have hydrogen in plasma form].

It is astonishing and amazing that thousands of years back Rishis of Sanskrit Speaking civilization were aware of this scientific fact! Modern day civilization is unable to interpret the language properly is not their fault. This must be understood properly after abandoning the religious mind set about the Veda and Purana. Rather it be attempted with research topic and analysed scientifically.

All the above qualities of Hydrogen described in chemistry of Hydrogen are narrated in Sanskrit literature about the Varun. Therefore, the Varun of Sanskrit is Hydrogen. Let us see more:

अष्टाचक्रं वर्तत एकनेमि सहस्राक्षरं प्र पुरो नि पश्चा। अर्धेन विश्वं भुवनं जजान यदस्यार्धं कतमः स केतुः ॥ **अथर्ववेद काण्ड -» 11; सूक्त » 4; मन्त्र » 22.** (See also अथर्व० १०।८।७। तथा १३ ॥

Ashtachakram vartat eknemi sahastraksharam pra puro ni pashcha I Ardhena vishvam bhuvanam jajaan yadasyardham katamah sa ketuh II 22 II Atharva ved. 11-4- 22. Read Atharva ved. 10-8-7 and 13.

Bound with unbreakable laws of nature in the universe, omnipresent, in past and future, and is responsible for the creation, and its presence manifests all elements of nature. On analysing scientifically as per modern science knowledge the above mantra is symbolic and descriptive. Mantras 7 and 13 are similar to 22 mantras.

Prana, the Prana of Prana, all-comprehending presence, and power like the felly (or outer circumference -) of a wheel moves and turns the eight-wheeled, thousand axled chariot of the universe round and round, up and down, out and in. With half of its potential, it creates the entire manifest world. What the other half remains transcendent, highest pure bliss, self-existent omniscience.

एकचक्रं वर्तत एकनेमि सहस्राक्षरं प्र पुरो नि पश्चा। अर्धेन विश्वं भुवनं जजान यदस्यार्धं क्वS तद्बभूव ॥ अथर्ववेद - काण्ड » 10; सूक्त » 8; मन्त्र » 7.

Ek chakram vartat eknemi sahastraksharam pra puro ni pashcha I Ardhen vishvam bhuvanam jajan yadasyardham kva tadbabhuv II 7 II Atharv Ved. 10-8-7.

The absolute truth with its uniformly applicable and unbreakable laws of Nature is omnipresent and omniscient, in past, present, and future. With a fractional energy of this absolute truth, the boundless cosmos has been created.

One is the wheel of the universe, has the outer circumference - the transcendent Brahma, has the central axis, the immanent Brahma), yet thousands are the spokes and axes, wheels within wheels, moving up and down, forward, and backward, east, and west. With one part of his Shakti, Prakrti, Brahma has formed the entire universe, where is the rest of it? What happened?

प्रजापतिश्चरति गर्भे अन्तरदृश्यमानो बहुधा वि जायते। अर्धेन विश्वं भुवनं जजान यदस्यार्धं कतमः स केतुः ॥ अथर्ववेद - काण्ड » 10; सूक्त » 8; मन्त्र » 13.

Prajapatishchyarti garbhe Antardrashyamano bahudha vi jayate I ardhen vishvam bhuvanam jajaan yadasyaardham katamah sa ketuh II13 II Atharv ved. 10-8-13

Absolute truth (the Prajapati), omniscient and omnipresent in the (**गर्भे**(vast space of the evolving, boundaryless universe. It is unseen(**अदृश्यमानः**(, yet manifests (**वि जायते**(as Prakriti, and creates (**जजान**(the entire universe using only a fraction(**अर्धम्**(of HIS energy. Where is the rest of its energy. Where and how the rest (**सः कतमः**(is? **Speed of Sound in Various Gases:**

All for 20 °C, 1 Atm, audible frequencies. Extrapolated from tables in the reference below. Consult that reference for other conditions.

From above comparison one can conclude the truth or fact, and correctness of Vedic science. The scientific inferences as well as achievements of the Sanskrit Speaking Civilization. Rig Veda Mandala 1, Hymn 136, Mantra1-7 speaks about the Varun, Mitra, Varun, and Aryama, are in atmosphere since eternity: -

प्र सु ज्येष्ठं निचिराभ्यां बृहन् नमो हव्यं मतिं भरता मळयद्भ्यां स्वादिष्ठं मळयद्भ्याम् । ता सम्राजाघ्रतासुती यज्ञे-यज्ञ उपास्तुता । अथैनोः कषत्रं न कुतश्चनाध्र्षे देनत्वं नू चिदाध्र्षे **II1II Rigved. 1-136-1.**

Pra su jyeshtham nichirabhyam brihan namo havyam matim Bharata maralaydabhyam I ta samrajya rdhata suti yadne yadnya upastuta I Atheinoh kashatram na kutashchya naghrashe denatvam nu chidaghrashe II rigved. 1-136-1

Since eternity the Varun-H_2, Mitra-O_2, and Aryama-N_2, are pervading on earth, and are worth the prayers and respect as they are the provider of prosperity, food, energy, life, progeny etc., and enliven the living beings on earth. Their virtues, Godliness, and energy cannot be challenged by any means II1II. Rigved. 1-136-1.

Gas	Speed of Sound (m/s)
Argon	319
Helium	1007
Krypton	221
Xenon	178
Hydrogen	1270 - Varun
Nitrogen	349 - Aryama
Oxygen	326 - Mitra
Carbon Dioxide	267
Sulfur Dioxide	201
Ethylene	327
Methane	446
Propane	258
Reference: "Handbook of the Speed of sound in Real Gases," by A. J. Zuckerwar (AcademicPress,2002). Questions / Commentsto: suits@mtu.edu	

अदर्शी गातुरुरवे वरीयसी पन्था रतस्य समयस्त रश्मि भिश्चक्षुर्भगस्य रश्मिभिः । दयुक्षं मित्रस्यस्य सादनम्र्यम्णो च । अथा दधाते बृहदुक्थ्हं वयौपस्तुत्यं बृहद् वयः ॥2॥
Rigved. 1-136-2.

Adarshi gaturukhe variyasi patha ratasya samayasta Rashmi bhishchakshurbhgasya rashmibhih I dyuksahm mitrasyasya sadanamryamno cha I atha dadhate brihadukthham vyoupastutyam brihad vyah II 2 II Rigved. 1-136-2.

Dwelling arena (**सादन**) of celestial Varun, Mitra, and Aryama (**दयुक्षं मित्रस्यस्य सादनमृर्यम्णो**), as per the law of cosmos (**रतस्य समयस्त रश्मि**), is enlightened by rays of the Sun.

Scientifically the arena of celestial gasses Hydrogen, Oxygen and Nitrogen is governed by the laws of nature of cosmos. The rays, radiation etc. of the sun enlighten the three gasses. On understanding the work and importance of Varun, Mitra, and Aryama the interested reader must read and analyse, statement scientifically. The rest of the four mantras are mentioned here for an interested reader for analysis and interpretation. The following Mantras of Rigved be interpreted on the lines of science and not with any tinge of religion.

[जयोतिष्मतीमदितिं धारयत्क्षितिं सवर्वतीमा सचेते दिवे-दिवे जाग्रवांसा दिवे-दिवे| जयोतिष्मत कषत्रमाशाते आदित्या दानुनस पती |मित्रस्तयोर्वरुणो यातयज्जनो .अर्यमा यातयज्जनः ||3

अयं मित्राय वरुणाय शन्तमः सोमो भूत्ववपानेष्वाभगो देवो देवेष्वाभगः | तं देवासो जुषेरत विश्वे अद्य सजोषसः | तथा राजाना करथो यदिमह रतावाना यदीमहे || 4 ||

यो मित्राय वरुणायाविधज्जनो.अनर्वाणं तं परि पातोंहसो दाश्वांसं मर्तमंहसः | तमर्यमाभि रक्षत्य रजूयन्तमनु वरतम | उक्थैर्य एनोः परिभूषति वरतं सतोमैराभूषति वरतम || 5 II

नमो दिवे बर्हते रोदसीभ्यां मित्राय वोचं वरुणाय मीळ्हुषे सुम्ळीकाय मीळ्हुषे | इन्द्रमग्निमुप सतुहि दयुक्षमर्यमणं भगम | जयोग जीवन्तः परजया सचेमहि सोमस्योती सचेमहि || 6 II

ऊती देवानां वयमिन्द्रवन्तो मंसीमहि सवयशसो मरुद्भिः |अग्निर्मित्रो वरुणः शर्म यंसन तदश्याम मघवानो वयं च II7II].

Sun provides the energy, strength, and instigate the three to work. Aryama, stimulate Varun and Mitra to work as per the law of nature.

After understanding the facts of nature and cosmos it is a hint to younger generation of scientists, for research and analysis. The Aryama stimulates the Varun and Mitra to work as per the laws of nature, The sun provides the energy, and instigate the three for work. See below the function of Aryama which keeps Agni vayu and Pran vayu separate from each other- (अजायथाः॥ 1-141-9). The research can be attempted, for human benefits. The artificial rains, provide ample water for human consumption etc. can be worked out.

Birth and Functions of Varun in Rigveda: -

धीरा त्वस्य महिना जनूंषि वि यस्तस्तम्भ रोदसी चिदुर्वी । प्र नाकमृष्वं नुनुदे बृहन्तं दविता नक्षत्रं पप्रथच्च भूम ॥ धीरा त्वस्य महिना जनूंषि वि यस्तस्तम्भ रोदसी चिदुर्वी । प्र नाकमृष्वं नुनुदे बृहन्तं दविता नक्षत्रं पप्रथच्च भूम ॥ 1 ॥ Rigveda 7-86-1.

Dhira tvasya mahina janushi vi yastastmbha rodasi chidurvi I pra nakamrushvam nunude brihanta m dvita nkshatram paprathcya bhum II 1 II Rigved. 7-86-1.

All pervading and cause of manifest cosmos the Varun's birth and existence is most important. It is pillar. Varun is responsible for stability of heaven and earth, stabilise and station them in their places. It provides speed and mobility to nakshatra, bhumi etc. The Sun and constellations are inspired by Varun. Responsible for expansion of Earth. Cool, comfortable, and intelligent people (Dhira) know this.

Why we need this knowledge? After understanding the creation of cosmos and the nature or Prakriti, the knowledge about that how the unit of human or living beings are created? How the cell came to exists? This knowledge can be utilised for creating an artificial CELL.

In Rigveda mantra, offerings (Havi-हवि अर्पण) are provided, to fulfil the request prayer to invited deities in Yadnya **(It is not sacrifice. It is action with purpose).** In a similar way, the mantra of Rigveda 10-121-1 to 10, Offering mentioned but there are scientific facts hidden. Study mantras below: -

About enlivened energy- Pran, "Hiranyagarbha", Aaditi:

हिरण्यगर्भः समवर्तताग्रे भूतस्य जातः पतिरेक असोत । सदाधार पृथवीं द्यामुतेमा कस्मै देवाय हविषा विधेम ॥ 1 ॥

Hiranyagarbhah samavrtataagre bhutasya jatah patirek Asota I sada aadhar prithvim dyomutema kasme devay havisha vidhem II 1 II Rigved. 10-121-1.

The Controller who was present even before (**समवर्तताग्रे**) newly manifest Nature- (**सृष्टि**). The energy Pran- **प्राण रुप हिरण्यगर्भ - परमेश्वर,** the absolute truth or Parm Ishwar, is the enlivening energy and the creator as well as supporter of all the living beings on earth. We offer Him the Havi – **हवि्.** Havi is havan samagri or materials used for havan or YAJNYA - **यज्ञ.**

Param Atma Tattva is the cause of nature and the living beings. All is created (**भूतस्य जतः**), nourished and enlivened by Him. Example cited is, sparks coming out of burning fire, carry energy and fire with it so is the life appears from Param Aatma Tattva. Manifester of Earth, Antariksha, Aditya, and Udak – Liquid-Aap in Aakash is the provider of energy, courage, and happiness. As gratitude the offer is extended to deities (Mantra 2,3,4,5,6).

In the same context,

रथः। न। यातः। शिक्वऽभिः। कृतः। द्याम्। अङ्गेभिः। अरुषेभिः। ईयते। आत्। अस्य। ते। कृष्णासः। धक्षि। सूरयः। शूरस्यऽइव। त्वेषथात्। ईषते। वयः ॥ १.१४१.८

Rathah na yatah shikvabhih krutah dyam angebhih Iyate aat Asya te krishnash dhakshi soorayah shoorayah shoorasyah eiva tveshthat eishate vayahh II 8 II Rigved. 1-141-8

The chariot once made ready, deft hands and actions (शिक्वSभिः कृतः) of driver fly it in sky (द्याम्) using the parts of Chariot (अङ्गेभिः। अरुषेभिः।). Similarly, Sun – Agni-अग्नि, rises in sky and removes darkness and ignorance.

In this the example of chariot is full of science and space travel. Example is only quoted for understanding. Hence it must be known and prevalent in the society and understood by common man. Space travel was commonly known to the Sanskrit Speaking civilization. (see chapter on Space travel)

Next mantra talks about the Sun, Varun, Mitra, and Aryama giving an example of wheel and spokes, concurrent just like the rim of a wheel holding the spokes together running and working together. Like the wheel of chariot, the work of cosmos is supported and functions.

त्वया। हि । अग्ने। वरुणः। ध्रुतSव्रतः । मित्रः । शाशद्रे। अर्यमा । सुSदानवः । यत् । सीम्। अनु। क्रतुना । विश्वSथा। विSभुः । अरान् । न । नेमिः परिSभूः । अजायथाः ॥ **1-141-9.**

Tvaya hi agne Varunah dhrutvr+ata mitrah shashadre Aryama sudanvah yat seem anu kratuna vishvatha vibhuh aran na nemi paribhuh II Ajayathah 1-141-9.

Agni, with light, life, power, regulate Varun, and Mitra, who abide by the laws of Nature, removes darkness, while Aryama, with abundant and dynamic nature staying in between the two, keep them separate (see text above). In summary, their functions and encompassing them all, like the circumference encompasses the spokes of a wheel. Wheel has an iron circumference and spokes (अरान्) unite at the hub (नेमिः) similarly the soul or Aatma manifests elements-tattva which is surrounded by the Pran – life energy, like iron circumference of a wheel. Thus, protects and controls as well.

This indicates the existing knowledge in Sanskrit civilization about wheel, spokes, and their function. The manifestation of super soul / the absolute truth, regulated by the laws of nature and governed by those laws efficiently. The regulation in nature is explained in Rigveda. 5-29-1

त्र्यर्यमा मनुषो देवताता त्री रोचना दिव्या धारयन्त। अर्चन्ति त्वा मरुतः पूतदक्षास्त्वमेषामृषिरिन्द्रासि धीरः ॥१॥ ऋग्वेद. 5-29-1

Tryaryama manusho devtata tri rochana divya dharayant I archanti tva marutah pootadakshastva meshamrushirindraasi dhirah II 1 II Rigved.5-29- 1.

The three 'Ahuti' for Yadnya – the three effulgence, Marut – (wind) with speed, strength, and governance, Marut uphold in space the three luminaries- Sun, wind, Fire, "Tryarma" **त्र्यर्यमा** - are serving Indra- the powerful ruler. (**मृषिरिन्द्रासि धीरः**)

Three luminaries: the sun, the wind, and fire; the same trio may be intended by the earlier phrase tryaryamā trīṇi aryamāṇi tejāṃsi. The nature is interdependent on all the existing elements – tatvas. The description is symbolic. The sun, Maruts, and Agni symbolically used to explain the regulation of nature.

CHAPTER 4

THE SCIENTIFIC MEANING OF NOMENCLATURES USED IN GITA, RIGVEDA, AND PURAN

The study of Vedic Mantras, reveal that the Sanskrit literature of Vedas and Puranas are obscure and enigmatic. The presentation of Rigveda in this book is based on:

1. Logic and arguments,
2. Meditation, deep Thinking on the topic
3. Discussions by learned Acharyas of Sanskrit
4. **Reading Sanskrit Vedic Literature and translations by Acharyas like** Shankarachayas, Sayanacharyas, etc., and from internet, Wikipedia etc.

Each Sukta in 10 Mandals, is described in a very particular fashion. Sukta has DEVATA, RISHI, CHHANDA. and Swar - **स्वर**. Majority have same last heads, i.e., Rishi and Chhanda. Some places Rishi and Chhanda are different. Some places Rishis are females too. Apart from this the Rishis are from different CHATUR VARNA system, i.e., Brahman, Kshatriya, Vaishya, and Shudra.

Meaning of MANDAL, SUKTA, and DEVATA

Rigveda has described variety of modern subjects, to mention a few like, Flying Machines that too auto propelled or capable of flying with energy from mind, at a speed more than mind. Description of wheels, hub, spokes etc, and the horse driven vehicles. On the medical fronts the artificial limbs made from metals, youthful life to elders, Blinds provided with vision, creating cows and horses from skin, Creating human clone from dead person, viz. Nishad, Prithu, Vasishtha, Agustya etc. Prohibition of inter-related marriages (Discussion between brother and sister-Yam-Yami). Instruments of warfare, Potter, Farmer, Weavers, Needles, Irrigation system, etc indicate the overall development of civilization during Vedic era. Architecture or Vaastu shastra was highly developed.

The different names used in Rigveda are symbolic. The names used are confusing due to present day understanding which is different from that of Vedic era. The meanings of names used are conceptually different, but if analysed after reading more mantras of Rigveda, the clarity is obvious and the real meaning Rigveda intended, can be derived. Following description will certainly clear the doubt.

There is a mention of Panch-mahambhut (पंच महा भूत), the basic five primordial elements. These are Earth, Water, Fire, Air, and Aakash. This is the reverse order of their manifestation. Fractions of these all elements are incorporated in manifested "moving and Non-moving beings – Char-achar – (चराचर). Hence their real meaning must be understood as per the use by Rishi, Sages, or Scientists of Sanskrit Speaking Civilization. The following paragraphs are the authors understanding. The meaning may raise controversies. But the meaning sounds appropriate as per the overall Vedic scriptures.

The word Panchmahabhut (पंचमहाभूत) is used repeatedly in Sanskrit literature. What is the meaning of this word? How are these manifested?

There are five basic primordial elements of the whole cosmos responsible for the manifestation of nature – Srishti - सृष्टि.

The five basic primordial elements are:

Bhumi – Earth.

Aap – liquid element. (Not water which is a pat of Aap)

Nala – Agni – Fire element, anything which has heat and light.

Nilo – vayu – speed element Air is a part of Vayu.

Nabh – Aakash – space element.

Aakash Tattva – Nabh – नभ:, All pervading basic element. Bhutakash and Sarvakash.

Vedic connotation (in Sanskrit it is लक्ष्यार्थ) of Aakash is not just a space. It is envelope and surrounds everything in nature. Maintains original state which is everywhere. Space or Aakash is of two types. It is in all manifest beings called Bhuta-Aakash (भूताकाश), and a dome for cosmos called Vyom-Aakash (व्योमाकाश). The Aakash Tattva is space and time both. It is beyond speed, or it encompasses speed. It is primordial and pulsating. How one perceives it? It is by sense of hearing and feeling of sound vibrations (शब्द ब्रम्ह). At the same time, perceived by shape and colour (रूप), which is Blueish or blue-black. As per the NASADIYA Sukta of Rigved, it is the first primordial manifest cover and for containment of the manifest cosmos.

VAYU – Neel – (नील).

It is not air or gas. Air and gas are the component of Vayu. It is another primordial element with speed. It can travel to extremity within the same moment. The Vayu is the second expression after Aakash. It has speed. sense of touch can recognize it. It is with mixture of many gasses out of which few are still unknown to science. In Bhagwat Gita 7-4, Shri Krishna says about eight aspects of Prakriti or Nature. The separated energies or fractioned energy of "Paramatma Tatva" or Super Soul is pervading everything in this manifest cosmos.

भूमिरापोऽनलो वायु: खं मनो बुद्धिरेव च । अहङ्कार इतीयं मे भिन्ना प्रकृतिरष्टधा ||4|| Shrimad Bhagwadgita 7-4.

Bhumiraponalo vayuh kham mano budjireva cha I Ahangkar itiyam me bhinna prakritirshtadha II 4 II Shrimad bhagwad Gita. 7-4.

Prakriti has eight ingredients: bhumi, Aap, Agni, Vayu, Space, mann, budhi and Ahangkar.

Vayu is one of the basic the element. Prana Vayu is one of the five pranas as per Vedic knowledge the "Panch-Prana". These are the part of the main Vayu which is in the Aakash. Aakash is not an empty space but filled with Aether Vedic knowledge considers that Aakash is occupied by ocean of micro particles, Samudrarnav (समुद्रार्णव). Vayu is also an ingredient of the total aether. The five pranas can cover the day-to-day requirements of most human and living beings. These Pancha pranas are sufficient to keep your body and mind healthy, normal, and living spiritually alive. Highly evolved yogi can live without any food and water for many days. This makes it clear that the Vayu is not only air and gases. Prana Vayu is not just Oxygen. Rigved. Mandal 1, Sukta 2. Shlok 4 indicates that Indra and Vayu are the provider of food for living beings, are worshiped and praised for provider of the same to the Yadnya performers. Yadnya is efforts in those directions.

Ṛiṣhi (sage or seer): madhucchandāḥ vaiśvāmitraḥ, Devatā (deity or subject-matter): Indra Vāyūḥ;Chandas (meter): gāyatrī; Svara (tone/note): Swar;

The DEVATA is VAYU. Rishi is Vishwamitra. Chhanda is Gayatri, Devata are Vayu, Indra-Vayu, Mitra-Varuna. In this Sukta 2, INDRA and Vayu are invited to provide Food and Water.

इन्द्रवायू इमे सुता उप परयोभिरा गतम | इन्दवो वामुशन्ति हि II 2 II Rigveda. 1-2-4.

"Indra and Vāyu, the libations are ready for you, grant us food verily the drops of Soma juice await you both.

Movements of Celestial bodies in Space or Aakash.

The movements of the celestial bodies decide time cycle (काल चक्र). The text is also referred in medieval Indian literature as the Vayaviya Purana or Vayaviya Brahmanda. Vayu Purana is one of the eighteen Puranas of Sanskrit Speaking Civilization. It is in the Mahabharata manuscript. It analyses manifestation of cosmos, the time as a dimension and also about the time scale, Kalpa and Yuga the life span of Brahma, Vishnu, Rudra-Shiv, and Param Shiv. Their manifestation and time of their annihilation. It includes the subject of evolution of cosmos and basic elements.

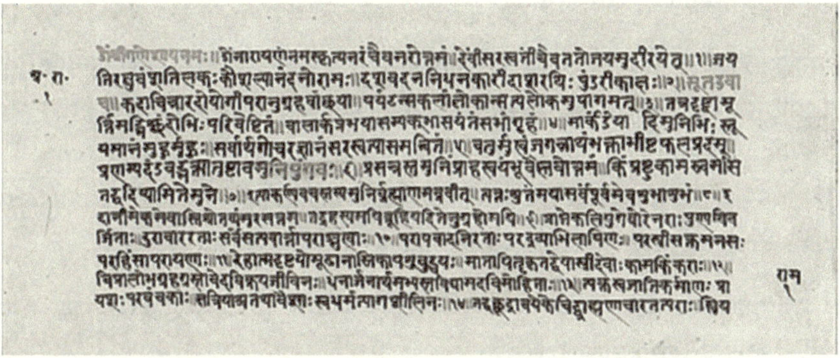

The evolution of cosmos is cosmic expression of basic elements. These are the PANCHMAHABHUT - 5 basic elements, which are – Earth, Water, Fire, Air, Space (BHUMIRAPONALONILONABHA). In fact, these are the expressional existence of elements. No one knows the original state of existence as expressed in NASADIYA SUKTA of Rigveda Mandal 10. The Vayu is recognized by sense of touch. It is not the air with mixture of gasses. Some of the gasses are still unknown to science. In Bhagwadgita 7-4, Shri Krishna says about 8 aspects of Prakriti or Nature. The separated energies of Paramatma Tatva or Super Soul (see above).

SUKTA 2 the DEVATA is VAYU. In this Sukta 2, INDRA and Vayu are invited to provide Food and Water. How are they considered the food provider? Food is possible due to the presence of Nitrogen element - PUSHNA VAYU (Aryama). Modern science knows this. It is amazing that the Vedic science was aware of this fact! Rigved maintains that the

Nitrogen cycle is important. The stock of nitrogen remains constant. (See nitrogen cycle elsewhere in this book)

AGNI – Nala - (नल).

Third stage of creation is Agni - (Tejah- Nala-नल:). Light is TEJ which has tremendous speed. Agni is a destructive element. But "Sankhya shastra" believes that the Agni has the quality to create. Electron movement is the energy which makes it move around in the orbit. So, the stars and the manifest cosmos.

The conceptual understanding of Rigveda is possible with deep thinking and meditating on each stanza of Rigveda. The obvious meaning of every Mantra may connote a different meaning than its original intent. 1st Mandal is 1st section, Sukta 1 is chapter, Devata is Topic or Subject matter. Mandal 1 Rishi is Vishva mitra, Chhanda is Gayatri, Devta is AGNI.

Here the topic or subject matter is AGNI. To quote an example the Rigveda Mandal 1, Sukta 1, Mantra 1. Says: -

ओम अग्निमीळे पुरोहितं यज्ञस्य देवमृत्विजम् । होतारं रत्न धामताम् II 1 II **Rigveda 1-1-1.**

Agnimile purohitam yadnyasya devam ritvijam I hotaram ratna dhamtam II1 II rigved. 1-1-1.

The word AGNI is discussed here:

The common understanding about the word AGNI is FIRE. The fire connotes that it emits light and heat. In fact, the virtues or DHARM of fire is heat and light. It is a sort of energy. What Veda considers about AGNI.

Agni (अग्नि)- : responsible for the manifestation of Brahma (Galaxies and stars, constellations etc.) and living beings (Praja) at the same time providing energy and speed to everything. Such energy is praiseworthy and worth to be worshipped (इळे). Has power for the creation of the universe. The question arises that how this is possible when the fire can destroy everything coming in contact? The meaning gets unfolded when you ponder on other Mantras elsewhere in Rigveda. The description about AGNI is available in Rigveda, 4- 58- 3.

चत्वारि शृङ्गा त्रयो अस्य पादा द्वे शीर्षे सप्त हस्तासो अस्य । त्रिधा बद्धो वृषभो रोरवीति महो देवो मर्त्यां आ विवेश ॥ Rigveda, 4- 58- 3.

Chatvari shringa trayo asya pada, dvei sheershe sapta hastaso asya I tridha baddho vrishabho rorviti maho devo martyam aa vivesh II 3 II Rigved, 4-58-3.

Meaning of mantra is Four horns (चत्वारी श्रृंगा), three legs (त्रयो अस्य पादा), two heads (व्दै शीर्षे), and seven hands (सप्त हस्तासो), the bull tied at three sites (त्रिधा बध्दो वृषभो), the great God enters from all around in mortal's abode and creates sound.

This is an enigmatic explanation about fire – the AGNI. It is an obscure picture. It is certainly symbolic. How it is so? The analysis is as follows:

It does not fit in the ordinary fire or flames of the fire, is obvious. If one considers AGNI (Flames or "Jwala") as SUN God, the meaning can be clear. The SUN showers energy or brilliance all around on earth. It energises all living beings when Sun rises in the morning. Sun is responsible for all types of seasons (three main Summer, Winter, and Rains.) on earth. Sun illuminates three abodes – BHUH, BHUVAH, SWAH. Sun Solstices are two – Summer and Winter or moves in two heads. Sun light beam, or Surya-Prakash, can be split into seven colours VIBGYOR is known to modern science.

Apart from this in Sanskrit literature Sun is as Agni.

In 10th Mandal, Sukta 1, Mantra 1, the explanation exists that:

अग्रे बर्हन्नुषसामूर्ध्वो अस्थान निर्जगन्वान तमसोज्योतिषागात | अग्निर्भानुना रुशता सवङ्ग आ जातोविश्वा सद्मान्यप्राः || 1 II Rigveda. 10-1-1.

Agre barhNnushsamoordhvo Asthan nirjagNvan tamasoJyotishagat I Agnirbhanuna rushata savanga Aa jatovishva sadmanyaprah IIb1 II Rigved. 10-1-1.

The great AGNI in the morning brings world, enlightenment from darkness using its TEJ (heat and light). This is directly indicating AGNI as Sun God.

Another explanation is in In Mundakopnishad, Mundak 1- Khand 2 – mantra 4:

काली कराली च मनोजवा च सुलोहिता या च सुधूम्रवर्णा ।
स्फुल्लिंगिनी विश्वरुची च देवी लेलायमाना इति सप्त जिव्हाः ॥
Mundakopnishad. 1-2- 4

Kaali karali cha manojava cha sulohita ya cha sudhumravarna I sfullingini vishvaruchi cha devi lelayamana iti sapta jivha II 4 II Mundakopnishad. 1-2-4

Seven types of flames (Seven tongues - **सप्त जिव्हाः**) are described in Mundakopnishad. All are having speed. In Yadnya Homkunda – **यज्ञकुन्ड** when Agni has established such flames are not visible. What is the meaning of such names for the flames is again an enigma? The interpretation is as follows:

KALI is related to kaal or TIME. Time depends upon the movement of the SUN. Agni again is from SUN. (refer to 'Mahasamhita' from Uma Samhita of Shiv Purana– Song of science – Shrimad Bhagwat Gita, Notion Press. Agni energy is from wood, wood is from a tree. The fire energy in wood is from Sun). The details about the 7 tongues or 7 flames of fire are as follows:

1. Kaali (**काली**) is kaal (**काल, मृत्यु,**) or time. This depends upon movement or rotation effect. (see Kalchakra chapter). Time is outcome of earth rotating around Sun. AGNI or fire is daependent upon Sun. (See Mahasamhita mantra of Uma Samhita of Shiv Puran). One gets fire from wood. Wood s from tree. In tree fire element is from sun via Chlorophyll, which is from

(Deleted line) sunrays. It is stored in the form of oil in wood. The energy all living beings get is from Sun or living force or life. Sun rotates around centre of Galaxy, obviously the energy is from somewhere else i.e., PARAM BRAHMA. Therefore, the energy of KAALI is from PARAM BRAHMA.

2. Karali (कराली) means Fierce and terrifying (भयंकर or विकराल). This energy can perform multiple work and functions. Sun's heat and brightness can perform multitude of functions. KARALI is KAR+ALI or) KAR in SANSKRIT is ARM which performs multitude of functions.

   A. Manojava (मनोजवा). Moving like mind. (Energy which flows like Mind)- The energy having a speed of mind, which is greater than speed of light. Einstein never agreed that there is element faster than the light. Prof. E.C.G. Sudarshan, Theoretical Physics, Syracuse University, New York, USA. (1956), proved this fact. He could not publish till 1962. The particle is TACHYON. Following paragraph is interesting.

[Quantum Field Theory of Interacting Tachyons. Article Oct 1968. J. Dhar. E. C. G. Sudarshan

A quantum field theory of spin-0 particles traveling with speeds greater than that of light has been constructed. The theory constructed here is explicitly Lorentz-invariant; and the quanta of the field obey Bose statistics. Formalism developed for the free field has been extended to the case of interaction of these particles with nucleons.

Another article in 1968 by Jacob Kuriyan. N. Mukunda. E. C. G. Sudarshan

The representation theory of the groups SO (5), SO (4, 1),SO (6) and SO(5, 1) is studied using the method of Master Analytic Representations (MAR). It is shown that a single analytic expression for the matrix elements of the generators ofSO(n+1) andSO(n, 1) in anSO(n) basis yields all the unitary representations (forn=4,5); and that the compact and non-c

The light is harnessed by man for his benefits. The following quote is from an article Science **Today Vol. 3, (july-june) 1968**"

But that was many million years ago. From the time Man got around, he's been trying to Improve upon nature with fire, torches, candles, and what-not. Then Edison came along and invented the electric lamp — and turned night into day. And since then, Man has progressed with light almost with the speed of light. Today, light is used for communication, health, entertainment, weaponry engineering, surgery, even for measuring distances! Light is just one aspect of science. light was harnessed with the progress of science. Man has advanced through understanding science. And there's no looking back] And then there was light...

1. Sulohita –(सु + लोहिता), Infra-red vibrations - light? Heat and radio waves are present in it. This needs targeted study and research.

2. Sudhumravarna – (सु धूम्रवर्णा) Smoke has bluish – Violet hue. Ultra-violet radiation? Beyond this is X-rays and cosmic rays.

3. Sfullingini –(स्फुल्लिंगिनी) Sphuran means flutter, spark (ठिणगी). Vibration with speed is Sphuran. It is a spark. Lightening in clouds, atomic energy. Pulsatile with strong movement. In an atom, electrons, protons, are pulsatile and vibrate. Hence it is atomic power.

4. Vishwa ruchi – (विश्व रुचि) energy with extremely strong power. It is topmost energy. It has power to destroy the world.

These seven energies are in Agni. Can these be in the fire? Obviously, this is in Super NATURE or Param Brahma. The AGNI in HOMKUNDA – Pious pyre site is just a representative of PARAMBRAHMA AGNI.

The 5th mantra of Mundakopnishad clearly indicates SUN Rays as Agni:

एतेषु यश्चरते भ्राजमानेषु यथाकालं चाहुतयोह्याददायन् । तन्नयन्त्येताः सूर्यस्य रश्मयो यत्र देवानां पतिरेको'धिवासः ॥ ५ ॥ Mundakopnishad, Mundak 1- Khand 2 - mantra 5.

Eteshu yashchrate bhrajmaneshu yathakaalam chahutyohyadadayan I tannayantyetah Sooryasya rashmayo yatra devanam patirekodhivasah II 5 II Mundakopnishad. 1-2-5.

One who performed good deeds (-pious *karma)*, at the proper time, **carry him through the rays of the sun** to a place where the Supreme soul or energy exists.

It is not the fire. But is more than fire. AGNI is Shakti or energy from Superpower. The Agni attracts or invites the Dev and RITVIJ (देवमृत्विजम् = Devam + Ritvijam) by performing YADNYA Karma. In turn, the wealth and useful things are provided by DEVTA. Wealth for living beings is food. The food is from Sun. All vegetation on earth is due to sun rays and the rain. Rain is due to sun is well known to humans. It is as per modern science.

The mantra five Equoted above, clearly indicates that in the AGNI from YADNYA KUNDA, at a proper time acts and behaves then these fire flames, in the form of sunrays, takes the performer to the Supreme energy level of PARAM BRAHMA.

एह्येहीति तमाहुतयः सुवर्चसः सूर्यस्य रश्मिभिर्यजमानं वहन्ति । प्रियां चमभिवदन्त्योऽर्चयन्त्य एष वः पुण्यः सुकृतो ब्रह्मलोकः ॥ ६ ॥
Mundakopnishad 1-2-6.

Ehyehiti tamahutayah suvarchasah sooryasya rashmibhiryajamanam vahanti I priyam chamabhivadantyorchayantya esha vah punyah sukruto brahmalokah II 6 II mundakopnishad. 1-2-6.

These oblations shining bright carry the performer of Yadnya, through the rays of the sun bidding him welcome, propitiating him and greeting him with pleasing words. This is the well-laid path of virtue leading to Brahmaloka.

The above 7 energies are highly scientific. Some energies are known to modern science like X-Rays, Infra-red, Ultraviolet rays, Radiation etc but others are to be researched out. The Supersonic flying machines push the sound waves to reach beyond sound speed but light waves pushing light speed waves and going beyond light speed is unknown even today. Modern science is speedily progressing to attain that knowledge.

How the oblations through the rays of the Sun carry the YADNYA performer to Brahma Lok is still enigmatic!! It is interesting for the researchers to investigate the details of 7 split fire waves described above. Above explanation is just a small understanding as per the intellect and experience of the author. Detailed investigations are essential to get more possibilities.

VAYU – Neel – (नील).

The Vayu Purana discusses its theories of cosmology, genealogy of gods and kings of solar and lunar dynasties, mythology, geography, Manvantaras, the solar system and the movements of the celestial bodies. The text is also referred in medieval Indian literature as the Vayaviya Purana or Vayaviya Brahmanda. It includes creation of cosmos, discussion about the time as a dimension and details of Kalpa and Yuga, etc. (as discussed above). It is repeated again for ease and clarity

The evolution of cosmos is cosmic expression of basic elements. These are the PANCHMAHABHUT- 5 basic elements, which are – Earth, Water, Fire, Air, Space (BHUMIRAPONALONILONABHA). In fact, these are the expressional existence of elements. No one knows the original state of existence as expressed in NASADIYA SUKTA of Rigveda Mandal 10. The

Vayu is the 2nd expression after Aakash. It has speed. It is recognized by sense of touch. It is not the air with mixture of gasses some of which are still unknown to science. In Bhagwadgita 7-4, Shri Krishna says about 8 aspects of Prakriti or Nature. The separated energies of Paramatma Tatva or Super Soul.

भूमिरापोऽनलो वायु: खं मनो बुद्धिरेव च | अहङ्कार इतीयं मे भिन्ना प्रकृतिरष्टधा ||**4**|| Shrimad Bhagwadgita 7-4.

SUKTA 2 the DEVATA is VAYU. Rishi is Vishwamitra. Chhanda is Gayatri, Devata are Vayu, Indra-Vayu, Mitra-Varuna. In this Sukta 2, INDRA and Vayu are invited to provide Food and Water.

इन्द्रवायू इमे सुता उप परयोभिरा गतम | इन्दवो वामुशन्ति हि ll 2 ll Rigveda. 1-2-4.

Indravayu ime suta upa parayobhira gatam I indavo vamushanti hi II 2 II

INDRA, MITRA - VARUNA:

Details have been explained above in the beginning of this chapter.

In Rigveda these two words are frequently used together. The following explanation is worth the reading:

ता मा॒ता वि॒श्ववे॑दसासु॒र्या॑य॒ प्रम॑हसा । म॒ही ज॑जा॒नादि॑तिर्ऋ॒ताव॑री ॥3॥ Rigveda 8-25-3.

Ta mata vishvavedsasuryay pramahasa I mahi jajaanaditi rutavari II3 II

Mother Aditi (ज॑जा॒नादि॑ति) manifested all-knowing bright and righteous MITRA-VARUNA, for vanquishing / killing asuras. The adverse effects are nullified (Asuras) and virtues supported. Specific virtues of Varun and supportive association of Mitra, both are incorporated in water. These both are having opposite nature but in combination control and regulate the manifested world.

सं॒सृष्टं॒ धन॑मु॒भयं॑ स॒माकृ॑तम॒स्मभ्यं॑ दत्तां॒ वरु॑णश्च म॒न्युः । भियं॒ दधा॑ना॒ हृद॑येषु॒ शत्र॑वः॒ परा॑जितासो॒ अप॒ नि ल॑यन्ताम् ॥7॥ Rigveda. १०.०८४.०७ मन्युसूक्तं,

Sansrushtam dhanamubhayam samakrutamsmabhyam dattam varunashchya manyuh I bhiyam dadhanam hridyeshu xtravah parajitaso Ap ni layantam II7 II Rigved. 10-84-7 (Manyusukta)

Both (मु॒भयं॑ =उभयं) these elements (*saṃsṛṣṭaṃ* - "mix; saṃsṛj; combine; accompany) Mitra and Varun are of opposite nature and behaviour, one is + ive while the other is – ive, One easily burns (Inflammable). (Dattam Varunasya= ignite;; fuel). दत्तां वरुणस्य), Energy of both is helpful to refrain enemies. the other is helpful in burning (Mitra).

धीरा॒ त्व॑स्य महि॒ना ज॒नूंषि॒ वि यस्त॒स्तम्भ॒ रोद॑सी चिदु॒र्वी । प्र नाक॑मृ॒ष्वं नु॑नुदे बृ॒हन्तं॑ द्वि॒ता नक्ष॑त्रं प॒प्रथ॑च्च॒ भूम॑ ॥1॥ Rigveda 7-86-1

Dhira tvasya mahina jnushi vi yastastambha rodasi chidurvi I pra nakmrushvam nunude brihantamdavita nakshatram paprathchcha bhum II 1 II Rigved. 7-86-1.

Omnipresent Varun's birth (ज॒नूंषि॒) and its presence is important. This Varun has stabilized Earth and Celestial sphere / Antariksha (द्वि॒ता नक्ष॑त्रं), in place and helped in the propagation of earth and celestial bodies (*rodasī* = "heaven and Earth). At the same time Sun and Constellations are also helped by Varun. The Varun has expanded nature - prakriti on earth floor (भूम॑). The presence of Hydrogen is important for the manifest Nature (Prakriti- प्रकृति) on earth floor, is known to present-day scientists.

नी॒चीन॑बारं॒ वरु॑णः॒ कव॑न्धं॒ प्र स॑सर्ज॒ रोद॑सी अ॒न्तरि॑क्षम् । तेन॒ विश्व॑स्य॒ भुव॑नस्य॒ राजा॒ यवं॒ न वृ॒ष्टिर्व्यु॑नत्ति॒ भूम॑ ॥3॥ Rigveda 5-85-3

Nichinbaram varunah kavandham pra sasrja rodasi Antariksham I ten vishvasya bhuvanasya raja yavam na vrushtirvyanatti bhuma II 3 II Rigved. 5-85-3.

Varuṇa is responsible for rain or downward opening cloud for the (benefit of the) heaven, the earth, and the firmament, thence is king (RAJA) of all the world, watering the soil (भूम), as the rain on barleycorn (यवंम्). Manifestation of clouds having down pouring capacity (नीचीनबारं वरूण) is by Varun.

What is the scientific explanation of all this statement?

The qualities and the actions of Varun as descried in Sanskrit literature (Rigveda. 5-85-3, 7-86-1, 7-35-13, 10-84-7, 8-25-3, and b1-25-20) are: -

1. It has control over Earth and DYU lok (Antariksha-अन्तरिक्ष),
2. Stabilises both and provides energy to move,
3. Provide energy to Nakshatra to move in speed,
4. Provide speed to Sun and Nakshatra,
5. Expands Earth floor – Bhum भूम,
6. Creates clouds.
7. Atomic number is one – Aja ekpad – अज एकपादयो

If one considers Varun as Hydrogen the properties of Varun are explainable. Hydrogen is inflammable. The Mitra or supportive element is Oxygen then the support for burning is Oxygen. Hydrogen and Oxygen make water. Both Mitra and Varun are in water. Why water-Emperor (JALA-Samrat) Varun created Clouds? (See mantra above Rigveda. १०.०८४.०७ मन्युसूक्त).

Varun has extra intellectual power and possess knowledge about the whole world. Celestial space, and the earth both enlightened by Varun. Accede the request and bless the devotees. Everything manifests due to Varun. Hence it is called “King” (**Raja**), Creator of all the elements. Atomic number is one. (See Rigveda. 7-35-13):

शं नौ अ॒ज एक॑पाद्दे॒वो अ॑स्तु॒ शं नोऽहि॑र्बु॒ध्न्य१: शं स॑मु॒द्रः । शं नौ अ॒पां नपा॑त्पे॒रुर॑स्तु॒ शं न॒: पृश्नि॑र्भवतु दे॒वगो॑पा ॥13॥ Rigveda 7-35-13.

Sham no aja ekpad devo Astu sham no hirbudhnhyah sham samudrah I sham no apam napat parurastu sham nah prushnirbhavatu deva gopah II 13 II

The scientific meaning of the word "AJAEKPAD" (अ॒ज एक॑पाद्दे॒वो) will be clear after knowing modern chemistry of Hydrogen. (See below).

[Chemistry details about Hydrogen: Hydrogen. symbol is H, is a highly flammable gas (Formula is H2) and the most common component of the universe. It is the lightest element ever and is colourless, odourless, and tasteless. **It's also in most organic compounds.** Hydrogen is non-metallic element with the **atomic number 1, and it is also roughly 75% of the universe's mass.** It's also the most abundant chemical element on the periodic table. Hydrogen(H) is a gas and is the first element on the periodic table. It is highly flammable. It is an elemental gas present in a trace amount in earth's atmosphere. Hydrogen is somewhat reactive because of its flammability. It is used as a component in fertilizer and fossil fuels. Hydrogen is one of the most important elements on our planet earth. Hydrogen can make a very essential molecule called water once the hydrogen has a covalent bond with oxygen. Hydrogen is the first element on the periodic table. It is also the most abundant element in the universe; stars in the main sequence have hydrogen in plasma form].

All the above qualities of Hydrogen described in chemistry of Hydrogen are narrated in Sanskrit literature about the Varun. Therefore, the Varun of Sanskrit is Hydrogen. Let us see more:

अष्टाचक्रं वर्तत एकनेमि सहस्राक्षरं प्र पुरो नि पश्चा। अर्धेन विश्वं भुवनं जजान यदस्यार्धं कतमः स केतुः ॥ अथर्ववेद - काण्ड » 11; सूक्त » 4; मन्त्र » 22.
Read also अथर्व० १०।८।७। तथा १३

Ashtachakram vartat eknemi sahastraksharam pra puro ni pashchya I Ardhen vishvam bhuvanam jajaan yadasyardham katamah sa ketuh II22 II Atharva ved 11-4-22.

Bound with unbreakable laws of nature in the universe, omnipresent, in past and future, and is responsible for the creation, and its presence manifests all elements of nature. On analysing scientifically as per modern science knowledge the above mantra is symbolic and descriptive:

Oxygen (Mitra Pran) or Pran Vayu has eight electrons and have VAM (वाम, opposite) nature i.e. electro Negative. Around its Nucleus are 8 Marut revolving. It can be illustrated by 8 spoked wheels (see figure below and the Mantra above). Wooden wheel has hub in the centre which support spokes and to stabilize spokes there is Iron wheel over wooden circumference. Prana has the power like the outer rim of a wheel moves and turns the eight-wheeled Chakra. thousand axled chariot of the universe moving. With half of its potential (अर्धेन विश्वं भुवनं जजान), it creates the entire manifest world. What the other half is unknown. In Atharva Veda it is expressed differently:

एकचक्रं वर्तत एकनेमि सहस्राक्षरं प्र पुरो नि पश्चा। अर्धेन विश्वं भुवनं जजान यदस्यार्धं क्व तद्बभूव ॥ अथर्ववेद - काण्ड » 10; सूक्त » 8; मन्त्र » 7.

Ek chakram vartat eknemi sahastraksharam pra puro ni pashcha I Ardhen Vishvam jajaana yadasyardham kva tababuha II 7 II 10-8-7.

The absolute truth with its uniformly applicable and unbreakable laws of Nature is omnipresent and omniscient, in past, present, and future. With a fractional energy of this absolute truth, the boundless cosmos has been created. The above mantra is again objective, symbolic, enigmatic, and obscure. Scientifically as per modern science, it can be explained by a diagram given below:

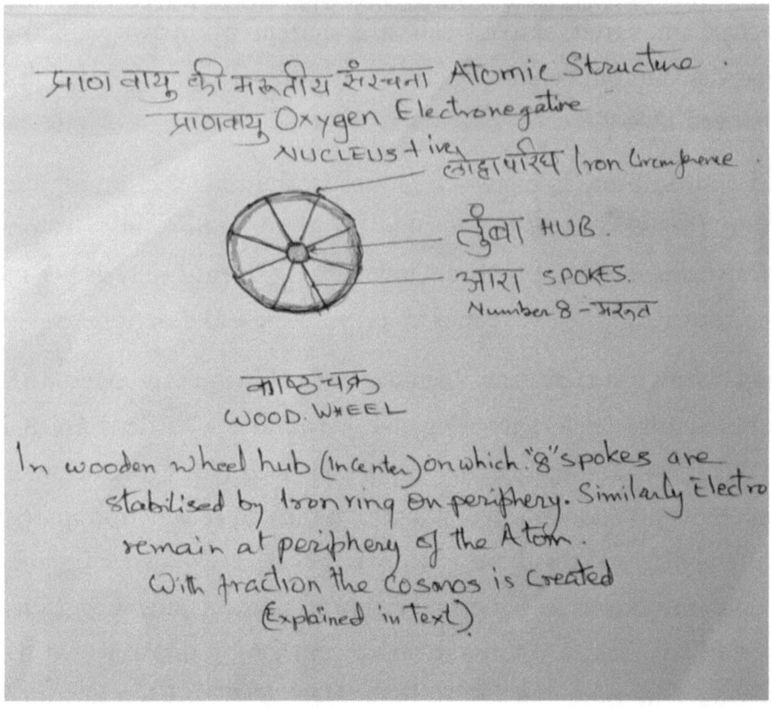

The above figure is as per the mantra of अथर्ववेद - काण्ड » 11; सूक्त » 4; मन्त्र » 22. Read also अथर्व० १०।८।७। and १३.

One is the wheel of the universe, one is the felly -the circumference, the transcendent Brahma, (so one is the central axis, the same one immanent Brahma), yet thousands are the spokes and axes, wheels within wheels, moving up and down, forward, and backward, east, and west. With one part of his Shakti, Prakrti, Brahma has formed the entire universe, where is the rest of it? What happened? Separate expression in Mantra 13.

प्रजापतिश्चरति गर्भे अन्तरदृश्यमानो बहुधा वि जायते। अर्धेन विश्वं भुवनं जजान यदस्यार्धं कतमः स केतुः ॥ अथर्ववेद - काण्ड » 10; सूक्त » 8; मन्त्र » 13.

Prajapatishcharati garbhe antardrishyamano bahudha vijayate I Arhen vishvam bhuvanam jajan yadasyardham katamah sa ketuh II 13 II Atharv Ved. 10-8-13.

Absolute truth (the Prajapati), omniscient and omnipresent in the (गर्भे) vast space of the evolving, boundaryless universe. It is unseen (अदृश्यमान:), yet manifests (वि जायते) as Prakriti, and creates (जजान(the entire universe using only a fraction (अर्धम्(of HIS energy. What is the rest of its energy. Where and how the rest (स: कतम:) is?

To understand the modern scientific meaning of all this enigmatic explanation.

Hydrogen (Varun)	**1270**
Nitrogen (Aryama, Pushna vayu)	**349**
Oxygen (Mitra, Pran-vayu)	**326**
Speed of Sound in Various Gases (See page 58):	
Reference: "Handbook of the Speed of Sound in Real Gases," by A. J. Zuckerwar (Academic Press, 2002).Questions/Commentsto: suits@mtu.edu	

From above comparison one can conclude the truth and correctness of Vedic science and the scientific inferences as well as achievements of the Sanskrit Speaking Civilization.

But the question of another half remains unanswered. Author could not trace the details of this statement in Ved or puranas. Should we not explore?

Ashvini Kumars:

Who is Ashwini Kumaras? There is mention of birth of Ashwini Kumaras in Rigveda:

यमा चिदत्रं यमसूरंसूत जिह्वाया अग्रं पतदा ह्यस्थांत् । वपूंषि जाता मिथुना संचेते तमोहना तपुंषो बुध्न एतां ॥

Yama chidatra yamasoora soota jihvaya Agram patada hyasythat I Vapushi jata mithuna sachet tamohana tapusho budhna eta II

"The parent of twins (the dawn), has brought forth the twin (Aśvins) on this occasion, (in the praise of whom) the tip of my tongue remains tremulous; they two, the dispersers of darkness, combine, assuming bodies as a pair (of twins) at the origin of the day."

The Ashwini Kumars (Asvini Kumaras) are **two twin brothers mentioned in Rigveda, sons of the sun god Surya**. They are the Physicians of God. They may also be referred to as the 'Horsemen' and are forever young, handsome, and athletic. They possess a celestial chariot with three wheels (**त्रिचकेण**, Rigveda.1-118-2), capable of travelling to DUE-lok (Swarga -lok). रथो ह वाम्... परि द्यावापृथिवी याति सद्यः। (Rigveda. 3-58-8). The chariot is having the speed of mind (**मनसो जवीयान्तिवन्धुरो**).

अश्विना परि वामिषः पुरूचीरीयुर्गीर्भिर्यतमाना अमृध्राः | रथो ह वां रतजा अद्रिजूतः परि द्यावापृथिवी याति सद्यः ||(८)|| Rigveda. 3-58-8.

Ashvina pari vamishah puruchiriyurgrbhiryatmana amrardhah ratho ha vam rataja adrijutah pari dyavav Prithivi yati sadyah II 8 II Rigved. 3-58-8.

या सुरथा रथीतमोभा देवा दिविस्प्रशा .अश्विना ता हवामहे ||२|| (Rigved 1- 22- 2).

Ya suratha rathitamobha deva divisprasha ashvina ta havanahe II 2 II Rigved. 1-22-2.

"We invoke and request to solicit, the two Aśvins, who are both divine, the best of charioteers (modern day pilot), riding in an excellent car and attaining heaven."

त्रिवन्धुरेणं त्रिवृता रथेंन त्रिचक्रेणं सुवृता यांतमर्वाक्। पिन्वंतं गा जिन्वंतमर्वतो नो वर्धयंतमश्विना वीरमस्मे ||2|| Rigveda. 1-118-2.

Trivandhuna trivrita rathena suvruta yatamarvak I pinvatam ga jinvatamvarato no vardhayatamashvina virmasme II 2 II Rigved. 1-118-2.

आ वां रथो अश्विना श्येनपत्वा सुमृळीकः स्ववाँ यात्वर्वाङ् । यो मर्त्यस्य मनसो जवीयान्त्रिबन्धुरो वृषणा वातरंहाः॥1॥ Rigveda.1-118-1

Aa vam ratho Ashvina Shyenpatva sumrulikah svavam yatvrvanga I yo martaSya manaso javiya ntribandhuro vrushana vatarahah II 1 II Rigved. 1-118-1.

Oh, Ashvini Kumar both, your chariot (RATH) has seats which are pleasant having more speed than of mind able to go in sky (in three abodes-BHUH, BHUVAH, SWAHA) like GARUD (श्येनपत्वा), are summoned to attend the YADNYA.

An event in Shrimad Bhagwatam too, mentions about Air vehicle (Vimana) during Mahabharat era:

स लब्ध्वा कामगं यानं तमोधाम दुरासदम् । ययौ द्वारवतीं शाल्वो वैरं वृष्णिकृतं स्मरन् ॥ ८ ॥ Śrīmad-Bhāgavatam ŚB 10.76.8

Sa labdhva kamagam Yanam tamodham durasadam I yayou dvarvatim shalvo veiram vrushnikrutam smaran II 8 II Shrimad Bhagvatam. 10-76-8.

saḥ — he; *labdhvā* — obtaining; *kāma-gam* — moving at his will; *yānam* — the vehicle; *tamaḥ* — of darkness; *dhāma* — abode; *durāsadam* — unapproachable; *yayau* — went; *dvāravatīm* — to Dvārakā; *śālvaḥ* — Śālva; *vairam* — the enmity; *vṛṣṇi-kṛtam* — shown by the Vṛṣṇis; *smaran* — remembering.

This unassailable vehicle was filled with darkness and could go anywhere (यानं तमोधाम). Upon obtaining it, Śhālva went to Dvārakā, remembering the Vṛṣṇis' enmity toward him.

निरुध्य सेनया शाल्वो महत्या भरतर्षभ। पुरीं बभञ्जोपवनानुद्यानानि च सर्वश॥ ९॥ :

Nirudhya senayo Shalvo mahatya bharatshabha I purim babhanjo pavanano dyanani cha sarvashah II 9 II

सगोपुराणि द्वाराणि प्रासादाट्टालतोलिका :न्निपेतुविमानाग्न्या स ।विहारान् : शस्त्रवृष्टय॥ १० ॥ :

Sagopurani dvarani prasadattalatolikah I viharan s vimanagrya nnipetuh shastravrushtyah II 10 II

शिला द्रुमाश्चाशनय :सर्पा आसारशर्करा :। प्रचण्डश्चक्रवातोऽभूद् रजसाच्छादिता दिश :॥ ११ ॥ ŚB 10.76.9-11.

Shila drumashchashanayah sarpa aasarasharkarah I Prachandashchkra-vatobhuda rajasa chhadita dishah II11 II SB 10-76- 9 to 11.

Śhālva besieged the city with a large army, O best of the Bharatas, decimating the outlying parks and gardens, the mansions along with their observatories, towering gateways, (पुरीं बभञ्जोपवनानुद्यानानि च सर्वशः) and surrounding walls, and the public recreational areas. From his excellent airship he threw down a torrent of weapons (शस्त्रवृष्टयः), including stones, tree trunks, thunderbolts (प्रचण्डश्चक्रवातोऽभूद्), snakes and hailstones. A fierce whirlwind arose and blanketed all directions with dust and created darkness in the city.

इत्यर्द्यमाना सौभेन कृष्णस्य नगरी भृशम् ।नाभ्यपद्यत शं राजं स्त्रिपुरेण यथा मही ॥ १२ ॥

Ityardyamana saubhen krishnasya nagari bhrusham I nabhyapadyat sham rajam stripurena yatha mahi II 12 II

Thus, terribly tormented by the airship named 'Saubha', Lord Kṛiṣhṇa's city had no peace, O King, just like the earth when it was attacked by the three aerial cities of the demons.

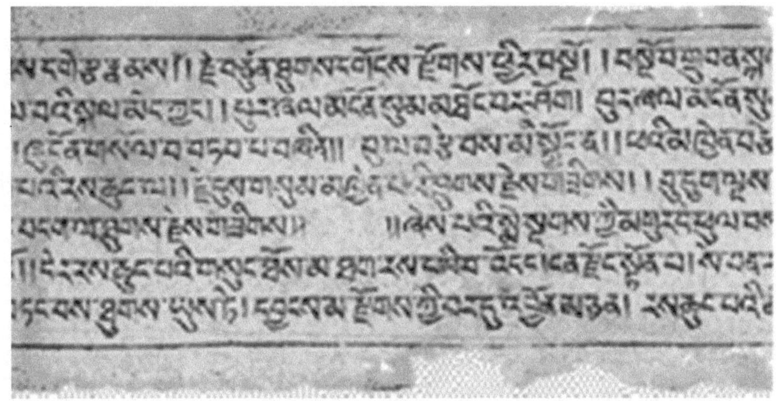

https://wishawaft.blogspot.com/2017/01/vimanas-flying-machines-01.html

A Sanskrit book by Raja Bhoj of Dhar. SAMARANGAN SUTRADHAR. After gaining knowledge from this book about flying machine, Shri Shivkar Bapuji Talpade prepared a machine in 1895, which flew 1500 feet in the sky. He named it as **MARUTSAKHA.** Right brothers purchased the knowledge from Mr Talpade of Bombay. The right brothers were successful in 1903 in Europe.

Raja Bhoja's Samarangana Sutradhara, ancient Engineering Science – Translator. by Prabhakar Apte

One of his books, 'Samarangana Sutradhara', written in Sanskrit, is in 80 chapters, on civil engineering, detailing construction of buildings, forts, temples, idols of deities and mechanical devices. It devotes one full chapter on building of flying machines Chapter 31. Being the only ancient Indian source known about building airplanes, Raja Bhoj's work has attracted much attention. But the book does not explain process of building airplanes and says that it has been done purposely, for sake of secrecy.

Sukta-सूक्त 108 Deity-देवता = Indra and Agni (ईंद्र, अग्निं).

य इन्द्राग्नी चित्रतमो रथो वामभि विश्वानि भुवनानि चष्टे | तेना यातं सरथं तस्थिवांसाथा सोमस्य पिबतं सुतस्य II १ II (Rigved 1-108-1).

Ya indragni chitratamo ratho vamabhi vishvani bhuvanani chashte I tena yatam saratham tasthivansatha somasya pibatam sutasya II 1 II Rigved. 1-108-1.

The amazing chariot of Indra and Agni, which illuminates the world, is invited to attend the Yadnya where Som Ras is ready for consumption. (१(

अश्विनोरसनं रथमनश्वं वाजिनावतोः| तेनाहं भूरि चाकन ||१0 (Rigved 1- 120-10).

Ashvinorasanam rathamanashvam vajinavatoh I tenaham bhuri Chakan II10 II Rigved. 1-120-10.

अयं समह मा तनूह्याते जनाननु| सोमपेयं सुखो रथः||11|| (Rigved 1- 120-11).

Ayam samaha ma tanuhyate janaananu I soma peyam sokho rathah II 11 II Rigved. 1-121 11

Above mantra indicates the RATH without horses (रथमनश्वं = रथम् + अनश्वम्) used by ASHVINI Kumar. See below the various actions of the RATH: flying like birds, it moves in Aakash and moves on water and taking off from water to fly. A self-propelled flying machine (See mantra below).

युवमेतं चक्रथुः सिन्धुषु पलवमात्मन्वन्तं पक्षिणन्तौग्र्याय कम | येन देवत्रा मनसा निरूहथुः सुपप्तनीपेतथुः कषोदसो महः ||५|| (Rigved 1- 182- 5).

Yuvametam chakrathuh sindhushu palavamatmanvantam pakshinanto-gryaya kam I yen devatra manasa niruhathuh supaptanipetathuh kashodaso mah II5 II Rigved. 1-182-5.

Ashvini kumar made a Chariot which was self-propelled and could go through sea (SINDHU) – सिन्धुषु प्लवमात्मन्वन्तं at the same time fly in Aakash like bird (पक्षिणन्तौग्र्याय). It could propel and fly also on sea take off to sky. This was to save son of Tugra (न्तौग्र्याय).

Sutra 183, devta— Ashvini Kumar

तम्। युञ्जाथाम्। मनसः। यः। जवीयान्। त्रिऽवन्धुरः। वृषणा। यः। त्रिऽचक्रः। येन। उपऽयाथः। सुऽकृतः। दुरोणम्। त्रिऽधातुना। पतथः। विः। न। पर्णैः ॥ ११.१८३.

Tam yunjatham manasah yah javiyan trivandhrah vrushna yah tri chakrah yen upayathah sukrutah duronam tri dhatuna patathah vih na parneih II 1 II Rigved. 1-183- 1.

A 3 wheeled chariot with speed more than mind, has 3 seats for the driver/Pilot, and is made from 3 metals, in which you come like a bird, to the Yadnya site.

(As per Dr. Tulsi Ram, the meaning of mantra has multiple possibilities for interpretation. An expert who would be of the order of a Rshi, a visionary of the dynamics of Nature in his own field in the context for example in Physics, Astrophysics, Aeronautics, Medicine and Meditation. The meaning, can be better in the unified field of comprehensive reality.)

अनश्वो जातो अनभीशुर उक्थ्यो रथस तरिचक्रः परि वर्तते रजः |महत तद वो देव्यस्य परवाचनं दयाम रभवः पर्थिवीं यच च पुष्यथ ||1 || Rigved. 4-32-1.

Anashvo jato anabhishura ukthyo rathasa tarichakrah pari vartate rajah I mahat tada vo devasya paravachanam dyam rabhavahparthivim yach cha pushyatha II 1 II Rigved. 4-32-1.

रथं ये चक्रुः सुव्रतं सुचेतसो ऽविह्वरन्तम मनसस परि धयया |तां ऊ नव अस्य सवनस्य पीतय आ वो वाजा रभवो वेदयामसि II 2 II (Rigved 4-36-2)

Ratham ye chakruh suvratam suchetaso vivharantam manasas pari dhayaya I tan u nava asya savanasya pitaya aa vo vaja rabhavo vedyamasi II 2 II Rigved. 4-36-2.

RIBHUs made chariot, which runs with power of mind, for use of Ashvini Kumars. This chariot had three seats for the Sarathi – (driver or Pilot), Had three wheels. The chariot was constructed with three types of metals (त्रिऽधातुना। पतथः) Oh Ribhu you have made chariot for Ashwini kumaras which has three wheels, runs without horses, and without reigns in space - Akash, and thus nourish earth and Swarga.

Sun Solstices in Rigveda: Sun solstices or Summer and Winter solstices were known to Vedic Rishis.

परं मृत्यो अनु परेहि पन्थां यस्ते स्व इतरो देवयानात् । चक्षुष्मते शृण्वते ते ब्रवीमि मा नंप्रजां : रीरिषो मोत वीरान् ॥ Rigved 10-18-1.

Param mrutyo anu parahi pantha yaste sva itaro **devyanat** I chakshushmate shruvate te bravimi ma nah prajam ririsho mot viran II 1 II rigved. 10-18-1.

देवयानात् (dev+Ayan. डेव + अयन) = Uttar ayan =Summer Solstice. Death God (yam यम) adopt different path and avoid killing of our brave soldiers and our progeny. 1.

Manifestation of SUN. and its solstices. Stabilization of Sun in space is described in Rigveda Mantra Rigved 6- 67- 1. below: -

विश्वेषां वः सतां ज्येष्ठतमा गीर्भिर्मित्रां वरूणा वा वृषध्यै । सं या रश्मेव यमतुर्यमिष्ठा व्दा जनां असमा बाहुभिः स्वैः II1II Rigved. 6-67-1.

viśveṣāṁ vaḥ satāṁ jyeṣṭhatamā gīrbhir mitrāvaruṇā vāvṛdhadhyai I saṁ yā raśmeva yamatur yamiṣṭhā dvā janām̐ asamā bāhubhiḥ svaiḥ II 1 II Rigved. 6-67-1.

Mitra and Varun even though are different under control like reigns of horses, the two elements right and left reigns, responsible for Sun's solstices. **These two elements + ive and – ive, concentrate to form Star, like SUN.**

विद्युतो ज्योतिः परिसजिहान मित्रावरूणा विद्युत्सर्वे समाहिता (ऋगवेद. तैत्तरीय आरण्यक).

Vidyuto Jyotih parisajihan mitra Varuna Vidyut sarve samahita II Rigved. Taittariya Aranyaka.

VARUN is responsible for stationing Sun in space - Antariksha (Rigved. Taittariya Aaranyak. Upanishad).

वनेषु व्यंतरिक्षं ततान वाजं मर्वत्सु पय उस्त्रियासु । हृत्सु ऋतं वरुणो अप्स्वग्निं दिवि सूर्य मदधात् सोमभद्रौ II 2 II Rigved 5-85-2

Vaneshu Vyantariksham tataan Vajam marvatsu paya ustriyasu I hrutsu rutam Varuno Apsavagnim divi surya maddhat soubhadrou II 2 II Rigved. 5-85-2.

Varun manifests or establishes above trees of forest the Antariksha, intellect in humans, Fire – agni in water and Sun in antariksha, water in rivers, milk in cows, and strength in horses. Because of all this Varun is as Raja-SAMRAT in Rigved. 7-87-5.

तिस्त्रो द्यावो निहिता अन्तरस्मिन् तिस्त्रो भूमि रुपरा षडविधानाः । गुत्सो राजा वरुणश्चक्र एतं दिवि हिरण्यम् शुमेकम II5II

Tistro dyavo nihita antarsmin tistro bhumi rupara shadvidhanah I gutso raja varunashchakra etam divi hiranyam shumekam II 5 II Rigved 7-87-5.

In other words, all actions in the universe or multiverse, are dependent upon VARUN i.e., Rigveda 8-41 – 6

यस्मिन विश्वानि काव्या चक्रे नाभिरिवश्रिता । त्रितं जूति सपर्यत व्रजे गावो न संयुजे युजे अश्र्वाँ अयुक्षत नभन्ता मन्यके समें II 6 II Rigveda 8-41 – 6.

yashmin viśvāni kāvyā chakre nābhir iva śritā | tritaṃ jūtī saparyata vraje gāvo na saṃyuje yuje aśhravām̐ ayukṣhata nabhantā manyake same || Rigveda 8-41 – 6

Like in a wheel the axel supports wheel, similarly like nave of church, Varun is support of the nature - Srishti

"In whom all pious acts are concentrated, like the nave in the (centre of the church) wheel, worship him quickly who abides in the three worlds; as men assemble the cattle in their pasture, so do (our foes) collect their horses(to assail us); may all our adversaries perish."

Considering all the above statements in Rigveda about Varun it is Hydrogen gas. This is endorsed by the modern science by Chemist – W. Prout. As per the hypothesis of William Prout, the Varun Chakra must be the Hydrogen Cycle like the PUSHNA CHAKRA, i.e., Nitrogen cycle.

Mid-19th century earliest use found in William A. Miller (1817–1870), chemist. From the genitive of the name of William Prout, English chemist, and physician and his hypothesis.

The due credit of Scientific knowledge, to Rigveda is missing, instead the knowledge which got revealed and understood in 19th Century by modern Science gets the credit while thousands of years back it was acknowledged by Rigveda. And the due credit is ignored. It is due to APATHY of the descendants of Rigvedic Rishis. Terms and conditions are always dictated by the winner. Invaders never wanted any supremacy of slave country. Slave country population is always at receiving end. The obscure knowledge of the Rigveda literature could not be understood by the invaders. Their aim was only loot and grab the wealth and knowledge of Bharat varsha.

द्वे स्रुती अंशृणवं पितृणामहं देवानामुत मर्त्यानाम् । ताभ्यामिदं विश्वमेजत्समेति यदन्तरा पितरं मातरं च ॥15॥ Rigveda. 10- 88 - 15(

Dve sruti ashrunavam pitruna maham I Tabhyamidam vishvamejatsameti yadantara pitaram mataram cha II 5 II
Rigved. 10-88-15.

Living beings or mortals born through parents have two paths – Pitruyan and Devyan marg.) १५(

इन्द्राय । गिरः । अनिशितऽसर्गाः । अपः । प्र । ईरयम् । सगरस्य । बुध्नात् । यः । अक्षेणऽइव । चक्रिया । शचीभिः । विष्वक् । तस्तम्भ । पृथिवीम् । उत । द्याम् ॥ १०.८९.४

Indraya girah anishita sarga h Apah pra iryam sagarasya budhnat yah aksheniva chakriya shachibhih vishvak tastambh prithivim uta dyam II 4 II Rigved. 10-89-4.

In this mantra it is symbolically explained giving example of wheel. Prayers for Indra, by which the deeds of Indra support Earth and Swarga like hub of a wheel.)४(

Antariksha Swarg and Earth are invaded and entangled by Indra in such a way as the hub supports the wheel.

Rigved indicates the wheel and its hub which supports wheel, relation as an example which reveals that the wheel was invented even before the script of Rigveda.

In the mantra **Rigved 8-41-6. Mentioned above,** again, the example of wheel is used. Chakra and its spokes depend upon the support of central Hub. In similar way the world depends upon Varun. Hence worship Varun who pervades the 3 abodes. All elements are manifest due to Varun. II 6II

Hub of wheel of chariot, supports the wheel with spokes similarly all the work actions of universe, are supported and are dependent upon the Varun (hydrogen Vayu). Varun moves in the three lokas, and manifestation of all the elements of the world. This flows in 3 lokas (त्रितं जूति सपर्यत, - त्रैलोक्यगामि वरूण - Bhuh, Bhuvah, Swah). How it can be explained by modern science: -

Modern physics considers the elements are multiples of HYDROGEN. See the modern hypothesis by William Prout: -

"Definition of W. Prout hypothesis (a hypothesis in chemistry): **the atomic weights of all other elements are exact multiples of that of hydrogen** and hence hydrogen is the primary substance from which the other elements have been formed".

This hypothesis was affirmatively established thousands of years back by Rishis of Sanskrit Speaking Civilization. Following is the proof of this: -

अस्तभ्नाद् द्याम् असुरोविश्ववेदा अमिमीत वरिमाणं पृथिव्याः । आसीदत् विश्वाभुवनानि सम्राट विश्वेत् तानि वरुणस्य व्रतानि ॥1॥ Rigveda 8- 42 -1.

Astabhnad dyam asurovishva veda amimita varimanam pruthivyah I aasidat vishvabhvanani samrat vishvet tani Varunasya vratani II 1 II Rigved. 8-42-1.

One who is responsible for the manifestation of Nature created elements, one who infuses life force in everything in nature, and one who controls and guides the Swarga Lok or Antariksha (**द्यु लोक**) as well as Earth (i.e., expands and limits) is known as the VARUN (Hydrogen). Hence it is known as the SAMRAT.

All above is the handy work of VARUN therefore it is difficult to be described. Therefore, Gita explains that whatever is there in nature of this universe or multiverse, is the result of interaction of nature KASHETRA and the soul or KSHETRADNYA -the knower of the KSHETRA.

यावत्सञ्जायते किञ्चित्सत्वं स्थावर जंगमम् क्षेत्र क्षेत्रज्ञ संयोगात्तद्विध्दि भरतर्षभ II27|| Gita 13-26.

Yavatsanjayte kinchitsatvam sthavarjangamam kshetra kshetradnya sanyogatta dvidhi bharatarsham II 27 II Gita. 13-26, 27

In the early twentieth century, Sir J.C. Bose established through experiments that even plants, which are non-moving life forms, can feel and respond to emotions. His experiments proved that soothing music could enhance the growth of plants. When a hunter shoots a bird sitting on a tree, the vibrations of the tree seem to indicate that it weeps for the bird. And when a loving gardener enters the garden, the trees feel joyous. The changes in the vibrations of the tree reveal that it also possesses consciousness and can experience semblances of emotions. Thousands of years back Ved and Puran classified living beings into 4 groups, according to the birth of the living being, – Udbeej (from seeds), Swedaj (from larva), Andaj (from eggs), and jarayuj (membrane covered body).

तन्मित्रस्य वरूणस्या भिचक्षे सूर्यो रूपं कृणुते द्योरूपस्थे । अनंतमन्य द्रुश दस्य पाजः कृष्ण मन्यधरितः II 5 II Rigved 1- 115- 5.

Tanmitrasya varunasya bhichakshe suryo rupam krunute dyorupsthe I anantmanya drush dasya pajah krishna manyadharitah II 5 II Rigved. 1-115-5.

Sun is the chief source of light, heat, energy. The matter is wave energy has been accepted by modern science.

Fractional energy from the Super soul energy source, intensely condensate (a product of condensation especially a liquid obtained by condensation of a gas or vapor steam condensate.) and form a thick liquidate substance. It again retrogradely transform into soul energy. Modern science now understands matter as wave energy instead of substance. Vedic understanding has been the same for so many years (Refer Song of Science Shrimad Bhagwat Gita, Notion Press, Chennai, Singapore, Malaysia 2022, B. G. Matapurkar)

Mitra-Varun element which manifest SUN (as mentioned above) which is conducive and provides energy, light, and heat to all. This has enlightened Antariksha and earth. Gita mentions the same in the Stanza 14 of Chapter 15: -

अहं वैश्वानरो भूत्वा प्राणिनाम् देहमाश्रितः । प्रणापानसमायुक्तः पचाम्यत्रं चतुर्विधम् II 14 II Gita. 15-14.

Aham veishvanaro bhutva praninam deh mashritah I pranapana samayuktah pachamyatram chaturvidham II 14 II Gita 15-14.

All living beings have digestive fire, which helps digestion is also a fraction of energy of SUN.

Sukta 83, Devata – Parjanya. This word PARJANYA is very scientific and appropriately created. (PAR + JANYA) This means which is born of different source. Atmospheric conditions are secondary to something else. See below: -

अच्छा वद तवसं गीर्भिराभिः स्तुहि पर्जन्यं नमस विवास । कनिक्रद्द वृषभो जीरदानु रेतो दधात्योषधीषु गर्भम्).(Rigvada. 5-83-1

Achha vad tavasam girbhirabhih stuhi parjanyam namasa vivasa I kanikdad vrishbho jirdanu reto dadhatyo oushadhishu garbham II 1 II Rigved. 5-83-1.

Parjanya is due to Sun. Sun effect is Parjanya. Parjanya responsible for thunderous rains, impregnate medicinal plants (**रेतो दधात्योषधीषु गर्भम्**). Energy of Mitra-Varun effect is morning light of golden hue, which spreads (**कनिक्रद्द वृषभो**) all around earth.

ऋतस्य बुध्न उषसा मिषण्यन्वृषो मही रोदसी आ विवेश । मही मित्रस्य वरूणस्य माया चन्द्रेव भानुं विदधे पुरूत्रा II 7 II Rigved 3-61-7.

Ritasya budhna ushasa mishanyanvusho mahi rodasi Aa vivesha I mahi mitrasya varunasya maya chandrev bjanum vidadhe purutra II 7 II Rived. 3-61-7.

Vivaha Sukta of Rigveda 10- 85- 16 to 27.

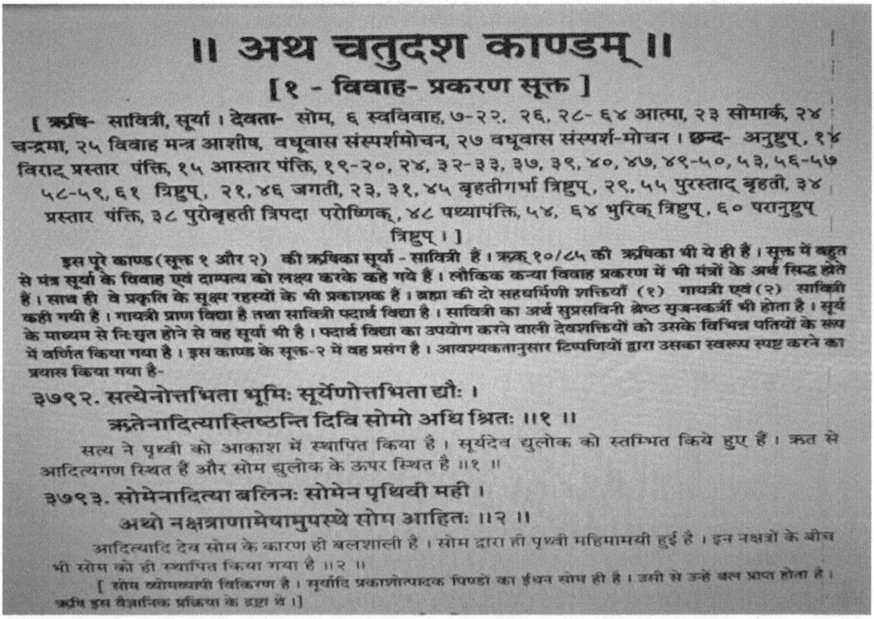

॥ अथ चतुदश काण्डम् ॥

[१ - विवाह- प्रकरण सूक्त]

[ऋषि- सावित्री, सूर्या । देवता- सोम, ६ स्वविवाह, ७-२२, २६, २८- ६४ आत्मा, २३ सोमार्क, २४ चन्द्रमा, २५ विवाह मन्त्र आशीष, वधूवास संस्पर्शमोचन, २७ वधूवास संस्पर्श-मोचन । छन्द- अनुष्टुप्, १४ विराट् प्रस्तार पंक्ति, १५ आस्तार पंक्ति, १९-२०, २४, ३२-३३, ३७, ३९, ४०, ४७, ४९-५०, ५३, ५६-५७ ५८-५९, ६१ त्रिष्टुप्, २१, ४६ जगती, २३, ३१, ४५ बृहतीगर्भा त्रिष्टुप्, २९, ५५ पुरस्ताद् बृहती, ३४ प्रस्तार पंक्ति, ३८ पुरोबृहती त्रिपदा परोष्णिक्, ४८ पथ्यापंक्ति, ५४, ६४ भुरिक् त्रिष्टुप्, ६० परानुष्टुप त्रिष्टुप् ।]

इस पूरे काण्ड (सूक्त १ और २) की ऋषिका सूर्या - सावित्री हैं । ऋक् १०/८५ की ऋषिका भी ये ही हैं । सूक्त में बहुत से मंत्र सूर्या के विवाह एवं दाम्पत्य को लक्ष्य करके कहे गये हैं । लौकिक कन्या विवाह प्रकरण में भी मंत्रों के अर्थ सिद्ध होते हैं । साथ ही वे प्रकृति के सूक्ष्म रहस्यों के भी प्रकाशक हैं । ब्रह्मा की दो सहधर्मिणी शक्तियाँ (१) गायत्री एवं (२) सावित्री कही गयी हैं । गायत्री प्राण विद्या है तथा सावित्री पदार्थ विद्या है । सावित्री का अर्थ सुप्रसविनी श्रेष्ठ सृजनकर्त्री भी होता है । सूर्य के माध्यम से निःसृत होने से वह सूर्या भी है । पदार्थ विद्या का उपयोग करने वाली देवशक्तियों को उसके विभिन्न पतियों के रूप में वर्णित किया गया है । इस काण्ड के सूक्त-२ में वह प्रसंग है । आवश्यकतानुसार टिप्पणियों द्वारा उसका स्वरूप स्पष्ट करने का प्रयास किया गया है-

३७९२. सत्येनोत्तभिता भूमिः सूर्येणोत्तभिता द्यौः ।
ऋतेनादित्यास्तिष्ठन्ति दिवि सोमो अधि श्रितः ॥१ ॥

सत्य ने पृथ्वी को आकाश में स्थापित किया है । सूर्यदेव द्युलोक को स्तम्भित किये हुए हैं । ऋत से आदित्यगण स्थित हैं और सोम द्युलोक के ऊपर स्थित है ॥१ ॥

३७९३. सोमेनादित्या बलिनः सोमेन पृथिवी मही ।
अथो नक्षत्राणामेषामुपस्थे सोम आहितः ॥२ ॥

आदित्यादि देव सोम के कारण ही बलशाली हैं । सोम द्वारा ही पृथ्वी महिमामयी हुई है । इन नक्षत्रों के बीच भी सोम को ही स्थापित किया गया है ॥२ ॥

[सोम व्योमव्यापी विकिरण है । सूर्यादि प्रकाशोत्पादक पिण्डों का ईंधन सोम ही है । उसी से उन्हें बल प्राप्त होता है । ऋषि इस वैज्ञानिक प्रक्रिया के द्रष्टा थे ।]

सुकिंशुकं शल्मलिं विश्वरूपं हिरण्यवर्णं सुवृतं सुचक्रम् । आरोह सूर्ये अमृतस्य लोकं स्योनं पत्ये वहतुं कृणुष्व ॥२०॥

Sukim Shukam shalmalim Vishva rupam Hiranya varnam suvrutam suchakram I Aaroh surye Anrutasya lokam syonam patye vahatum krishnaushva II 20 II Rigved. 10-85-20.

Sukim Shukam and Shalmali are names of plants, Palash and Dhak or Padhok Red wood tree, and Shalmali, for wood to construct chariot. Amṛtasya = "amṛta; immortality. lokaṃ = "Loka; Earth; world; syonam = "benevolent; agreeable; pleasant; agreeable. patye = pati = "husband; vahatuṃ = "marriage." kṛṇuṣva = kṛ = "make; perform; duplicate; plant; kṛu; concentrate; knot; join;

The Mantra is recited at the time when the bride enters the house of the husband. amṛtasya lokam = the world of immortality; or, the Soma- moon, an object which ascends - aroha,- आरोह.

उदीर्ष्वातः पतिवती ह्येषा विश्वावसुं नमसा गीर्भिरीळे ।अन्यामिच्छ पितृषदं व्यक्तां स ते भागो जनुषा तस्य विद्धि ॥२१॥ Rigved. 21 -85-10.

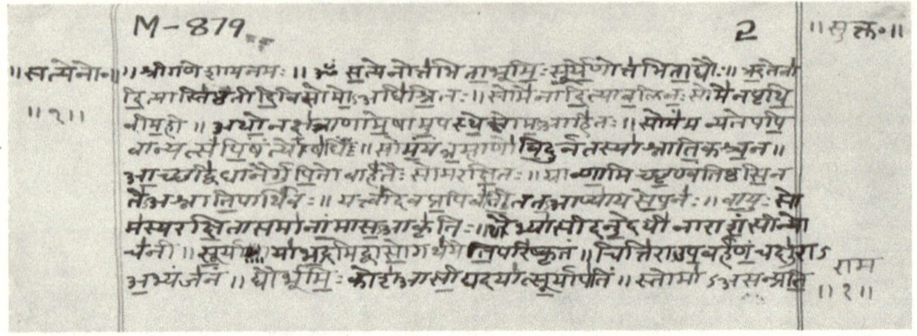

Vivaha sukta, Rigveda 10.85.1-8, Sanskrit, in **Devanagari** script. 1500-1200 BCE (Wikipedia)

उदीर्ष्वातो विश्वावसो नमसेळा महे त्वा ।अन्यामिच्छ प्रफर्व्यं सं जायां पत्या सृज ॥२२॥ Rigved. 10-85-22.

Udirshvato vishvavaso nmsela mahe tva I anyamichha prafarvyam sam jayam patya sruja ॥२२॥ Rigved. 10-85-22.

Get up: the girl has her husband. O Visvavasu. Find if her father has another marriageable girl for arranging ceremony for her.

The request is to Visvavasu the gandharva who is King of the gandharva. The Vivah Shuktam is for wedding hymns. Gandharva are musicians to help couples to get married in the form of Gandharva Vivaha or love marriage which is without the consent of families. Vasvavasu is requested that this couple got married now. Kindly go and find a suitable husband for another unmarried woman. So, basically asking that here your work is done now move on to the next matrimonial project.

These statements are approximately over 3000 years old. The sanctity is with marriage ceremony if properly performed, for arranged or love marriages. The Vedic ceremony is symbolic. The marriage of daughter of Surya deity has been celebrated in this Vivaha-sukta, so that the similar ritual is followed in the society. This is for the immortality or Amritatva -

अमृतत्व. How the immortality is achieved by marriages? Marriage is bond between the couple. The progeny is well protected, cared with love and affection. There is security to the off springs. Mother and the father both take the responsibility to rear up the children, educate them and provide financial security till they start earning. Thus, through forth coming generation, the continuity of chain of self is assured thus the immortality is achieved. Animals also have immortality. But the humans handle it intellectually and with financial security, as well as by both the parents. The live-in-relationship and homosexuality does not provide these scientific facts. The life may go berserk. To prevent this, the institution of marriage is important and essential.

The Vedic "Suktas" from Rigveda are more important in current societies where the trend has started to not to enter marriage bonds. Live-in-relationship is harmful for the society.

YAM-YAMI SAMVAD: -

Marriages between close relatives like brothers and sisters is not to be consummated. As it leads to the abnormalities in progeny. See relevant mantras below: -

Yam-Yami dialogue condemned physical relationship between brother and Sister. Rigveda. 10-10-1-1to 14

परेयिवांसं प्रवतों महीरनुं बहुभ्यपन्थांमनुपस्पशानम् । वैवस्वतं संगमंनं जनांनां यमं राजांनं : हविषां दुवस्य ॥ Rigveda. 10-14-1.

Pareyivansam pravto mahiranu bahubhyah panthamanupspashanam I veivasvtam sangamanam jananam yamam rajanam havisha duvasya Rigveda. 10-14-1.

Well-wisher, preventer of sin, controller of forefathers, the YAM must be worshiped by all.

यमो नौ गातुं प्रथमो विवेद नैषा गव्यूतिरपभर्तवा उं । यत्रा नः पूर्वे पितरः परेयुरेना जज्ञानाः पथ्या अनु स्वाः ॥ 2 II Rigveda. 10-14-2.

Yamo no gatum prathamo viveda Neisha gavyutirapbhartava um I yatra nah purve pitarah pareyurena jadnyanah pathya anu avah ॥ 2 II Rigveda. 10-14-2.

"Yama, the chief (of all), knows our well-being; this pasture no one can take from us; by the road by which our forefathers have gone, all who are born (proceed) along the paths they have made for themselves"

मातली कव्यैर्यमो अङ्गिरोभिर्बृहस्पतिऋक्वभिर्वावृधानः । यांश्च देवा वावृधुर्ये च देवान्त्स्वाहान्ये स्वधयान्ये मदन्ति ॥ 3 II Rigveda. 10- 14- 3.

Matali kavyeiryamo angirobhirbruhaspatirukvabhirvavrudhanah I yanshcha deva vavrudhurye cha devantsvahanye svadhayanye madanti II 3II Rigveda. 10- 14- 3.

The dialog between YAM and YAMI who are real brother and Sister is an interesting episode described in 10th Mandal and Sukta 10, Mantra1-14. It is perfect model of writing in Rigveda. Basically, the Rigveda is obscure, enigmatic, camouflaged scientific discussion which needs great pondering on the subject.

The names of brother and sister are important. YAM is first of ASHTANG YOG system (Yam, Niyam, Asteya, Asan, pratyahara, Dharana Dhyan and Samadhi). Yam is a controlling factor. The God of death is YAM which controls the excessive population of the universe. Yami is a feminine element interested in the continuity of PRAJAH – the population.

It cannot be considered a pornographic discussion. It expresses scientific facts prevalent in the society of that time. It is a psychoanalytical, logical expression to be understood by every person.

ओ चित्सखायं सख्या ववृत्यां तिरः पुरू चिदर्णवं जगन्वान् । पितुर्नपातमा दधीत वेधा अधि क्षमि प्रतरं दीध्यानः ॥ 1 II Rigveda. 10-10-1.

Ao chitsakhayam sakhya vavrutyam tirah puru chidarnavam jaganvan I piturnapatama dadhita vedha adhi kshami prataram didhyanah || 1 II Rigveda. 10-10-1.

Brother and sister "Yami and Yam" are placed in isolated surroundings. Indulges in carnal relation for continuity of progeny, which is an animal instinct. But YAM categorically insists and denies such a relation between brother and sister. It is a sin to be in a relative sexual relationship. This is to avoid genetic defects in progeny. This is acceptable to the modern science of today. Some of the Mantras are mentioned below: -

न वा उं ते तन्वां तन्वं१ सं पंपृच्यां पापमांहुर्यः स्वसांरं निगच्छांत् । अन्येन मत्प्रमुदं : कल्पयस्व न ते भ्रातां सुभगे वष्टयेतत् || Rigveda 10-10-12

बतो बंतासि यम नैव ते मनो हृदंयं चाविदाम । अन्या किल त्वां कक्ष्येव युक्तं परिं ष्वजाते लिबुंजेव वृक्षम् || Rigveda, 10-10-13.

अन्यमू षु त्वं यंम्यन्य उ त्वां परिं ष्वजाते लिबुंजेव वृक्षम् । तस्यं वा त्वं मनं इच्छा स वा तवाधां कृणुष्व संविदं सुभंद्राम् || Rigveda 10-10-14.

Oh Sister be in love with other man and he be in love with you and have family of yours with progeny of both of you.

Artificial limbs

In war injury the leg amputated and replaced by Iron leg to continue the war fight. See following mantra:

चरित्रं हि वेरिवाच्छेदि पणमाजा खेलस्य परितक्म्यायाम् । सद्यो जंघामायसीम् विश्पलायैधने हिते सतवे प्रत्यधत्तम् II 15 II **ऋग्वेद - मण्डल** » 1; **सूक्त** » 116; **मन्त्र** » 15.

Charitram hi verivachhedi panamaja khelasya paritakmyayam I sadyo jaghamayasim vishpalayeidhane hite satve pratyadhattam II 15 II Rigved. 1-116-15.

In a war VISHPALA wife of KHEL King, lost her leg. VISHPALA was provided with a functioning Iron Leg and that too in one night. (१५(. She fought the war next day. In modern time such aa feat is almost impossible and unbelievable. If it is considered as a fictional story, even then research can be attempted.

Mind is Brahma: -

The Rishis of Sanskrit era recognized Mind – मन. Bhrigu rishi after hard work, penance, Yadnya and Tap-तप, realized that the mind is Brahma. To understand Brahma, he again performed Tap. He realized that superior to mind is Vidnyan. Everything of manifest nature is from Vidnyan and all merges back in Vidnayan. The Vidnyan is a special knowledge or Vishesh Dnyan (ज्ञान). In Sanskrit it is recognized as Pradnya dnyan (प्रज्ञा ज्ञान). It is present in everything in manifest world or nature, including micro-organisms. The Pradnya dnyan can be called as automation but it is a function of brain. This dnyan decides future outcome in stem Cells, organisms, celestial bodies, stars, constellations, galaxies, and plants. Automation is outcome of Pradnya and not pradnya it-self. This can be explained by the fact that the cell decides when and how the division, duplication memory be executed. Single celled Amoeba with such Dnyan divides and propagates. If a child is taken to the edge of terrace of 4th floor, immediately he pushes himself backwards with such Pradnya dnyan. He has no experience of fear or death by falling but he recedes back. This is Pradnya dnyan. The mantra below connotes such a knowledge. Plants have mind and pradnya dnyan. It is proved by experiments by Cleve Backster in 1966 (See Appendix 3). He talked to plants. And they talked back.

स तपोऽतप्यत । स तपस्तत्वा । विज्ञानम् ब्रम्हेति व्यजानात । विज्ञानाध्द्येव खल्विदानि भूतानि जायन्ते । विज्ञानेन जातानि जीवन्ति । विज्ञानं प्रयन्त्यभिसंविशन्तीति । Bhriguvalli Anuvak 5.

Sa tapo tapyat sa tapastatva vidnynam brahmeti Vyajanat vidnyanadheva khalvidani Bhutani jayante vidnyanen jatani jivanti vidnyanam prayantyabhisamvishantiti II Bhriguvalli Anuvak 5.

तव्दिज्ञाय I पुनरेव वरुणं पितरमुपससार I अधिहि भगवो ब्रम्हेति I तं होवाच I तपसा ब्रम्ह विजिज्ञासस्व I तपो ब्रम्हेति I स तपोऽतप्यत I स तपस्तत्वा II 1 II **Briguvalli Anuvak 4.**

Tadvidnyaya punarev varunam pitaramupasara adhihi bhagavo bramheti sa tapotapyata sa tapastatva II Bhriguvalli Anuvak 4.

The same is reiterated in Brahmanand Valli, Anuwak 5, of Tattariyopnishad: (**तैत्तरिय उपनिषद् ब्रम्हानंदवल्ली, अनुवाक** 5, Mantra 1.

विज्ञानं यज्ञं तनुते । कर्माणि तनुतेऽपि च । विज्ञानं देवाः सर्वे। ब्रह्म ज्येष्ठमुपासते । विज्ञानं ब्रह्म चेद्वेद। तस्माच्चेन्न प्रमाद्यति । शरीरे पाप्मनो हित्वा।सर्वान् कामान् समश्नुत इति । तस्यैष एव शारीर आत्मा। यःपूर्वस्य। Brahmanand Valli, Anuwak 5, Mantra 1, of Tattariyopnishad.

Vidnyanam yadnyam tanute I karmani tanutepi cha I vidnyanam devah sarve I bramha jyeshthamupasate I vidnyanam II Tattariyopnishad. Brahmanand Valli, Anuwak 5.

तस्माद्वा एतस्माद्विज्ञानमयात् । अन्योऽन्तर आत्माऽऽनन्दमयः तेनैष वा एष पुरुषविध एव । तस्य पुरुषविधताम् । अन्वयं पुरुषविधः । तस्य प्रियमेव शिरः।

This mantra is in continuity with above mantra. It is a long statement.

Tasmadva etasmadvidnyanmayat I Anyontara Atma Anandmayah teneisha va esh pirushvidha ev I tasya purushvidhatam I Anvayam purushvidhah I tasya pryameva shirah I

It is interesting to note the intent of Vedic verse of the Brahmanand valli:

One of the five subtle sheaths of Aatma- the Vidnyan (**विज्ञान = विशेष ज्ञान**) is real agent of actions. This is when the determination faculty or Buddhi (**बुध्दि**) or analytical mindset, sanctions permission or decision, for mind and senses to work together through the gross instrument or vehicle the body, (Annamay sharir- food body). This sanction is for the Mind or Aatma.

Mind is waves. Ditermination faculty – the Buddhi, directs and stimulates these waves for ultimate action of gross body.

Karmas (कर्म) are any deed sacred or worldly, are done after sanction rom Buddhi.

Brahman is referred as Hiranyagarbha (हिरण्यगर्भ) or Cosmic – Mind. All life actions are dependent on mind and influenced by waves of cosmic mind. This cosmic mind decides fruits of all actions. Once one concentrates on cosmic mind, all objects of desire in the world, can be attained. After understanding all this the Ved further contemplates that body is cause of all sins. Identification of mind with body, one suffers from sin and miseries. If identified with cosmic mind, the person is liberated.

Vedic knowledge (वैदिकज्ञान = वेद ग्यान), had disciplined peoples of Sanskrit Speaking Civilization. Because of the invaders, the descendants of this civilization in modern times are considered as the HINDU population and have become HINGLISH Speaking Civilization (Hindi + English). This is the targeted and calculated attempt to assassinate and extinguish the civilization. But roots of RISHI culture are still smouldering and influencing them. The VEDIK DNYAN is for the welfare of the whole of the humanity. Unfortunately, humanity now, in modern time, has been fractioned. The division is by the colour of skin, eyes, and different religions, cults, faith, sects or sampradaya, etc. Hence the superiority or inferiority element is assumed in human minds. Vedic knowledge holds that all the living beings belong to one family- "वसुधेव कुटुंम्बकम्". The living beings may be from different origins as per Vedic knowledge, like: उद्बीज (from seeds), स्वेदज (from Larvae), अण्डज (from eggs), जरायुज (born with membrane).

All living beings and the so-called non-living (in fact as per Vedic knowledge everything manifest in Nature is living) and are DEVTA, and must be respected Everything manifest like plants, Stone, animals, etc., are DEVTA and are worth the worship.

The conceptual understanding of Rigveda is possible with deep thinking and meditating on each stanza of Rigveda. The obvious meaning of every Mantra may connote a different meaning than its original intent. Rigveda Mandal 1, Sukta 1, Mantra 1. Says: -

ओम अग्निमीळे पुरोहितम् यज्ञस्य देवम् ऋत्विजम् I **होतेरम् रत्नधामताम्** II1 II Rigved. 1-1-1.

Om Agnimile purohitam yadnyasya devam ritvijam I hoteram ratnadhamtam II 1 II

Agni (**अग्नि**)- : responsible for the manifestation of Brahma (Galaxies and stars, constellations etc.) and living beings (Praja) at the same time providing speed to everything. Such energy is praiseworthy and worth to be worshipped (**इळे**). Has power for the creation of the universe. The question arises that how this is possible when the fire can destroy everything coming in contact? The description about AGNI is available in Rigveda, 4- 58- 3.

चत्वारी श्रृंगा त्रयो अस्य पादा, व्दै शीर्षे सप्त हस्तासो अस्य । क्ष्रोरवीती महो देवो मर्त्या आ विवेश ॥

Four horns (**चत्वारी श्रृंगा**), three legs (**त्रयो अस्य पादा**), two heads (**व्दै शीर्षे**), and seven hands (**सप्त हस्तासो**), the bull tied at three sites (**त्रिधा बध्दो वृषभो**), the great God enters from all around in mortal's abode and creates sound.

This has been interpreted religiously about Veda 4, Yadnya 3, Ceremonies 2, and so on. But scientifically meaning can be different.

This is an enigmatic explanation about fire – the AGNI. It is an obscure picture. It does not fit in the ordinary fire or flames of the fire, is obvious.

If one considers AGNI (Flames or "Jwala") as SUN God, the meaning can be clear. The SUN showers energy or brilliance all around on earth. Hence great God (Mahadev). It energises all living beings when Sun rises in the morning. Sun is responsible for all types of seasons (three main Summer, Winter, and Rains.) on earth. Sun illuminates three abodes. The Sun light illuminates – BHUH, BHUVAH, SWAH. In space beyond three abodes light is absent. Sun Solstices are two – Summer and Winter or moves in two heads. Sun light beam, or Surya-Prakash, can be split into seven colours VIBGYOR is known to modern science. In Mundakopnishad, it is suggested that the Sun has seven flames. See below.

Apart from this in Sanskrit literature Sun is as Agni.

In 10th Mandal, Sukta 1, Mantra 1, it is further explained that:

अग्रे बर्हन्नुषसामूर्ध्वो अस्थान निर्जगन्वान तमसोज्योतिषागात |अग्निर्भानुना रुशता सवङ्ग आ जातोविश्वा सद्मान्यप्राः II1II Rigveda 1-1-10

Agre barhannushusamurdhvo asthan nirjaganvan tamasojyotishagat I Agnirbhanuna rushata savanga aa jatovishva sadamanyprah II 1 II Rigved. 10-1-1.

The great AGNI in the morning brings light on earth, enlightenment world from darkness using its TEJ (heat and light). This is directly indicating AGNI as Sun God.

In Mundakopnishad, Mundak 1- Khand 2 – mantra 4, it is stated that, there are seven flames, flares or toungues coming out of Sun God:

काली कराली च मनोजवा च सुलोहिता या च सुधूर्मवर्णा । स्फुल्लिंगिनी विश्वरुची च देवी लेलायमाना इति सप्त जिव्हाः Ii 4 II Mundakopnishad, Mundak 1- Khand 2 – mantra 4.

Kali karali cha manojava cha sulohita ya cha sudhumravarna I sfullingini vishvaruchi cha devi lelayamana iti sapta jivha II 4 II Mundakopnishad, Mundak 1- Khand 2 – mantra 4.

Seven types of flames (Seven tongues - सप्त जिव्हा:) are described in Mundakopnishad. All are having speed. In Yadnya Homkunda – यज्ञकुन्ड when Agni has established such flames are not visible. What is the meaning of such names for the flames is again an enigma? The scientific explanation can be:

1. KALI is related to kaal or TIME. Time depends upon the movement of the SUN. Agni again is from SUN. (refer to Mahasamhita from Uma Samhita of Shiv Purana– Song of science – Shrimad Bhagwat Gita, Notion Press. Agni energy is from wood, wood is from a tree. The fire energy in wood is from Sun).

2. Karali means -- Fierce and terrifying (भयंकर किंवा विकराल). This energy can perform multiple work and functions. Sun's heat and brightness can perform multitude of functions.

3. Manojava- an energy having a speed of mind (मन), which is greater than speed of light.

4. Sulohita – Infra red vibrations (colour of rusted Iron)- light? Needs targeted study.

5. Sudhumravarna – Smoke has bluish – Violet hue. Ultra-violet radiation?

6. Sfullingini – is a spark. Atomic energy. Pulsatile with strong movement. In an atom, electrons, protons, and neutrons are pulsatile and vibrate.

7. Vishwa Ruchi – energy with extremely strong power.

These seven energies are in Agni. Can these be in the fire? Obviously, this is in NATURE or Param Brahma.

The 5th mantra of Mundakopnishad clearly indicates SUN Rays as Agni:

एतेषु यश्चरते भ्राजमानेषु यथाकालं चाहुतयोहयाददायन् । तन्नयन्त्येताः सूर्यस्य रश्मयो यत्र देवानां पतिरेकोऽधिवासः ॥ ५ ॥

Eteshu yashcharate bhrajamaneshu yathakalam chahutayohya-dadaantyetah suryasya rashmayo yatra devanam patirekodhivasah II 5 II

Him who performed good deeds-pious *karma* performed by him, at the proper time, **conduct through the rays of the sun (सूर्यस्य रश्मयो)** where the Lord of the *Devas* is sole sovereign.

It is not the fire. But is more than fire. AGNI is Shakti or energy from Superpower. The Agni attracts or invites the Dev and RITVIJ (देवमृत्विजम् = Devam + Ritvijam) by performing YADNYA Karma. In turn the wealth and useful things are provided by DEVTA.

AGNI (**अग्नि**) or the fire god or one of the 5 basic elements (**पंच्चमाहाभूत**), whose eternal virtues are heat and light, without which, the fire has no meaning. Fire as PUROHIT or priest, to organize YADNYA (**यज्ञ कर्म**) and invite Gods. Praise and worship Gods to provide benefits of YADNYA KARMA. A sensible question that crops up is, How Agni can be PUROHIT (Who organizes YADNYA karma - work action and invite or attract devata and Ritvij - देवमृत्विजम् (Ritviz means "The most superior amongst all sages".) to provide wealth and needful commodities (रत्नधातमम्)? The answer is provided in Rigved itself.

The Scientific analysis and meaning can be: -

To understand, the meaning of AGNI, one must refer to Mandal 3, Sukta 1, Mantra 1-12. It needs detailed understanding of the meaning of the twelve mantras. 12th is very significant in the above context.

वव्रजा सीमनदतीरदब्धा दिवो यहनीरवसाना अनह्वनाः सना अत्र युवतयः सयोनीरेकं गर्भदधिरे सप्त वाणीः II6II.

अक्रो न बभ्रिः समिथे महिना दिदृक्षयः सूनवे भात्रऋजीकः उदुस्त्रिया जनिता यो जजानापां गर्भो नृतमो यहवो अग्निः **(१२).**

Vavraja simandatiradabdha divo yahaniravasana anahrinah sana atra yuvatayah sayonirekam Garbha dadhire sapta vanih II 6 II

Akro na babhrih samithe mahina didrukshayah soonave bharujikah udustriya janita yo jajanapam garbho nrutamo yahavo agnih II 12 II

The Sun is responsible for creating liquid water using his rays, with efforts generate rains, is worth the worship like parents are responsible for care and education of progeny.

As described above, gaining knowledge after doing hard work (Karmopasana -**कर्मोपासना**) and enlighten people, like females with their husbands, provide progeny, with protection teaching and training, at the same time educate them, and enjoy happy family life.

Agni is present in water (गर्भदधिरे) in a secret manner (समिथे महीनां) and provides nutritive value to it. (See Mantra below). Agni dev (**अग्निदेव**) retrieved from the water of rivers, but Agni does not harm water. It is distributed all over Antariksha (**अंतरिक्ष**). Agni is present in water (गर्भदधिरे) in a secret manner (समिथे महीनां) yrays, electromagnetic waves. It prepares clouds, responsible for rain and produces vegetation and food for the living beings. This is reiterated with the example of mothers educating children or their progeny.

प्र य आरुः शितिपृष्ठस्य धासेरा मातरा विविशुः सप्त वाणीः परिक्षिता पितरा संचरेते प्र सस्त्रिते दीर्घमायुः प्रयक्षे II 1 II Rigveda. 3-7- 1.

Pra ya Aaruh shiti prushthasya dhasera matara vivishuh sapta vanih prikshita pitara sanchrete pra sastrite dirghamayuh prayakshe II 1 II Rigveda. 3-7- 1

Energy in the form of Rays (of light and sound both), vibrations, radiation from galaxies, stars, and planets are in space emit a bluish-white aura, provide long life to it, spread such bluish white rays on earth and space from where these get generated. Like those who preserve energy with celibacy and Brahmacharya and save energy and prolong their life.

All this suggest that Agni is not only fire but in Rigveda it is electromagnetic waves, energy, heat, radiation, and light element of nature.

दिवक्षसो धेनवो वृष्णो अश्वा देवीरा तस्थौ मधुमव्दहन्तीः ऋतस्य त्वा सदसि क्षेमयंन्तं पर्येका चरति वतनि गौः II 2 II

divakshaso dhenavo vrushnao ashva devira tasthou madhumdvahantih rutasya tva sadasi kshemayantam paryeka charati vatani gauh II 2 II

Established in Aakash, the rays like cows, are speedy horses of Agni. Agni in micro form exists in sweet water of rivers. In close association with water, self-enlightened Agni in rays' forms spread all around are not harmful to water. The Earth moves in its sanctioned orbit (truthful path), like men with profound knowledge (**ऋतस्य**) with soft speech, and truthful pious behaviour, are not harmed in anyway.

इन्द्र वायू मनोजुवा विप्रा हवन्त ऊतये सहस्त्राक्षा धियस्पती II 3 II

Indra vayu manojuva vipra hvanta utaye sahastraksha dhiyaspati II 3 II

Indra and Vayu are like 'Mind' (**मनोजुवा**), has speed like mind. He has 1000 eyes (**सहस्त्राक्षा**). Intelligent people invite Indra for their protection.

Indra has spread in Aakash and receives liquid water (**जल**) like Ocean receives river water. A huge quantity is accepted by the ocean, without changing itself. Scientifically speaking the rays, radiation, and vibrations of all galaxies and stars, accommodate water without disturbing itself. Its level, quality, or virtues, remain undisturbed. At the same time do not cause any harm to water or moisture level below that sphere towards the earth. (Rigved, 1, 7, 1).

इन्द्रंमिद्गाथिनो बृहदिन्द्रमर्केभिरर्किणः । इन्द्रं वाणीरनूषत II 1 II Rigveda. 1-7-1.

Indramidgathino brihadindramarkebhirkirnah I indram vanirnushat II 1 II Rigveda. 1-7-1.

Knowledge about the Sun and Vayu with their properties and virtues, utilization for human benefits must be attempted. Hence praise Indra, with songs and Ved mantra.

ऋचो अक्षरे परमे व्योमन्यस्मिन्देवा अधि विश्वे निषेदुः । यस्तन्न वेद किमृचा करिष्यति य इत्तद्विदुस्त इमे समति॥39॥ Rigveda. 1-64-39.

Richo Akshsre parame vyomanyasmindeva adhi vishve nisheduh I yastanna ved kimrucha karishyati ya ittadvidusta ime samati II 39 II Rigveda. 1-64-39.

Supreme truth or "paramvyoman" the supreme heaven provides primordial elements or devata, one who do not understand Ved richas or imperishable Ved literature, what is he going to do with it? Those who know it are perfect.

इन्द्र मित्र वरूणमग्निमाहुरथो दिव्य स सुपणो गरुत्मान् । एकं सद्विप्रा बहुधा वदंन्त्यग्नि यमं मातरिश्वानमाहुः II 46 II Rigveda. 1-64-46.

Indra mitra varunam agnimahuratho divya sa supano garutman I ekam sadvipra bahudha vadantya Agni, yamam, matarishvan mahuh II II 46 II Rigveda. 1-64-46.

Sanskrit Rishis called him (this energy) by different names, Indra, Mitra, Varuna, Agni. This energy is like heavenly Garuda, who has beautiful wings. The truth is one, but the sages (or learned ones) call it by many names or describe him in many ways; they called him Agni, Yama, Mātariśvan (**मातारिश्वान**). Indra has thousands of eyes. Transmitted in Akasha, his presence, provide food and riches to all living beings, humans. How this is possible? How is this achieved scientifically achieved?

Scientifically, when rays, radiation, vibrations of BRAHMA (Galaxies, Stars, constellations, etc.), in the form of Shakti- which can be VIDYUT (Electricity), vibrations, rays, light, heat, present in the GARBHA (-centre) of water particles, enhance the productive capacity and nutritional power of water. This happens when INDRA enters in moisture – a sphere below the radiation sphere, which provides the electric charge to clouds. Rain with the thunderous sound of clouds, the nutrients get dissolved or get attached to rainwater droplets and fall on earth which enrich the soil and provides nourishments to vegetation on earth. At the same time change the elements on earth, in a useful manner as precious stones, diamonds, iron, metals, calcium, zinc, phosphorus, etc. for human utilization. Indirectly provide riches and wealth. In other words, Veda has described science in an obscure and camouflaged way.

The following mantras of Rigveda authenticate the above statement.

How the productive capacity of water, gets enhanced, gets answered in Mandal 1, Sutra 23, Mantra 12.

हस्कारादि विद्युत स्पर्यतो जाता अवन्तु नः मरूतो मृळयन्तु नः II 12 II Rigved. 1-23-12.

Haskaradi Vidyut sparyato jata avantu nah maruto mrulayantu nah II 12 II Rigved. 1-23-12.

Shining VIDYUT responsible for MARUT (-VAYU), or Marutgana manifest due to Vidyut. by invigorating productivity and provide food and nourishment, thus protect living beings on earth.

दिवश्चिदस्य वरिमा वि पप्रथ इन्द्र न मन्हा पृथिवि चन प्रति भीमस्तुविष्माषणिभ्य आतपः शिशीते वज्रम तेजसे न वंसगः II 1 II Rived 1, 55, 1.

Divashchidasya varima vi paprath Indra na manha pruthavi chana prati bhimastuvishmashanibhya aatapah shishite vajram tejase na vansagah II 1 II Rived 1, 55, 1

The effective influence of Indra is much more than Aakash. Earth is also unable to match the same (Greatness-Mahanta), of Indra. Indra protects people from enemies. Indra sharpens weapons like a bull sharpens horns for YUDDHA purposes, getting ready for fight.

अभिमवन्व नत्स्वभिष्टिभूतयोस्न्तरिक्ष प्रान्तविषीभिरा वृतम् इन्द्र द्रक्षासस ऋभवो मदच्चुतं शतक्रतु जवनि सुनृतारुहतं II2 II. Rigved 1, 51, 2.

Abhibhavanva natsvabhishtibhuta yosnantariksha prantavishibhira vrutam Indra drakshasas ribhaavo madachcytam shatakratu javani sunrutaruhatam II2 II. Rigved 1, 51, 2.

Marut named RIBHAVO came for the help of Indra, which have spread in Akash and are considered very strong.

युञ्जन्ति बरग्नमरूषं चरन्ति परि तस्थुषः रोचन्ते रोचना दिवी II 1 II. Rigved 1-6-1

Yunjanti baragnamarusham charanti pari tastushah rochante rochana divi II 1 II. Rigved 1-6-1

Indra (अरुषम्) exists and pervades everywhere(चरन्तम्) in the form of a Brilliant and energetic Sun (सूर्य), non-violent energy, and Fire-(AGNI). It is also in the form of (रोचना) speedy (चरन्तम्) wind (VAYU). It is spread in abundance(ब्रध्नम्) in all living and non-living beings of all the first three abodes out of 7 abodes (Bhu, BHuvah, Swaha, Maha, Janah, Tapah, Satyah). Indra is seen in all the constellations in space (– the Antariksha). This reiterates the fact that the radiation, electromagnetic waves, light and sound waves are spread everywhere in antariksha.

The above mantra clearly indicates that the Indra is not Devta in human form as considered or depicted and understood. It must be, understood scientifically, as a natural, elemental sphere around Earth. Being supernatural elements, termed as Devata, Indra-devata. Indra devata is concerned to induce rain by energizing moisture and clouds.

यदङ्ग दाशुषे त्वमग्ने भद्रं करिष्यसि। तवेत्तत्सत्यमङ्गिरः|| 6 || (Rigved.(6-1-1

Yadang dashushe tvam agne bhadram karishyasi I tavettatsatyamangirah || 6 || (Rigved 1-1-6).

Energy-God - the Agni – the Sun, is the life of all living beings. You (त्वम) bless the persons. You are generous, helping and giving. You are the breath of life. This is the truth about your divine nature. Based on this the Sun god is Devata and invited to help and provide benefits.

This is expressed in first mandal of Rigved.

Agni Devta invited to Yadnya and help the progression of the Yadnya at the same time bestow the profit to the performer of Yadnya. Bless like father who blesses his sons without any demand from sons.

ॐअग्निमीळे पुरोहितं यज्ञस्य देवमृत्विजम् | होतारं रत्नधातमम् || 1 || Rigved. 1-1-1.

Yadnya - यज्ञ: is Highest quality of work for the salvation, for spiritual knowledge, and knowing truth.

Purohit - पुरोहित: Persons who perform the Yadnya-karma.

Devta- - देवता: Celestial Gods, who grant happiness.

Ritvij - ऋत्विज: Who accomplish the Yadnya.

Hota - होता: Hota are people who extend invitation to Gods

Yajak- - याजक: those who indulge in the Yadnya.

Ratna- - रत्न: Benefits of Yadnya-karma.

The cause of Clouds, Rain, Rain drop precipitation.

Rigved 1-79-1,2,3, it is very clearly indicated that Agni is responsible for rain. How it instigates clouds to precipitate rain drops.

आ ते सुपर्णा अमिनन्तम् एवैः कृष्णो वृषभो यदीदम् । शिवाभिर्न स्मयमानाभिरागात्पतन्ति मिहः स्तनयन्त्यभ्रा II 2 II Rigved 1- 79- 2.

Aa te Suparna aminantam eveih krishno vrushabho yadidam I shivabhirna smayamannabhiragatpatanti mihah stanayantyabhra II 2 II Rigved 1-79- 2.

The Sun rays, waves (सुपर्णाः किरणें - like Garuda; Suparṇa; bird of prey eagle) etc provoke rain fall. Perceived virtues of space aether in those rain drops, fall on earth. the clouds thunder (अभ्रा मेघ स्तनयन्ति गर्जते) and rainwater with dissolved nutrients, drop down (आ पतन्ति) on earth ॥ २ ॥

यदीमृतस्य पयसा पियानो नयन्नृतस्य पथिभी रजिष्ठैः। अर्यमा मित्रो वरुणः परिज्मा त्वचं पृञ्चन्त्युपरस्य योनौ ॥ 3 II Rigveda. 1-79-3.

Yadimrutasya payasa piyano nayannrutasya pathibhi rajishtheh I Aryama mitro varunah parijma Tvacha prunchantyuparasya yonou ǁ 3 II Rigveda. 1-79-3.

When action and the cause (अर्यमा मित्रो वरुणः परिज्मा त्वचं – Parijma is UDAN, Outer part of truth = Tvacham), the Pran, and the Jal or Aap or water, get together in life, then only the body manifests and life begins. ॥३॥

वायवा याहि दर्शतेमे सोमा अरंकृताः। तेषां पाहि श्रुधी हवम् ॥ 1 ॥ Rigved 1-2-1

Vayava yahi darshateme soma arankrutah I tesham pahi shrudhi havam ॥ 1 II Rigved 1-2-1

Vayu can be only experienced and revealed in the heart (दर्शतेमे), having virtues of touch, and the knowledge only, with which the physical presence of Vayu, can be felt (वायवा याहि – वायव + आयाहि), which made all manifest materials of nature (Prakriti) and protect them. The belief is that the wind is responsible to erosion and cause weathering of material things around. How can Vayu protect materials of nature? Is it scientifically true? It can be explained by scientifically by:

Actions and interactions of PANCHMAHABHUT (भुमिरापोनलोनिलोनभः) are responsible for the manifestation of materials in nature (See "brahmotpatti" and "prajotpatti"). Vayu is essential in this. Thus, Vayu made all manifest materials of nature (Prakriti) and protect them.

The living beings can live and listen as well as speak (पाहि श्रुधी हवम्) due to the presence of Vayu, is as per the modern science. The science of this Sanskrit statement is given below. "Vayu" exists in all living and non-living matter of this universe. In other words, Vayu is everywhere in Space and all the living and non-living matters of the Prakriti or nature.

How living beings can speak and listen? Scientifically it can be explained as under:

The sound waves float in the air medium thereby reaching our ears and so our speech. When we expel air from the lungs and push it through the larynx, the vocal cords vibrate, making the sound. The cords are mostly made up of cartilage and muscle. Stretched across the top are the vocal cords, which are two folds of the mucous membrane.

A sound is a form of energy produced by the vibration of particles in a medium. Let us understand how sound waves are produced with the help of an example: In a drum, when drumsticks hit the drum, the outer membrane of the drum vibrates up and down. Whenever the drum membrane moves up it compresses the air just above it. While the air molecules expand when the drum membrane vibrates down. This compression and expansion of air produce a difference in air pressure. This pressure difference in the air is carried like ripples in ponds and results in the production of sound by a drum. Why do sound waves need a medium for their propagation? Sound needs a material medium for its propagation like solid, liquid, or gas to travel because the molecules of solid, liquid, and gases carry sound waves from one point to another. Sound cannot progress through the vacuum because the vacuum has no molecules which can vibrate and carry the sound waves. In a small Sanskrit hymn, how much science is hidden which needs to be explored for the human generations to come?!

Word-Meaning of Mantra Rigveda 1-2-1: -(दर्शत(Vayu can be experienced with knowledge, has limitless energy- force, and is life for all living and non-living manifestations of nature.)इमे(who has, adorned and ornated)अरंकृताः (the manifest material world of nature)सोमाः(. All material manifest world is pervaded by VAYU. With meditative practice, man can reveal the virtues of components of manifest material world can get unfolded. Even the work actions inside the materials get unfolded to meditating person. So is the ultimate energy (God-Parmeshwar) in all manifest material world gets revealed (वायवा याहि दर्शनीये॰).

मि॒त्रं हु॑वे पू॒तद॑क्षं॒ वरु॑णं च रि॒शाद॑सम्। धियं॑ घृ॒ताचीं॒ साध॑न्ता ॥7॥ (Rigved, 1-2-7).

Mitram huve putadaksham Varunam cha rishadsm I dhiyam ghritachim sadhanta ॥7II Rigved, 1-2-7.

Like Sun in space and Vayu (Pran), in the living body, which provides pleasure and protection from enemies like diseases, outside as well as inside. The (VARUN) that is PRAN and APAN which are inside and outside the body, human beings must utilize for their welfare. It can further be explained that Sun along with Vayu are responsible for rain by heating water in collections of water on earth and with Vayu, the water vapours are taken up in the sky resulting in the rain for the benefit of living beings.

यः श्वेताँ अधिनिर्णिजश्चक्रे कृष्णाँ अनु व्रता । स धाम पूर्व्यं ममे यः स्कम्भेन वि रोदसी अजो न द्यामधारयन्नभन्तामन्यके समे ॥ 10 ॥ Rigved. 8-41-10.

Yah shvetam adhinirnijashchakre krushnam anu vrata I sad ham pUrvyam mame yah skambha vi rodasi ajo na dyamadhar yannabhantamanyake same II 10 II Rigved. 8-41-10.

यस्मिन्विश्वानि काव्या चक्रे नाभिरिव श्रिता । त्रितं जूती सपर्यत व्रजे गावो न संयुजे युजे अश्वाँ अयुक्षत नभन्तामन्यके समे ॥ 1 ॥ Rigved 8-41-6.

As the spokes of a wheel are resting on the hub in the centre of the wheel, similarly whole work actions in universe depends upon VARUN. All the elements in universe, are manifest from – Hydrogen (Varun). This is as per the modern Science.

अस्मा ऊ षु प्रभूतये वरुणाय मरुद्भ्योऽर्चा विदुष्टरेभ्यः । यो धीता मानुषाणां पश्वो गा इव रक्षति नभन्तामन्यके समे ॥ 1 II Rigved. 8-41-1.

Asma uoo shu prabhutaye varunaya marudbhyorcha vidushatarebhyah I yo dhita manushanam pashvo gaa eiva rakshati nabhantamanyake same || 1 II Rigved. 8-41-1.

Worship Varuna for prosperity, honour. With his powers, judgement and actions, protects and promotes humans, animals, birds, etc., just as he protects and regulates stars, planets and satellites, all like the sacred cow.

तिस्रो द्‌यावो निहिता अन्तरस्मिन्तिस्रो भूमीरुपरा :षड्‌विधानाः । गृत्सो राजा वरुणश्चक्र एतं दिवि प्रेङ्खं हिरण्ययं शुभे कम् ॥ 5 II Rigved. 7-87-5.

Bhuh, Bhuvah, Svah are three regions- bhuvans or lok out of seven, which are illuminated by Sun. Three heavens of light are contained in the presence of this lord Varuna and there are three orders of the earth globe over which there are six variations. The omnipotent ruler – raja, Varuna created all this universe including the sun. All work and actions are inter-dependent on Varun.

In fact, the space above earth is divided into various planes. Each plane has different gods. It is worth mentioning here that the thirty-three deities or godsmentioned in Ved include: -

According to "Shathpath Brahman" these are

Vasu 8,

Rudra 11,

Aditya 12,

Dyoe 1,

Prithvi 1.

But Rishi Yagyavalkya considered 'The eight Vasus, eleven Rudras, twelve Adityas, Indra and Prajapati are the thirty-three gods".

According to Yaksha, the original thirty-three gods (eight Vasus, eleven Rudras, twelve Adityas and two Asvinis) are divided equally in three different planes of existence namely the celestial plane (dyuloka) the intermediate region (antarikshaloka) and the terrestrial plane (bhurloka) each plane having eleven gods.

The dyu loka (celestial plane) is presided over by Savitra or Surya; while Antariksha loka (intermediary space) is presided over by Indra or Vayu; and the bhurloka (terrestrial plane) is presided over by Agni.

There is misunderstanding about different Gods and deities.

Vedic understanding is very clear. All the gods lead to One God. And, one should make a distinction between a path and the goal. The goal is consciousness of the Supreme in all its manifestations.

Another misunderstanding is about the form of Gods or deities.

All gods mentioned in the Rig-Veda have human features such as the face, limbs etc, their forms are shadowy and unique colour. At the same time, deities have distinct power and personality. Indra has strength and vigour; Pushan has protecting power; so is Vishnu. The sun stands for many forms of brilliance, while Rudra represents the anger.

The physical features represent a specific form of nature.

Different gods are the primordial elements but supreme energy is one and the only one – The Tejahpunjah (तेजःपुञ्ज).

CHAPTER 5

FIRE – AGNI. THE ENERGY

Rigveda has given highest importance to FIRE-AGNI -the energy. It is called AGNI by Rigveda. Is Agni and Fire being the same? In Rigveda meaning of Agni is not fire, it is much more than the fire. In fact, author could not find exact translation of the word in English. Word energy is to some extent matches the word AGNI. Agni is "VIRAT SHAKTI" (विराट शक्ति) – unfathomable **Power or energy.** No God - Devata, is approachable without the medium of Agni, and no divinity is without the presence of Agni. Hence AGNI is main essential for YAJNYA KUND and the ceremony. **Therefore, the word AGNI is used in this chapter.** Agni can be symbolized as the natural element fire and aspiring for knowledge. Heat, combustion, light, and energy are DHARMA of Agni. It can convert gross to the subtle. Agni gives energy. Once the primordial AGNI released from the "absolute truth" it pervades in all the basic elements. One can say manifestation of 5 basic elements, the Agni plays an important role. Some classify Agni into 5 types. There are five Agnis in each of the five basic elements, namely – Parthiva (earth), Aap (liquid, water), Tejas (Agni), Vayavya (vayu) and Nabha (akash).

Rigveda has classified the agni into three. The Rigvedic classification from human point of view can be:

1. Un-harnessed or Cosmic Agni or Primordial Agni. Agni which is in the Absolute truth and the whole cosmos. Rigveda calls it AADILOKIK AGNI.

2. Harnessed Agni or Agni in Yagya or Yadnya Kund, Agni harnessed for cooking (Firewood Natural gas, electricity, Solar energy, Sonic energy,

Hydro-electric agni, Radiation agni, Solar Agni, ultrasonic Agni, Atomic Agni, etc. Rigveda calls it LOKIK AGNI or GRAHAPATYA (for general domestic usage),

3. Entrapped Agni in Living beings, Agni for day-to-day activities to perpetuate life in all living beings. Rigveda calls it PRANAGNI (Pran is of 10 types. Details are in book published by Author-SONG of Science Shrimad Bhagwat Gita. Notion Press, 2020 edition). Hence Rigveda nick names Agni as AGNI DEVATA. Maximum mantras are devoted to AGNI. Even in YAGYA process the word used as JATVEDASE honour to Agni, a knower of everything. Because Agni provides location for life to exist, Congenial environment for perpetuation of life. Planets like earth and surrounding atmosphere, weather, provide environment, food, or energy for activities to living beings. Veda has gone further to say that the Stars like SUN are the firewood for the YADNYA of cosmos. How are such conclusions arrived at? How interesting is VEDA RICHAS? How scientific are the different mantras of Rigveda?

The SANATAN DHARMA of AGNI, has heat, energy, and light. Symbolic description of Sun light – energy is it driven by seven horses. Or one horse with seven names. It also described as having seven tongues. What is this symbolic expression in Rigveda? On analysis and from the knowledge of PURAN RICHAS the following description is valuable: -

Rigveda 1-1-1. Richa(श्रृचा), अ॒ग्निमी॑ळे पु॒रोहि॑तं य॒ज्ञस्य॑ दे॒वमृ॒त्विज॑म् । होता॑रं रत्न॒धात॑मम् ॥

The mantras are praises for AGNI. Agni is PUROHIT and RITVIJ who conducts, administers, and offers work-KARMA, for the YAJNYA (-YADNYA), for the creation and the creature. Agni is possessor of wealth and wealth giver. This means the Agni has all the power for manifestation of nature-PRAKRITI. YAJNA is considered as the religious ceremony, but scientifically how can it be a religious? The

above narration sounds more scientific. Yes, of course, the above-mentioned scientific KARMA is attended religiously for the manifestation of cosmos. Agni's offerings which it is in possession, for oblations, are for creation and creature. Next nine Mantras - 'Richas' are more explanatory in this context. Though Agni is purohit still invite to the 'Yadnya-Karma' along with Gods. (Rigveda. 1-1-5). In Rigveda. 1-19-1, Agni and Maruta - (Vayu), are together. MARUTA are SAPTA GANA means 7 individuals. Not only this but the other gods who are helpful and protector are also invited along with Agni. Creation of prakriti, vegetation, food etc, is not possible by one but all together are responsible for the manifestations, hence multiple helpful elements are invited for Yajnya karma. This is what appears from subsequent Suktas of Mandal one of Rigvedas. Analyse it scientifically:

Indra Devata being powerful and can devour enemies like VRITRASUR. Indra is helpful supporter and protector is expressed as leader amongst all. Details about Vritrasur could not be interpreted scientifically but the Vritrasur is expressed as a demon in literature. From all this expression it becomes clear that, the Vedic Scientific consideration is that the scientific development was in co-ordination with society, environment, and Prakriti or Nature, so that it is of utmost benefit for humanity at large.

Utilization of all supernatural elements 'God' in scientific development and progress without any harm to the elements. It reminds author, reminiscences of his childhood, the system of using service plates for serving food was on Banana leaves and PATTALs or plates made from MAHUA plant leaves. Water served in mud glasses 'DABULA'. Such material was for one time use only or were disposable, and easily recyclable. All natural products and recyclable. Banana leaves or PATTALS along with left-over food is given to domesticated animals to eat, e.g., cows, buffaloes, goats etc, which after 24 hours becomes

manure from cow-dung. What a wonderful waste management!!! One may not like to revert to that system, but trial will not be out of context. It will save collection of unmanageable garbage heaps and recycling problems. Washing metallic plates used for food serving need chemicals which drain into rivers and polluting river water. Civilized societies of urban cities the animal domestication is almost impossible, but villages where animal rearing is easy such trials can be adopted?

रतेनाद्रिं वय असन भिदन्तः सम अङगिरसो नवन्त गोभिः | शुनं नरः परि षदन्न उषासम आविः सवर अभवज जाते अग्नौ ||11|| Rigveda. 4-3-11.

Ratenadrim vaya asan bhidantah sama Angiraso navanta gobhih I shunam narah parishadanna ushasama aavih savara abhavaja jate agnou II 11 II Rigveda. 4-3-11

The RICHA narrates the AGNI manifested much earlier than Sun or before SUN, or sun came to existence after Agni. Sukta 12 of Mandal 1 of Rigveda again discus AGNI. Agni being messenger of Gods, selected as invoker of gods and invited along with Gods to Yajna place. This is for the **defence from evil spirit.**

"घर्ताहवन दीदिवः परति षम रिषतो दह| अग्ने तवं रक्षस्विनः" (Rigveda. 1-12-5).

Symbolic depiction can scientifically, be explained evils as Viruses or bacteria. (How YAJNYA helps, and the scientific explanation is given in authors book- "Song of Science Shrimad Bhagwadgita" 2020 ed. Notion Press. The ingredients of oblations to YAJNA KUND fire on Page 108-110, Chapter 3. Interested reader can read details in the book).

Sukta 95 of Mandal 1, subject matter of the Sukta (1-95 below) is "AGNI" nick named as Devata. Hence the matter of the Sukta be discussed with the subject of AGNI in mind only.

"SATYAGUNA VISHISHTOGNIH SHUDDHOGNIRVA.

सत्यागुणविशिष्टोसग्निः शुध्दोSग्निर्वा"

Accordingly, the meaning of the mantra is discussed keeping AGNI in mind. Relevant mantra is mentioned below:

आविष्ट्यो वर्धते चारुरासु जिह्मानामूर्ध्वः स्वयंशा उपस्थे । उभे त्वष्टुर्बिभ्यतुर्जायमानात्प्रतीची सिंहं प्रति जोषयेते ॥ 5 ॥

Avishtayo vardhayate charurasu jihamanamurdhavah svayasha upasthe I obhe tvshturbibhya tujayamanatpratichi simhampratijoshayate II5 II Rigved. 1-95-5.

Rigved understands that the Agni (fire) is born from the time of the creation of the cosmos. It is in woods and as disintegrator going upwards and being in the wood it grows and is in the form of the sun. It comes into existence at a certain time and perishes at the appointed time. (See Uma Samhita of Shiv puran).

धन्वन्त्स्रोतः कृणुते गातुमूर्मिं शुक्रैरूर्मिभिरभि नक्षति क्षाम्। विश्वा सनानि जठरेषु धत्तेऽन्तर्नवासु चरति प्रसूषु ॥ १० ॥ Rigveda 1-95-10.

Dhanvanstrotah krunute gaturmurmi shukrerurmibhirabhi nkshati ksham I Vishva sanani jathareshu dhattentarnavasu charatiprasushu II 10 II Rigveda 1-95-10.

Agni is energy the electric power and vital heat of life, creates paths over the deserts and in the skies, makes waterways to flow with rippling waves, and with bright rays of light illuminates the earth. It creates all the foods and vitalities for the internal organs of the living body systems and vibrates in all the new and upcoming forms of nature and human generations.

According to VEDIC concept, environment surrounding our earth, includes all the basic elements (Earth, Liquid, fire, Air, Space, भूमिरापोनालोनिलोनभः), animate and in-animate, manifestation in the cosmos. The VEDAS have paid all the attention and concentration on basic subjects and analysed scientifically. Rigveda, 1-95-10 above, is the testimony to this statement. There is a deep concern about AGNI its origin, function, and purpose of existence of AGNI must be investigated for the human benefit. How such a thinking be ritual, orthodox, or religious as it is thought, in modern sense? Before condemning without understanding it, such derogatory statements are unscholarly. The younger descendants of Sanskrit Speaking Civilization must understand, investigate, confirm, before following the statements by scholars with wasted interest.

Details about AGNI is in Mandala 10, Sukta 124: -

अदेवात् । देवः । प्रऽचता । गुहा । यन् । प्रऽपश्यमानः । अमृतऽत्वम् । एमि । शिवम् । यत् । सन्तम् । अशिवः । जहामि । स्वात् । सख्यात् । अरणीम् । नाभिम् । एमि ॥2॥ Rigveda 10-124-2.

Agni secretly travels from inauspicious (**अदेवा**) to auspicious (**देवा**) wisely (**प्रऽचता** PRA-CHTA), from secret (**गुहा गुप्त स्थान**), become visible (PASHYAMANA), get immortal state, and holy -pious, when born.

Primordial Agni released from the Absolute truth, gets immortality. The birth or origin of AGNI is from the ultimate source of all manifestations in nature.

इमम् न अगने ्प यज्ञम् आ इहि पंञ्चऽयामम् त्रिऽवृतम् सप्त तंतुम् असः हव्यऽवाट् उत नः पुरःऽगाः ज्योक् एव दीर्घम् तमः आ अशयिष्ठाः **॥1॥ Rigveda 10-124-1.**

Imam na Agnep yadnyam Aa ihi **panchayamam** trivitram sapta tantum Asah havyavat uta nah puragah jyok eva dirgham Tamah Aa ashyishthah II 1 II Rigveda 10-124-1.

To understand this above mantra, one must know the word PANCHAYAMAM or also called as PRAHAR (**प्रहर**). *pañcayāmam* (**पञ्चऽयामम्**) = "prahara; watch; travel; path. Prahar details are as under:

(Indian timings are divided into PRAHAR-**प्रहर-घडी** which means watch. Day-night segment of 24 hours is divided into 3 segments of 8 hour each and have their names as well-

1st prahar is 6-9PM called PRADOSH,

2nd prahar 9PM to midnight called NISHITA.

3rd PRAHAR is Midnight to 3AM is called TRIYAMA.

Similarly other prahar are PURVANHA, MADHYAMA, APARANHA, SAYANHA, and USHA. TRIVRITAM (त्रिऽवृतंम्)=TREBLE.

SAPTATANTUM (सप्तऽतंन्तुम्) = 7 threads.)

AGNI invited to YAJNYA. YAJNYA fire has 5 oblations as per the PRAHAR (प्रहर) timings. It spreads by 7 TANTUS (सप्तऽतंन्तुम्) or rays and be the bearer of our oblations, lead us, you have long been sleeping in profound darkness." Co-relate with the 2nd stanza above.

The scientific analysis of this is that the AGNI has 7 rays, 7 colours, and 7 tongues-means 7 flares. The scientific explanation is available in other Sanskrit literature. In MUNDAK upanishd 1, KHANDA 2, MANTRA 4. Seven tongues or flares are described. The seven flames of fire are Kaali, Karali, Manojava, Sulohita, Sudhumravarna, Sphulingini and Vishvaruchi. Mantra below is about seven flares of Agni. This has been discussed earlier.

काली कराली च मनोजवा च सुलोहिता या च सुधूम्रवर्णा । स्फुलिंन्गिनी विश्वरुची च देवी लेलायमाना इति सप्त जिह्वा: II 4 II Mundak 1, Khanda 2, Mantra 4.

Kali karali cha mnojava cha sulohita ya cha sudhumravarna I sfulingini vishvaruchi cha devi leilaymana iti saptajivhah II 4 II Mundakopnishad 1-2-4.

Following discussion is about all the seven flares, one by one: -

It is to be noted here that the RISHI talk here about BRAMHAGNI i.e. primordial AGNI and not agni of yajna kunda. One hardly sees 7 flares in Agni of YAJNA Kund.

Kali is kal feminine. Kal is time. Kal is death too. On earth the source of energy is SUN. Vegetation on earth is due to SUN. Vegetation is food for living beings. SUN gets energy from "absolute truth" is accepted by modern science now. Hence KALI is energy of "absolute truth". KAALI is 'KAAL' as well, which means death.

KARALI energy has many hands to perform work. Sun rays and heat also performs many tasks. Like heat, light. Harnessed solar energy performs many tasks, creates clouds, helps vegetation to produce chlorophyll etc.

MANOJAVA means having speed like mind or MANN (mn). There are particles faster than light (Faster-than-Light Particles. M. E. Arons and E. C. G. Sudarshan Phys. Rev. **173**, 1622 – Published 25 September 968). Tachyon is such particle. Obviously, mind is faster than all. This is MANOJAVA.

SULOHITA. Loha is Iron. Rusty coloured flare from AGNI. Scientifically can be Infra-red rays.

SUDHUMRAVARNA. DHUMRA is smoke. Rays having hue of smoke. Scientifically such flares can be Ultraviolet rays or cosmic rays.

SPHULLINGINI. i.e., spark (**ठिणगी**). Having vibrating particles are such "sphullingini" flares. Atomic rays can be such rays.

VISHVARUCHI. Very powerful energy which can destroy the universe. It is still unknown to modern science.

एतेषु यश्चरते भ्राजमानेषु यथाकाल चाहुतयो ह्याददायन् । तं नयन्त्येताः सूर्यस्य श्मयो यत्र (तन्नयन्त्येता) देवानां पतिरेकोऽधिवासः II 5 II Mundak 1, Khanda 2, Mantra 5.

एतेषु यश्चरते भ्राजमानेषु यथाकाल चाहुतयो ह्याददायन् ी तं नयन्त्येताः सूर्यस्य श्मयो यत्र क्षतन्नयन्त्येता) devana. pitrekoSi2vas: II 5 II Mundak 1, Khanda 2, Mantra 5.

Eteṣu yaścarate bhrājamāneṣu yathākālaṃ cāhutayohyādadāyan |tannayantyetāḥ sūryasya raśmayo yatra devānāṃ patireko'dhivāsaḥ || 5 || Mundakopnishad 1-2-5.

Timely oblations help persons with the help of such flare and Sun rays (सूर्यस्य रश्मयो) to the abode of "Absolute truth" PARAMBRAHMA. Thus achieve liberation and success. (Co-relate with mantra 6).

The following interpretation is important from the comparative analysis of fire from different civilizations of the world.

[An abstract from Britannica, about Fire in religion and philosophy: -

The sacred fires and fire drills of religious rituals and the numerous fire-gods of world mythology must be interpreted as additional evidence of both the antiquity and the importance of fire in human history. In the ancient Vedic scriptures, Agni, or Fire, is the messenger between the people and their gods and the personification of the sacrificial fire. Brahman households today are supposed to maintain a sacred fire for the worship of Agni, much as the ancient Romans kept a holy perpetual fire cared for by the vestal virgins and as the Greeks tended and transported the sacred fire of Hestia during migrations. The Zoroastrians of Iran placed fire at the centre of their religion and worshiped it as the most subtle and ethereal principle and the most potent and sacred power, thought to have been presented to man directly from heaven and kindled by the Deity himself. Among the Israelites, Abraham might be viewed as a reformer who resisted the ancient worship of Moloch, the god of fire, by child sacrifice. In Siberia both the primitive Koryak and Chuckchi and the more civilized Buryat honoured the fire-god by keeping all filth and impurities away from their fires and hearths. The need to protect fire from contamination was also a belief in parts of Africa, North and South America, and elsewhere. The Aztec of Mexico and the Inca of Peru worshiped gods of fire with sacred flames, which the Inca ignited by concentrating the Sun's rays with a concave metallic mirror.

The great Greek scientists and philosophers found fire just as significant as did the mystics of religion. Aristotle, for example, declared fire, along with water, earth, and air, to be one of the four general and essential elements of life and of all things. Plato asserted that God used the four elements in the creation of the world. Heraclitus attributed to fire the essential force for creation].

Reader can scrutinize, verify, and compare it with the scientific way the AGNI has been described. Fire is not a synonym of Agni. It is much more than the fire. Hence word AGNI has been used in Vedic descriptions.

Agni is an energy or SHAKTI. Shakti being a feminine word, hence it is symbolized as female or DEVI or DURGA. Markandeya Purana (Publisher- Khemraj Shrikrishna das, Shrivenkateshvar press, Mumbai.) is emphasizing on the physics of the energy on DEVI only. But the Mantras focus on the energy or AGNI.

आधार भूता जगतत्स्व मेका महीस्वरूपेण यतः स्थितांसि । अपांस्वरुपस्थितयात्वयैतद् आप्याय्यते कृत्स्नमलंघ्य वीर्ये II 3 II Markandeya Puran, Chapter 88- mantra 3.

Aadhrbhuta jagatastvameka mahisvrupena yatah sthitamsi I Apansvrupasthitayatvayeitad Aapyayate kritsna malanghya veerye II 3 II Markandeya Puran, Chapter 88- mantra 3.

Energy SHAKTI is supportive to every manifest thing in nature and cosmos. This Shakti is omnipresent in subtle form. In water the Shakti satisfies the manifest world. Shakti's power cannot be skipped or controlled or jumped over.

त्वम् वैष्णवी शक्तिर अनंत वीर्या विश्वस्यबीजंपरमासि। मायासंम्मोहितं देवी समस्त मेतत्वं वै प्रसन्नाभुवि मुक्ति हेतु II 4 II Markandeya Puran, Chapter 88- mantra 4.

Tvam veishnavishaktir Ananta virvishvasya bijamparamasi I mayasammohitam devi samastametatva vei prasannabhuvi mukti hetu II 4 II Markandeya Puran, Chapter 88- mantra 4.

Agni is energy or 'shakti-rup' of VISHNU, the primordial gas layer (see diagram). Agni is endless power and is seed of the whole cosmos. Nature's camouflaging effect is due to the Agni energy and is responsible for the liberation from the effect of camouflaging. This idea seems intriguing. But

Agni-shakti stimulates mind and soul to develop understanding to break the network of camouflaging effect of nature or Prakriti, called MAYA JAAL. Once mind decides the individual is no more lured for sense satisfaction. The greed vanishes. This is the psycho-physiological effect and thinking of Sanskrit Speaking civilization. In this context the GOD PARTICLE or Soul as particle is explained below: -

According to Rishi Kanaad (7000 BC) the nine elements are Matter (DRAVYA) e.g., namely – Parthiva (earth), Aap (liquid as water), Tejas (Agni), Vayavya (vayu) and Nabhasa (akash), along with Time, Disha-direction, Soul, and Mind. The mantra is:

पृथ्विय आप स्तेजो वायुर आकाशं कालो दिग् आत्मा मन इति द्रव्याणि II5II Vaisheshik Darshan 1-1-5.

Prithviyapostejaovayurakasham kalodigatma mann iti dr avyani II5II Vaisheshik Darshan 1-1-5.

What is the scientific meaning of this?

1. Earth- Prithvi. Minute inner composition of earth is Atom. Inside it is AGNI -energy.

2. Aap- Liquid Jal, Water. Composed of small particles. Agni in the form of electricity is in the water without harming. The existing force – the energy which exists, binds the particles to-gather.

3. Nala- Fire – Agni. It has particles. It has form, heat, light. It has subtle atomic particles.

4. Vayu- element of speed. Small particles of Vayu are responsible for speed.

5. Nabha- Aakash- Space. It has no body. But is perpetual. It is recognized by word. Wherever there is word, Aakash is there. It is formless hence perpetual.

6. Kaal- Samaya- Time. It is imaginary. It is one but for practical purpose it is Past, present, future. The cause, maintenance, and annihilation of all works are the result of time.

   नित्येष्वभावाद् नित्येषु भावात् कारणे कालाख्येति II9II Vaisheshik Darshan 2-2-9.

   Nityeshvamadad nityeshu bhavat karne kalakhyeti II9II VaisheshikDarshan 2-2-9.

   The eternity and non-eternity both exist due to time, or the cause is time.

7. DISHA- direction. It is the 10 directions. (The 10 directions are East, west, north south, along with Eshan, Agneys, Neiritya, vayavya, Urdhva -Top, Pataal-Down). The cause, maintenance, and annihilation are the result of Kaal and along with Kaal, Disha is also involved in the process. It is imaginary.

8. Aatma- soul. Is consciousness (**चैतन्य**). What is consciousness? From modern physics point of view, it is electromagnetic physiological concept of higher states. Knowledge is souls' virtue. How? Body has no consciousness because it is made of five elements which have no consciousness (**ज्ञान**). Senses have no knowledge because consciousness remains even after the loss of senses. Consciousness is not a virtue of mind as well. Because mind is a tool to know knowledge. Hence it can be concluded that knowledge is virtue of Soul-ATMA. After knowing beneficial and harmful, to gain benefit and avoid harm, body attempts which indicates that there is something different to drive the body and that is soul-ATMA. Aatma is like Aakash. It is comprehensive, extensive, and vast (Vibhu- **विभु**) like Aakash. See mantra below: -

   विभवान्महानाकाशस्तथा चात्मा II 22 II वसिहेसहकि डारसहान छ-ऋ-धधं

Vibhavanmahanakashastatha chatma II 22 II Vaisheshik Darshan 7-1-22.

9. Mind- Mann- **मन.** Mind is atom or compared to vastness it is small. Rishi Kanad says: -

तद्भावादणु मनः ॥ 23 ॥ वसिहेसहकि डारसहानं छ-ऋ-धटं

Tadbhavadanu mannah II 23 II Vaisheshik Darshan. 7-1-23.

If one concentrates on soul, and from above discussion, the soul is a matter-DRAVYA – **द्रव्य.** It is made up of particles. The particles have Agni as constituent. It is AGNI or energy. The soul or Aatma, in living beings is JEEVATMA which is a fraction of supreme soul or PARAM AATMA. In fact, both are same but appear different. It is as good as electricity at power station and electricity at utility point like electric gadgets viz. bulbs or electric press. It is one and the same and not different. At generation and at utility, electric current appears different. Basically, and functionally electricity is one. So is the JEEVATMA and PARAM AATMA. It is nothing but energy like electricity which is invisible and formless. Electricity in a straight wire is different than when it is wound around as armature. When wound in circle it produces magnetic power. So is the soul in humans is different functionally then in insects. One may call it by different names, but it is the same energy.

Each and everything in this universe albeit Multiverse try to maintain its form, shape, function etc., with the help of inbuilt virtues (Dharma), unless and until it is interfered with external or internal force influencing the original nature. But in the process, it manifests new product. To illustrate, water is an example. Water tries to maintain as water, till heat convert into steam (gas). Or low temperature of zero degree condenses it into solid and forms ice. Here the water is the same everywhere but form and shape changes. Similarly, Aatma- soul is same but Jeevatma- a fractioned absolute truth or PARAM AATMA. Form and shape of the different living beings is different, and soul is same which is AGNI – driving force to live life. Analyse the diagram in chapter of Brahmotpatti on page. Absolute truth or PARAM SHIV is a TEJAHPUNJA- (तेजःपुंज), It has everything as its constituent. It means Gas, Solid, Liquid in different form. When the gas released it forms gaseous layer around it. It needs time factor and the pressure inside the Absolute truth. It is released. This gas layer contains everything in it which is to be manifested in future in nature or PRAKRITI – with a time factor. The gas particles act and interact with each other by methods already described earlier. Modern science is still analysing the different gaseous factors in this primordial gas layer called by RISHI as KSHIR SAGAR or sea of whitish hue which gases emit. How was this interpreted is not available in Sanskrit literature or in fact author could not trace it, or manuscripts were destroyed by the invaders of Sanskrit land. If so, it is a great loss for the humanity at large. The gas layer and its composition have liquid and solid and all that is to be manifested in future cosmos and nature. The massive gas balls emitted from this primordial gas layer. With SAMAY-CHAKRA or time cycle, and with gravitational force due to revolution around it-self, everything in emitted balls kept to itself. With invisible time element, interacting particles of gases and environment of temperature solidification manifested. It formed Stars and groups of stars. With further time and different temperature environment different elements manifested like gold, Silver and so on. **This is not the end. Future time scale may give rise to more manifestations.**

It is important to note that the "Automated expression" of 'Absolute Truth' the infinite creation is from unknown and unmanifest matter. It is the consciousness of the PARAMATMA TATTVA which expresses it-self. The self-interacting dynamics which is responsible for manifest cosmos and Prakriti. Natural laws of the constitution, of absolute truth are applicable. How is this effectively carried out? What governs the constitution? Some force must be involved in this. It is the consciousness or Aatma which is force, energy, the primordial energy. This in other word is AGNI.

In all these manifestations AGNI plays its role efficiently cannot be ignored. Rather it plays main role in all manifestations of Prakriti. Hence RISHIS stressed more importance to AGNI. The prayers to invite DEVATAS to YAJNYA-KARMA or research and analysis act, sounds eminent. How can such acts be of religious nature? Do such thing be condemned or ignored. One must change his mind-set, that is what author likes to emphasize. Rigveda has devoted many Mantras in praise for AGNI, because of its essential role in manifestation of ever-expanding multiverses, the cosmos, and the Nature.

CHAPTER 6

GITA, VEDA, PURAN AND SCIENCE OF SIGNS OF ZODIAC

"RASHI" (राशि)

It is astonishing to note that the "Khagol Shastra" or Cosmic knowledge was well studied and established before the Rigved era, or Vedic literature was scripted down. The Vedic scientists were knowledgeable with Spheres moving in space like free pendulum and could influence the life on earth.

Rashi (राशि, समूह, ढीग) means collection or group. In night sky the stars glitter like precious Gems or RATNA रत्न. In Astrology Rashis are the twelve signs of Zodiac. Basically, these are the groups of stars in a particular figure and shape. Rishis have provided names for the purpose of understanding as well as spreading knowledge to future generations. What the Rigveda speaks about these Rashis (heaps of stars).

The Sun is the provider of the riches and the dwellings for living beings and men; the giver of the instrumental action, the smite or hit hard enemy in battles, and the distributor of riches. All these riches are possible by making land fertile with rains and needed environment. This is provided by Sun and Varun.

ईक्षे । रायः । क्षयस्य । चर्षणीनाम् । उत । व्रजम् । अपऽवर्ता । असि । गोनाम् ।
शिक्षाऽनरः । समऽइथेषु । प्रहाऽवान् । वस्वः । राशिम् । अभिऽनेता । असि । भूरिम् ॥8॥
Rigveda. 4-20-8.

This is in praise of INDRA, a Commander (ईक्षे) a distributer of wealth, dwelling units of humans (क्षयस्य), herd of cows (गोनाम्), men (शिक्षाऽनरः) and the distributor of great heaps of riches, Rashi (राशिम्) of wealth (*rāśim*, "pile;

quantity; sign of the zodiac; mass), abhinetā asi (future, bhūrim ="much; abundant; rich;). A note about understanding about modern astronomy is worth mentioning here.

astronomy -

http://hinduonline.co › FactsAboutHinduism › Astrono...

The paper of **John Playfair** (1748-1819) (FRS and Professor of Mathematics at the University... The observations on which the astronomy of **India** is founded.

Ancient observation, modern confirmation

That Hindu astronomical lore about ancient times cannot be based on later back-calculation, was also argued by Playfair's contemporary, the French astronomer jean-Sylvain Bailly: The motions of the stars calculated by the Hindus before some 4500 years vary not even a single minute from the [modem] tables of Cassini and Meyer. The Indian tables give the same annual variation of the moon as that discovered by Tycho Brahe - a variation unknown to the school of Alexandria and the Arabs.

Quoted in S. Sathe: In Search for the Year of the Bharata War, Navabharati, Hyderabad 1982, p.32.

द्वादशारं नहि तज्जराय वर्वर्ति चक्रं परि द्यामृतस्य । आ पुत्रा अग्ने मिथुनासो अत्र सप्त शतानि विंशतिश्च तस्थुः ‖11‖ Rigveda.1-164-11.

"The telve-spoked wheel (द्वादश आरं), of the Sun (सूर्य) revolves round the heavens, and never decays; seven hundred and twenty children (360X2= 720,Day and Night in a year. सप्त शतानि विंशतिश्च), Agni, abide in it." On this Mantra, **Commentary by Sāyaṇa: Ṛgveda-bhāṣya opines that** twelve-spoked wheel: the **twelve signs of the zodiac:** the term may also mean twelve months; seven hundred and twenty children: nights and days; (three hundred and sixty multiply with two):

sapta ca vai śatāni viṃśatiśca saṃvatsarasyāhorātrāḥ sa eṣohaḥ smmānaḥ (Aitareya Āraṇyaka-a part of Rigveda 3.2.1)

In Rigveda.The description of Rashis clearly exists

पञ्चंपादं पितरं द्वादंशाकृतिं दिव आंहु :परे अर्धे पुरीषिणंम्। अथेमे अन्य उपंरे विचक्षणं सप्तचंक्रे षळंर आहुरर्पितम् ॥12 ॥ Rigved. 1-164-12.

"They have termed the five-footed, parent with twelve-forms (द्वादश आकृति), Purișhinam, in the half hemisphere of the sky; and others have termed in Arpita (अर्पितम), in rest portion of the sky; shining in his seven-wheeled car, each (wheel) having six spokes (षळंर)." Explanation is as under:

One must understand the Five legs of time (i.e., astrologically it is Kshan, Muhurta, Prahar, Divas, Paksha). Twelve months It can be five seasons-(5 ऋतु, Hemant- हेमन्त and Shishir- शिशिर taken together) and twelve months. Sun solstices, and Seasons, are the fractions of time cycle. Twelve months is one Samvatsar -संवत्सर. Samvatsar has two AYANS अयन, of six months each. In half the sky is clear (दिव आंहुपरे अर्धे :) so that one can see far away (उपंरे विचक्षणं) while in other half of sky it has rains. It has twelve figures in the sky (द्वादंशाकृतिं दिव आंहु:). Sun passes through these figures every month. These are the twelve signs of Zodiac. Which in Sanskrit language are called RASHIS. This is the clear evidence of Rashis in Rigveda.

Popular Word-Meaning: - Oh humans, understand that the Time- Cycle has 5 legs, 12 months, separated by solar Solstices of 6 months each on one side the sky is clear while the other half is not clear due to clouds, and has 6 seasons, 7 days (सप्तचंक्रे). One must understand it with efforts and Yagya. ॥ १२ ॥

Are there names of Rashis signs of Zodiac indicated in Rigveda?

There are some names available in Rigveda Mantras. There are 12 Rashis or signs of Zodiac in Astrological description. These are Mesh – Aries, Vrishabh – Taurus, Mithun – Gemini, Kark – Cancer, Simha – Leo, Kanya – Virgo, Tula - Libra, Vrishchik – Scorpio, Dhanu - Sagittarius, Makar - Capricorn, Kumbha – Aquarius, Mein – Pisces.

Aries or Mesha.

नेमिं नमन्ति चक्षसा मेषं विप्रा अभिस्वरा । सुदीतयो वो अद्रुहोऽपि कर्णे तरस्विनः : समृक्वभिः ॥12॥ Rigveda. 8-97-12

Nemim namanti chakshasa mesham vipra abhisvara I suditayo vo adruhopi karne tarasvinah samrukvbhi ॥12॥ Rigveda. 8-97-12

Taurus Vrishabh

अयं **विदच्चित्रद्र्शीकमर्णः** शुक्रसद्मनामुषसामनीके | अयं महान महता सकम्भनेनोद दयामस्तभ्नाद **वृ8**र्भोमरुत्वान || Rigveda 6-47-5.

Ayam vidachchitrardrarshikam shukrasadmanamushsamnike I Ayam mahan mahata sakambhanenod dayamstabhnad vrusharbhomrutvan Rigveda 6-47-5.

Understand that the beautiful looking (**च्चित्रद्र्शीकम**) Vrishabha due to Nakshatra and forming group of stars - a constellation (Taurus), speedy Vayu is generated by Vrishabha which is responsible for rains. The same situation exists when Sun passes through Taurus sign -Vrishabha Rashi causes rain. In modern time also rainy season is when Sun is in Vrishabha rashi ॥५॥ See Mantra of Rigveda 6-49-6, below: -

पर्जन्यवाता वृषभा पृथिव्याः पुरिषाणि जिन्वतमप्यानि ी सत्यश्रुतः कवयो यस्य गीर्भिर्जगत सथातर्जगदाक्रणुध्वम् ‘ीघी ‘गिवेदां घ-थक्ष-घं

Parjanyavata vrishabha pruthivyah purishani jivantamapyani I satyashrutah kavayo ysya girbhirjagat sathatrjagadakranudhvam ||6II Rigveda. 6-49-6.

Vrishabha sign of zodiac is responsible for rains. It stimulates Vayu- Marut)पर्जन्यवाता (in clouds to arrive on earth)पृथिव्याः(. Knowledgeable and truthful persons)कवयः(can achieve the same goal)आ, कृणुध्वम्(and stabilize the clouds by their song. Such persons must be praised. ||६||

Similar evidence is in Rigveda 8-93-1

उद घेदभि शरुतामघं वर्षभं नर्यापसम | अस्तारमेषि सूर्य || नव यो नवतिं पुरो बिभेद बाह्वोजसा | अहिं च वर्त्रहावधीत || 1 II Rigveda 8-93-1.

Uda ghedabhi sharutamagham varshabham naryapasam I Astarmeshi surya I nava yo navatim puro bibheda bahavojasa I ahim cha vartrahavadhita || 1 II Rigveda 8-93-1.

The Sun disappears (अस्तारमेषि सूर्य) due to clouds as a result when Vrishabha Rashi rises (वर्षभं नर्यापसम) which is responsible for cloudy sky.

It is clear from above description that the science of space was developed hence the Rashis are quoted as example to explain. Therefore, the knowledge of Rigveda has become enigmatic.

CHAPTER 7

SHILPKALA - ARCHITECTURE

Whatever could be retrieved from the pages of Rigveda, it can be concluded that the Shilp Vidya or Architecture was well developed even before the poetry of Gita, Veda, Puran was composed. In this context the following script is worth reading and understanding.

Nakṣatra (नक्षत्र, "planet") refers to the third of *āyādiṣaḍvarga*, six principles that constitute the "horoscope" of an architectural or iconographic object, according to the Mānasāra (IX, 63-73). Their application is intended to "verify" the measurements of the architectural and iconographic object against the dictates of astrology that lay out the conditions of auspiciousness.

Nakṣatra and *ṛkṣa*, sometimes used interchangeably as synonyms in the text, however, are different in a strict technical sense. Ṛkṣa is the Plaedis or constellation of seven stars (the Great Bear, Seven Sages), while *nakṣatra* literally means a star, asterism (that is, a constellation of heavenly bodies), 27 number.

They are in order as follows:

1. Aśvinī;
2. Bharaṇī;
3. Kārttikā;
4. Rohiṇī or Brāhmī;
5. Mṛgaśiras;
6. Ārdrā;
7. Punarvāsū or Yāmakau;

8. Puṣya or Siddhya;
9. Āśleṣā;
10. Māghā;
11. Pūrva-phālguṇī;
12. Uttara-phālguṇī;
13. Hasta;
14. Citrā;
15. Svāti;
16. Viśākhā;
17. Anurādhā;
18. Jyeṣṭha;
19. Mūla;
20. Pūrvāṣāḍhā;
21. Uttarāṣāḍhā;
22. Abhijit;
23. Śravaṇa;
24. Śraviṣṭā;
25. Śatabhiṣaj;
26. Bhādrapāda;
27. Revati.

In the context of village planning and measurement, the text sates that among the stars, the ones that are *pūrṇa*, odd (literally, "full, complete"), are auspicious and the ones that are *karṇa*, even (literally, "ear"), inauspicious. In iconographic measurement, however, the role given is that all except the sixth, eighth and ninth *nakṣatras* are auspicious. In both cases, the *janmanakṣatra*, birth-star of the patron or of the *sthapati*, as applies, even if in itself an inauspicious star, is always considered as auspicious for the architectural and iconographic object.

Source: OpenEdition books: Architectural terms contained in Ajitāgama and Rauravāgama

The script indicates the basics about Architecture.

प्रातःऽयुजा। वि। बोधय। अश्विनौ। आ। इह। गच्छताम्। अस्य। सोमस्य। पीतये
॥ गिवेदां ऋ-धध-ऋं

Pratahyja vi bodhay I Ashvino Aa eih gachhyatam asya somasya pitaye ll Rigveda. 1-22-1.

In first part of Mantra the Virtues of Ashvin is described.

Ashvins are expert in the knowledge (बोधय) of (प्रातःऽयुजा) in Shilp Vidya and Yantra kala (Architecture and technology), at the same time impress upon the knowledge, meaning there by the Earth and energy both are important in the Shilp Vidya and Yantra kala (गच्छताम्). Both are essential. Hence Ashvins are requested (विबोधय) to provide the essentials needed (अस्य सोमस्य). ॥१॥

The Palace for VARUN: 1000 pillars and 1000 doors of dwelling unit for VARUN (Rigveda. 2-41-5). This is described in the following Mantra: -

कव तयानि नौ सख्या बभूवः सचावहे यदवकं पुरा चित । बृहन्तं मनं वरुण स्वधावः सहस्त्रद्वारं जगमा गहँ ते ll5 ll **Rigveda. 7-88-5.**

Kava tayani nau sakhya babuvah sachavahe yadavakram purachit I bruhantam manam varuna svadhavah sahastrdvaram jagama graham te II5 II Rigveda. 7-88-5.

The word meaning analysed. bṛhantam = large; great; huge. mānaṃ = "house." svadhāvaḥ, Sva + dhāvas svadhāvat "autonomous; independent." sahasradvāraṃ Sahasra [noun], one-thousandth;."sahasra+dvāraṃ, dvāram dvāra, "aperture; gate; door.

In above Mantra a word (स्वधाव सहस्त्र द्वारम्) has been used which means automated or independently operable. स्वधावः = running automatically. Does that mean the doors were operated automatically? Were there the self-operable doors existed during Rigveda era? This is a subject of future research. The Mantra reads like, the old friendship be protected (यदवकं) as before. Let visit to automatic 1000 doored great house.

Rig Veda has references to 1000 Pillar Hall (2700 years ago), Panini wrote Ashtadhyayi, first grammar book in the world. Interpreting on some Sutras later commentators add owl shaped buildings, eagle shaped buildings etc. (Please see the links below). Before that, Agastya laid a road route though the Vindhya Hills to South India. The Puranas describe it Agastya subduing the arrogance of Vindhyas-a Mountain range in India. Hindus were great civil engineers long before any other civilization in the world. This is proved by continuous references to architectural matters in our literature. In Ramayana we come across building a bridge over sea. In addition, we hear about the spatial palace of Ravana.

In Mahabharata era, there was the Wax Palace. - Laksha-griha, with tunnels for escape. But the description in the Sabha Parva about the palace built by Maya Danava at Indraprastha is extraordinary about 3000 years to 5000 years ago. The time is not important here, but the Shilp Vidya feats exist even in later period. This must be the carried forward knowledge from ancient to modern era. Apart from this, some of the old temple buildings available are carved into the Rocky Mountains itself. If one puts all the building references from Hindu scriptures in chronological order the following statement will be an eye opener.

Rig Veda has references to 1000 Pillar Hall. There are owl shaped buildings, eagle shaped buildings etc. The Crystal Palace in Sabha Parva of Mahabharata was a unique construction. In later period, the road constructions in difficult terrains of south rocky area of south India, was amazing. The old Sangam Tamil literature mentions about Mauryan laid road route in mountainous area to come to South India. That should have happened during Chandra Gupta Maurya time (3rd century BCE). The Puranas describe it Agastya subduing the arrogance of Vindhyas, Agastya laid a road route though the Vindhya Hills to South India.

There is evidence in Sanskrit literature about engineering feats of diverting River routs. Two great River diversions in the stories of Bhageeratha and Agastya. Bhageeratha diverted River Ganges and Agastya diverted River Kaveri.

The great engineering feats are worth the mention in this context. Danava, Asura, Daitya, were the community who specialised in the field of Architecture. Mayan- were the Great builders of South and Central America came from the building community whose chief was Maya. He was the one who built the most famous building during Mahabharat era. Understanding this. Dhritarashtra also wanted one such building with 1000 Pillars. The 1000 pillar halls in many Tamil Nadu and Andhra temples today are engineering wonders of the world. This is also in the Rig Veda. In Khadavaprastha which is now Gondwana Land. (Khandava-vana= Gondwana)

The burning of Khandava Vana near Delhi was a historical event. That lead to a big clash between the Kuru Dynasty and the Nagas who were living in the forest. Maya who was also living in the Khandava forest was rescued by Arjuna and Krishna. The discussion they had after the Forest burning incident is as follows.

राजानावनभिद्रुहा धरुवे सदस्युत्तमे सहस्त्रस्थूण आसाते II5II Rigveda 2-41-5.

Janavanbhidruha dharuve sadasyuttame sahastrasthuna aasate ||5|| Rigveda 2-41-5.

Oh elite, dignified persons (राजानावनभिद्रुहा), members of the royal dynasty (सदस्युत्तमे), meet in a hall having 1000 pillars. In an Auditorium (SABHAGRUHA-सभागृह-) **where 1000 pillars** (सहस्रस्थूणे) exist, and the hall is occupied by best members - SHRESHTHA-श्रेष्ठ सदस्य (सदस्युत्तमे) II5II

अत्यासो न ये मरुतः स्वञ्चो यक्षदृशो न शुभयन्त मर्याः । ते हर्म्येष्ठाः शिशवो न शुभ्रा वत्सासो न क्रीळिनः पयोधाः II16 II Rigveda 7-56-16.

Atyaso na ye marutah svncho yakshdrasho na shbhyanta marya I te harmeshthah shishavo na Shubhra vatsaso na krilinah payodhah II16 II Rigveda 7-56-16.

"Speedy Vayu- Maruts like horses (अत्यासो), shining like men gazing as children in mansion (हर्म्येष्ठाः), Playful (क्रीळिनः) children and frolicsome as calves (शिशवो न शुभ्रा वत्सासो न क्रीळिनः), they are the dispensers of water (पयोधाः)." Is it something like fire-Brigade of modern era? Dispensers of water to extinguish the fire.

इन्द्र त्रिधातु शरणं त्रिवरूथं स्वस्तिमत् । छर्दिर्यच्छ मघवद्भ्यश्च मह्यं च यावया दिद्युमेभ्यः II9II Rig Veda 6.46.9.

Indra tridhatu sharanam trivautham svastimat I chhardiryaChha maghavadbhyashchhya mahyam cha yavaya didyumebhyah II9II Rig Veda 6.46.9.

Enemies use fire weapons to destroy the mansion. Indra (leader) is requested to provide three-dimensional (त्रिवरूथं स्वस्तिमत्) protection and shelter (शरणं) made from three elements (त्रिधातु), so that the blazing weapons ("defence; protective covering) are nullified.

All these mantras are of architectural importance. These indicate the expertise of the Sanskrit era in Shilpa Vidya. And need further research.

CHAPTER 8

VEDIC ASTRONOMY, ASTROLOGY, AND SPACE SCIENCE

Astronomy - KHAGOL SHASTRA (खगोल शास्त्र), Astrology Jyotish shastra (ज्योतिष शास्त्र), and Space sciences were highly developed during the era of Sanskrit Speaking civilization. Bharat varsha was agriculturally well-developed country. Astronomy was developed to support, develop, and plan the agriculture, as it was essential for day-to-day activity. It is the branch which deals with the physics that study the celestial and cosmic agni and -multiverse bodies. Rigveda has discussed this branch at many places but because of symbolic and obscure narration it is difficult to understand. The knowledge of astronomy was based on direct observation from multiple observatories in the country. (Reference "An Account of the Brahmin's Observatory at Benares. By Sir Robert Barker, Knt. F. R. S.; In a Letter to Sir John Pringle, Bart. P. R. S.").

The Rigveda statement about Sun in Mantra 1-71-9.

मनो न योअध्वनः सद्य एत्येकः सत्रा सूरो वस्व ईशे | राजाना मित्रावरुणा सुपाणी गोषु परियमम्र्तं रक्षमाणा || Rigveda 1-71-9.

Mano na yoadhvanah sadya etyekah satra sooro vasva eishe I Rajan Mitra-Varuna supani goshu pariyammratam rakshamana II 9 II Rigveda 1-71-9.

Mitra-Varun protect earth and provide necessities of life. As conscious and intuitive mind travels without any help like lightning or electricity travels quickly through its path. Persons with good moral virtues, achieve all needed sense satisfaction in life. Similarly, it is as good as without science and knowledgeable people, one cannot construct or fly Planes, to travel around quickly. It is must for people to have healthy body and mind without which happiness of life cannot be achieved.

Sun moves in Aakash alone like mind.

तरणिर्विश्वदर्शतो जयोतिष्क्रदसि सूर्य | विश्वमा भासिरोचनम || 4 || Rigved. 1=50-4.

Taranirvishva darshato jyotishkradasi soorya I vishvama bhasirochsnam I taranirvishvadarshito II Rigveda 1-50-4.

Sun provides light and heat to the whole world.

अयुक्त सप्त शुन्ध्युवः सूरो रथस्य नप्त्यः | ताभिर्याति सवयुक्तिभिः || Rigved 1-50-9.

Ayukta sapta shundhyuvah sooro rathasya naptyah I tabhiryati svayuktibhih || Rigved 1-50-9.

Analytically the meaning of above mantras is:

Sun's mobility is the result of 7 horses. Horse is symbolic here. The sun rotates due to the rays, attraction, waves and the gravitation, and radiation spread in the cosmos from various stars and planets and constellations at the same time the energy provided to sun from the absolute truth – Paramshiva. It is surprizing that even the speed of light was calculated. Based on the Rigveda Mantras Acharya Sayana (Sri Sayanacharya was born to Māyaṇācārya and Śrīmatīdevī in Pampakṣhetra (modern day Hampi) in a Brahmin family **around 1270 CE.**) concludes: -

Sri Sayanacharya was born to Māyaṇācārya and Śrīmatīdevī in Pampakṣetra (modern day Hampi) in a Brahmin family around 1270 CE. He was one of the chief commentators on the Vedas during his time & was a court advisor to the King of the newly established Vijayanagar kingdom. More than a hundred works are attributed to him, among which are commentaries on nearly all parts of the Vedas. In a statement on the Rigveda given by Sayanacharya, he says,

तथा च स्मर्यते योजनानाम सहस्त्रे द्वे द्वे शते द्वे च योजने एकेनं निमशारदधेन कम मान नामोस्तुते

"tatha ca smaryate yojananam. sahasre dve dve sate dve ca yojane ekena nimishardhena kramaman Namostute."

This means "It is remembered here that Sun (light) traverses 2,202 yojanas in half a nimisha."

My salute to sun who spreads light with the speed of 2,202 yojanas in half a Nimesh. Nimesh is time taken for eyelid to blink.

Below is a print from the journal of 1790. It is worth reading for the understanding that the science was very well developed and advanced when west science was in a primitive stage. It is a false notion that, India got science from western countries. It is on the contrary that India has given science to west. Of course, west has furthered the knowledge in a definitive way on basic concepts of science from India. This is at the cost of sovereignty of the country. The GURUKUL and Sanskrit teachings made illegal by invaders. The teaching was as per the desire of the invaders. (Read Lord Macaulay's statement in early 1800 in British parliament). In support of this the following page from 1790 publication is important. While reading the following document use the Error! Hyperlink reference not valid. Read alphabet 'S' instead of 'F'

REMARKS ON THE ASTRONOMY OF THE BRAHMINS.

BY JOHN PLAYFAIR, A. M. F. R. S. OF EDINBURGH, AND PROFESSOR OF MATHEMATICS IN THE UNIVERSITY OF EDINBURGH.

1. SINCE the time when Aftronomy emerged from the obfcurity of ancient fable, nothing is better known than its progrefs through the different nations of the earth. With the era of Nabonaffar regular, obfervations began to be made in Chaldea, the earlieft which have merited the attention of fucceeding ages. The curiofity of the Greeks was foon after directed to the fame object; they were the firft who endeavoured to explain and connect by theory, the various phenomena of the heavens, and the fyntaxis of Ptolemy continued for more than five hundred years, without oppofition or improvement, to direct the aftronomers of Egypt, Italy, and Greece. After the fciences were banifhed from Alexandria, his writings made their way into the Eaft, and the caliphs of Bagdat cultivated aftronomy with fuccefs. The Perfians followed their example, borrowing whatever mathematical knowledge was ftill preferved among the ruins of the Grecian empire. The conquefts of Zingis and Timour retarded, but did not ftop the progrefs of aftronomy in the Eaft; their grandfons were renowned for their love of fcience. Mean time, being brought by the Arabs into Spain, it likewife found in Alphonfo of Caftille, both a difciple and a patron. Soon after, being carried into the North, it exercifed the genius of Copernicus, of Kepler, and of Newton, and became the moft perfect of all fciences.

2. In the progrefs of aftronomy from the Indus to the Ganges, there is fcarce a ftep which cannot be accurately traced. The various fyftems that have prevailed in all thofe countries are vifibly connected with each other; they are all derived from one original, and would incline us to believe that the manner in which men begin to obferve the heavens and to reafon about them, is an experiment of the human race which has been made but once.

It is therefore matter of curiofity to find beyond the Indus, a fyftem of aftronomical knowledge which appears to make no part of the great body of fcience which has enlightened other countries of the earth; a fyftem in the hands of men which follow its rules without underftanding its principles, and who can give no account of its origin, except that it lays claim to an antiquity far beyond the period to which with us the hiftory of the heroic ages is fuppofed to extend.

3. We owe our firft knowledge of this aftronomy to Mr. La Loubere, who returning in 1687, from an embaffy to Siam, brought with him an extract from a Siamefe manufcript, which contained tables and rules for calculating the places of the fun and moon. The manner in which the rules are laid down rendered the principles on which they are founded obfcure. After that two other fets of aftronomical tables were fent to Paris, by the miffionaries of Indoftan, but they remained unnoticed till the return of M. le Gentil from India, where he had been to obferve the tranfit of Venus, in 1769. This academician employed himfelf, during the long ftay which his zeal for fcience induced him to make in that country, in acquiring a knowledge of the Indian aftronomy. The Brahmins thought they faw in the bufinefs of an aftronomer, the marks of a *caft* that had fome affinity to their own, and began to converfe with M. Le Gentil more familiarly than with other ftrangers. A learned Brahmin of Trivalore, having made a vifit to the French aftronomer, inftructed him in the methods which he ufed for calculating eclipfes of the fun and moon, and communicated to him the tables and rules that

VOL. V. D

A page from an original article from the Literary Magazine & British Review, 1790. John Playfair. Published by Literary Magazine & British Review, London, 1790. John Playfair (1748–1819) was a Scottish mathematician and geologist.

Table of KAAL CHAKRA as per Veda is 1 Yojan = 9 miles, 160 Yards = 9.11 miles1 Day+night (Ahoratra – अहोरात्र) = 810000 Half Nimesh. Or 1 Second = 9.41 Half Nimesh. As per Mantra (योजनानाम सहस्त्रे द्वे द्वे शते द्वे च योजने) 2202 X 9.11 = 20060.22 miles per Half Nimesh. 20060.22 X 9.41 = 188766.67Miles per Second. Almost equal to modern calculations. The currently agreed value of the speed of light is 186282.397 miles per second, that too being an approximation! How deep was the study of RISHIS that the difference between NAKSHATRA and TARA and Planets:

उपप्लवांस्तथा घोराञ्शशिनस्तेजसस्तथा । ताराणां पतनं दृष्ट्वा नक्षत्राणां च पर्ययम् ॥ ३६ ॥

Upaplavanstatha ghoranshashistejstatha I taranam patanam drashtava nakshatranam cha paryayam

घोराञ्शशिनस्तेजसस्तथा Moon and Sun. ताराणां Celestial bodies. नक्षत्राणां 27 constellations

सत्येन॑ । उत्त॑भिता । भूमि॑ः । सूर्ये॑ण । उत्त॑भिता । द्यौः । ऋतेन॑ । आ॒दि॒त्याः । ति॒ष्ठ॒न्ति॒ । दि॒वि । सोम॑ः । अधि॑ । श्रि॒तः ॥ Rigveda. १०.८५.१ (Similar mantra in Atharva Veda).

Satyen uttabhita bhumih suryen uttabhita dayouh ruten aadityah tishthanti divi somah adhi shritah I **Rigveda.10-85-1.** (Similar mantra is in AtharvaVeda).

“Earth is upheld by absolute truth; heaven (स्वर्ग) is upheld by the sun; the Ādityas are supported by sacrifice, Soma is supreme in heaven.” In other words the earth is sustained by the force of its own identity within the truth of laws of nature, the heaven is sustained by the sun (sun light prevails up to three lokas i.e. Bhuh, Bhuvah, and Svahah together called vyarhiti – व्याहृति) within the same truth of nature’s divine law, the Adityas are sustained by Rutam (ऋतेन॑), the natural law of Divinity, and Soma-moon is sustained in the highest heaven of the same law.

Compared to Soma - moon, the Ādityas (Sun and 12 functions, hence 12 different names) are strong, in comparison to Soma the earth is mighty: Thus Soma is in the lap of all these constellations which is the abode and home of Moon. || 2 ||

सोमेन । आदित्याः । बलिनः । सोमेन । पृथिवी । मही । अथो इति । नक्षत्राणाम् । एषाम् । उपऽस्थे । सोमः । आऽहितः ॥ Rigved. १०२.८५..

Somen aaditya blinah somen Pruthvi mahi Atho iti I nakshatranam esham upasthe somah aahitah II Rigved. १०.८५.२.

Rays generated from its originator are stronger than the source of origin. Moon is responsible for manifesting medicinal elements in vegetation and sustain life on earth. Moon shines in Rewati nakshatra ॥२॥

Similar Mantra are in Atharva Veda is below: The explanation is for the marriage institution but express the scientifically the size, shape, distance, difference between Stars and Nakshatra. The facsimile below is in Hindi language. It is for understanding of Hindi and Sanskrit. It Authenticate the statement above.

It is clear from the analysis of above mantra that SUN is a Star. Sun and stars are powerful than Moon. Earth is much bigger than moon. These facts were known to Rishis of Vedic era. Sun moves but Nakashtra doesn't move. Nakashtra are big but appear small due to the distance from the earth. In the later era of Mahabharat era, the above statement in Mantra 290- 36. It is repeated below for better analysis: -

It is interesting to note that the constellations and the Names of different Nakashatras have appeared in Rigveda. Following mantras are to show the names of nakshatra in Rigved mantras shown in red colour: -

नि वर्तध्वं मानु गातास्मान सिषक्त रेवतीः |अग्नीषोमापुनर्वसू अस्मे धारयतं रयिम || 10-19-1

तरिः सप्त सस्रा नद्यो महीरपो वनस्पतीन पर्वतानग्निमूतये |कर्शानुमस्तृन तिष्यं (पुष्य) सधस्थ आरुद्रंरुद्रेषु रुद्रियं हवामहे || 10-64-8

अभि शयावं न कर्शनेभिरश्वं नक्षत्रेभिः पितरोद्यामपिंशन | रात्र्यां तमो अदधुर्ज्योतिरहन्ब्रहस्पतिर्भिनदद्रिं विदद गाः || 10-68-11

सूर्याया वहतुः परागात सविता यमवारूजत | अघासुहन्यन्ते गावो अर्जुन्योः (फाल्गुनि) पर्युह्यते || 10-85-13

कुवित स देवीः सनयो नवो वा यामो बभूयाद उषसो वो अद्य |येना नवग्वे अङगिरे दशग्वे सप्तास्ये रेवती रेवद ऊष || 4-51-4.

युष्मादत्तस्य मरुतो विचेतसो रायः स्याम रथ्यो वयस्वतः I न यो युच्छति तिष्यो (पुष्य) यथा दिवो स्मे रारन्त मरुतः सहस्त्रिणम् II 5 -54 -13.

अस्थुरु चित्रा उषसः पुरस्तान्मिता इव स्वरवोऽध्वरेषु । व्यू व्रजस्य तमसो द्वारोच्छन्तीरव्रञ्छुचयः पावकाः ॥ 4 – 51 -2.

The above mantras are mentioned only to realize the names of some nakshatras. Mantras are not translated. Interested reader can translate and v erify.

Six seasons are provided by nakshatras and utilised by men for agricultural produce.

उतो स मह्यमिन्दुभि :षड्युक्ताँ अनुसेषिधत् । गोभिर्यवं न चर्कृषत् ॥ Rig Veda 1.23.15

uto sa mahyamindubhiḥ ṣhaḍyuktan anuseṣidhat | ghobhiryavaṃ na chakrushat ||

"Verily he has brought to me successively the six seasons, connected with the drops of the juice due to Moon, (See the origin of Moon in next chapter) as farmer (कृषक) repeatedly ploughs the earth for growing barley and different crops, with the help of cattle "

Signs of Zodiac and their names:

Twelve signs of Zodiac. RASHI shapes and names. How groups of stars are arranged giving shapes and named accordingly

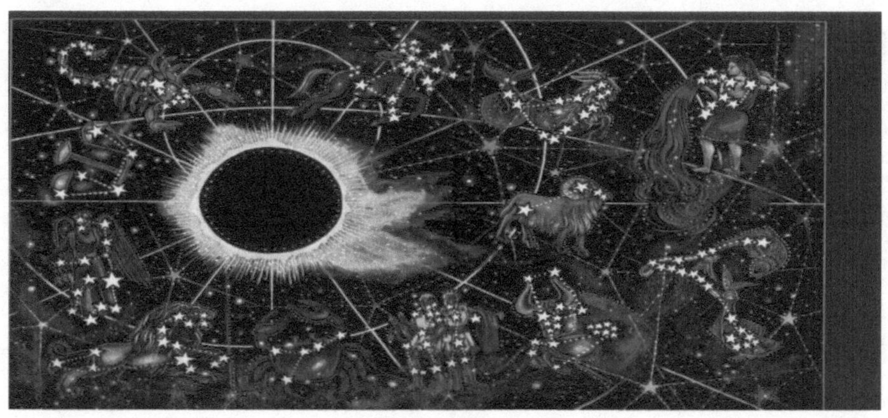

Source Wikipedia

Nakshatras

The Rigveda describes the universe to be infinite. Of the five planets it mentions Brihaspati (Jupiter) and Vena (Venus) by name. The moon's path was divided into 27 equal parts, although the moon takes about 27 1/3 days to complete it. Each of these parts was called a nakshatra. Specific stars or asterisms were also termed nakshatras. Satapatha Brahman a relates a story about the nakshatras being as powerful as the sun in earlier times but that they have lost this power to the sun. In view of this the etymology na + kshatra, 'no power,' is proposed. A favoured modern etymology is nak-kshatra, 'ruler overnight.' One ancient name of astronomer is naksatra-dar´sa. Nakshatras are mentioned in the Rigveda and Taittarıya Samhita specifically consider that they are linked to the moon's path. The Rigvedic reference to 34 lights apparently means the sun, the moon, the five planets, and the 27 nakshatras. In later literature the list of nakshatras was increased to 28. Constellations other than the nakshatras were also known; these include the Rakshas (the Bears), the two divine Dogs (Canis Major and Canis Minor), and the Boat (Argo Navis). Aitreya Brahman. a speaks of Mriga (Orion) and Mriga vyadha (Sirius). The moon is called surya rashmi, one that shines by sunlight. Satapatha Brahman provides an overview of the broad aspects of Vedic astronomy. The sixth chapter (Kanda) of the book provides significant clues. Speaking of creation under the aegis of the Prajapati (reference either to a star or to abstract time) mention is made of the emergence of Asva, Rishabha, Aja and Kurma before the emergence of the earth. It has been argued that these refer to stars or constellations. Visvanatha Vidyalankar suggests that these should be identified as the sun (Ashva), Gemini (Rishabha), Aja (Capricorn) and Kurma (Cassiopeia). This identification is supported by etymological considerations. RV 1.164.2 and Nirukta 4.4.27 define Asva as the sun. Riasabha which literally means the twin asses are defined in Nighantu 1.15 as A´svinau which later usage suggests are Castor and Pollux in Gemini. In Western astronomy the twin asses are to be found in the next constellation ofChancer as Asellus Borealis and Asellus Australis. Aja (goat) is defined by Nighant.u 1.15 as a sun and owing to the continuity that we see in the Vedic and later European names for constellations (as in the case of the Great Bear) it is reasonable to identify it as the constellation Capricorn (caper goat + cornu horn). Kurma is a synonym of Ka´syapa (tortoise) which is linguistically close to Cassiopeia (from Greek Kassiopeia). Etymologically Kashyap¯ıya, slow like a tortoise, seems appropriate for Cassiopeia (from Greek Kassiopeia) since it is near the pole. This last name may point to an epoch when this constellation was even closer to the north pole. Vedic ritual was based on the times for the full and the new moons, solstices, and the equinoxes. The year was known to be somewhat more than 365 days and a bit less than 366 days. The solar year was marked variously in the many different astronomical traditions that marked the Vedic world. In one tradition, an extra eleven days, marked by ekadas ratra or elevenday sacrifice, were added to the lunar year of 354 days. According to the Taittarıya Samhita five more days are required over the nominal year of 360 days to complete the seasons, adding that four days are too short and six days are too long. In other traditions, Gavam ayana, 'the walk of cows or 8 intercalary periods,' varied from 36 days of the lunar sidereal year of 12 months of 27 days, to 9 days for the lunar sidereal year of 13 months of 27 days to bring the year in line with the ideal year of 360 days; additional days were required to be in accord with the solar year. The year was divided into two halves: uttar¯ayana, when the sun travels north, and dakshin. ¯ayana, when the sun travels south. According to Kausıtaki Brahman, the year-long sacrifices began with the winter solstice, noting the occurrence of the summer solstice, vesuvian, after six months. The twelve tropical months, and the six seasons, are named in the Yajurveda:

Rivers Saraswati and Dridhaswati disappearance

(14. H.P. Frankfort, "Evidence for Harappan irrigation system in Haryana and Rajasthan," Eastern Anthropologist, 45, 87-103, 1992. 15. PB 25.10.16. This also fixes this Brahman. a as posterior to 1900 B.C.E)

Recent archaeological discoveries establish that the Saraswati River dried up around 1900 B.C.E. which led to the collapse of the Harappan civilization that was principally located in the Saraswati region. Frankfort has even argued that the Drishadvati was already dry before 2600 B.C.E. The region of the Saraswati and the Drishadvati rivers, called Brahmavarta, (ब्रम्हावर्त) was especially sanctified and Saraswati was one of the mightiest rivers of the Rigvedic period. On the other hand, Pancavimsa Brahman describes the disappearance of Saraswati in the sands. The Rigvedic hymns are generally before 1900 B.C.E but if one accepts Frankfort's interpretation of the data on the Drishadvati then the Rigvedic period includes the period before 2600 B.C.E.

The above descriptions indicate the study of the space Constellations, galaxies etc was profound, and the knowledge was highly developed during Vedic era, even before Rigveda poetry was scripted. The Vedic era name for astronomy is **Jyotish Shastra**, 'the science of light,' and Jyotish Vidya, 'the science of stars.' The classification of knowledge is in terms of apara (material) and para (transcendental). Speech and language are considered to have four forms (RV 1.164.45 – quoted previously), of which one kind, the para, is unmanifest.

Rigvedic Rishis calculated the time cycle depending upon the rotation of cosmic manifest organelle. The time was divided into earth year and Divya year. The day and night of Brahma – the manifest universe and multiverses. They named it as Kalp. Day and night of Brahma when the count is 365 days is One year of Brahma. Such 100 years is the life span of Brahma. For detailed understanding see the clip below: -

[The Astronomy of the Classical period. The Puran talks about Kalpa, a day of Brahma which is taken to equal 12,000 thousand of divine years, each of which equals 360 human years, for a total of 4,320 million human years. Krita, Treta, Dwapar and Kali are 4 yugas, supposed to last 4,000, 3,000, 2,000, 1,000 divine years respectively. In addition, there are sandhyas (twilights or joint period between the two yugas) of 800 (two twilights of 400 years), 600, 400, 200 on the yugas, in order, to give a total span of 12,000 divine years. Brahma, the creator of time, is a personification of the beginning of the sustaining principle, to be taken either as Vishnu or Shiva. Each day of Brahma is followed by a night of the same duration. A year of Brahma equals such 360 day and nights, and the duration of the universe is the span of 100 Brahma years. The largest cycle is 311,040,000 million years. We are supposed to be in the 55th year of the current Brahma. The large cycle is nested in still larger cycles. Within each Kalpa are fourteen secondary cycles, called manvantaras, each lasting 306,720,000 years. In each manvantara, humans begin with a new Manu. We are now in the seventh manvantara of the kalpa, started by Manu Vaivasvata. A Kalpa equals a thousand Maha yugas, each of which has the four yugas Krita, Treta, Dvapara, and Kali. Each manvantara may be divided into 71 Maha yugas. While the yugas, as defined in the Puranic literature of the first millennium C.E. have extremely large periods in multiples of the 'years of the gods,' it is likely that the four yugas were originally 4,800, 3,600, 2,400, and 1,200 ordinary years, respectively. The Rigveda are: Mercury: 87 days Venus: 225 days Mars: 687 days Jupiter: 4,340 or 4,350 days Saturn: 10,816 days. (S.C. Kak, "The astronomical code of the Rigveda," Current Science, 66, 323-326, 1994.)

Such mammoth calculations indicate how deep was the study and vast knowledge of Sanskrit Speaking civilization. The knowledge of the cosmic celestial movements to calculate the Time cycle. Modern science is inching towards the same goal.

CHAPTER 9

PLANETS OF SUN AND NAVAGRAHA STOTRA

Nine planets of Sun, the Vedic Navagraha of Solar family and their effect on living beings on earth is scientifically studied by scientists of Sanskrit Speaking Civilization. This subject has been dealt very scientifically in Rigveda. The Solar system with its 9 planets is part of the whole Brahmanda. The living beings have evolved from cosmos therefore are a part of Brahmanda. Rigveda hence considers that the AHAM BRAHMASMIN or YATHA Brahmande tatha pinde. This means whatever is in brahmand is in living body.

Rigveda is a deep study and observation of night sky by Rishis of Sanskrit Speaking Civilization. The following observation proves this:

अबुध्ने राजा वरुणो वनस्योर्ध्वं स्तूपं ददते पूतदक्षः। नीचीनाः स्थुरुपरि बुध्न एषामस्मे अन्तर्निहिताः केतवः स्युः॥ 7 II Rigveda 1-24-7.

abudhne rājā varuṇo vanasyordhvaṁ stūpaṁ dadate pūtadakṣaḥ | nīcīnāḥ sthur upari budhna eṣām asme antar nihitāḥ ketavaḥ syuḥ ||

The space science was well developed. In above Mantra it is said that the Space is a dome without pillars. It is a huge STUPA (स्तूपं) having no support of pillars but strongly upholds everything in place. All stars are suspended and rotating! This is considered as the KING VARUNA who is symbolic description of Space. Varuna has created a path for sun to move.

Because of the multitude of functions of which Sun must perform, Rigveda considers various names. See Mantra below: -

इन्द्रं मित्रं वरुणमग्निमाहुरथो दिव्यः स सुपर्णो गरुत्मान् । एकं सद्विप्रा बहुधा वदन्त्यग्निं यमं मातरिश्वानमाहुः ॥ थघ ी 'गिवेदां ऋ-ऋघथ-थघं

indram mitraṃ varuṇam agnim āhur atho divyaḥ sa suparṇo garutmān | ekaṃ sad viprā bahudhā vadanty agniṃ yamam mātariśvānam āhuḥ II 46 II Rigved. 1-164-46

Rishis have named the Sun according to the functions sun has to perform. Indra, Mitra, Varuṇa, Agni, and he is the celestial, well-winged Garutmat, for learned priests call one by many names as they speak of gni, Yama, Mātariśvan."

उरुं हि राजा वरुणश्चकार सूर्याय पन्थामन्वेतवा उ । अपदे पादा प्रति धातवेऽकरुता पवक्ता हृदयाविधश्चित् ॥

Before we discuss about Sun and its planetary system, we must explore what makes Sun move. For this the bigger Stars in cosmos -the Brahmanda must be explored.

There are 27 NAKSHATRAS which have been discussed in previous chapter.

Rigveda Pramana – **प्रमाण:** -

अमी य ऋक्षा निहितास उच्चा नक्तं दहश्रे कुह चिद्दिवेयुः । अदब्धानि वरुणस्य व्रतानि विचाकशच्चन्द्रमा नक्तमेति ॥ 10 II Rigveda 1-24-10.

amī ya ṛukṣā nihitāsa ucchā naktaṃ dadṛaśhre kuha chid diveyuḥ | adabdhāni varuṇasya vratāni vichākaśacha candramā naktam eti || Rigveda 1-24-10.

Commentary by Sāyaṇa: Ṛgveda-bhāṣya

Ṛkṣāḥ, constellations may be seven Ṛiṣhis, Ursa Major or constellations, Constellations, and the moon shine because of Varuṇa's piety (varuṇasya vratāni) since they shine by his command. A reference to asterisms: varuṇasya karmāṇi nakṣatra-darśanādirūpāṇi

The meaning of above is the SAPTA RISHI ere called as ऋक्षा i. e. the bear hence the name as URSA MAJOR. This name later changed to SAPTA RISHI. There is no shape of Bear in those 7 stars hence Rigvedic Rishi changed the name to SAPTA RISHI. West failed to recognize this change by RIGVEDA. So, the name continued as URSA.

In above Mantra, it clearly states that, in night-time, only the stars, RUKSHA - ऋक्षा निहिंतास, and galaxies are visible. One cannot see them during daytime due to the Sun light. But exist there. Only Moon is visible during day and night. This is in question form (कुहं चिद्दिवेयुः).

This is much clearer from the statement from SHATPATH BRAHMANA means 'having hundred paths' (by Sayanacharya):

atha yasmānna kṛttikāsvādadhīta | ṛkṣāṇāṃ ha vā etā agre patnya āsuḥ saptarṣīnu ha sma vai purarkṣā ityācakṣate tā mithunena vyārdhyantāmī II SHATPATH BRAHMANA Verse 2.1.2.4

Analysis of above mantra. This narration is symbolic. Sapta Rishis and Krittikas are separated by distance. The fires under the Krittikas The Krittikas were the wives of the Bears (riksha); the seven Rishis. (The original name of the Rikshas means bears). They were, however, precluded from intermixing with their husbands, for the latter, the seven Rishis, **rise in the north, and the Krittikas in the east.** Now it is a misfortune for one to be precluded from interaction with his wife. Therefore, not set up his fires under the Krittikas, lest he should thereby be precluded from intermixing.

Here the MAITHUNA word is used for intermixing. The meaning has no sexual intent but the action and interaction between the two elements. The whole manifestation is basically MAITHUNIC. This has been explained in earlier chapters.

यौ ते श्वानौ यम रक्षितारौ चतुरक्षौ पंथिरक्षी नृचक्षंसौ । ताभ्यांमेनं परिं देहि राजन्त्स्वस्ति चांस्मा अनमीवं चं धेहि ॥ Rigveda 10-14-11.

yau te śvānau yama rakṣitārau caturakṣau pathirakṣī nṛcakṣasau | tābhyām enam pari dehi rājan svasti cāsmā anamīvaṃ ca dhehi || Rigveda 10-14-11.

Entrust him, O king, to your two dogs, which are your protectors, Yama, the four-eyed guardians of the road, renowned by men, and grant him prosperity and health. ॥११॥

The above DOGS are symbolic expression of Rigveda. On both sides of Milky-way galaxy are two stars as two DOGS with 4 eyes (श्वानौ यम रक्षितारौ चतुरक्षौ), who are protectors. In English these expressions are as CANNIS MAJOR and MINOR. Sanskrit Rishi changed these names and changed to PUNARVASU and VYADH

उरूणसावसुतृपा उदुम्बलौ यमस्य दूतौ चरतो जनाँ अनु । तावस्मभ्यं दृशये सूर्याय पुनर्दातामसुमद्येह भद्रम् ॥ Rigveda 10-14-12.

The messengers of Yama, having massive strength, take away the life of mortals. May allow humans to live a prosperous existence. So that men may look upon the sun. ॥१२॥

In summary, the above descriptive statement of Rigveda, inform that the stars and constellations are named by Sanskrit rishis of Rigveda era. The Names were changed as per the scientific developments later. A testimony to this is the name of JYESHTHA Nakshatra is due to its size i.e., biggest size. It is oldest i.e., JYESHTHA. The names of stars and constellations are the nomenclature from the RISHI and SAGES of the Sanskrit Speaking Civilization. Modern science how so ever considered most developed but the contributions by RISHIS need not be ignored. They deserve full credit for their achievements. Discovery of Particle Physics in 19th Century by modern science, was well developed propagated, and established 7000 years before by Rishi KANAAD (See Song of Science Shrimad Bhagwad gita. Notion Press 2020 ed. By B. G. Matapurkar). The proposition of modern physics in 19th Century, the thermodynamic balance and the ENTHALPY and ENTROPY which are closely related concepts. **They are**

in fact energy conversion during chemical reactions. The disturbance in balance may be chaotic and everything may go very wrong. The concept is in SPACE too. Every possible position of object in space when it is in microstate. Energy is stored in small particles of liquid or solids. This is called QUANTA by modern science. Energy is distributed in bonding. This concept has been established in 1875 by Ludwig Boltzmann (Physics. THERMODYNEMIC BALANCE OYLA magazine, 9th September issue 2019. www.oylaindia.org).This is what the concept propagated in Shrimad Bhagwadgita as:

यदा यदा हि धर्मस्य ग्लानिर्भवति भारत ।अभ्युत्थानमधर्मस्य तदात्मानं सृजाम्यहम् ॥७II Shrimad Bhagwadgita, 4, 7.परित्राणाय साधूनां विनाशाय च दुष्कृताम् धर्मसंस्थापनार्थाय सम्भवामि युगे युगे II 8 II Shrimad Bhagwadgita, ४-८

Yada yada hi dharmasya glanirbhavati Bharata Abhythanamadha rmasya tadatmanam srijamyaham II Gita 4-7 & 8.

(For details consult the "Exploration of science in Shrimad Bhagwadgita. Analytical study by B. G. Matapurkar, 1st ed. 2020, ISBN: 978-93-89339-47-5).

Different names of same objects in space in different literary work create confusion and thereby clarity of the subject. To explain:

The SOLAR SYSTEM is a negligible object in MILKYWAY galaxy. Sun with all planets rotate around the STAR MOOLBARHI (**मूलबर्हि**) or MOOL NAKSHATRA. Milky Way Galaxy is indicated as PATHIRAKSHI (**पथिरक्षि**) refer to Rigveda Mantra quoted above-10-14-11. In same Rigveda 1-164-43, it is SHAKAMAYAM DHUMAM.

शकमयं धूममारादपश्यं विषूवता पर एनावरेण |उक्षाणं पश्निमपचन्त वीरास्तानि धर्माणि परथमान्यासन ||43II. Rigveda 1-164-43.

śakamayaṁ dhūmamārāda paśyaṁ viṣūvatā para enāvareṇa | ukṣāṇam pṛśnim apacanta vīrās tāni dharmāṇi prathamāny āsan || Rigveda 1-164-43.

The Milky Way galaxy is termed as "Shakamaya Dhuma (शकमयं धूममारादपश्यं)". This statement is by Aacharya Dirghatamas Auchitya.

This very Milkyway Galaxy is termed as GHRUMA in VALMIKI RAMAYANA: When ladies grief over the exile of Rama for 14 years. The citizens of Ayodhya too undergo a miserable state. All Nature (प्रकृति) mourns at Rama's departure. The timing here has been narrated with stars position in space.

(nakshatraani gata arciimshi grahaah ca gata tejasah |vishaakhaah ca **sadhuumaah** ca nabhasi pracakaashire || 2-41-12).

All the shine and splendour of STARS IN space was lost in the mist as Shri RAM proceeds to forest for 14 years.

There is a comparative statement in Rigveda about the Stars and Constellations. See the mantra Rigveda. 10-85-2, below:

सत्येनोत्तभिता भूमिः सूर्येणोत्तभिता दयौः .रतेनादित्यास्तिष्ठन्ति दिवि सोमो अधि शरितः ।। 1 || Rigveda. 10-85-1

satyenottabhitā bhūmiḥ sūryeṇottabhitā dyauḥ | ṛtenādityās tiṣṭhanti divi somo adhi śritaḥ ||

"Earth is upheld by absolute truth; heaven is upheld by the sun; the Ādityas are supported by the laws of nature, sacrifice, Soma – Moon is supreme in heaven."

सोमेनादित्या बलिनः सोमेन पर्थिवी मही .अथोनक्षत्राणामेषामुपस्थे सोम आहितः ||2|| ||10-85-2.

somenādityā balinaḥ somena pṛthivī mahī | atho nakṣatrāṇām eṣām upasthe soma āhitaḥ || Rigveda. 10-85-2

Sun is powerful than Moon. The Earth is bigger than the moon. Moon is with NAKSHATRA (अथो नक्षत्राणामेषामुपस्थे सोम आहितः) i.e., has different origin. It is highly surprising that the scientific knowledge of Rigveda era seems as good as modern science even it was more advanced than the modern science. The origin of Moon is still debated but they knew the origin of moon. This is a subject of further research. Rocks brought from Mars and analysis of such rocks proves that it is like earth! Hence recognized as BHUMI PUTRA (See NAVAGRAHA STOTRA given below).

Rays are more powerful than the manifest element. Rays of the moon produce juice or soma in vegetation and produce medicines. Moon moves in the centre of the Nakshatra ॥२॥

Rigveda indicates five planets-5 Graha, in following Mantra:

महत तन नाम गुह्यं पुरुस्प्रग येन भूतं जनयो येनभव्यम | परत्नं जातं जयोतिर्यदस्य परियं परियाः समविशन्त पञ्च || Rigveda 10- 55 -2.

mahat tan nāma guhyam puruspṛg yena bhūtaṃ janayo yena bhavyam | pratnaṃ jātaṃ jyotir yadasya priyam priyāḥ sam aviśanta pañcha || Rigveda 10- 55 -2.

Great supreme element creator of nature's existing elements of past present and future is known to knowledgeable men. With efforts the ultimate absolute truth highly illumined but secret place, can be achieved by any without any bias.

आ रोदसी अप्रणादोत मध्यं पञ्च देवान रतुशः सप्त सप्त |चतुस्त्रिंशता पुरुधा वि चष्टे सरूपेण जयोतिषाविव्रतेन || Rigveda 10- 55 -3.

āa rodasī apṛṇādot madhyam pañcha devām̐ ṛatuśhaḥ sapta-sapta | chatustriṃśhatā purudhā vi chaṣṭe sarūpeṇa jyotiṣhā vivratena || Rigveda 10- 55 -3

Indra with his RAYS from his body created SWARG, Earth, and 5 DEV, 7 elements, 30 DEVGANA. (३(

अयं वेनश्चोदयत पश्निगर्भा जयोतिर्जरायू रजसोविमाने | इममपां संगमे सूर्यस्य शिशुं न विप्रामतिभी रिहन्ति II 1 II Rigveda. 10- 123- 1.

ayaṁ venaś chodayat pṛśnigarbhā jyotirjarāyū rajaso vimāne | imam apāṁ saṁgame sūryasya śiśuṁ na viprā matibhī rihanti II 1 II Rigveda. 10- 1231.

Surrounded by bright light, VEN DEV (अयं वेन) send water to earth which is raised by Sun rays on earth. (What is VEN DEV? It is planet VENOUS but in later era this name was changed to SHUKRA. But the name VENOUS continued in the knowledge of west world. What was the need of changing the name? The King VEN of ISHVAKU dynasty, was a very cruel king). The planet VENUS is very bright hence named bright or TEJASVI or SHUKRA. SHUKRACHARYA is GURU of RAKSHASA clan is very bright, brilliant, and intelligent too. Hence name replacement established. (see figure below)

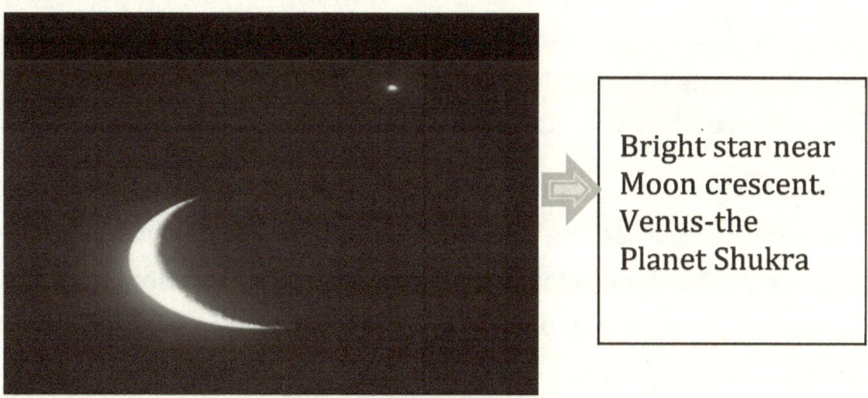

Moon with Bright STAR - SHUKRA – Venus. (WIKIPEDIA)

समुद्राद्रूर्मिमुदियर्ति वेनो नभोजाः पर्ष्ठंहर्यतस्य दर्शि | रतस्य सानावधि विष्टपि भराट्समानं योनिमभ्यनूषत वराः II 2 II Rigveda 10- 123- 2.

samudrādūrmim udiyarti veno nabhojāḥ parṣṭhaṃ haryatasya darśhi | ṛatasya sānāvadhi viṣhṭapi bharāṭ samānaṃ yonimbhyanūṣhaata vrāḥ ||2 II Rigveda 10- 123- 2.

A statement that "from space one can see the back of Venus" from space only back (पर्ष्ठहर्यतस्य दर्शि) of Venus is visible. It forces one to think that men from space have visualized the Venus. Or there was space travel. Ocean water by Surya taken up in space where it remains stable due to AGNI and Electricity or VIDYUT energy. See 3rd stanza Rigveda 10-123-3.

समानं पूर्वीरभि वावशानास्तिष्ठन्वत्सस्य मातरः सनीळाः ।ऋतस्य सानावधि चक्रमाणा रिहंति मध्वो अमृतस्य वाणीः ॥ Rigveda 10-123-3.

samānam pūrvīrabhi vāvśāhnāstiṣṭh anvatsasya mātaraḥ sanīḻāḥ | ṛtasya sānāvadhi cakramāṇā rihanti madhvo amṛtasya vāṇīḥ || Rigveda 10-123-3.

The mantra has symbolic and obscure meaning. Like eternal God and the statements of Veda, (पूर्वी) शाश्वती वाणीः(and pleasantly describing glory of originator of Veda, appreciating sweet taste, moving in space. The water occupies a common station, clamouring around like the assembled mothers of the calf; wandering above the summit of the water they utter the praises of the sweet-flavoured ambrosia (food of God). ॥३॥.

Scientifically the analysis could be Dark allusions indicatively refer to the thunder-clouds in sending rain; like the mothers cows around their calves, vatsa = vaidyutāgni, agni as the lightning. The knowledge of clouds generated from earth and the rains and electricity in clouds and the rain precipitation due to Indra-Varun effect (still unknown to modern science) was known to Rishis. This knowledge is not from western civilization.

Statement about Jupiter - BRIHASPATI Planet in Rigveda. 4-50-1 to 4.

यस्तम्भसहसा विज्मो अन्तान ब्रहस्पति स्त्रिषधस्थो रवेण । तम प्रत्नास दीध्यानाः पुरो विप्रा दधिरे मन्द्र जिह्वम ॥ 1 ॥ Rigveda. 4-50-1

yastastambha sahasā vijmo antān bṛhaspatistriṣadhastho raveṇa | tam pratnāsa dīdhyānāḥ puro viprā dadhire mandrajihvam || Rigveda. 4-50-1.

Jupiter with its power and rays and energy (स्त्रिषधस्थो) flames like tongues (जिह्वम), settled in all directions. Jupiter with might established the earth. Brihaspati, in the triple world of our fulfilment.

धुनतेयः सुप्रकेतम मदन्तो ब्रहस्पते अभि ये नस ततस्त्रे I पर्षन्तं सर्प्रम अदब्धम ऊर्वम ब्रहस्पते रक्षताद अस्यनयोनिम II 2 II Rigveda. 4-50-2.

dhunteyaḥ supraketam madanto bṛhaspate abhi ye nas tatasre | parṣhantaṁ saṛpram adabdham ūrvam bṛhaspate rakṣatād asyanayonim || Rigveda. 4-50-2.

Jupiter the Brihaspati protect the vibrations and impulses, generated due to consciousness of Supreme energy or God, which are useful for the living beings. **Rigveda. 4-50-2.**

ब्रहस्पते या परमा परावद अत आ त ऋत्स्पृशो नि षेदुः । तुभ्यम् खाता अवता अद्रिदुग्धा मध्व श्चोतन्य अभितो विरप्शम II3 II **Rigveda. 4-50-3.**

bṛhaspate yā paramā parāvad ata ā ta ṛtaspṛśo ni ṣeduḥ | tubhyaṁ khātā avatā adridugdhā madhvaḥ ścotanty abhito virapśam || **Rigveda. 4-50-3**

Oh Jupiter the ruler of big state, with your best skill and principled policy (परमा), touching the truth (ऋतस्पृशः)of clouds (अद्रिदुग्धाः)with Water (the JAL) you irrigate)श्चोतन्ति(the world and establish. We must respect that. Or like clouds provide pleasure to living being II ३ II

ब्रहस्पतिः प्रथमं जायमानो महो ज्योतिषः परमे व्योमन । सप्तास्यस तुविजातो रवेण वि सप्तरश्मिर अधमत तमांसि II4 II

bṛhaspatiḥ prathamaṁ jāyamāno maho jyotiṣaḥ parame vyoman | saptāsyas tuvijāto raveṇa vi saptaraśmir adhamat tamāṁsi || 4 || **Rigveda. 4-50-4**

Brihaspati from the vast light, was born first, in the highest heavenly space, with his seven fronts, and seven rays, vanished the darknesses of the space.

Brhaspati, the cosmic sun, born from absolute truth the primordial ultimate energy source. Seven rays of light for creation of energy, dispel darkness.

NAVAGRUHA STOTRA composed by VYAS RISHI is a highly scientific which includes origin of planets of Sun. Sri Navagraha Stotra is in Sanskrit and it is written by Maharishi Vyas. The nine mantras for nine planets. It is a prayer addressed to the Nine Planets which is believed to influence human's ups and downs in life as per the Astrology. By reciting Sri Navagraha Stotra all troubles, difficulties get vanished from our life. This is the belief which is religious and orthodox way of life. This is true (as explained earlier in prayer section of this book). Original Stotra is written by RISHI VYAS. Each mantra of the poetical Stotra is highly scientifically composed. The astrology, astrophysics and the "KHAGOL SHASTRA" was prevalent even before the Mahabharat era. What science is involved was prevalent before the composition. But it is interesting to know that the origin and source of each planet has been described in the poetical composition, the Navagraha Stotra. Following description of Stotra and its scientific bent has been analysed by the author and presented. Some scientific analysis could not be presented here because the authentic proof could not be ascertained hence not described. It is requested to the readers for further research and analysis on the subject. Author hopes that some scholar will certainly undertake this task and complete the analysis. The photographic presentation given below is from internet. It is presented as it is, in Sanskrit and Marathi for better understanding. Even though the description is not from Rigveda, but the scientific explanation is relevant as per the above statements, it is discussed below.

II नवग्रह स्तोत्र II

अथ नवग्रह स्तोत्र II श्री गणेशाय नमः II

जपाकुसुम संकाशं काश्यपेयं महदद्युतिम् Iतमोरिंसर्वपापघ्नं प्रणतोऽस्मि दिवाकरम् II १ II

दधिशंखतुषाराभं क्षीरोदार्णव संभवम् Iनमामि शशिनं सोमं शंभोर्मुकुट |भूषणम् II २ II

धरणीगर्भ संभूतं विद्युत्कांति समप्रभम् Iकुमारं शक्तिहस्तं तं मंगलं प्रणाम्यहम् II ३ II

प्रियंगुकलिकाश्यामं रुपेणाप्रतिमं बुधम् Iसौम्यं सौम्यगुणोपेतं तं बुधं प्रणमाम्यहम् II ४ II

देवानांच ऋषीनांच गुरुं कांचन सन्निभम् Iबुद्धिभूतं त्रिलोकेशं तं नमामि बृहस्पतिम् II ५ II

हिमकुंद मृणालाभं दैत्यानां परमं गुरुम् Iसर्वशास्त्र प्रवक्तारं भार्गवं प्रणमाम्यहम् II ६ II

नीलांजन समाभासं रविपुत्रं यमाग्रजम् Iछायामार्तंड संभूतं तं नमामि शनैश्चरम् II ७ II

अर्धकायं महावीर्यं चंद्रादित्य विमर्दनम् Iसिंहिकागर्भसंभूतं तं राहुं प्रणमाम्यहम् II ८ II

पलाशपुष्पसंकाशं तारकाग्रह मस्तकम् Iरौद्रंरौद्रात्मकं घोरं तं केतुं प्रणमाम्यहम् II ९ II

II इति श्रीव्यास विरचितम् आदित्यादी नवग्रह स्तोत्रं संपूर्ण II

नवग्रह स्तोत्र मराठी अर्थः

The above line sketches are the figures for concentration of all persons of different mind-set and development. This is for the benefit for every person of the different human societies of the world. All figures are scientifically developed but this is beyond the scope of this book. What science is hidden in each Navagraha Stotra mantras is explained as follows: MOON (चंद्र) Interestingly the origin of MOON is still debated by modern science. International investigations by different countries -USA, USSR-Russia, China, Japan, India etc remain inconclusive. But as thought previously moon is separated from Earth and revolving around Earth. This is doubted now after rock analysis of moon rocks. Mantra below clearly states that the moon is not from earth but from the NAKSHATRA of the Milky-way galaxy (Origin of moon has been discussed earlier).

MOON:

दधिशंखतुषाराभं क्षीरोदार्णव संभवम्। नमामि शशिनं सोमं शंभोर्मुकुट भूषणम् II 2 II

Navagraha Stotra

Dadhi Shankha tushaa-raabham Khseero Darnava Sambhavam I Namaami Shashinam Somam Shambhor Mukuta Bhooshanam II2II

I bow to Soma, the Moon God, who is white in color like curd, conch shell and snow, who rose from the Ksheerasagara (ocean of milk) and who adorns the head of Lord Shiva.

Another mantra for Moon is:

रोहिणीशः सुधामूर्तिः सुधागात्रः सुधाशनः I विषमस्थानसंभूतां पीडां हरतु मे विधुः II

Rohineeshah sudha murtih Sudha gatrah sudhasana I Vishama sthana sambhootam Peedam haratu me vidhuh II

Other mantra speaks about the origin of Moon is from different place (**विषमस्थानसंभूता**).

The one who has the whitish yellow hue, possibly evolved from Milky-way galaxy or from the milky ocean (See red words above), Chandra is adorned by deity Shiva, My salute to that Chandra.

MANGAL:

धरणीगर्भ संभूतं विद्युत्कांति समप्रभम् I कुमारं शक्तिहस्तं तं मंगलं प्रणाम्यहम् II 3 II

Navagrah Stotra 3

Dharanee garbha Sambhootham I Vidhyuth kanti Samaprabham Kumaaram Sakthi Hasthancha I Mangalam Pranamaam Yaham II 3 II

The other mantra is

भूमिपुत्रो महातेजा जगतां भ्यकृत्सदा । वृष्टिकृद् वृष्टिहर्ता च पीडां हरतु मे कुजः ॥

Bhoomi puthro maha thejaa,Jagatham bhayakruth sada,Vrushtikrud vrushtihartha, Cha peeadam harathu may Kuja., 3

MARS in Sanskrit is BHOUMA or MANGAL or Kujah. BHOUMA name is very scientific as the birth of mars is from the depth of Earth. Hence called son of Bhumi- the earth. BHUMIPUTRA (**भूमिपुत्रो**). It is also termed as BHUMI PUTRA. At UJJAIN city of Madhya Pradesh of India there is birthplace of Mars. It is famous as birthplace of mars, the mangal planet has been ejected out at this place and thrown in space. The one who is the son of Bhooma Devi, one who has the lustre of lightning, one who has Shakti in his hand (see line diagram above), and the auspicious one, my salute to that Angaraka (**अंगारक**-another name of Mars).

प्रियंगुकलिकाश्यामं रुपेणाप्रतिमं बुधम् I **सौम्यं सौम्यगुणोपेतं तं बुधंप्रणमाम्यहम्** II 4 II

Piryangu kali Kaasyaamam – Roope'naa Prathamam Budham

Sowmyam sowmya Gunopetham – Tham Buddham Pranamamyaham

Another mantra is: -

उत्पातरुपो जगतां चंद्रपुत्रो महाद्युतिः । सूर्यप्रियकरो विद्वान पीडां हरतु मे बुधः ॥

Utpatrupo jagatam Chandra putro mahadutih I surya priyakaro vidvan peedam haratu me budhah:

The one who is dark like the bud of Priyangu flower (Priyangu Callicarpa Macrophylla), one who is unequalled in beauty and is intelligent, And the son of Chandra, one who is like moon and peaceful, I prostrate that Budha planet (– **बुध ग्रह**).

JUPITER:

देवानांच ऋषीनांच गुरुं कांचन सन्निभम् I **बुद्धिभूतं त्रिलोकेशं तं नमामि बृहस्पतिम्** II 5II

Lord Guru (Brihaspati or Jupiter)

Deva-naam cha Rishi Naam cha Gurum kaanchana sannibham,Buddhi Bhootam Trilokesham Tam Namaami Brihaspatim

My salute to Brihaspathi, the Lord of the three lokas. Guru is the source of knowledge and wisdom for Devas and Rishis, and wise persons.

Another mantra is more scientific: -

देवमंत्री विशालाक्षः सदा लोकहिते रतः । अनेकशिष्यसंपूर्णः पीडां हरतु मे गुरुः ।।

Dev mantri vishalakshah sada lokhite ratah I Anek shishya Sampoornah peedam haratu me guru II

Jupiter is minister to Gods or deities. Always busy in the welfare of of people or living beings. The Jupiter has many satellites (**अनेकशिष्यसंपूर्णः**). Modern science previously thought that the Jupiter Planet has only 11 Satellites, but now it is found that the Jupiter has innumerable satellites. Jupiter has **80 moons.** Fifty-seven moons have been given official names by the International Astronomical Union (IAU). Another 23 moons are awaiting official names.

Montage of Voyager 1 images showing the Galilean satellites

From farthest out, the Galilean satellites are Callisto, Ganymede, Europa, and Io. They are shown here in their correct positions relative to Jupiter but are not to scale. The largest moon in the solar system, Ganymede, is larger than the planet Mercury.

This is a clear indication that the modern science is achieving the knowledge about the Jupiter and inching gradually to the findings of Rishis of Vedic era. Is it not an amazing fact? The Rishis are deprived of due recognition? Bharat Varsha – the country of Hindus the Hindustan, are looted by invaders of everything wealth, knowledge, precious lives, learned man, and culture.

The one who is the Guru of the Devas and Rishis, the one who is radiant and intelligent, The Lord of all the three worlds, I prostrate that Brihaspati. The Lord of three worlds (BHUH, BHUVAH, SVAH). It says that the JUPITER was at the Centre of the SOLAR System and not the SUN. The

SUN and the JUPITER formed a BINARY system in the beginning of the UNIVERSE. SUN being evolved from JUPITER (Science to day 1974 - JUPITER a DETHRONED king).

Jupiter has held the title of 'Moon King' until the discover of the 20 new moons orbiting Saturn. Pic: Shutterstock.

The planet Jupiter has been dethroned of its 'Moon King' status, following the discovery of 20 new moons orbiting Saturn. The discovery was made by a team from Carnegie Institution for Science in Washington DC, led by astronomer Scott S. Sheppard.

What Rigved states about Planet Guru 0r Jupiter?

अनर्वाणं वर्षभं मन्द्रजिव्हं ब्रहस्पतिं वर्धया नव्यमर्कैः । गाथान्यः सुरुचो यस्य देवा आश्र्ण्वन्ति नवमानस्य मर्ताः ॥ 1 ॥ **Rigveda.** ऋ-ऋक्षए-ऋ

anarvāṇaṁ vṛṣabham mandrajihvam bṛhaspatiṁ vardhayā navyam arkaiḥ | gāthānyaḥ suruco yasya devā āśṛṇvanti navamānasya martāḥ II 1 II Rigveda. 1-190-1

तं रत्विया उप वाचः सचन्ते सर्गो न यो देवयतामसर्जि I ब्रहस्पतिः स हयञ्जो वरांसि विभ्वाभवत सं रते मातरिश्र्वा II 2 II **Rigveda.** ऋ-ऋक्षए- **2**

tam ṛtviyā upa vācaḥ sacante sargo na yo devayatām asarji | bṛhaspatiḥ sa hy añjo varāṁsi vibhvābhavat sam ṛte mātariśvā II 2 II Rigveda. 1-190- 2

By singing hymns in praise of Brihaspati who is provider of knowledge and intellect, get benefited.

SATURN:

नीलांजन समाभासं रविपुत्रं यमाग्रजम्। छायामार्तंड संभूतं तं नमामि शनैश्चरम् ॥७॥

Saturn is SHANI is a slow planet, its movement is slow compared to other planets. Its origin is from SUN; hence it is SURYA PUTRA. Planet with bluish hue, brother of God of death my salute to you.

Chhaya graha Rahu

अर्धकायं महावीर्यं चंद्रादित्य विमर्दनम्। सिंहिकागर्भसंभूतं तं राहुं प्रणमाम्यहम् ॥८॥

Ardha kaayam mahaveeram – Chandra Aditya vimarshanam I Simhikaagarba Sambhootham – Tam Raahum Pranamamyaham II

Respects to Rahu, a half-body, the fearless opponent of Chandra and Surya, Rahu is born of Singha Rashi, or Simhika's womb or centre of Simha constellation.

Planet with half body capable of reducing the glory of Moon and Sun. SIMHA Rashi nakshatra are Magha, Purvaphalguni and Uttaraphalguni. Lord of this Rashi is Sun. Out of the nine planets Sun is considered as the King. Is it that the RAHU planet is born from such NAKSHATRA constellations? Rahu is born from the centre of Simha Rashi. It is a subject of further research. What is Nakshatra?

NAKSHATRA in Rigveda: **The 27 Nakshatras in Vedic astrology.** One can divide Nakshatras into various categories, depending on their attributes, the planet that rules them, and much more. The SUN star moves in 12 signs of RASHI 0r signs of zodiac, for one month period. Each RASHI has its relationship with stars of NAKSHATRA. In the Sun movement through SIMHA RASHI which has the influence of 3 different NAKSHATRA e.g., Magha, Purvaphalguni and Uttaraphalguni as stated above, Planet RAHU is born. The two planets RAHU and KETU are not true planets as per the Astrological consideration. These are considered as the CHCHAYA GRUHA (छाया ग्रह). Birth of RAHU planet and its birth from SIMHIKA is authors understanding. Author could not find any conclusive confirmation of this scientific understanding. Hence it is requested that the Scholars and readers of this understanding need to explore the subject. It is a matter of research and be treated as it is.

Astrological View about Rahu and Ketu:

The five instincts as per Vedic understanding, that keep us attached to the materialistic purpose of life are Desire, passions (Kaam - काम), Anger (Krodh – क्रोध), and intoxicants (Madh - मद, drugs, alcohol, etc.), Attachment (Moh - मोह), Lobh (Greed), and Matsara - मत्सर (Jealousy). We need to control our instincts rather than allow ourselves to be controlled by them. **Rahu and Ketu can keep our minds focused on these instincts- by exaggerating and obscuring or blocking.**

The invisible line is Rahu and Ketu. The soul's purpose in this life is to act out his given Karma, destroy the illusions of the worldly life and move towards self-realization. To live on the astral planes where pleasure and pain cannot hurt, the mind is still and at peace. The position of Rahu and Ketu indicates the soul's journey in a particular lifetime and its connection with eternal life. Ketu deals with the past Karma and Rahu with the future. We are tied to the cycle of unhappiness and dissatisfaction as we cannot break away from animal nature in us, our lower selves with animal instinct. This entangles into Birth- death cycle. We are born again and again to experience the pleasures and pains of earthly life until we recognize them to be the illusions that truly they are. On a subconscious level, we are afraid that we will lose out if we give up these desires. One continues with greed and sense satisfaction in life. Spirituality teaches us to abandon the greed and sense satisfaction and liberate by achieving the goal of our incarnation – Moksha. The conflict between our attachment to materialistic achievements (this gives us momentary pleasure, which is a fantasy as it has no factual basis, the domain of Rahu) and liberation of the soul, finding bliss and tranquillity which is eternal (Ketu is the Moksha karaka significator for spiritual realization).

अत्र॑। अह॑। गोः। अ॒म॒न्व॒त॒। नाम॑। त्वष्टुः॑। अ॒पी॒च्य॑म्। इ॒त्था। च॒न्द्रम॑सः। गृ॒हे ॥ 15॥ **Rigveda:1:84:15.**

atrāha gor amanvata nāma tvaṣṭur apīcyam | itthā candramaso gṛhe II Rigveda:1:84:15.

"The (solar rays) found on this occasion the light of Tvaṣṭā verily concealed in the mansion of the moving moon."

Commentary by Sāyaṇa: Ṛgveda-bhāṣya

'The rays of the sun are reflected back in the moon ,the solar radiance, concealed by the night, enters into the moon, and thus dispels darkness by night, as well as by day'. One ray of the sun that named śuṣumnā lights up the moon; therefore, moon's light is derived from the sun (Nirukta 2,6)(cf. Viṣṇu Purāṇa 36)

There is also a 28th Nakshatra, which astrologers take into consideration. It is the **Abhijit Nakshatra.** Sun is the ruler of this constellation, and the deity that governs it, is Lord Brahma

तरीणि (त्रिणि) जाना परि भूषन्त्यस्य समुद्र एकं दिव्येकमप्सु | पूर्वामनु पर दिशं पार्थिवानां रतून परशासद विदधावनुष्ठु ॥3॥ Rigveda. 1-95-3 trīṇi jānā pari bhūṣhanty asya samudra ekaṃ divy ekam apsu | pūrvāmanu par diśam pārthivānām ṛtūn praśāsad vidadhāv anuṣṭhu II3II Rigveda. 1-95-3.

In absence of primordial time, day and night, past, present and future, difficult to establish. Without this no Ritu (1tu) can establish. Day and night are due to Sun's speed in space.

Rigveda and Seasons, RITUS:

Sun creates and controls the seasons in relation to the sun and earth and, in relation to the earth and her people, it creates the directions such as east and others.

Seasons or RITUS of the year, are indicated in Rigveda. Rigveda. 10-90-6. Indicate 3 Seasons - Ritus.

यत्पुरुषेण हविषा देवा यज्ञमतन्वत । वसन्तो अस्यासीदाज्यं ग्रीष्म इध्मः शरद्धविः ॥6॥

yat puruṣeṇa haviṣā devā yajñam atanvata | vasanto asyāsīd ājyaṃ grīṣma idhmaḥ śarad dhaviḥ II6II Rigveda. 10-90-6.

Research and analysis efforts (हविषा) of Rishis, (यज्ञमतन्वत), reveal that vegetation is supported by Vasant Ritu or spring season. Medicinal plants grow and later in summer season these vegetations increase, as this Ritu acts like energy for the vegetations. In later season of Sharad Ritu, it becomes consumable (शरद्धविः).

हिमेवं पर्णा मुषिता वनानि बृहस्पतिनाकृपयद्वलो गाः । अनानुकृत्यमपुनश्चकार यात्सूर्यामासा मिथ उच्चरातः ॥10॥ Rigveda 10-68-10.

himeva parṇā muṣitā vanāni bṛhaspatinākṛpayad valo gāḥ | anānukṛtyam apunaśhcakāra yāt sūryāmāsā mitha uchcharātaḥ ||

Just as the leaves of forest trees are made to fall by winter, so darkness is dispelled and light is created, so is ignorance dispelled and the light of Vedic revelation revealed by Brhaspati and illuminate the days and nights.

मधुश्च माधवश्च वासंतिकावृतु शुक्रश्च शुचिश्च ग्रैष्मावृतु नभश्च नभस्यश्च वार्षिकावृतु इषश्चोर्जश्च शारदावृतु सहश्व सहस्यश्च हेमन्तिकावृतु तपश्च तपस्यश्च शैशिरावृतु अग्नेरन्तः श्लेषोस्सि कल्पेतां द्यावापृथिवि

(https://maghaa.com/wp-content/uploads/2019/02/TS_4-4-11.png)

Names of 6 RITUS are mentioned in YAJUVEDA, TAITTARIYA SAMHITA - 4-4-11. Mantra above. Rigveda further decides year or VARSHA – वर्ष from one Varsha ritu to next Varsha ritu.

Eclips and Rigveda,:

यत्त्वां सूर्य स्वर्भानुस्तमसाविध्यदासुरः । अक्षेत्रविद्यथा मुग्धो भुवनान्यदीधयुः ॥ Rigveda 5-40-5.

yat tvā sūrya svarbhānus tamasāvidhyad āsuraḥ | akṣetravid yathā mugdho bhuvanāny adīdhayuḥ || Rigveda 5-40-5.

O Sun! When you are blocked by the one whom you gifted your own light (moon), then earth gets scared by sudden darkness. O Sūrya, when the Asura's descendant Svarbhanu, (name of Rahu) pierced thee through and through with darkness, all creatures looked like one who is bewildered, who knows not the place where he is standing, because of darkness.

Photo from Internet. Wikipedia

In Rigveda the movement of earth has been clearly described. It is scientific as per the modern science standards.

Before one proceed ahead, for knowing the inter celestial attraction let us understand the earth was first mapped out by Sage Ramanujacharya after reading the Bhishma Parva from Mahabharat.

यथा हि पुरुषः पश्येदादर्शे मुखमात्मनः। - एवं सुदर्शनद्व -द्वीपो दृश्यते चन्द्रमण्डले॥ रंशद्वै पिप्पलस्तत द्विरंशे च शशो महान्।।- (भीष्म पर्व, महाभारत(

Just like a man sees his face in the mirror, so does the Earth appears in the Universe. In the first phase, you see Peepal leaves and the next phase you see a rabbit. Based on this shloka, Sage Ramanuj Acharya sketched out the map, but the world laughed it off on seeing some leaves and a rabbit. Much later, when the picture was switched upside down, the reality struck in. reverse picture and realize the result.

If one reverses the picture the modern map of earth continents is revealed.

MOTION OF EARTH, and inter-celestial attraction:

अ॒हस्ता॒ यद॒पदी॒ वर्ध॑त॒ क्षाः शची॑भिर्वे॒द्याना॑म् । शुष्णं॒ परि॑ प्रद॒क्षिणिद्वि॒श्वाय॑वे॒ नि शि॑श्नथः ॥ 14 ॥ Rig Veda 10.22.14,

ahastā yad apadī vardhata kṣāḥ śacībhir vedyānām | śuṣṇam pari pradakṣiṇid viśvāyave ni śiśnathaḥ || Rig Veda 10.22.14,

"This earth is devoid of hands and legs (अहस्ता यद्पदी), yet it moves ahead. All the objects over the earth also move with it. It moves around the sun.

In this mantra,Kshaa क्षाः = Earth (refer Nigantu 1.1), Ahastaa अ-हस्ता = without hands, Apadee अ-पदी= without legs. Vardhat = moves ahead, Shushnam Pari = Around the sun, Pradakshinit प्रदक्षिणि= revolves.

(Nighantu: Nighaṇṭu is a Sanskrit term for **a traditional collection of words**, grouped into thematic categories, often with brief annotations).

सविता यन्त्रैः पृथिवीमरम्णादस्कम्भने सविता द्यामदृंहत् । अश्वमिवाधुक्षद्धुनिमन्तरिक्षमतूर्ते बद्धं सविता समुद्रम् ॥10.149.1॥

savitā yantraiḥ pṛthivīm aramṇād askambhane savitā dyām adṛṃhat | aśvam ivādhukṣad dhunim antarikṣam atūrte baddhaṃ savitā samudram || ॥Rig Veda 10.149.1

"The sun tied Earth and other planets through attraction. All move around the Sun in a balance manner, as if a trainer moves newly trained horses around itself holding their reins."

This indicates the attraction by gravity. Example of Horse in training is cited here to explain the earth movement around Sun.

In above mantra, Savita (सविता)= Sun, Yantraih (यन्त्रैः) = through reins, Prithiveem (पृथि वीम्) = Earth, Aramnaat (अरम्णात्)= Ties, अस्कम्भने=in a balanced manner, Dyaam Andahat (द्यामदृंहत्)= Other planets in sky as well, Atoorte (अतूर्ते)= Unbreakable, Baddham (बद्धम्)= Holds, Ashwam Adhukshat (अश्वंम्ऽइव, अधुक्षत्)= Like horses

GRAVITATIONAL FORCE

यदा ते हर्यता हरी वावृधाते दिवेदिवे । आदित्ते विश्वा भुवनानि येमिरे ॥28॥ Rig Veda 8.12.28.

yadā te haryatā harī vāvṛdhāte dive-dive | āditte viśvā bhuvanāni yemire ||28|| Rig Veda 8.12.28.

Oh, super-power, the whole cosmos in small and big form, is under your control. It is gradually advancing every moment. The laws of Nature are governing the events. The laws of attraction influence each thing in cosmos. As and when the development progresses, the laws of nature influence all. The Super-power ties all under the same nature's laws. ॥२८॥

As this happens and understood by the knower his faith deepens in the super-power. ॥२८॥

"O God! by putting forth your mighty rays, which possess the qualities of gravitation and attraction-illumination and motion – keep up the entire universe in order through the Power of your attraction."

The gravitational force and attraction of all spheres in cosmos is explained in next mantra.

यदा सूर्यममुं दिवि शुक्रं ज्योतिरधारयः । आदित्ते विश्वा भुवनानि येमिरे ||30|| Rig Veda 8.12.30.

yadā sūryam amuṃ divi śukraṃ jyotir adhārayaḥ | ād it te viśvā bhuvanāni yemire || Rig Veda 8.12.30.

"O God, you have created this Sun. You possess infinite power. You are upholding the sun and other spheres and render them steadfast by your power of attraction.

Similar view is expressed in Yajurved. Yajur Veda 33.43.

आ कृष्णेन रजसा वर्त्तमानो निवेशयन्नमृतं मर्त्यं च। हिरण्ययेन सविता रथेना देवो याति भुवनानि पश्यन् ॥ Yajurved. Yajur Veda 33.43.

"The sun moves in its own orbit in space taking along with itself the mortal bodies like earth through force of attraction (आकर्षणेन)."

हिरण्यपाणिः सविता विचर्षणिरुभे द्यावापृथिवी अन्तरीयते । अपामीवां बाधते वेति सूर्यमभि कृष्णेन रजसा द्यामृणोति ॥ Rig Veda 1.35.9.

hiraṇyapāṇiḥ savitā vicarṣaṇir ubhe dyāvāpṛthivī antar īyate | apāmīvām bādhate veti sūryam abhi kṛṣṇena rajasā dyām ṛṇoti || Rig Veda 1.35.9.

"The sun moves in its own orbit but holding earth and other heavenly bodies in a manner that they do not collide with each other through force of attraction.

पञ्चारे चक्रे परिवर्तमाने तस्मिन्ना तस्थुर्भुवनानि विश्वा । तस्य नाक्षस्तप्यते भूरिभारः सनादेव न शीर्यते सनाभिः ॥ Rig Veda 1.164.13.

pañcāre cakre parivartamāne tasminn ā tasthur bhuvanāni viśvā | tasya nākṣas tapyate bhūribhāraḥ sanād eva na śīryate sanābhiḥ || Rig Veda 1.164.13.

"Sun moves in its orbit which itself is moving. Earth and other bodies move around sun due to force of attraction, because sun is heavier than them.

Rig Veda 1.6.5 & Rig Veda 8.12.30. The mantra reveals: "The Sun, created by God, is kept in its orbit through divine gravitational force." Quote: "The Sun is anchored in space through divine gravitational force."

THE SUN's ORBIT: In summery Vedic rishis were fully aware of the origin of Sun, its position in galaxy, and moving in an orbit which itself is moving. The light of the Moon. Rig Veda 1.84.15. The mantra mentions: "The Moon receives its light from the Sun." Quote: "Moonlight is sunlight in disguise."

ECLIPSE

यत्त्वा सूर्य स्वर्भानुस्तमसाविध्यदासुरः । अक्षेत्रविद्यथा मुग्धो भुवनान्यदीधयुः ॥ Rig Veda 5.40.5

yat tvā sūrya svarbhānustamasāvidhyad āsuraḥ | akṣetravid yathā mugdho bhuvanānya dīdhayuḥ || Rig Veda 5.40.5.

"O Sun! When you are blocked by the one whom you gifted your own light (moon), then earth gets scared by sudden darkness."

The above statements of Rigveda indicate that the scientific facts were known to Rishis of Rigvedic era. Arya Bhatta must have followed it and advanced it further. This cosmic science knowledge is as old as Rigveda. It is not a gift from West civilization as it is thought by present generation.

CHAPTER 10

SCIENTIFIC MEDICAL STATEMENTS IN RIGVEDA

Genetics and embryology

The oldest and the most developed life sciences which are the natural therapeutic medical sciences in the world. It is called Ayurveda a Sanskrit word. It means Ayur-life and Veda -knowledge or Dnyan or Gyan. According to modern medical drugs system each drug has a harmful effect on body, but natural ayurvedic drugs have no toxic effects on body. Nature has its own protective and healing effects on body. It offers the critical instructions for health and long life. This is encouraged in Ayurvedic medical system. Ayurveda system is the most holistic and natural health care system compared to the available medical health care systems in the world. It is a gift of India to the whole humanity of the world. This system has been condemned to promote the drugs developed by invaders of the west.

Rig Veda, the oldest record of virtues of manifest nature and human history, is full of mysteries. Foreign "scholars" who translated it have added footnote at every other page, 'the meaning is uncertain', 'the meaning is not clear', 'the meaning is obscure'. Ancient literature is full of medical details and knowledge, **treatments, techniques but in this book only the statements in Rigveda will be discussed.**

Before one explores the scientific medical statements in Rigveda it will be of interest to know what health means. In YOG VASISHTHA when child Shri RAM was taught by Rishi VASISHTHA for continuously 18 days, he explains Adhi and Vyadhi. He teaches Shri Ram the following:

Health of human being depends upon the cravings, desires, and passions which if unsatisfied the MIND is saddened. That is the soul is saddened. The sadness spreads in body. This upsets digestion, in turn cause maladies in the body. The immunity is jeopardised. This makes body vulnerable to external attacks by pathogens in environment.

श्री वसिष्ठौवाच I आधयो व्याधयश्चैव व्दयं दुःखस्य कारणम् I तन्निवृत्तिः सुखं विद्यात्तत्क्षयो मोक्ष उच्चते II12II YogVasishtha 6-81 -12.

Aadhyo Vyadhyashcheiva dvayam duhkhasya Karanam I tannivruttih sukham vidyattatkshayo moksha uchchyate II12II YogVasishtha 6-81 -12.

Health to Disease. Unfulfilled Desire. Ailments to Health Treatment of disease = Moksha. Aadhi to Vyadhi (Aa2yo Vya2yXcEv), Disturbed Mind, Vyadhi to Aadhi. NIVRITTI from Vyadhi = moksha. Ashvini Kumar are the doctors of Vedic period. The Medical Science was well developed during Vedic period. Ashvini Kumars are considered as DEVTAS because of the superhuman qualities in them. While praising doctors Ashvini Kumars many medical treatments and medical facilities have been described. Some of them are discussed below: -

Mandal 1, Sukta 116, Mantra 10, 12-16, 22. And 117-24.

Providing youth to elderly persons. Rishi Chyavan (**ऋषि च्यवन**) was given the youthful life so that he could marry a young female.

हिरण्यहस्तमश्विना रराणा पुत्रं नरा वध्रिमत्या अदत्तम्। त्रिधा ह श्यावमश्विना विकस्तमुज्जीवस ऐरयतं सुदानू II 24 II Rigveda 1-117-24.

hiraṇyahastam aśvinā rarāṇā putraṁ narā vadhrimatyā adattam | tridhā ha śyāvam aśvinā vikastam uj jīvasa airayataṁ sudānū || 24 II Rigveda 1-117-24.

Ashvins, rejuvenated wedded couple, blessed woman with son. Divided into three pieces. He was brought back to life by Ashvins. He was risen to full stature again. Griffith's interpretation given below. With liberal bounty to the weakling's consorts ye, Heroes, gave a son Hiranyahasta (13); 1-117-24. And Syava, cut into three pieces, ye brought to life again, O bounteous Ashvins. Ye from Chyavana worn with age removed his skin, as were a robe. So, when ye made him young again, he stirred the longing of a dame (Griffith).

जुजुरुषो नासत्योत वव्रिं प्रामुञ्चतं द्रापिमिव च्यवानात्। प्रातिरतं जहितस्यायुर्दस्रादित्पतिमकृणुतं कनीनाम् ॥ Rigveda. 1- 116- 10.

jujuruṣo nāsatyota vavrim prāmuñcataṁ drāpim iva cyavānāt | prātiratam̐ jahitasyāyur dasrād it patim akṛṇutaṁ kanīnām || Rigveda. 1- 116- 10.

Ashvini kumaras are capable and responsible of destroying enemies, removed the old and wrinkled skin of Rishi Chyavana and provided new youthful skin, at the same time long life to Rishi Chyavana. Thus, helped him in getting married. Read Rigved 5-74-5: -

Like a physician and surgeon, you discard the debility of age, like an old and worn-out garment when you renew it back to youth, so that he could marry a young female II 5 II.

प्र च्यवानाज्जुजुरुषो वव्रिमत्कं न मुञ्चथः। युवा यदी कृथः पुनरा काममृण्वे वध्वः ॥५॥ ऋग्वेद 5; 74; 5.

pra cyavānāj jujuruṣo vavrim atkaṁ na muñcathaḥ | yuvā yadī kṛthaḥ punarā kāmam mṛuṇve vadhvaḥ II5II Rigved. 5-74-5.

Rigved 1-20-4. Describes the event of rejuvenating parents by rishi Ribhu:

युवानां पितरा पुन: सत्यमंत्रा ऋजुयवः ऋभवो विष्ट्यकत ॥ 4 ॥ Rigved 1-20-4.

yuvānām pitarā punaḥ satyamantrā ṛjūyavaḥ | ṛbhavo viṣhṭyakrata || Rigved 1-20-4.

The Rubhus with effectual prayers, honest, with constant labour, made parents (iptra) young again.

शतं मेषान्वृक्ये मामहानं तम :प्रणीतमशिवेन पित्रा। आक्षी ऋज्राश्वे अश्विनावधत्तं ज्योतिरन्धाय चक्रथुर्विचक्षे ॥ Rigved 1-117-17.

śhatam meṣhānvṛukye māmahānaṁ tamaḥ praṇītamaśivena pitrā | ākṣhī ṛujrāśhve aśhvināvadhattaṁ jyotirandhāya chakrathurvichakṣe || Rigved 1-117-17.

Ashvins, creators of light and givers of eyes, bring eyes for the injured of the swift army of horse, in short, create and bring light for the blind who may then see the light of truth.

अमाजुरश्चिद्भवथो युवं भगोऽनाशोश्चिदवितारापमस्य चित् । अन्धस्य चिन्नासत्या कृशस्य द्युवामिदाहुर्भिषजा रुतस्य चित् ॥ Rigved 10- 39- 3.

amājuraś cid bhavatho yuvam bhago nāśoś cid avitārāpamasya cit | andhasya cin nāsatyā kṛśasya cid yuvām id āhur bhiṣajā rutasya cit || Rigved 10- 39- 3

O lovers and observers of the truth and law of nature, you bring light for the blind, strength for the anaemic and health for the chronic sufferers. That is what people call you, "saviours of life".

युवम् । विप्रस्य । जरणाम् । उपऽईयुषः । पुनरिति । कलेः । अकृणुतम् । युवत् । वयः । युवम् । वन्दनम् । ऋश्यऽदात् । उत् । ऊपथुः । युवम् । सद्यः । विश्पलाम् । एतवे । कृथः ॥ **ऋग्वेद -10; 39; 8.**

yuvaṁ viprasya jaraṇām upeyuṣaḥ punaḥ kaler akṛṇutaṁ yuvad vayaḥ | yuvaṁ vandanam ṛśyadād ud ūpathur yuvaṁ sadyo viśpalām etave kṛthaḥ ||ऋग्वेद - 10; 39; 8

You rejuvenate and restore to vibrant youthful ness the aging veteran scholar in pursuit of research. You raise the man of holiness from chronic ailment to renewed life. And you help the public health authority in community health programmes so that they may go on with their normal activity. Interestingly, in Rigveda, the statement is repeatedly mentioned hence not ignorable.

Horse headed- Dadhyanka

Now let us look at the interesting story of the horse headed Dadhayank! His story is in RV 1-84-16; 1-116-12; 1-117-22; 10-48-8, Satapatha Brahmana 14-4-5-13; Brhad Aranyaka Upanishad 2-5; Bhagavatam 6-10 Adhyaya. His story is found in many places in the Vedas.

Dadhyank was the son of Atharvan Rishi. He and his father were regarded as the founders of Vedic sacrifice. They knew a secret mantra known as Madhu Vidhya. Dadhyank taught this to all his devoted students. Those who learn this knowledge – vidya, gets free from all miseries of life. Indra also came to the seer and learnt the vidya. But the seer warned him that he should lead a life worthy of it. Indra became angry at his advice and told him that he would cut off the Rishi's head if he had taught it to anyone else. Later on the Vedic era twins, the Aswinikumar's came and asked the seer to teach them the Madhu Vidya. But Rishi told them about Indra's curse, the Asvins cut his head off and preserved it in a safe place and learnt the Madhu Vidya. During that study, they replaced a horse's head on Dadhyank. The technique and the method of head transplant is not mentioned in the literature. This is beyond the scope of this article. When he finished teaching them, Indra's thunderbolt came and cut off Dadhyank's head. Later Asvini kumaras fixed his preserved original head, back on him.

Rishi Kakshivan has glorified Ashwinikumar's in his Rig Vedic hymns. Ashvins are attributed with mystical powers throughout the Vedas. What is Madhu Vidya? It is modern zoonotransplant surgery. See evidence below:

Madhu VIDYA Rigved, 1-116-12, 164-46, 3-53-8, 4-47-8,

तव्दां नरा सनयेदंस उग्रमाविष्कृणोमि तन्यतुर्ण विष्टिम् । दध्यंग हयन्मध्वाथर्वणो वामश्र्वस्य शिष्र्णा प्र यदीमुवाच **II 12 II Rigveda 1-116-12.**

tad vāṁ narā sanaye daṁsa ugram āviṣ kṛṇomi tanyatur na vṛṣṭim | dadhyaṅ ha yan madhv ātharvaṇo vām aśvasya śīrṣṇā pra yad īm uvāca **II 12 II Rigveda 1-116-12.**

Son of Atharvarn, Dadhynka Rishi, on acquiring horse head in place of human head, spoke like thunder of clouds.

इन्द्रं मित्रं वरुणमग्निमाहुरथो दिव्यः स सुपर्णो गरुत्मान्। एकं सद्विप्रा बहुधा वदन्त्यग्निं यमं मातरिश्वानमाहुः **II Rigveda. 1-164-46**

indram mitraṁ varuṇam agnim āhur atho divyaḥ sa suparṇo garutmān | ekaṁ sad viprā bahudhā vadanty agniṁ yamam mātariśvānam āhuḥ || **Rigveda. 1-164-46**

About head replacement evidence: See note on excavation in KHMER Cambodia: -

Hayagreeva from Khmer (Cambodia), 10th century CE. I will try to list the mysteries of R.V., one by one.

One of the mysteries of Rig Veda that puzzled the westerners is the Story of Dadhyank Atharvan, a Rishi with a horse head. Until the year 2000, they wrote that they have discovered his grave in Potapovka near Samara in Russia. By 2010 they have changed their view!

Excavations of 1985-86 of a Kurgan burial dated 2200 BCE at Potapovka revealed in grave shaft of kurgan no.3, a decapitated man with a horse skull replacing his head. In simple terms, the man's head was removed, and a horse head was fixed. They thought that it was the grave of Rig Vedic seer Dadhyank. Later research showed that the skeleton of both the horse and the human being were not of male, but of female. They also found the horse head was fixed 1000 years after the human being's death. This shows that we can't jump to conclusion by listening to archaeologists! They only "interpret" it and confirm in what they have already believed. In this case they started talking Aryan migration from the Steppes. It may be otherwise. Needs research.

Similar description is available in Brihadaranyak Upanishad, 2- 5- 19 and 2-5-16.

In this with head of horse DADYANK Rishi taught ASHWINI kumars.

Horse faced Vajimuka in Guimet Museum, France.

Here the perpetual question arises that how human language came through the horse' mouth and head?

For Hindus, head replacement or transplant is nothing new. We have Lord Ganesh with elephant head, Hayagriva with horse head, Daksha with a goat's head, lord Narasimha with lion's head and vishnu's avatars with fish, tortoise, and pig forms. Horse headed Hayagreeva sculptures are available even in Cambodia.

The afferent and efferent messages which flow in nerves are only some flowing currents only through nerves. There is no difference in flowing current in nerves between horse head or human head. Hence is it not a possibility? All this needs to be investigated.

यः । ऋते । चित् । अभिऽश्रिषः । पुरा । जत्रुऽभ्यः । आऽतृदः । सम्ऽधाता । सन्धिम् । मघऽवा । पुरुऽवसुः । इष्कर्ता । विऽह्रुतम् । पुनरिति ॥ १२ ॥ **ऋग्वेद** ८-१-ऋधं

ya ṛute cht abhiśhriṣhaḥ purā jatrubhyah āatṛudaḥ | saṁdhātā sandhim maghavā purūvasuh iṣhkartā vihrutam punah || Rigved 8-1-12.

Indra is that vibrant lord of assertive life energy who, without piercing and without ligatures, provides treatment for collar bones (clavicle - **जत्रुऽभ्यः । आऽतृदः = स्कंध सन्धि से ग्रीवा तक**) and then, later, heals and sets the same back into healthy order if they get dislocated or fractured.

In modern medical treatment of fracture Clavicle is treated by providing figure of 8 bandage. The bandage is kept for 4-6 weeks.

तद्वां नरा सनये दंस उग्रमाविष्कृणोमि तन्यतुर्न वृष्टिम् । दध्यङ्ह यन्मध्वाथर्वणो वामश्वस्य शीर्ष्णा प्र यदीमुवाच ॥ Rig Veda 1.116.12

tad vāṃ narā sanaye daṃsa ugram āviṣ kṛṇomi tanyatur na vṛṣṭim | dadhyaṅ ha yan madhv ātharvaṇo vām aśvasya śīrṣṇā pra yad īm uvāca || Rig Veda 1.116.12

Tongue of horse provided with your help to rishi Atharva's son, Dadhyank RISHI, so that he could talk like a normal person (12).

आथर्वणायाश्रिवना दधीचेऽश्रश्वं शीरेः प्रत्येरयतम् । स वां मधु प्र वोचदृतायन्त्वाष्ट्रं य्द्दस्त्रावपि कक्ष्यम् वाम् ॥12॥

śarasya cid ārcatkasyāvatād ā nīcād uccā cakrathuḥ pātave vāḥ | śayave chinnāsatyā śachībhir jasuraye staryam pipyathurgām || **Rigveda. 1- 116-22.**

Not only this but Horse's head fixed on Rishi Dadhichi and Taught MADHU VIDYA (Deals with zoono transplant surgery?).

उतस्या वां मधुमक्षिकारपन्मदे सोमस्यौशिजो हुवन्यति । युवं दधिचो मन आ विवासथोऽथा शिरः प्रति वामश्यंम् वदत **II 9 II Rigveda. 1- 119-9.**

uta syā vām madhumakṣikārapanmade somasyauśijo huvanyati | yuvaṁ dadhīcho man aā vivāsathothā śhiraḥ prati vāmaśvyaṁ vadat **II 9 II Rigveda. 1- 119-9.**

Dadhichi was provided with good health and taught Madhu Vidya with his grafted horse head. This is an example of Xeno-transplants currently performed? Xenotransplantation or heterologous transplant is the **transplantation** of living cells, tissues, or organs from one species to another. What xenotransplants have been done in the modern era? There have only been a few attempts at human xenografting over the years, but no human solid organ xenograft projects are currently approved by the FDA (Food and Drug Administration of USA). "Baby Fae", a child born with a malformed heart survived for a brief period with a baboon heart. At the beginning of the 20th century when studies in xenotransplantation were just beginning, few questioned the morality of it, turning to animals as a "natural" alternative to allografts. Xenotransplantation was not taken seriously, at least in France, during the first half of the 20th century. In India Pigs heart used in Assam (Dr Barua) but punished legally by contemporary ethical team. Ashvini Kumar attempts are praised below.

अजोहवीन्नासत्या करा वां महे यामन्पुरुभुजा पुरन्धिः। श्रुतं तच्छासुरिव वध्रिमत्या हिरण्यहस्तमश्विनावदत्तम् II Rigved 1- 116-13.

ajohavīn nāsatyā karā vām mahe yāman purubhujā puraṁdhiḥ | śrutaṁ tac chāsur iva vadhrimatyā hiraṇyahastam aśvināv adattam II Rigved 1- 116-13

Wise wife of a Rishi VADHRIMATI became mother of son Hiranyahastha, because of your treatment (13).

During the battle between VRIK and VARTIKA, you saved VRIK and provided vision to VRIK (14).

आस्नो वृकस्य वर्तिकामभीके युवं नरा नासत्यामुमुक्तम्। उतो कविं पुरुभुजा युवं ह कृपमाणमकृणुतं विचक्षे ॥ Rigveda. 1-116- 14.

āsno vṛkasya vartikām abhīke yuvaṁ narā nāsatyāmumuktam | uto kavim purubhujā yuvaṁ ha kṛpamāṇam akṛṇvicakṣe ||Rigveda. 1-116- 14.

You provided eyesight to RIJASHVA when he lost his eyesight (16).

शतं मेषान्वृक्ये चक्षदानमृज्राश्वं तं पितान्धं चकार। Rigveda. 1-116- 14.

तस्मा अक्षी नासत्या विचक्ष आधत्तं दस्रा भिषजावनर्वन् ॥ Rigved.1-116-16

This verse talks about Aswinikumar, giving vision to blind people. Three instances are mentioned as follows: - Rijrasva got his vision back. - An unnamed poet got his vision back. - are being praised as the healers of the blind.

When VISHPALA wife of king lost her leg in a battle, you provided Iron leg to her so that she could walk normally (15).

चरित्रं हि वेरिवाच्छेदि पर्णमाजा खेलस्य परितक्म्यायाम्। सद्यो जङ्घामायसीं विश्पलायै धने हिते सर्तवे प्रत्यधत्तम् ॥ Rigved 1- 116-15

This verse talks about a warrior queen named Vishpalayei. Her lower limb was lost in the battle and Ashwini kumara chopped that limb and attached a prosthetic metal limb. Next day she took part in the war. In a way the prosthetic limb was instantly effective. In modern scientific medicine such an instant use is almost difficult.

तद्वां नरा सनये दंस उग्रमाविष्कृणोमि तन्यतुर्न वृष्टिम्। दध्यङ्ह यन्मध्वाथर्वणो वामश्वस्य शीर्ष्णा प्र यदीमुवाच ॥ Rigveda. 1- 116- 12.

Split hymn as above is: तत्। वाम्। नरा। सनये। दंसः। उग्रम्। आविः। कृणोमि। तन्यतुः। न। वृष्टिम्। दध्यङ्। ह। यत्। मधु। आथर्वणः। वाम्। अश्वस्य। शीर्ष्णा। प्र। यत्। ईम्। उवाच ॥ १.११६.१२) ऋग्वेद 1- 116- 12

One of the mysteries of Rig Veda that puzzled the westerners is the Story of Dadhyang Atharvan, a Rishi with a horse head. Until the year 2000, they wrote that they have discovered his grave in Potapovka near Samara in Russia. By 2010 they have changed their view!

You could convert a cow which reached non childbearing age, was without childbirth, to provide milk (22).

शरस्यं चिदार्चत्कस्यावतादा नीचादुच्चा चक्रथुपातवे वाः। शयवे : चिन्नासत्या शचीभिर्जसुरये स्तर्यं पिप्यथुर्गाम् ॥ Rigved. 1- 116- 22.

śarasya cid ārcatkasyāvatād ā nīcād uccā cakrathuḥ pātave vāḥ | śayave chinnāsatyā śachībhir jasuraye staryam pipyathurgām || Rigveda. 1-116-22.

This verse talks about how Ashwini kumaras produced lactation in an infertile cow. Modern science use medical kits on a regular basis, to reinduce lactation in cows.

Rigved 1-161 Mantra 1-14: - Description about Ribhu Gana is interesting. Agni the messenger of God came to Ribhu Gana and gave a piece of advice to them. The sons of Sudhanva, divide the CHAMAS patra (vessel) into four. This is the message to you from God. If you do so you shall be at par with God. On this Ribhu Gana said, to messenger Agni (अग्नि दूतं), apart from what you gave message we have to create horses, cow from skinless cow, and provide youthful life to our old parents. After that we shall come to you. See 3rd stanza below:

अग्निं दूतं प्रति यदब्रवीतनाश्वः कर्त्वो रथ उतेह कर्त्वः । धेनुः कर्त्वा युवशा कर्त्वा द्वा तानि भ्रातरनु वः कृत्व्येमसि ॥ Rigved. 1-161-3.

agniṃ dūtam prati yad abravītanāśvaḥ kartvo ratha uteha kartvaḥ | dhenuḥ kartvā yuvaśā kartvā dvā tāni bhrātar anu vaḥ kṛtvy emasi || Rigved.1-161-3.

Messenger Agni was furious on seeing 4 parts of Chamas Patra. He wanted to punish and kill the person who divided the Patra. Indra and Brihaspati liked the work. Hence the three brothers Ribhu, Vibhu and Vaaj, your research has been accepted by Indra, Brihaspati therefore now you go to Indra devata and enjoy the Yadnya offerings. Because of their research work they were placed at the level of Gods.

इन्द्रो हरी युयुजे अश्विना रथं बृहस्पतिर्विश्वरूपामुपाजत । ऋभुर्विभ्वा वाजो देवाँ अगच्छत स्वपसो यज्ञियं भागमैतन ॥ Rigved. 1-161-6

indro harī yuyuje aśvinā ratham bṛhaspatir viśvarūpām upājata | ṛbhur vibhvā vājo devām̐ agacchata svapaso yajñiyam bhāgam aitana || RIGVED. 1-161-6

"Indra decorated his horses; the Aśvins have harnessed their car; Bṛhaspati has accepted the omniform (cow); Rishi Ribhu and his two brothers achieved this scientific research, therefore, Ṛbhu, Vibhva and Vāja, got place with deities. doers of good deeds, enjoy your sacrificial portion."

Similar expression is also In following mantras. Rigved 3- 60- 1 to 7. In these mantras, Rigveda reiterate the work done by sons of Sodhanva and Angira due to the scientific success and Ribhu Gana got the Devatva position.

Rigveda 1-111-8. Ribhu gana, sons of Sodhanva created cow from skin and provided mother to calf. They also rejuvenated their old parents and made them young who lived long life.

निश्चर्मण ऋभवों गामपिंशत सं वत्सेना सृजता मातरं पुन्हः । सौधन्वनासः स्वपस्यया नरो जिंव्रीयुवाना पितरा कृणोतन II 8 II Rigveda. 1-110-8.

niś carmaṇa ṛbhavo gām apiṁśata saṁ vatsenāsṛjatā mātaram punaḥ | saudhanvanāsaḥ svapasyayā naro jivrī yuvānā pitarākṛṇotana || Rigved. 1-110-8

Rigved. 4- 33- Mantra 1 to 11. sUKt ३३ Devata Ribhu Gana. In this chapter of Rigveda, how the scientific feats achieved by Ribhu, Vibhu and Vaj three brothers became friend to Devta Gana despite being mortal became immortal.

प्र ऋभुभ्यो दूतमिव वाचमिष्य उपस्तिरे श्र्वैतिरिंधेनुमिळे । ये वातजूता स्तरिणिभिरेवैः परिद्याम सद्यो अपसोबभूवुः ॥ 1 ॥ ऋग्वेदं **4-33-1**

To prepare SOMRAS we praise Ribhu Gana to provide milk giving Cows.

Ribhu's parents all the time lying down due to weakened and energy less body due to old age. Ribhu's carefully attended them and provided with youth and young body with tremendous energy. Ribhu Gana becoming like Indra accept our prayers and must attend to our invitation.

पुनर्येचक्रुः पितरा युवाना सना यूपेव जरणा शयाना । तेवाजो विभ्वाँ ऋतोरिंद्रवन्तो मधुप्सरसों नोSवन्तु यज्ञम् ॥ 3 ॥ **Rigveda. 4-33- 3.**

punar ye cakruḥ pitarā yuvānā sanā yūpeva jaraṇā śayānā | te vājo vibhvām̐ ṛbhur indravanto madhupsaraso no vantu yajñam || Rigved. 4-33-3

Utilising their intellect Ribhu, Vibh and Vaj created Horse named Hari for Indra. (Rigveda. 4-33-10).

Following mantra is about RIBHU Devata. The sukta has Rishi: medhātithiḥ kāṇvaḥ. Devatā: Rbhavaḥ; Chandas: gāyatrī. Hence the mantra is on Ribhu. Ribhu name is not there in mantra.

ये । इन्द्राय । वचःऽयुजा । ततक्षुः । मनसा । हरी इति । शमाईभिः । यज्ञम् । आशत ॥धीी 'गिवेदा ऋ-धए-धं

ya indrāya vacoyujā tatakṣur manasā harī | śamībhir yajñam āśata || Rigveda 1-20-2.

This means the persons who created Horse, with mind and intellect, with holy actions and hard work (यज्ञम्)'Yadnya' (śamībhiḥ (शमाईभिः) = they performed with tongs, ladles (ततक्षुः invent), and mechanical skills. Created horse named HARI (हरी इति), for Indra Devata.

Rigveda. 4-36-1, Interestingly, enough Ribhu's scientific achievement is developing a vehicle which is automatically driven, horse less, self-propelled, having three wheels: - **मण्डल** 4, **सूक्त** 36, **मंत्र** 1, **देवता** = **ऋभुगण.** The vehicle can move in Aakash- sky also. See Mantra below: -

अनश्र्वो जातो अनभीशु शयरूक्थ्यो रथस्त्रिचकः परि वर्तते रजः I महतत्व्दो देव्यस्य प्रवाचनं द्‍यामृभवम् पृथ्वीं यच्च पुष्यथः **II 1 II Rigved. 4-36-1.**

anaśvo jāto anabhīśur ukthyo rathas tricakraḥ pari vartate rajaḥ | mahat tad vo devyasya pravācanaṁ dyām ṛbhavaḥ pṛthivīṁ yac ca puṣyatha || Rigved. 4-36-1.

Rigveda.1-111 -1. Ribhu Gana (**ऋभु गण**) created vehicle for the use of Ashvini Kumars and created two horses for that vehicle. They created cow -mother to calf, and youthful life to their parents.

तत्क्षन्नथम् सुवृतम् विद्मनापस्तक्षन्हरी इन्द्रवाहा वृषण्वसू I तत्क्षणपितृभ्यामृभवो युवद्‍वयस्तक्षण्वस्ताय मातरम् सचाभुवम् **II1II Rigveda. 1- 111-1**

takṣan rathaṁ suvṛtaṁ vidmanāpasas takṣan harī indravāhā vṛṣaṇvasū| takṣan pitṛbhyām ṛbhavo yuvad vayas takṣan vatsāya mātaraṁ sacābhuvam||

In Rigved Mandal 1, Sukta 20 the scientific achievements by Ribhu Rishi are discussed:

य इन्द्राय वचोयुजा ततक्षुर्मनसा हरी शमीभर्यज्ञमाशत II2 II Rigveda 1-20-2.

ya indrāya vacoyujā tatakṣur manasā harī | śamībhir yajñam āśata ||

Rishi Ribhu made horses capable of getting in the vehicle on command by themselves, to run it.

ततक्षन्नासत्याभ्याम परिज्मानं सुखं रथं तक्षन्धेनुं सबर्दुघाम II3 II Rigveda 1- 20-3.

takṣan nāsatyābhyām parijmānaṁ sukhaṁ ratham | takṣan dhenuṁ sabardughām II3 II Rigveda 1- 20-3

Rishi Ribhu made a vehicle for Ashwini Kumars, which runs with uniform speed. At the same time developed a cow which gives milk all the time.

अधारयन्त वहनयोस्भजन्त सुकु त्यया भागंदेवेशु यज्ञियम् II8II Rigveda. 1-20-8.

adhārayanta vahnayo bhajanta sukṛtyayā | bhāgaṁ deveṣu yajñiyam ||II8II Rigveda. 1-20-8

Mortal Rishi Ribhu became immortal as he made 4 CHAMAS from one Chamas, for Yadnya. Hence came to the level of Devata (८).

Rishi Ribhu received Godly status (DEAVATVA) due to his scientific achievements. The most difficult of these achievements is division of one "patra" or vessel into 4. What metal the Chamas was made of is not clear. Division of metal into 4 is possible but such work may not uplift the mortal to God-DEVATVA level. Details of the Chamas the Patra is unclear. The vessel divided and made fit for drinking SOMRAS. See mantra below: -

किंमयः स्विच्चमस एष आस यंकाव्येन चतुरो विंचकः । अथा सुनुध्वं सवनंवदाय पात ऋभवो मधुनः सोम्यस्य II 4 II Rigveda, 4-35-4.

kimmayaḥ svic camasa eṣa āsa yaṁ kāvyena caturo vicakra | athā sunudhvaṁ savanam madāya pāta ṛbhavo madhunaḥ somyasya II 4 II Rigveda, 4-35-4.

How the Chamas was? With deft action and intelligence, you divided it into four. Technology not mentioned. Following web site addresses the problem to some extent.

हिरण्मयेन पात्रेण सत्यस्यापिहितं मुखम् । तत्वं पूषन्नपावृणु सत्यधर्माय दृष्टये II 15 II Ishavasya Upanishad

In short, the meaning is "GOLD VESSEL CLOSES THE MOUTH OF TRUTH". How is it so?

It is an every-day experience that the riches hide the truth in all walks of life. The above prayer is to Pushna or SUN (commonly understood) but another meaning in Rigveda is Nitrogen cycle or PUSHNA-CHAKRA as described earlier. If PUSHNA chakra blessings are bestowed on someone he will not be afraid of persons with riches or power. He will be bold as his daily needs be met with availability of food and available wealth in his life. He can expose the truth hidden behind the activities of rich scoundrels.

HIRANMAY PATRA is HIREN is RETA or -**रेत**, which means semen or sperm. What is vessel made from sperm? It is body which is composed of multitude of cells. Formation of Patra is by fertilization of ovum with sperm. Once fertilized it is termed as KALAL-**कलल**. (See Song of science Shrimad Bhagwat Gita, Notion press, Chinnai, Singapore, and Malaysia, 2022 edition by the Author).

This 'KALAL PATRA' (CHAMAS), was divided into 4 by RISHI Ribhu and his brothers Vibhu and Vaj.

ज्येष्ठ आह चमसा द्वा करेति कनीयान् त्रीण्कृणवा मे तयाह । कनिष्ठ आह चतुरस् करेति त्वष्ट ऋभव स्तत्पनय व्दचो वहः II 5 II Rigveda 4-33 -5.

Elder brother said two division can be made, younger brother said three can be made from this, youngest said 4 can be made from this Chamas Patra.

If one considers the "kalal-patra" as Chamas patra then as per modern science of embryology, the zygote cells divide into 2, which become 4 and so on and forms the whole body. In other word the cell consists of a cell wall membrane which contains the cellular ingredients, thus becomes a vessel or patra i.e., CHAMAS patra. A vessel enclosed in a membrane or cell membrane. It is divisible which was divided by RIBHU GANA with a Sharp instrument. See below: -

क्षेत्रमिव वि ममुस्तेजनेनँएकं पात्मृभवो **जेहमानम्** । उपस्तुता उपम् नाधमाना अमर्त्येषु श्रव इच्छमानाः II 5 II Rigveda. 1- 110 – 5.

kṣetram iva vi mamus tejanenam̐ ekam pātram ṛbhavo jehamānam | upastutā upamaṁ nādhamānā amartyeṣu śrava icchamānāḥ || II 5 II Rigveda. 1- 110 – 5.

In a comparable way as one measures the field, the Rishi Ribhu divided Chamas Patra with the help of sharp instrument, into 4 parts, in presence of immortal God.

Next is what is the meaning of Chamas Patra or HIREN in this mantra.

It can emphatically be said that Ribhu rishi and two brothers- Vibhu and Vaj have achieved a remarkable success in Medical and engineering subjects. In modern Science it is a subject of tissue engineering. This is reiterated in Rigveda literature. In modern science there is no evidence about providing youth to elderly humans. There is evidence in Rigveda that Rishi Ribhu and brothers have experimented on cows and developed breed to produce more milk. How this was achieved is not clearly stated in Rigveda. But it is certain that Rishi Ribhu had performed great research on creating cows, Horses etc from skin of dead animals. (Rigved 1-111-1; 1-161-7 and 3; 3-60-2; 4-36-4 see mantra above). All this has come to be acceptable to modern science. Because all such research work has been attempted by modern scientists. But above literature had appeared thousands of years before. Before cloning of Sheep-Dolly, the description was not acceptable and considered as fiction only. Creation of horse from horse was not an idea only but use of intellect and challenging work had been mentioned in the literature. On pondering, on the above Rigveda subject, it is obvious that the Ribhu Rishi's achievements are equally true as per modern science. Even the names are also mentioned in Rigveda rhymes. Created horse named as HARI and cow mentioned as DHENU. It involved great time span for the research outcome that is, it was not an instant success. See the following Mantras: - Mantra is repeated for better understanding. Rigveda 1- 161-3 and 7:

अग्नि दूतं प्रति यद्ब्रवीतनाश्र्वः **कर्त्वोरथे** उतहे कर्त्वः । धेनुः कर्त्वा युवशा कर्त्वा व्दा तानि भ्रातरनु वः कृत्व्येमसि II3II Rigveda 1- 161-3 agniṁ dūtam prati yad abravītanāśvaḥ kartvo ratha uteha kartvaḥ | dhenuḥ kartvā yuvaśā kartvā dvā tāni bhrātar anu vaḥ kṛtvy emasi II3II Rigveda 1-161-3

Ribhu Rishi needed time to create cow etc. After success only Ribhu wanted to appear before the Messenger- Agni. This indicates that he wanted time for the research.

निश्र्चर्मणो गामरिणीत धीतिभिर्या जरंता युवशा ताकृणोतन । सौधन्वना अश्र्वादश्र्वमतक्षत युक्त्वा रथमुप देवाँ अयातन II7II Rigveda 1- 161-7

niś carmaṇo gām ariṇīta dhītibhir yā jarantā yuvaśā tākṛṇotana | saudhanvanā aśvād aśvam atakṣata yuktvā ratham upa devām̐ ayātana II7II Rigveda 1- 161-7

With intellect you created cow from dead cow. Provided youth full life to your old parents, created horse from horse. Take your time and reach Indra.

आपो भूयिष्ठा इत्येको अब्रवीदग्निर्भूयिष्ठम् इत्यन्यो अब्रवीत् । वधर्यन्तीं बहुभ्य प्रैको अब्रवींदृता वदन्तश्चतमसाँ अपिंशत II 9 II Rigved. 1- 161-9.

āpo bhūyiṣṭhā ity eko abravīd agnir bhūyiṣṭha ity anyo abravīt | vadharyantīm bahubhyaḥ praiko abravīd ṛtā vadantaś camasām̐ apiṁśata || Rigveda, 1-161-9: -

One of the three RIBHUS one said that Aap (0r **जल**) is the best, other said Fire or (**अग्नि**) as the best while the third said Earth is the best. Considering this they divided the Hiranyamay Patra the Chamas.

श्रोणामेक उदकम् गामवाजति मांसमेकः पिंशति सूनयामृतम् ी आ निम्रुचः शकृदेको अपाभरत्किंम् स्वित्पुत्रेभ्यः पितरा उपावतु ीऋए ी ंगिवेदां ऋ-ऋघऋ- ऋएं

śroṇām eka udakaṁ gām avājati māṁsam ekaḥ piṁśati sūnayābhṛtam | ā nimrucaḥ śakṛd eko apābharat kiṁ svit putrebhyaḥ pitarā upāvatuḥ ||II10 II Rigveda. 1-161- 10.

One of the Ribhus kept UDAK- water (watery blood) on earth. Other kept flesh and the third cleans the flesh.

What parents get from three Ribhus?

In summary it can be said that the works done by Rishi Ribhus are:

1. Parents were provided with youthful life. it seems the science was undoubtedly advance, yet in modern science no such treatment is available.

2. Ribhus created cows who can provide great quantity of milk. It seems this is an experiment of genetic engineering. Rishi Ribhus worked on live animals.

3. Created cows from skin, as mother to the calf whose mother had died. Also created calf for cows whose calves had died.

अनश्वो जातो अनभीशुर उक्थ्यो रथस तरिचक्रः परि वर्तते रजः |

महत तद वो देव्यस्य परवाचनं दयाम रभवःपर्थिवीं यच च पुष्यथ || Rigved 4-36-1.

anaśvo jāto anabhīśur ukthyo rathas tricakraḥ pari vartate rajaḥ | mahat tad vo devyasya pravācanaṁ dyām ṛbhavaḥ pṛthivīṁ yac ca puṣyatha || Rigved 4- 36- 1.

Created Rath, who moves without Reigns or without Horses, having three wheels, capable of blowing dust around in huge amounts, or created an Aeroplane. The Rath can move on earth and Space both (दयाम रभवः पर्थिवीं). These Godly achievements placed you at par with Gods.

1. Divided Chamas into 4. As explained earlier Chamas Patra is not made of metal of not an earthenware vessel. It is "Kalal" or fertilized ovum, zygot. Evidence of this is clear in Rigveda, 1- 110-3. The word used is Chit Chamas (चिच्चमचमसुरस्य). Which means living container or Patra. A cell with covering membrane becomes a container or PATRA (पात्र). A container made of mud, wood, or

any metal like Gold, Silver etc., cannot be divided into 4 with the capacity to contain.

तत्सविता वोमृऽतत्वमासुवदगोह्यं यच्छ्रवयंत ऐतन । त्यं चिच्चमसमसुरस्य भक्षणमैकंम् सन्तमकृणुता चतुर्वयम् II Rigved. 1- 110- 3.

tat savitā vo mṛtatvam āsuvad agohyaṁ yac chravayanta aitana | tyaṁ cic camasam asurasya bhakṣaṇam ekaṁ santam akṛṇutā caturvayam || **Rigved. 1- 110- 3.**

On reaching lord of light the Savita, the lord creates the nectar of bliss fand food or you. Like water is held in the cloud or soul in the body, He increases fourfold for the living and eathing souls in existence. **चिच्चमसम = चित्त + चमस, is a PATRA or cup having CHITTA i.e., life or is a living entity.**

Rishi Ribhu used (TEJAN) sharp weapon (**ममुस्तेजनेनमेकं**) to divide the Patra -Chamas into 4. (Rigveda. 1-110- 5). Later, after Rigveda period the similar weapon might have been used to divide the aborted embryo of Gandhari into 101 parts in AADI PARVA of Mahabharat. (See under lined word in mantra below).

कषेत्रमिव वि ममुस्तेजनेनमेकं पात्रं रभवो जेहमानम ी उपस्तुता उपमं नाधमाना अमर्त्येषु शरव इछमानाः ीत्री ॑गिवेदां ऋ-ऋऋए- त्र

kṣetram iva vi mamus tejanenam ekam pātram ṛbhavo jehamānam | upastutā upamaṁ nādhamānā amartyeṣu śrava icchamānāḥ II5II Rigveda. 1-110- 5

Cloning and other medical achievements of Vedic era: -

The Vedic era enumerates the cloning in animals. The following statement in hymns confirms this fact.

सत्रे ह जाताविषिता नमोभिः कुम्भे रेतः सिषिचतुः समानम | ततो ह मान उदियाय मध्यात ततो जातं रषिमाहुर्वसिष्ठम II13II Rigveda 7- 33- 13.

satre ha jātāv iṣitā namobhiḥ kumbhe retaḥ siṣicatuḥ samānam | tato ha māna ud iyāya madhyāt tato jātam ṛṣim āhur vasiṣṭham II13II Rigveda 7-33- 13

Details in Rigveda 7- 33 Mantra from 10-14.

History goes back to King VEN. He is of ISHVAKU dynasty. He was a cruel king. Hence killed by public-PRAJA. He existed sixty-two generations before RAM. Rishis or scientists of that time created human clone from the thigh of dead king VEN. The child thus created was very black and ugly or VIKRUT (Nishad). The living Child was sent to Jungle. The race became NISHAD race. Even now this race is called NISHAD JATI.

Therefore, the second child human clone was created from the hand of VEN. The child was called PRITHU. The word used as MANTHAN for creating clone. Prithu is a scientific name as the child is separated (PRITHAK) from dead king VEN.

From VEN dead king a daughter was also created.

Vasishtha and AGASTI (रषिमाहुर्वसिष्ठम) were created by MITRA and VARUN. See mantra below and the above mantra from RIGVEDA.

This is from the semen (कुम्भे रेतः सिषिचतुः). At the same time the details of cloning are in Mantra below from Rigveda 7-33-10 to 13

विद्युतो जयोतिः परि संजिहानं मित्रावरुणा यदपश्यतां तवा | तत ते जन्मोतैकं वसिष्ठागस्त्यो यत तवा विशाजभार || 10. Rigveda 7- 33.

उतासि मैत्रावरुणो वसिष्ठोर्वश्या बरह्मन मनसो.अधि जातः |

दरप्सं सकन्नं बरह्मणा दैव्येन विश्वे देवाः पुष्करे तवाददन्त II 11 II. Rigveda 7- 33-11. Next mantra states the birth of Vasishtha (जज्ञे वसिष्ठः)

स प्रकेत उभयस्य प्रविद्वान्त्सहस्रदान उत वा सदानः। यमेन ततं परिधिं वयिष्यन्नप्सरसः परि जज्ञे वसिष्ठः ॥१२॥

The container in which the clone developed was called Kumbh, which was named as PUSHKAR. The pushkar word is meaningful. PUSH is nourishing growth. KAR is which creates, (KARANARE - करणारे) hence PUSHKAR. The Kumbha contains nourishing elements, (पोषकतत्व असलेले कुंभ).

उर्वषी has nothing to do with the generation of AGASTYA or VASISHTHA.

Since both are from KUNDA (कुंड) hence the KONDINYA GOTRA thus came from them and generations are of KONDINYA GOTRA.

A word about "CHAMAS PATRA":

आगन्न रभूणाम इह रत्नधेयम अभूत सोमस्य सुषुतस्य पीतिः |सुक्रत्यया यत सवपस्यया चं एकं विचक्र चमसं चतुर्धा II2II. Rigveda 4-35-2

āgann ṛbhūṇām iha ratnadheyam abhūt somasya suṣutasya pītiḥ | sukṛtyayā yat svapasyayā caṁ ekaṁ vicakra camasaṁ caturdhā II2II. Rigveda 4-35-2

Rishi Rubhus' performance let the joy of the soma success distilled from nature be here for the people to share who deserve the prize, since with their admirable action and brilliant intelligence and will they have designed and divided one patra into 4 from one CHAMAS.

वय अक्रणोत चमसं चतुर्धा सखे वि शिक्षेत्य अब्रवीत |अथैत वाजा अम्तस्य पन्थां गणं देवानाम रभवः सुहस्ताः II3II Rigveda 4-35- 3

Eminent scholars, dynamic scientists, dexterous technologists, join the fraternity of divines and move on to the path of immortality.

किम्मयः सविच चमस एष आस यं काव्येन चतुरो विचक्र | अथा सुनुध्वं सवनम मदाय पात रभवो मधुनः सोम्यस्य II4II Rigveda 4-35-4

A question can be asked 'what is the chamas patra'?

Chamas Patra is a divine container. A vessel used for drinking SOMA RASA -an extract from plants. See below:

अश्नापिनद्धं मधु पर्यपश्यन मत्स्यं न दीन उदनिक्षियन्तम |निष टज्जभार चमसं न वर्क्षादब्ह्रस्पतिर्विरवेणा विक्रत्य II8II Rigveda. 10-68-8.

Brhaspati sees the sweetness and beauty of human life caught up in the bonds of pleasure and sufferance in the body like a fish caught up in shallow waters, and he raises and refines it like a **cup of soma for the divinities**, crafted from rough wood, having refined and blest it by the resounding voice of revelation.

It is not from metal or earthenware, or wood etc. It is from a living material - plant. Rishi Ribhu and his two brothers used Chamas Patra to create cows and horses. Division of living vessel or container is possible. After division also it functions as a container. A membrane covered cell is a Patra where divine living material is contained inside. With division and multiplication only, the creation is possible.

The above statements from different mantra of different sutras, the CHAMAS Patra which contains divine and a living material/tissue which can be divided into four. A clear description about embryonic cell could not be obtained. But overall, it depicts as embryonic cell. Which could be divided by a sharp instrument. Experiments carried out by Rubhu rishi on animals which needed time. In later Sanskrit literature the human clones could also be possible. Such noble work placed Rubhu rishi to immortality.

SHAKAL branch of Rigveda has Aitareya Aranyaka and Aitareya Brahman. It is composed by Aitareya Rishi. He derived his name as he was son of a female called AITARA. He was popularly known as MAHI DAS, because he was worshiper of Prithvi or MAHI. Last part of Aitareya Aranyaka is Aitareya Upanishad. Aitareya Upanishad 1-1-4 and 1-2-4, deals with how the SOUL gets into manifest form as person. It is astonishing and baffling that thousands of years before man thought about all such knowledge. The Sanskrit civilization knew about the embryology and emphasized the similarity about manifestation of nature and human development in uterus. Sequence and chronological order of manifestation of Nature is dealt in this Upanishad. Aap is not just water as is commonly known, it is a liquid element is clarified in this Upanishad by Rishi Aitareya Mahi Das. The Aitareya Upanishad belongs to the Aitareya Aranyaka and is a part of the Rig Veda.) This Upanishad consists of 3 chapters; the first chapter has 3 sections and the remaining two chapters do not have any sections. In the earlier portions of the Aranyaka rituals for the attainment of oneness with Saguna Brahman and their interpretations are dealt with. It is the purpose of the Upanishad to lead the mind of the ritualist away from the outer ceremonials to their inner meaning. Sankara points out that there are three classes of men who wish to acquire wisdom. The highest consist of those who have turned away from the world, whose minds are freed and collected, who are eager for freedom. For such seekers this Upanishad is intended. (The other two classes of people are those who want to become free gradually and those who care only for worldly possessions).

Embryology or BHRUNA SHASTRA (भ्रूण शास्त्र):

The laws of Nature are intricate and camouflaged by illusion due to MAYA incorporated in whole cosmos, but Ved believe that the laws have uniform applicability may it be in universe or multiverses of the cosmos. This has been explained in the series of publications on science in Vedic literature by the author. The following description is an example of this uniform applicability of nature in the universe.

Even though there is no direct evidence about embryology in Rigveda scriptures, but a comparative statement about development of Nature and foetus, reveal the existing knowledge about embryological development of foetus in the uterus. The Manifestation of cosmic body - VIRAT PURUSHA (ivra3 pu+8) has been compared with the development of embryo body or PURUSH in the uterus. As the body of foetus grows and develops in uterus so the growth of cosmic body develops. Living being and the Nature (s<i*3) are related is intelligently expressed in the Richa

(1ca) of Rigvedic Upanishad – the Aitareya Upanishad. See the following Mantras: -

Sloka: 1.1.2. स इमाँ ल्लोकानसृजत । अम्भो मरीचीर्मापोऽदोऽम्भः परेण दिवं द्यौः प्रतिष्ठाऽन्तरिक्षं ॥पृथिवी मरो या अधस्तात्त आपः ॥ २॥ Aitareya Upanishad. 1-1-2.

Sa imam llokan srujat I Ambho marichiemapodombhah paren divam dyouh pratishthantariksham II Prithvi maro ya adhastatta aapah ॥ २॥ Aitareya Upanishad. 1-1-2.

In mantra 1 and 2 it is assumed that the absolute truth ultimate energy, is in human form and He decided to create the material world – Srishti, after overall glancing the entire material expression. It is a symbolic expression.

The super soul created world named Ambha. Marichi, Mara, Apah (अम्भो मरीचीर्मापोऽ). That which is beyond heaven (दिवं द्यौः) is Ambha and beyond Tejah. It is placed beyond Tejah. The Antariksha or sky is Marichi. The earth is Mara - Mrityu Loka (मृत्यु लोक). The worlds that are below (अधस्तात्त) are the Apah. Where is Ambh located.

Scientific analysis of this mantra is, initially there was only "Aatma Tattva". It created above mentioned loka. Ambha is superior location to Tejah or DIVAM (परेण दिवं). Superior to Tejah and inferior to Atma Tattva. Five elements are in order of Aakash- Vayu- Tejah. Or in between Atma-Tattva and Tejah there are Aakash + Vayu. Therefore, the combination of Aakash and Vayu is Ambha. Vayu is not air only. It is a speedy element. The element is full of hustle bustle. This is due to other elements like sound waves. Sound waves are not only which are heard with ears but there are sounds beyond the reach of listening capacity. Manifestation of Nature is from Ambha. But primary is Atama tattva, which has manifested Ambha. This is Aakash and Vayu tattva. The primordial gasses which are Ambha, rotating and circulating resulting into gravitational attraction, and pressure. This resulted in production of heat and light which is Tejah. Because of gravitational force and pressure in the ball of primordial gasses, the heavy material pushed to centre and lighter element remained at periphery. All this created reaction in small atomic particles which resulted in emission of heat and light surrounding the ball of gasses, which is Marichi in Antariksha. After this on cooling the BHUMI (solid) was manifested. These are PRITHVI like elements. The order is first Ambha then round balls which are emitting light and heat are SUN like stars. From Sun like stars the planets like earth (BHUMI- wUim) manifested. These are MAR lok, i.e., death is essential part of MAR. This MAR incorporates inside the Aakash, tejah, Aap (liquid element). The reaction inside resulted in manifestation of water on cooling of planets. This applies to all the universe and multiverses.

Modern science accepts this chronological order. From water element the living beings (or Prajotpatti) could manifest or is possible. How this interpretation could be derived thousands of years before is amazing. But is very much scientific and as per the modern science, or otherwise. The Rigveda's Aitareya Aranyaka, Mantra below compares the development of foetus (PURUSHA-पुरूष) with the development or manifestation of PRAKRITI PURUSHA (प्रकृति पुरूष, or विराट पुरूष).

Sloka: 1.1.4. तमभ्यतपत्तस्याभितप्तस्य मुखं निरभिद्यत यथाऽण्डं मुखाद्वाग्वाचोऽग्निर्नासिके निरभिद्येतं नासिकाभ्यां प्राणः ॥ प्राणाद्वायुरक्षिणी निरभिद्येतमक्षीभ्यां चक्षुश्चक्षुष आदित्यः कर्णौ निरभिद्येतां कर्णाभ्यां श्रोत्रं श्रोत्रद्दिशस्त्वङ्निरभिद्यत त्वचो लोमानि लोमभ्य ओषधिवनस्पतयो हृदयं निरभिद्यत हृदयान्मनो मनसश्चन्द्रमा नाभिर्निरभिद्यत नाभ्या अपानोऽपानान्मृत्युः शिश्नं निरभिद्यत शिश्नाद्रेतो रेतस आपः ॥ ४॥ ॥ इत्यैतरेयोपनिषदि प्रथमाध्याये प्रथमः खण्डः ॥Rigveda branch, SHAKAL SHAKHA, AITTAREYA ARANYAKA, 1-1-4

tamabhyad̓hyatapattasyād̓hitaptasya mukhaṃ nirad̓hidyata yathāṇḍaṃ

mukhādvāgvācho'gnirnāsike nirad̓hidyetāṃ nāsikād̓hyāṃ prāṇaḥ I prāṇādvāyurakṣiṇī niradhidyetāmakṣidhyāṃ chakṣuśchakṣuṣa ādityaḥ karṇau

nirabhidyetāṃ karṇādhyāṃ śhrotraṃ shrotr niradhidyata tvacho lomāni

lomabhya oṣhadhivanaspatayo hṛidayaṃ niradhidyata hṛdyānmano

manasaśchandramā nābhirniradhidyata nābhyā apānan mrityuḥ śhiśhnaṃ

nirabhidyata śiśnadreto retasa āpaḥ ॥ ४॥ ॥ इत्यैतरेयोपनिषदि प्रथमाध्याये प्रथमः खण्डः ॥Rigveda branch, SHAKAL SHAKHA, AITTAREYA ARANYAKA, 1-1-4

In this Mantra how the PRAKRITI PURUSH developed like a PURUSH developed in uterus, has been compared. The embryological development described is at par with modern embryology. Knowledge of embryology was existing in the society even before the Rigveda was written. The mouth is integral in the development of feeding, the initiation of digestion, and for speech and socialization. The order of development is first mouth, nose, eyes, ears, Skin, Heart, umbilicus and then Penis. Exactly same order is in above Mantra.

After development of Mouth in embryo, speech, or Vani (वाणी, वाक्) is possible. The development of mouth and the speech in Purush, Agni is manifested in Prakriti Purush. How it is so? If one considers the speech, (VAAK – वाक्), Speech has sound waves, electro-magnetic radio waves. One knows that the electromagnetic waves produce fire or Agni. First fire on earth was the result of electrocution in clouds that fell on earth. Thus, the development of Agni in nature, is possible with developed mouth. Therefore, it has been compared. Hence the Rishi's interpretation sounds correct in above mantra.

नसिके निरभेद्येतां दोधूयति नभस्वति । तत्र **वायुर्गन्धवहो** घ्राणो नसि जिघृक्षतः **॥ २०॥**
2-10-20 Śrīmad-Bhāgavatam » SB

Nāsike nirabhidyetāṁ dodhūyati nabhasvati I tatra vāyurgandha-vaho ghrāṇo nasi jighṛkṣataḥ II २० II 2-10-20 Śrīmad-Bhāgavatam » SB

Thereafter, when the supreme purusha desired to smell odours, the nostrils and respiration were generated, the nasal instrument and odours came into existence, and the controlling deity of air, carrying smell, also became manifested.

Next development by Atama is the nose. This needs air or Prana for life to sustain. With development of nose, PRANA got manifested or needed Oxygen. Thus, the Vayu having PRAN was manifested by Prakriti Purush.

After nose eyes appear in developing embryo. It is an instrument for vision. In a dead animal, organ of vision is there but dead body cannot see. That is fractioned Atama in body enlivens the living body. At the same time the supreme Atama manifests Aditya or Surya in cosmos. Without light the appreciation of vision is impossible. Hence light from Sun is essential.

After eyes Ears develop. This is sense organ of hearing. In cosmos manifests DISHA or direction. The direction can only be appreciated by the sense organ. Without which appreciation of direction is impossible. Balancing act of body depends upon ear. Aitareya Upanishad, a section of Rigveda, 1-1-4, 1-2-4. (Modern science recognizes Labyrinth and Vestibula apparatus in middle ear. It is responsible for balancing), clearly indicates that the sense of direction is in ear. The vestibular system is the sensory apparatus of the inner ear that helps the body maintain its postural equilibrium. One thing is clear that the positioning of self and the surrounding is only possible with instrument to recognize it. Similar statement is in Śrīmad-Bhāgavatam (Bhāgavata Purāṇa), Canto 2, The Cosmic Manifestation CHAPTER TEN, Mantra 6 to 32. Some relevant mantras are mentioned. See below:

बोध्यमानस्य ऋषिभिरात्मनस्तज्जिघृक्षत :। कर्णौ च निरभिद्येतां दिश :श्रोत्रं गुणग्रह :॥ २२ ॥ ŚB 2.10.22.

bodhyamānasya ṛṣibhir ātmanas taj jighṛkṣataḥ karṇau ca nirabhidyetāṁ diśaḥ śrotraṁ guṇa-grahaḥ ॥ २२ ॥ ŚB 2.10.22.

bodhyamānasya — desiring to understand; ṛṣibhiḥ — by the authorities; ātmanaḥ — of the Supreme Being; tat — that; jighṛkṣataḥ — when He desired to take up; karṇau — the ears; ca — also; nirabhidyetām — became manifested; diśaḥ — the direction or the god of air; śrotram — the power of hearing; guṇa-grahaḥ — and the objects of hearing.

There is clear mention of direction sense is present in ear.

"कर्णौ च निरभिद्येतां दिशः"

त्वक्चर्ममांसरुधिरमेदोमज्जास्थिधातव। : भूम्यप्तेजोमया सप्त :प्राणो व्योमाम्बुवायुभि॥ ३१॥ : ŚB 2.10.31.

tvak-charma-māṁsa-rudhira-medo-majjāsthi-dhātavaḥ bhūmyptejomayāḥ sapta prāṇo vyomāmbu-*vāyubhiḥ* ॥ 31 ॥ ŚB 2.10.31.

Thin layer on the skin, the skin itself, the flesh, blood, fat, marrow and bone, on earth, water and fire, whereas the life breath is produced by the sky, water and air.

Hair appears over skin and the vegetation manifests on the surface of the earth. Next sequence of order of development is Heart, Umbilicus, and Penis in developing embryo. How scientifically it is compared with Prakriti Purush is highly commendable. Doesn't it reveal that the knowledge of Embryology was existing even before the Rigveda?

Heart in Sanskrit is called HRIDAYA (हृदय). It is developed in 3rd month of gestation according to Rigveda SHAKAL branch, the Aitareya Aranyaka, of Aitareya Upanishad. But according to the Shrimad Bhagwat by Rishi Vyas, heart develops in 2nd month of pregnancy (See Song of Science

Shrimad Bhagwadgita, 2020 ed. Notion Press, India, Singapur, Malaysia). A baby's cardiovascular system begins developing during five weeks of pregnancy, or three weeks after conception. The heart starts to beat shortly afterward. But ultrasound study reveals beat by 5th month of pregnancy. It's not until around 17 to 20 weeks, when the four chambers of the heart have developed and can be detected on an ultrasound.

Even though the Rigveda is not an embryology work, but how accurate was the concept of heart development by Rishis of Veda is surprising. It must be prevalent in the society of the Sanskrit civilization. Hence set up as simile of Cosmos development. See below:

ŚB 2.10.30. निदिध्यासोरात्ममायां हृदयं निरभिद्यत । ततो मनश्चन्द्र इति सङ्कल्प॥ ३०काम एव च ॥ :

nididhyāsor ātma-māyāṁ hṛdayaṁ nirabhidyata tato manaś candra iti saṅkalpaḥ kāma eva ca II 30 II **ŚB 2.10.30.**

nididhyāsoḥ — being desirous to know; *ātma-māyām* own energy; *hṛdayam* —heart; *nirabhidyata* —manifested; *tataḥ* -thereafter; *manaḥ* themind *chandraḥ* controlling deity of the mind, the moon; *iti* — thus; *saṅkalpaḥ* — determination; *kāmaḥ* — desire; *eva* — as much as; *ca* — also.

The Heart, Mind, and Moon are interrelated is mentioned in the stanza. Outwardly it sounds absurd. But analyse it Scientifically and one finds appropriate. How?

Heart in Sanskrit is HRIDAYA (हृदय). On splitting the word HRI+ da+ ya. Hri is to receive+ Da is to give and ya is to control all. The control is from heart and brain. Here the mind is essentially needed. The moon mentioned in mantra is manifest in Prakriti Purush, by Param Aatma tattva. Moon controls mind. Common belief is that the mind is product of brain. But the living beings like plant, Amoeba have mind and the receiving and dispersal is controlled by heart. Every cell has heart in it which controls the receiving and dispersal of constituents and metabolic products.

With development of Umbilicus or Nabhi, the death manifests (नाभिर्निरभिद्यत नाभ्या अपानोऽपानान्मृत्युः).

The scientific analysis of this mantra is important. Nabhi is umbilicus, with this the APAN vayu (there are five types of main VAYU-Prana, Apana, Samana, Vyana, Udana, and other five Vayu are minor or subtle Pranas which are Naga, Kurma, Krukara, Devadutta, Dhananjaya. Each have different task and functions in the body. Details can be learned from Pantanjala Yog Sutra). Apana Vayu has definite task and function to perform. In summary it is excretory function like dispersal of urine, faeces, ejaculation, expulsion of foetus and so on. Apana Vayu the Death manifests. It's place in body is GUHYA PRADESH-Rectum, Anus, and Uterus etc. and it moves downwards. Umbilicus develops in 2nd month of pregnancy. (Umbilical cord development begins in the embryologic period around week 3 with the formation of the connecting stalk. By week 7, the umbilical cord has fully formed, composed of the connecting stalk, vitelline duct, and umbilical vessels surrounding the amniotic membrane).

What is the relation of Umbilicus to death?

After fertilization of Ovum the cell divides by it-self. And it has its own nourishment. It does not depend upon anything. All is automatic hence no death. But when placental cord and NABHI develop the food and nourishment is through mother's circulation. Thus grows the fetus in uterus. If this lifeline is severed or denied the death occurs. Hence Rishi has correctly defined the death and Nabhi – umbilicus relation.

What is Apana Vayu relation to death?

Apana Vayu helps digestion by degradation of food and pushes it downwards. "Pachan Shakti" or digestive power is due to Apana Vayu. This power reduces the food ingested to minute particles. This facilitates the absorption of vital food ingredients. In otherwards the as food the effect of Apana Vayu is on food body also or ANNAMAYA SHARIR. Hence it degrades body towards death. This develops after the manifestation of Umbilicus or Nabhi. Therefore, the Apana Vayu is related with death. In short, the Mantra by Rishi is correctly and scientifically composed. Modern science is still to advance in these medical facts which Rishis understood thousands of years before.

It is surprising to note that the death can be delayed or postponed by controlling this Apana Vayu. It has been described in Yoga and Pranayama books. If the direction of Apana Vayu from degradation to upgradation is achieved the death can be controlled is a statement available in Pranayama and Yoga Sutra.

After Nabhi – Umbilicus the SHISHNA (शीश्न) or Penis is manifested. Reta (ret) or seminal fluid with Sperms, is responsible for perpetuation of life. At the same time the Virat Purush manifested Aap which is for the perpetuation of life and life force or living beings. It is well known that the life is and exists due to Aap the liquid and water (शिश्नं निरभिद्यत शिश्नाद्रेतो रेतस आपः). Here the Aap or water is considered RETA. The development of the male external genitalia is typically complete by 14 weeks of development.

It is of interest to quote here the knowledge of Embryology was well utilised during Mahabharat period. The embryo cells or embryonic Stem Cells used to produce 101 children in an artificial Uterus (स्वनुगुपतेषु देशेषु – A self-operated artificial device). The technology used in creating human foetuses (See birth of Kauravas in Aadiparva of Bhagwatam by Rishi Vyas. Exploration of science in ShriMad Bhagwad Gita, Analytical study by dr. B. G. Matapurkar, Mahi Publication, 1st Ed. 2020, ISBN 978-93-89339-47-5.).

CHAPTER 11

NASADIYA SUKTA

(Rigveda Mandal 10, Sukta 129)

The Vedic rishis have created extremely wonderful hymn on earth, in the form of Ved. They have composed poetry on the subject of "not the non-existent" the Nasadiya - नासदीय. It is certain that the universe is a complex and mysterious entity. Humans have limited capacity to understand existence by available limited capacity of sense organs provided by nature – the Srishti. Vedic hymns challenge the reader to consider the limits of human knowledge and to contemplate the ultimate mysteries of existence. Nasadiya Sukta is not for the religion, Ishwar, or God. It is about only scientific way of understanding the origin of cosmos, existence, and creation.

The main Idea of this book is not to follow the writings of westerners or the written by Bharatiya following the writings of western scholars. On the contrary extract the hidden science in the Vedas. It has hardly any religious intentions of Rishis, in writings of original Veda. It is basically a scientific discussion and derivation.It deals with Creation, the origin of Universe and multiverse and cosmos. It is the **129th Sukta of the 10th mandala of the Rigveda** (10:129). It is concerned with cosmology and the origin of the cosmos -Srishti, Brahmana.

One does not understand that the intent of religion in Sanskrit literature from where, when and by whom the religious concept introduced? Why the education and learning were at the peak in India and available to population of entire world? Why were there multiple universities for international students' learning, especially for medical knowledge, with hostel, residential facility? Why India before invasion of looters and dacoit

- robbers with armed gang, was rich and prosperous with tremendous wealth and knowledge? They looted India on Gun point of everything wealth, Sanskrit knowledge, literature, technologies etc? Why Gurukul educational system became illegal? These are the questions worth pondering to really understand the hidden meaning in the Sanskrit Veda and Puranas. These questions need be answered by younger generation, before taking decision that the science is the gift of western civilization. The law of nature is whatever starts must end someday and not without reason.

10th Mandala of Rig Veda comprising **191 'suktas'** and 1754 mantras. The Rig Veda is the oldest of the 4 Vedas and considered as around **1500 - 2000 BC. (The time needs research and verification. It is beyond the purview of this book.)**. The time calculated differently by different scholars on the subject.

Before discussing the Rigveda, Nasadiya Sukta, Rigveda ideology about the Sukas needs a little pondering. Let us understand the modern science in relation to the VEDIC Science, for better exposure of the subject.

Nucleus (**नाभिक**) of an atom retains intrinsic nature and essential individuality of the substance. SEED can better explain this. BEEJ or seed is in a dormant phase of life and harbours knowledge about how to grow into the whole tree. Or waiting for the congenial environment. The MARUT or NILO or VAYU (not just an air but an element with speed) part of PANCHMAHABHUTAS which are the ingredients of the ATOM, of the substance, in modern science called as the ELECTRONS. If the electrons removed, the nucleus retains all individuality. If the nucleus removed, the atom ceases to exist. This has already been explained in Prayer mantra "Poorna madah - **ओम पूर्ण मदः पूर्ण मिदम्**". In other word, nucleus is the POORNATVA (**पूर्णत्व**) of the atom. Interference in ATOM, or tempered with, it creates or gives birth to a new one. This phenomenon is transmutation or disintegration (**विघटन**).

Evolution:

Every human realizes at some time or the other, that the life is lacking something. In persevering the happiness which is searching love, success, profit, peace etc. The goal of happiness is in gaining, success, fame, etc. Vedic literature mentions that Sorrow-pleasure, Success- failure, profit-loss, life – death, all are not within the reach of an individual. It is in the hands of destiny. The work and the attempts for achieving all these are only in one's reach. Who controls it? What governs the destiny? A phrase coined in Sanskrit literature is "BRAHMA BHAVATI SARATHI". This means the destiny guides the fate. (It is discussed in SONG of SCIENCE – SHRIMAD BHAGWAD GITA, Notion press, Chennai, Malaysia, Singapore, 10th chapter, 2022 edition, by Balkrishna Matapurkar). The worldly gain of any type is not an ultimate, or for gaining true happiness. If once success achieved, or gained, one longs for more or another. One is longing all the time. If not achieved is a cause of unhappiness. One remains dissatisfied. In sense satisfaction, true happiness is unperceivable by greed or sense satisfaction. The manifest world is as per yogic philosophy is not true. It is an illusion or MAYA. The world is a MAYA JAAL. It is not a reality. Manifest word itself signifies that the world has appeared on something else. Or super-imposed on something real or truth. What is that absolute truth?

Here lies the concept of evolution. It needs illumination, Prakash, Dnyan, Knowledge, or realization. This can be explained, by example of seeing prepared food on DINING table. Food is not reality, though it appears so. It evolved from seed, environment, growing vegetation, labour of the farmers, cooking etc. In dark environment you may pick up a snake presuming it as a piece of rope but on illumination, light, Prakash, Dnyan, knowledge one reveals it, as snake. This is MAYA or illusion.

If an individual is illumined, is realised, with knowledge, Prakash, Dynan, or realization, absolute truth gets exposed to the individual.

In an equivalent manner the spirit and matter can be realized. The manifest "Matter" of all types is superimposed on absolute truth. Hence it is an illusion or MAYA. How it is so? The MODERN Science is playing its role for realization. It is slowly progressing towards absolute reality and understanding and gaining knowledge of MATTER but slowly unravelling the energy or driving force behind all manifest matter. The fraction of energy from the penultimate energy source-TEJAPUNJAH, "(तेजः- पुन्जः)", force-point, or absolute truth. Science needs proof. SPIRIT or soul has no proof. Presence of soul or spirit needs realization.

YOGIS, RISHIS, and SAGES of Sanskrit Speaking Civilization well understood the process of realization. *In the phase of deep sleep, one is listless, without any state of consciousness, physical body is at rest. No activity of the body and mind. No thought teeming in mind. Mind is also at full resting attitude. Except the VITAL activity essential for life and life's processes to continue life, are active. On awakening one is fresh, active, rejuvenated, energetic, happy, joyous, and jubilant. In short, the body and mind during sleep was relaxed, inactive physically, and thoughtless or in a state of "NIRVICHARITA" a state of thoughtlessness. Sages and Rishis thought of achieving such a stage without sleep but in a state of full conscious stage, an awake state of body and mind. This thought propagated the meditation technique to achieve the still mind, even without any thought in mind – a stage of NIRVICHARITA. Full concentration inside and no external disturbance.* This can be compared with auto vehicle. A motorcar running without ups and down movements, without side wise movement, with uniform speed, without obstacles, achieves destination in record time, consuming less fuel, better mileage, and impressive economy. This is exactly the modus operando of meditation practice. Therefore, the RISHIS achieved knowledge about universe, Soul, etc. VIDYA and AVIDYA – developed PHYSICAL and SPIRITUAL wisdom. Vidya is spiritual and AVIDYA is physical science. Both are essential for life. Spiritual knowledge cannot benefit the ailments and physical comforts of body and Spiritual knowledge is for aim of life which is liberation or MOKSHA. Hence both are essential for life. See mantra below:

विद्यां च अविद्यां च यस्तव्दैदो भय ँ सह । अविद्याम् मृत्युंतीर्त्वा विद्याम् मृतंम् मश्नुते //**ईशोपनिषद्, मंत्र ११)**

vidyāṁ chāvidyāṁ cha yasta dvedobhayaṁ sahaavidyayā mṛituṁ tīrtvā vidyayāmṛtam aśnute II Ishavasyopnishad. 11.

Accordingly, the Sanskrit speaking civilization on realising above, developed both the sciences, and achieved success in all the branches of science, which is well known to the world.

The above understanding and the knowledge, the process of evolution analysed into the following stages:

Stage 1. Stage of Oneness. Before any manifestation everything was one and the only one. A source of unlimited energy - PARAM SHIVA. KAAL-CHAKRA non-existent at this site. Because the Param Shiv is self-manifest. It rotates around it-self. There is nothing for Param Shiv to rotate around. Hence Kaal dies here. Time exists due to rotation is well known.

Stage 2. Manifestation of Universe.

Stage 3. Living and non-moving i.e., CHAR-ACHAR manifestation. Mind or energy and Matter

Stage 4. Illusion or MAYA: All appears real. The camouflaging effect of nature.

Stage 5. Realization of illusion.

As per the "Nasadiys Sukta" of Rigveda, 10-129 1-7 statement, there was nothing before manifestation. But it mentions the existence of self-manifest point of source of energy or SWAYAMBHU SHIVA SHAKTI or TEJAH-PUNJAH. (यदासीत्तपंसस्तन्मंहिनाजांयतैकंम्॥३॥). It is with a HUMMING Sound likened to a slow and steady OHM sound. This is Ohm

Naad which is envisioned and elucidated by Sanskrit Speaking Civilization thousands of years back in Veda and Puranas. This energy or shakti FRACTIONS INTO RUDRA SHIV SHAKTI. In Shiva purana it is mentioned that (RUDRA's) calibration had been attempted by Vishnu and Brahma both but could not measure the dimensions. Rudra the SHIVA SHAKTI rotates around its origin. In Kaal CHAKRA the RUDRA manifests 11 times and unmanifest 11 times, before the ultimate annihilation. Various names of 11 Rudra are:

Mahan, mahatma, Gatiman, Bhishan, Bhayankar, Ritudhvaja, Urdhvakash, Pingalaksha, Ruchi, Shuchi and **Kalagni**. The last is main Rudra.

This SHAKTI is highly destructive. Because it has tremendous amount of heat, light, and high degree of radiations. Because of this heat, light, and radiation balls of GASSES emerge out. The balls of gasses thus generated rotate around the RUDRA because of the centrifugal force of Rudra.

The VISHNU are 14 in number. Or it manifests and unmanifest 14 times repeatedly. These are the PRIMORDIAL GASSES keep circulating around the RUDRA-SHIVA. In SANSKRIT literature these gasses are described as KSHIR-SAGAR. Or ocean of milk because of the whitish hue of the primordial gasses. On this Khirsagar, is depicted sleeping human figure-the VISHNU. Because, these gasses are in a dormant phase of manifestation, and evolution of the future universes. The description goes further that the VISHNU in sleeping position. Sleeps on the bed of coiled snake. Even today the snake is considered as the life protection symbol, In Medical Sciences the emblem bears the snake figure (Details are in Song of science Shrimad Bhagwadgita, Notion Press, 2020 ed. By B. Matapurkar). The human figure, Vishnu indicates the dormant phase of the manifestation of universe including elements, life, and the living beings. The symbolic representation of Vishnu on snake bed, sound scientific even by the standard of modern science. From this dormant phase, the of matter, life, and living beings manifest in due course of time. Again, the KAAL-

CHAKA is involved in the manifestation of Nature – the Prakriti. Therefore, KAAL CHAKRA provides proper, and congenial, environment is essential in all manifestations. It is like the fact that seeds do not sprout in a dry container for a long time but when proper temperature, moisture, fertile soil is provided the seeds start sprouting. Seeds are the dormant phase of future plant.

The point number 1 in evolution described above, Stage 1. Stage of Oneness. Before any manifestation everything is one and the only one. A source of unlimited energy, force, radiation, sonic waves etc. heat and light. Because it is rotating around it-self it produces slow humming sound waves. Which Sanskrit sages termed as OHM. It is self-manifest (**स्वयंभुवः**). If the laws of nature are uniformly applicable, then from where this self-manifestation is possible? Nothing manifests without cause. Possibility is the existing sea of primordial particles (**समुद्रार्णव**) got conglomerated into one central one-ness-the TEJAHPUNJAH. This primordial mixture as param-Shiv has the precursor of all future manifestations – like basic elements or PANCHMAHABHUTAS.

An interesting statement is in Devi Bhagwat Puran 12-10-1. It is about MANIDVEEPA, which is above Brahma Loka (Satya loka). As per Vedic knowledge there are Seven Swarga Loka. (These are discovered as the space travel advanced – Bhuh, Bhuvah, Swah, Maha, Janah, Tapaha, and Satyam). Brahma loka is satya loka as mentioned above). Above Satya loka is Manidveepa in ocean of minute atomic particles (**समुद्रार्णव**). In this Manidveepa is the residence of DEVI. See mantra below:

ब्रम्हलोकाद्उर्ध्वं भागे सर्वलोकोSस्ति यः श्रुतः । मणिव्दीपः स एवास्ति यत्र देवी विराजते II 12-10-1.

Shrimad devi Bhagwat mahapuran, part 2, No. 1898, page 57.

Bramhalokad Oordhva bhage sarva lokkosti yah shrutah I manidveepah sa evasti yatra devi virajate II 12-10-1

सर्वश्रृंगारवेषाढ्या सुकुमारांग वल्लरी ।सौंदर्यधारासर्वस्वा निर्व्याजकरूणामयी II 31 II

Sarva shringarveshadhya sukumarag vallari I soundaryadharasarvasva nirvyajakarunamayi II 31 II

निजसंलापमाधुर्यविनिर्भर्सितकच्छपी। कोटिकोटिरवीन्दूनां कान्तिं य बिभ्रती परा II 32 II

nija sanlaapmadhuryavinirbharsita kachhyapi I koti koti ra vinduna kanti ya bibhrati para II 32 II

नानासखीभिर्दासीभिस्तथा देवांगनादिभिः ।सर्वाभिर्देवताभिस्तुसमन्तात्परिवेष्टिता **II 33 II**

nana sakhi bhirdaasi bhistatha devaganadibhih I sarvabhirdevatabhistusamantatpri veshtata II 33 II

Shrimad devi Bhagwat mahapuran, part 2, No. 1898, page 848.

या यास्तु देवतास्त्र प्रतिब्रम्हाण्डवर्तिनाम् II 52 II

ya yastu devatastra prati brmhanda vartinaam II 52 II

समष्टयः स्थितास्तुसेवन्ते जगदीश्वरम् । सप्तकोटिमहामंत्रा मूर्तिमंन्त उपासते II 53 II

samashtayah sthitastusevante jagadeeshvaram I Saptakoti mahamahamantra moortumanta oopasate II 53 II

महाविद्याश्च सकलाः साम्यावस्थात्मिकां शिवाम् । कारणब्रम्हरूपां तां मयाशबलविग्रहाम् II 54 II

Mahavidyashcya sakalah samyavasthatmika Shivam I karana brahmarupa tam mashbalvigraham II 54 II

Shrimad devi Bhagwat mahapuran, part 2, No. 1898, page 849.

The religious meaning: Abode of Devi is known in Manidveep which is Sarva lok. Devi is well dressed and well-groomed and Devi has tender body, and is beautiful, and has soft sweet voice, is sincere, naïve, honest for everything without any bias to anything. All friends and service persons, Devatas are around Devi. This is in all multiverses (**प्रतिब्रम्हाण्ड**)of cosmos. All carryout the wishes of super truth (Jagdeeshvara). All surrounding persons serve the Maha Devi.

Scientific meaning: Manidveep is situated beyond the Satya loka or Brahma loka. As depicted in figure below, why a woman be in abode of Manidveep which is not congenial to life like earth? Everything gets straightened if one considers Devi as SHAKTI or energy. Which is surrounded by Rays, Waves, innumerable forms of radiations etc. and many unknown elements to human mind yet. Need exploration. This energy has become soft and providing congenial environment for manifest nature so that to enable manifestation of nature. This is the work of Super God or super energy or Absolute truth. This energy-Devi serves the purpose of Param Shiva – the Absolute Truth (कारणब्रम्हरूपां).

Diagrammatic representation of the mantra above (artists view).

In Manidveep the Devi in the center is surrounded by friends, Devtas, Brahma, Vishnu, Mahesh as per the hymn. This is symbolic for common understanding. It is obscure, enigmatic representation of scientific facts. Friends are supportive rays, waves, radiations, and still unknown elements rays etc. to human mind, from celestial bodies of cosmos and to carry out the aims and objectives of Jagadishwara.- the absolute truth. Devatas are supernatural elements like Vayu, Primordial form of Panchmahabhutas. Brahma – Vishnu- Mahesh and their presence for future manifestation of

Nature – the Prakriti. The Manidveep is above the Brahma loka or Satya loka. At this spot of Manidveep, the human form presence is just impossible. Obviously the Devi here is in the form Energy or Shakti which is feminine hence Devi has been depicted. This evolution is in all the Brahmandas for the future formation of maniest uni and Multi verss in developing Cosmos. This is the depiction of continuous evolution process in Brahmanda. **SPIRIT has become MATTER by crystallization. Self-limitation, or exclusive concentration or involution, or all. Exact scientific knowledge is still unknown till to date. The spirit undergoes mutation as per modern science language. That is SPIRIT or energy, terminates into MATTER. Similar is the return journey for annihilation of all manifestation. The evolution and demolition are a repeated process as expressed in GITA (which is a summary of VEDA). The world repeatedly manifests and unmanifest in a periodic cyclic manner. Such scientific explanations are available in the VEDA (See details in Kaal-Chakra).**

आब्रह्मभुवनात्, लोकाः, पुनरावर्तिनः, अर्जुन, माम्, उपेत्य, तु, कौन्तेय, पुनर्जन्म, न, विद्यते ।।16।। Shrimad Bhagwad Gita 8-16.

Aabramha bhvan lokah punar avartinah Arjuna mam oopetya tu kounteya punarjanma na vidyate II 16 II Chapter 8.

This exactly is the Vedic statement and that is how the universe or multiverse are manifest and unmanifest.

The other statement is the manifest evidence of spiritual energy is SUN. Manifest shape is provided by SUN, MITRA, VARUNA, UDAN (See Rigved sutra 1-115-5: -

तन मित्रस्य वरुणस्याभिचक्षे सूर्यो रूपं कर्णुते दयोरुपस्थे |अनन्तमन्यद रुशदस्य पाजः कर्ष्णमन्यद धरितःसंभरन्ति| अद्या देवा उदिता सूर्यस्य निरंहसः पिप्रता नरवद्यात |तन नो || 5 || Rigveda. 1-115-5 tan mitrasya varuṇasyābhicakṣe sūryo rūpaṁ kṛṇute dyor upasthe | anantam anyad ruśad asya pājaḥ kṛṣṇam anyad dharitaḥ sam bharanti Adya deva oodita sooryasya niramhasah piprata narvadyat tana no II 5 II Rigveda. 1-115-5

Manifestoing or enlightening the universe the SUN and VARUN created SAVITA in SWARG or DUELOK or Abode - **द्यु लोक**. The TEJ, prosperity, and wealth all are due to this. For the welfare of all living beings SAVITA DEVTA, manifest in Swarga loka with effect from SUN, MITRA. The cosmic radiation, electromagnetic waves, sound waves from cosmos are responsible for manifestation of nature.

Modern science has accepted that the matter is energy. (See Song of science Shrimad Bhagwad Gita, Notion Press. Chennai, Singapore, Malaysia. 2022 by B. Matapurkar).

विश्र्वा रूपाणि प्रति मुञ्चंते कविः प्रासावीद भद्रं व्दिपदे चतुष्पदे । विं नाक मख्यत् सविता वरेण्योSनु प्रयाणमुषसो विराजति II 2 II Rigveda 5- 83-2.

Diagram to show Manifastation of Universe

(Kaal Chakra exists here. Artists' presentation)

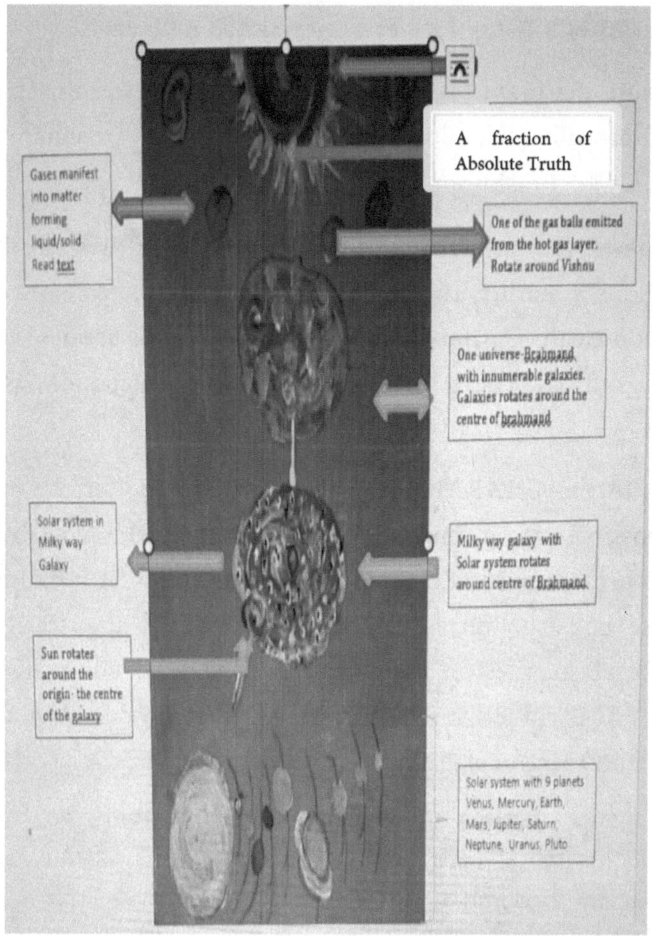

The SUN is the greatest source of JYOTI - TEJ, main and chief source of energy, light, and heat. Sun is the PRAN for all living beings. More clarification is in Prashnopnishad.

स एष वैश्वानरो विश्वरूपः प्राणोऽग्निरुदयते ।तदेतदृचाऽभ्युक्तम् ॥१.७॥
Prashnopnishad 1 - 7th Hymn.

Sa eva veishvanaro vishvarupah pranognirudayate I tadeta dracha bhyuktam Prashnopnishad 1 - 8th Hymn.

विश्वरूपं हरिणं जातवेदसंपरायणं ज्योतिरेकं तपन्तम् । सहस्त्ररश्मिः शतधा वर्तमानः प्राणः प्रजानामुदयत्येष सूर्यः ॥ १.८॥ Prashnopnishad 8th Hym.

Vishvarupam harinam jatavedsamprayanam jyotirekam tapantam I sahastra Rashmih shatadha artamanah pranah prajanamudayatyesh sootyah II ॥ १ ॥८. Prashnopnishad 8th Hym.

Sun manifests the Savita in Dueu (द्युलोक) lok, responsible for all manifestations in nature. It is source of energy, light, heat, and Prana -प्राण for all life on earth. Cosmos is grouped into lokas or abodes where life or living beings' dwell. There are 7 swarg kok, and 7 Patal lok, as per Vedic knowledge.

According to the CHARAK SAMHITA, without potter the earthenware pot is impossible even if mud, stick, and potter wheel is available. Building material is present but the technical expert to build the building is absent then house construction is impossible. Similarly, the spirit energy is essential for all manifest in the nature. KABANDHI, son of KATYAYAN questions YAMA in PRASHNOPNISHAD that how PRAJA manifest in nature. He the Yama explains:

तस्मै स होवाच प्रजाकामो वै प्रजापतिः स तपोस्तप्यत स तपस्तप्त्वा स मिथुनमुत्पादयते । रयिं च प्राणं चेत्येतौ मे बहुधा प्रजाः करिष्येत इति **॥1-4 ॥ Prashnopnishad 1- Hymn 4.**

Tasmei sa hovacha prajakamo vei prajapatih sa tapostapyat sa tapastatva sa mithunamutpadayate I rayim cha pranam chetyetou me bahudha prajah karishyet iti II1-4 II Prashnopnishad 1- Hymn 4.

The Brahma -lord of creatures wanted to manifest Prajah. He performed penance. The hard work and penance – Yadnya Karma, he could manifest Matter – RAYI रयी, and spirit energy – the Prana - प्राणं, with the hope that they together must produce creatures for him.

आदित्यो ह वै प्राणो रयिरेव चंन्द्रमा रयिर्वा एतत्सर्वं यन्मूंत चामूर्त च तस्मान्मूर्तिरेव रयिः II 1.5 II **Prashnopnishad 1- Hymn 5.**

Adityo ha vei prano rayireva chandrama rayirva etatsarvam yanmurta chamurta cha tasmanmoortireva rayih II 1.5 II Prashnopnishad 1- Hymn 5.

The Aaditya – Sun is Prana, Rayi is Moon – **चन्द्रमा**. Scientifically speaking the energy – Pran Shakti to all living beings is from Sun. Hence Sun is Pran. How the Moon is Rayi? One knows that the moon has no light of its own. It is due to Sun light. Or Moon has no Tej therefore moon is matter or Rayi. One can say the Sun is Pran of moon. Such explanation is in Mantra 5 of Prashnopnishad. In fact, in all manifest cosmos matter or Rayi exists. Hence Mantra explains both Murt **मूर्त**, and Amurt **अमूर्त** In other words, whatever is manifest is Rayi. The scientific explanation of mantra 5 is as per the modern science.

It will be easy to understand NASADIYA SUKTA with above background knowledge. It is basically a chronology of creation by the creator. Following is the mantra presentation in Rigveda in Sanskrit: -

नासदासीन्नो सदासीत्तदानीं नासीद्रजो नो व्योमा परो यत् । किमावरीवः कुह

कस्य शर्मन्नम्भः किमासीद्गहनं गभीरम् ॥ १॥

न मृत्युरासीदमृतं न तर्हि न रात्र्या अह्न आसीत्प्रकेतः ।आनीदवातं स्वधया तदेकं तस्माद्धान्यन्न परः किं चनास ॥ २॥

तम आसीत्तमसा गूळ्हमग्रेऽप्रकेतं सलिलं सर्वमा इदम् ।

तुच्छयेनाभ्वपिहितं यदासीत्तपसस्तन्महिनाजायतैकम् ॥ ३॥

कामस्तदग्रे समवर्तताधि मनसो रेतः प्रथमं यदासीत् ।

सतो बन्धुमसति निरविन्दन्हृदि प्रतीष्या कवयो मनीषा ॥ ४॥

तिरश्चीनो विततो रश्मिरेषामधः स्विदासी३दुपरि स्विदासी३त् ।

रेतोधा आसन्महिमान आसन्स्वधा अवस्तात्प्रयतिः परस्तात् ॥ ५॥

को अद्धा वेद क इह प्र वोचत्कुत आजाता कुत इयं विसृष्टिः ।

अर्वाग्देवा अस्य विसर्जनेनाथा को वेद यत आबभूव ॥ ६॥

इयं विसृष्टिर्यत आबभूव यदि वा दधे यदि वा न ।

यो अस्याध्यक्षः परमे व्योमन्सो अङ्ग वेद यदि वा न वेद ॥ ७॥

If Rigveda is about religion, then why it deals with Origin of nature and trying to understand the origin of manifest worlds. The inquisitive understanding seems to be to spread the knowledge. A deep thinker always questions what is all this where we are existing and why? "Nasadiya Sukta" is all about such revelation.

In the beginning of 10th Mandal Sukta 190, mantra 1,2,& 3

ऋतं च सत्यं चाभीध्दात्तपसोऽध्य जायत ।ततो रात्र्य जायत ततः समुद्रो अर्णवः II 1 II Rigved. 10-190-1

ṛtaṁ ca satyaṁ cābhīddhāt tapasodhya jāyata | tato rātry ajāyata tataḥ samudro arṇavaḥ || Rigved. 10-190-1

RITA – **ऋत,** is truth which is Nature's basic law. It is mind's inner desire. Workforce which manifested into nature, it is repeated in every KALP (Kalp is the time of cosmic cycle-from origin to annihilation of manifest nature). In other word the SUPER SOUL with hard work manifested the existence of nature and its ingredients- days, Night, oceans. (**प्रकृति तथा सृष्टि**). The super soul is the source for laws of nature, laws of activities of nature, manifest universe or multiverse, day-night (**अहोरात्र**), and SAMUDRA-oceans, etc.

समुद्रादर्णवादधि संवत्सरो अजायत । अहोरात्राणि विदधव्दिश्वस्य मिषतो वशी II2II Rigved. 10-190-2.

samudrād arṇavād adhi saṁvatsaro ajāyata | ahorātrāṇi vidadhad viśhvasya miṣhato vaśhī **II2II Rigved. 10-190-2.**

This is the truth and untruth in first mantra:

"Then, there was neither existence, nor non-existence. It contemplates that, why, and through what the nature got manifested or came into being. There is no definite answer, but only a question mark. At the end in 7th mantra, there is astonishing statement that, whether one can ever know the origins of the universe. This is in fact an absolute truth.

Origin of universe or manifestation of nature is a great cosmic mystery has been expressed by VEDA. Even the so understood creator really knows it or not is a surprizing note in the Sukta: अङ्ग वेद यदि वा न वेद II 7 II.

The following is the analysis of Nasadiya Sukta:

नासदासीन्नो सदासीत्तदानीं नासीद्रजो नो मा परो यत् । किमावरीवः कुह कस्य शर्मन्नम्भः किमासीद्गहनं गभीरम् ॥ १ ॥ Rigved. 10-129-1

nāsad āsīn no sad āsīt tadānīṁ nāsīd rajo no vyomā paro yat | kim āvarīvaḥ kuha kasya śarmann ambhaḥ kim āsīd gahanaṁ gabhīram II 1 II **Rigved. 10-129-1**

There was nothing before the manifestation of universe. The beginning was from zero. No space, wind, but only darkness existed. Why, that plasma, all pervading, deep and profound?

Modern scientific thought developed that the universe developed with a BIG BANG. It expanded from a tiny, superdense, and extremely hot point in space. This idea has often said to have originated in 1929 Edwin Hubble discovery of cosmic expansion. Before that Einstein assumed the universe as static. (Page 242, The Radius of Space Began at Zero, (Georges Lemaitre-1894-1966). The SCIENCE BOOK-Big ideas simply explained. DK-Penguin Random HOUSE.www.dk.com).

Scientific definitions for expanding universe theory. According to the theory, **galaxies are not moving through space but rather with space as it expands**. The expansion of the universe implies that all the matter of the universe was once concentrated in one place, which lends support to the big bang theory.

If Rigveda is the oldest literature available in the world, author feels that a due credit be given by all the scholars. Unfortunately, western science literature the Rigveda is categorically missing! It is the responsibility of all of us to highlight the fact that Veda have arrived at this conclusion thousands of years back.

In subsequent mantra 2, Veda states that,

न मृत्युरासीदमृतं न तर्हि न रात्र्या अह्न आसीत्प्रकेतः ।आनीदवातं स्वधया तदेकं तस्माद्धान्यन्न परः किं चनास II 2 II Rigved. 10-129-2

na mṛtyur āsīd amṛtaṁ na tarhi na rātryā ahna āsīt praketaḥ | ānīd avātaṁ svadhayā tad ekaṁ tasmād dhānyan na paraḥ kiṁ canāsa II 2 II **Rigved. 10-129-2.**

There was no death or immortality (न मृत्युरासीदमृतं). No earth no life. No immortals like in heaven. No day or night. But for that breathless one breathing on its own. Only eternal existed.

तम आसीत्तमसा गूळ्हमग्रेऽप्रकेतं सलिलं सर्वमा इदम् । तुच्छ्येनाभ्वपिहितं यदासीत्तपसस्तन्महिनाजायतैकम् II 3 II Rigved. 10-129-3.

tama āsīt tamasā gūlham agre praketaṁ salilaṁ sarvam ā idam | tucchyenābhv apihitaṁ yad āsīt tapasas tan mahinājāyataikam II 3 II Rigved. 10-129-3

In the beginning only darkness (आसीत्तमसा) was thereernal element - (PADARTH dravya) existed without any form.

कामस्तदग्रे समवर्तताधि मनसो रेतः प्रथमं यदासीत् । सतो बन्धुमसति निरविन्दन्हृदि प्रतीष्या कवयो मनीषा ॥ ४॥ Rigved. 10-129-4 kāmas tad agre sam avartatādhi manaso retaḥ prathamaṁ yad āsīt | sato bandhum asati nir avindan hṛdi pratīṣyā kavayo manīṣā II 4 II Rigved. 10-129-4

Creator of universe thought of establishing universe, from unmanifest to manifest world. In the cosmic mind, all pervading desire, the primal seed made its first appearance and the wise men, seeking deep in their heart Could see the link between 'that is' and 'that is not'.

तिरश्चीनो विततो रश्मिरेषामधः स्विदासीउदुपरि स्विदासीउत् । रेतोधा आसन्महिमानं आसन्स्वधा अवस्तात्प्रयतिः परस्तात् ॥ ५॥ Rigved. 10-129-5.

tiraścīno vitato raśmir eṣām adhaḥ svid āsī3d upari svid āsī3t | retodhā āsan mahimāna āsan svadhā avastāt prayatiḥ parastāt II 5 II Rigved. 10-129-5.

With such thought, **rays emerged, and energy established,** due to which using the nature/element, creation started. Reins of the link, a grid of crisscross lines, Holds all the seeds and mighty forces, Microcosmic forces within and macro forces out above. These forces are the rays and the waves (electromagnetic, sound waves, and energy forces, and many still unknown facts).

को अद्धा वेद क इह प्र वोचत्कुत आजाता कुत इयं विसृष्टिः । अर्वाग्देवा अस्य विसर्जनेनाथा को वेद यत आबभूव II 6 II Rigved. 10-129-6

ko addhā veda ka iha pra vocat kuta ājātā kuta iyaṁ visṛṣṭiḥ | arvāg devā asya visarjanenāthā ko veda yata ābabhūva II 6 II Rigved. 10-129-6.

No one can say when and how the world manifested. Because the scientists and knowledge-able came into existence after that. Before the manifest universe what it was and what was there and what is the cause of creation, is an all enigmatic?

इयं विसृष्टिर्यत आबभूव यदि वा दधे यदि वा न । यो अस्याध्यक्षः परमे व्योमन्सो अङ्ग वेद यदि वा न वेद II 7 II Rigved. 10-129-7.

iyaṁ visṛṣṭir yata ābabhūva yadi vā dadhe yadi vā na | yo asyādhyakṣaḥ parame vyoman so aṅga veda yadi vā na veda II 7 II Rigved. 10-129-7

What is the source of creation, who is responsible for creation, who is the concept propagator, observer, surveyor of this creation established in space or in heaven, or elsewhere? It is the responsibility of the humans you may call them RISHI, SAGES, of Sanskrit civilization, scientists of modern times of the universe!!! That one, out of which the creation came keeps it secret. But kept hidden due to camouflaging effect of the NATURE. One must unfold the mystery. It is kept secret for us to be unravelled by some of us. Secret May hold the reins or not, perceiving, all from above, 'That' one alone Knows the beginning - may not know too. Or it all is just a nature's process of manifestation.

CREATION OF NATURE:

Creation of Nature and the Living beings are interrelated. As mentioned above the 'Nasadiya Sukta' deals with 'Brahmotpatti' (Manifestation of Nature). Shrimad Bhagwat Gita Rishi Vyas describes same thing but in a different way.

महर्षय :सप्त पूर्वे चत्वारो मनवस्तथा | मद्भावा मानसा जाता येषां लोक इमा :प्रजा :|| 6 || Gita 10-6.

maharṣhayaḥ sapta pūrve chatvāro manavas tathā I mad-bhāvā mānasā jātā yeṣhāṁ loka imāḥ prajāḥ II gita 10-6

Above stanza (underlined word) speaks that: all living beings are developed "from mind of Shri Krishna" (Madbhava manasa jata). This sounds unscientific. How can mind manifest nature? Author investigated the Sanskrit literature elsewhere. It was written with scientific details in UPANISHAD. Author has tried to explain this statement that - "population developed from the MIND of Super soul (Here in Gita the Lord Shri Krishna)", and the details are from TAITTARIYOPNISHAD (see explanation later in this chapter). After understanding the facts of manifestation of population in Upnishad the MIND factor will be discussed. The discussion is long hence reader must have patience to understand it. In SHIKSHVALLI.of Upanishad ANUWAK 3, stanza 1 and 2, this knowledge is in five different groups.

संहितोपासनम् I सह नौ यशः । सह नौ ब्रह्मवर्चसम् । Teittariya Upanishad. Shikshavalli. 3-1.

In this stanza there is conversation between student and teacher. Students appeal for combined attempt – teacher and students, for understanding secret life on earth. Its birth and death. Glued words and sentences have five elements पञ्चस्वधिकरणेषु in the form of Mahasamhita.

अधिलोकमधिज्यौतिषमधिविद्यमधिप्रजमध्यात्मम् । ता महास.हिता इत्याचक्षते..|

This teaching is based on five perceptible objects: a) Universe, b) Luminaries, c) Learning, d) Progeny, e) Body. These they call 'the great combinations (or blending)'.

The complete mantra is below:

संहितोपासनम् । सह नौ यशः । सह नौ ब्रह्मवर्चसम् । अथातः स.हिताया उपनिषदम् व्याख्यास्यामः । पञ्चस्वधिकरणेषु । अधिलोकमधिज्यौतिषमधिविद्यमधिप्रजमध्यात्मम् । ता महास.हिता इत्याचक्षते । Taittariya Upanishad Shikshavalli, Anuwak 3, mantra 1-2.

Adhilokam adhijyotisham adhividyam adhiprajam adhyatmam I ta mahasamhita ityachakshate I Taittariya Upanishad Shikshavalli, Anuwak 3, mantra 1-2.

Mantra of Samhita in split form, one by one all 5 will be discussed.

1. ADHILOK – about worlds or universe.

2. ADHIJYOTISH – about PRAKAASH, Light or Tej.

3. ADHIVIDYAM – about Knowledge – VIDYA.

4. ADHIPRAJAM – about Population – PRAJA.

5. ADHYATM – about self or ATMA or Soul – the AATMA. All this makes MAHASAMHITA. Abstracts are selected.

The teachings concerning the universe is this: The earth is the prior form, the heaven (firmament) is the posterior form. Atmosphere is the junction. Air is the junction. Thus, one should meditate upon the Universe.

The above statement is of Aadi Shankaracharya. If one keeps it in background and think about the hidden science in the above stanza, it can be like this: -

(For details - See Song of Science Shrimad Bhagwad Gita, page 237, 1st Edition 2020, Notion Press. Chennai, Malaysia, Singhapour).and mentioned below.

In above mantra the MAHASAMHITA is explained. The knowledge is explained in 5 different sections. Mahasamhita is highly scientific but enigmatic, and symbolic. The following analysis will help in solving enigmatic presentation. On splitting the underlined part of the Mantra:

1. ADHILOK – about worlds or universe.

अथाधिलोकम् । पृथिवी पूर्वरूपम् । द्यौरुत्तररूपम् । आकाशः सन्धिः वायुः सन्धानम् । इत्यधिलोकम् ॥ १ ॥

Athadhilokam I pruthivi purva lokam I dyouruttarrupam I aakashah sandhihi I vayuh sandhanam I ityadhilokam II 1 II

The scientific detailed thinking is: -

Earth or PRITHVI is dwelling place for earthlings. Hence is 'purva lok' i.e., close or near to humans. DYUE – द्यु लोक, or SWARG lok, (A region between earth and below the north star), is away from earth hence UTTAR RUPA. Both purva + uttar are joined by Space or AKAASH. The VAYU or AIR collimates both i.e., sandhanam-संधानम्. This is end of Adhilok. The science can be corroborated here. The atmosphere around earth is 1000 Km. Out of this 15 Km is air. The 200 Km has light or Prakash. The rest is dark or has no light. The lighted space is swarg or DYUE LOK – द्युलोकं.

Second part of MAHASAMHITA: Aadhijyotisham:

अथाधिजौतिषम् । अग्निः पूर्वरूपम् ।आदित्य उत्तररूपम्। आपः सन्धिः ।वैद्युतः सन्धानम् । इत्यधिज्यौतिषम् II २॥

Athadijyotisham I Agnih poorva rupam I Aaditya uttar rupam I Aapah sandhih I vidyutah sandhanam I ityadhijyotisham II 2 II

What SHANKARBHASHYA says:

Now concerning the luminaries or meditations upon fire. Fire is the prior form; the sun is the posterior form. Water is the intermediate form and lightning is the connection. That one should meditate upon light.

The scientific explanation can be: -

Adi-JYOTI-sham = primordial light or JYOTI or Prakash or DNYAN – knowledge. Agni is on earth i.e., closer to humans. Hence "purva roopam". (In Rigved Agni is SUN = which radiates heat and light). The SUN is in antariksha, or space. - akash, away from humans, hence uttar roopam. AAPAH आपः - or liquid element, Joins the two- Agni and Sun. How this is possible? On pondering on this it is obscure presentation of science in Sanskrit literature. To unravel the hidden science, one must ponder on the following explanation. The SUN energy is essential for Vegetation on earth. Water provides energy and nutrition, or water is a medium for absorption of nutrition from soil. Hydroponics vegetation can grow only in water, without soil, hence the electric energy present in water which energises the water for plant nutrition. Sun rays help formation of CHLOROPHIL in leaves. In short, Vegetation or wood collects energy from SUN, the wood is a storehouse or Sun energy. Or solar energy is in the wood indirectly. Therefore, the fire is in the wood. This becomes CRUDE oil under earth in special environment. Again, a source of fuel energy. Now come back to Sanskrit Mantra- water is a joining element or Aapah – Aap:, is basic element out of 5 PANCHMAHABHUTAS, is a joining force between Agni on earth and Sun in ANTARIKSHA.

The electricity collimates both. The electricity is responsible for fire on earth. One knows that the electricity fell on earth to ignite fire in dried woods. To analyse it further, the Sun evaporates the water of oceans. The steam from oceans become clouds in space or Aakash. There is electricity in clouds responsible for lightening during rainy season. In short, the electricity is indirectly from the Sun. Now it is very clear that the electricity collimates Agni and the Sun.

The scientific obscurity needs to be unfolded by pondering on the Mantra of Sanskrit literature. The rishis and sages were highly scientific and presented science in an obscure manner. They were very clear scientifically and understanding was too, very clear to the contemporary population. Obviously, it is obscure to modern population and the modern scientists.

3. ADHIVIDYAM – about Knowledge – VIDYA. Next in Mahasamhita is: -

अथाधिविद्यम् । आचार्यः पूर्वरूपम् । अन्तेवास्युत्तररूपम् । विद्या सन्धिः । प्रवचनꣳसन्धानम् । इत्यधिविद्यम् ॥

Athadividyam I Aacharyah poorva rupam I Antevasyuttar rupam I vidya sandhih I pravachana sandhanam I ityadhi vidyam I

Now concerning knowledge: The teacher is the prior form, the taught subject is the posterior form, learning is the intermediate form, and the instruction is the means of joining them – thus one should meditate on learning.

Aadhividyam – **आधिविद्यम्** - Teacher is poorva roopam i.e. at the root level in imparting knowledge. Disciple is at the receiving end, so it is UTTAR ROOPAM or at a distance. Student takes time to learn. The topic or subject VIDYA – **विद्या**, of teaching is uniting the two. It is SANDHI – **संधीः**. The oration or lecture or PRAVACHAN -**प्रवचन**, is sandhanam - **संधानम्** i.e. collimate the two - Teacher and the student. End of VIDYAM **इत्याधिविद्यमं्**

4. ADHIPRAJAM – about Population – PRAJA.

अथाधिप्रजम् । माता पूर्वरूपम् । पितोत्तररूपम् । प्रजा सन्धिः ।प्रजनन >\सन्धानम् ।

इत्यधिप्रजम् ॥ ३॥

Athadi prajam I mata poorva rupam I pitottar rupam I praja sandhih I prajanan sandhanam I ityadhi prajam I

Now concerning Progeny: Mother is the prior form, father is the posterior form, progeny is the junction and procreation is the connection – thus one should meditate upon progeny.

Regarding living beings' mother is near to all prajah प्रजाः and father is at distance, even father may be unknown. Hence mother is purva rupa and Father is uttar rupa. The progeny unites the father and mother both. Hence progeny is SANDHI संन्धिः, Reproduction – prajanan-प्रजनन, obviously collimates the two. This is the law of nature and is followed by all prajah – the population.

5. ADHYATM – about self or ATMA or Soul – the AATMA. All this makes MAHASAMHITA. Abstracts are selected.

अथाध्यात्मम्। अधराहनुः पूर्वरूपम् । उत्तराहनूत्तररूपम् । वाक्सन्धिः । जिह्वासन्धानम् । इत्यध्यात्मम् । इतीमामहासहिताः९ । य एवमेता महासहिता व्याख्याता वेद । सन्धीयतेप्रजयापशुभिः। ब्रह्मवर्चसेनान्नाद्येन सुवर्ग्येण लोकेन॥४॥ इति तृतीयोऽनुवाकः ॥

Athadhyatmam I adhara hanuh poorva rupam I Uttara hanuttar rupam I vak sandhih I jivhasandhanam I ityadhyatmam I

Iti maha samhitah I ya eva meta mahasamhita vyakhyata ved I sandhiyate prajaya pashbhih I bramhavarchasennanadyen suvargyen lokena II 4 II iti tritiyonuvakah II

What follows is concerning the individual or the body. The lower jaw is the prior form, the upper jaw the posterior form, speech is the conjunction, the tongue the means of union – thus one should meditate upon oneself.

Lower jaw is under control of the person. Hence is close and near. The upper jaw is not under control. Hence is away. Voice connects the two. Tongue regulates or collimates the two.

The scientific overall view, about the above statement in above stanzas are important in the description of chronology of manifestation of universe, light, knowledge, population, and the supreme SOUL. Senses and sense organs are provided to living beings, for survival and maintenance of life of all living beings. But super-soul is beyond all this. No sense is perfect and capable of knowing the super-self. It can only be understood or felt at heart.

महर्षय :सप्त पूर्वे चत्वारो मनवस्तथा | मद्भावा मानसा जाता येषां लोक इमा :प्रजा :|| 6|| Gita 10-6.

Maharshayah sapta poorve chatvaro manavasttha I madbhava mansa jata yesham lok imah prajah II 6 II Gita 10-6

To explain in other words, the development of universe or manifestation of Nature, is the result of mindset of the super soul, is the decision for the effective interactions of Panch-maha-bhuta पंच महा भूत or 5 basic elements of the nature. Read below mentioned Mantra of Ishavasyopnishad:

हिरण्मयेन पात्रेण सत्यस्यापिहितं मुखम् । तत्त्वं पूषन्नपावृणु सत्यधर्माय दृष्टये ॥ १५ ॥ Ishavasyopnishad.

Truth is always kept hidden by covering it with golden cover. For example, any crime or 'untruth' undertaken by a rich and influential person remains hidden due to his wealth and prestige in the society. Uninfluential and poor person has no say. But the basic truth must be uncovered.

How the CREATION or manifestation is possible? Thoughtful efforts of RISHIS of Sanskrit Speaking Civilization, had uncovered the golden lid. The PRIMORDIAL gasses get precipitated or get crystallised by interactive processes between them. The gasses can precipitate into matter, sounds imaginative only. But it is true as the modern science discovered that HYDROGEN GAS when mixes or burns in OXYGEN gas, in a definitive temperature, it becomes liquid water or Aap. Similarly primordial gasses' interaction with each other, and at a definitive temperature and time, is water, AAP or liquid matter got precipitated or manifested in NATURE. Another example for conversion of gasses to liquids or AAP (one of the basic elements of PANCHMAHABHUT) is MERCURY. (Mercury is a liquid silver or quicksilver. Formula is Hg. It is considered as metal. It has a low melting point. It is mostly composed of Oxygen, Hydrogen, Helium, Sodium and Potassium. At room temperature Mercury can evaporate into invisible, odourless, toxic vapour. On heating it is converted to colourless, odourless GAS. In short, the mercury is a precipitation from gas). It is liquid at room temperature. Liquid or AAP "in mercury form" is from gasses and evaporates back to vapours or gasses. In other word gasses of primordial origin converts into or manifest into elements of nature. Later, at the time of annihilation or PRALAYA KAAL, gets converted back into gas. This is how, the manifest nature is generated and annihilated. Such law is uniformly applicable in NATURE or PRAKRITI. Here the time factor is involved too. Hence KAAL-CHAKRA is essential to be unfolded.

According to Jain understanding the matter is made up of SKANDHA (Molecule), Skandhadesh (Atom), Skandhapradesh (Ionised Atom), parmanu (elementary particles – e.g., Electron, Proton), Such Parmanus are in a state of motion. State of the matter depends upon Division, Union, or both (Read SARVARTH SIDDHI from JAIN literature). The negatively charged are Electron. Positively charged are Positrons, and having no charge are Neutrons.

Matter exists in the form of individual elementary particles. Properties of particles may unite, separate or both at the same time depending upon the qualities of particles.

स्निग्ध रुक्षत्वादबन्ध II33II Chapter 5, Tattvarthdhigama Sutra.

Positive elementary particles combine with other similar particles having different energy. Negative with negatively charged particles. Positive particles can combine with negatively charged particles and vice versa. Thus, summarily the molecules can be formed by Division –

भेद. **or** भेदादणु:, भेदात अणुरूत्पाद्यते **II27II. Union** - संघात. अणवः स्कन्धाश्च **II25II.**

Division and Union both. Combined effect of division and union. भेदसंघातेभ्य उत्पद्यन्ते II26II. भेदसंघाताभ्यां चाक्षुषः II28II

There are two types, "Karya Parmanu" and "Karan Parmanu". This is as per the Jain literature.

This is as per the Prof. Max Born (A book"Restless Universe", page 266,).

The following description from Jain literature is to present the clarity about how new matter manifests in nature. How two primordial elements unite. What technology is used by nature to establish the new products. The description is indicative of the possibilities of "maithunic" union or combination of nature or dharma of two diverse elements. The newly formed matter is different then the two primary basic matter.

The Gunas are always uniting, separating, uniting again. (see mantra below from "Sarvarth Siddhi").

अन्योन मिथुनाः सर्ब्बे नैषामादिसंप्रयोगो वियोगो वा उपलभ्यते **II Sarvarth siddhi from Jain literature.**

Anyon mithunah sarbbe neishamadisam prayogo viyogo va upalabhyate I sarvarth siddhi from jain literatre.

(Positive sciences of the ancient Hindus London, Chapter 1, page 4, Dr Brajendrenath Seal, LONGMAN S, Green and C O; 3 9 Paternoter Row, L ondon 4th Avenue, 30th Street New York, Bombay, Calcutta, and Madras).

Unions of Electron and Positrons to from different kinds of matter. Matter formation in nature is the result of differences in the degrees of SNIGDHA (greesy or Positive) and RUKSHA (dry or negative) properties of these particle in molecules. (SNIGDHARUKSHATVAD BANDHA.

स्निग्धरूक्षद्वाद बंधः सूत्र "पुद्गलानां स्निग्धरूक्षत्वाद् बन्धो भवति" II 33 II particles unite by the VIRTUE of the properties of SNIGDHA and RUKSHA associated with them. In SWETAMBHARA GRANTH (JAIN Literature) it is mentioned that.

बंधपापरिणामे दुविहे पण्णते णिध्दबंधणपरिणामे लुक्ख बंधणपरिणामे य II

Bandha papriname duvihe pannate niddah bandhanapariname ya II

The molecules of matter are formed by 3 different ways:

1. BHED (**भेद**) or DIVISION. (**भेदादणुः सूत्र** 27 – **भेदात अणुरूपसद्भुते** II27II TATTVARTH DHIGAMA SUTRA Adhyaya 5 SUTRA 27 and 28. Digambar and Shwetambar Jain literature).
2. SANGHAT **संघात** or Union.
3. BHED + SANGHAT or Division + UNION,Both combined together. **भेदसंघातेभ्यउसद्‌यन्ते** II26II (TATTVARTH DHIGAMA SUTRA Adhyaya 5).

Thus, when two different particles of different primordial gases come together by any of the means described above a LIQUID element is formed. One of the basic units of the manifest world of nature.

CHAPTER 12

TIME CYCLE OR KAAL CHAKRA

TIME CYCLE (KAAL-CHAKRA) of Universe:

Sanskrit Speaking Civilization has discussed about the time since the VEDIC period. The time is directly proportional to the rotation of earth on its own AXIS (धुरी, अक्ष). At the same time earth's rotation around Sun, and the speed of rotation. That is the time is different on different planets. This is because of their size, speed of rotation, and distance of orbit in space around the central nucleus point. This becomes massive in calculation as one goes deep in space. This was recognized by Rishis and sages.

This invites the knowledge about speed and motion of objects in space. It led Rishi Kanaad to formulate the laws of motion. A profound insight into the nature of motion and force. Vaisheshik Darshan by Rishi Kanaad has incorporated the knowledge of particle physics, atoms, gravity, and other important studies of the modern physics! Even the God Particle which modern science is still searching. In short, some sutras mentioned here:

1. वेगः निमित्तववशेषात किमणो जायते |

   (A change in motion is caused by a force.)

2. वेगः निमित्तापेत किमणो जायते नियतदिक क्रियाप्रबन्धहेतु |

   (An impressed force can cause a proportional change in Motion in the direction of the force.)

3. वेगः संयोगववशेषववरोधी |

   (Any motion is a sum of the action and reaction of forces.)

These laws are formulated by Rishi Kanaad thousands of years before Newton.

These are the three laws of motion in Vaisheshik Sutras as the principles that govern motion. Vaisheshika Sutra dates to at least 600 – 200 BCE. Nearly two thousand years before Newton presented his work! This explains why majority of western scientists cropped up after invasion of Bharat Varsha country.

The manifest Srishti or cosmos is bound by these laws of Rishi Kanaad. It is explained below:

In the manifestation of cosmos (se figure on Bramhotpatti) Rudra onward is discussed previously. How Rudra get manifested? The energy particles in PARAM SHIV, coalesce and grow together to form balls. Energy is always restless hence rotate and become round. There is change in motion as per 1st law of motion of Rishi Kanaad. The motion gets speed in the direction of force to get expelled out of Tejah Punj = the Param shiv energy source as per the 2nd law of Rishi Kanaad. As per the 3rd law the sum of action and reaction, the born Rudra starts rotating around the Tejah Punj or Param shiv. This decides the time scale of Rudra. (See calculation of time of Rudra). Similarly, laws are applicable to Vishnu and Bramha as well.

It will be of interest to understand that the laws of nature are uniformly applicable in manifest universe. Whatever is in Universe – Brahmanda, is in our manifest body. Hence Veda calls it as "Yatha brahmande tatha pinde" or "Aham brahmasmin". (This has been explained in detail in "Song of Science-Shrimad Bhagwadgita, Notion Press, Chennai, Malaysia, Singapore. Ed. 2020, Matapurkar, B. G.)

How the month, calculated from moon's movement is explained in the following Veda Richa: -

यत्त्वां देव प्रपिबन्ति तत आ प्यायसे पुनं :। वायुः सोमस्य रक्षिता समानां मास आकृतिः
|| Rigved. 10-85-5

yat tvā deva prapibanti tata ā pyāyase punaḥ | vāyuḥ somasya rakṣitā samānām māsa ākṛtiḥ || Rigved. 10-85-5.

As Moon advances on East side towards Sun, it darkens in 15 days of Krishna Paksha. The brightness comes back when Moon is in 15 days of Shukla Paksha. Thus creates Months and Seasons. ||5||

The following mantra from Vaisheshik Darshan by ACHARYA KANAD, considers the time as DRAVYA – substance.

पृथिव्यापस्तेजो वायुराकाशंम् कालो दिगात्मा मन इति द्रव्याणि **II5II Vasheshik. 1-1-5.**

Prithivyastejo vayurakasham kaalo digaatma mann iti dravyani tII5II Vasheshik. 1-1-5.

Other RISHIS and Jain Acharyas (Sutra 39 of 5th chapter of TATTVARTH SUTRA) uphold this view.

What is thc NATURE of timc? Time consists of units which always remain separate or do not mix with each other. These are subtle grains, invisible, inactive and without form.

If one thinks about the TIME, then prime question that how and when the manifest world came into existence, need be answered first then only time can be explained. Rigveda has devoted NASADIYA SUKTA for solving the birth of manifest world – the NATURE or SRISHTI (सृष्टि), in a very peculiar way. Rigveda 10-129. How PANCH MAHA BHUT got manifest? Manifest world has Stars, place for living organisms like earth. Exploration about all this started when MAN became knowledgeable in manifest world. In Rigveda the evolved RISHI in 10-129 Sukta explains questions. When the nature was manifested, there was nothing – no truth (सत्) or untruth (असत्). That is nothing was manifest. There was no living place – LOK (लोक = भू, भुवः, स्वहः, महं जनः, तपः:, सत्य). There was no space where manifest nature could dwell. There was no cover or AAKASH for protection of manifest world. If so, then suddenly who, what, where and for whom the protection cover Aakash got manifested? Next what created the AMBHA (अम्भ). Is it water or sound producing element? Meaning of AMBHA is debated. It is interesting to note the study of GALAXY by scientist HUBBLE who invented the telescope to visualize the galaxy. He concluded that the stars and constellations -components of galaxy are gradually distancing away. This means the Aakash is expanding along with components of the galaxy. The ever-expanding universe. (https://www.rmg.co.uk/stories/topics/what-has-hubble-space-telescope-discovered). It is astonishing that how the RISHI could conclude in NASADIYA SUKTA. Hubble discovered the age of universe as 13.8 billion yeas. This means there was nothing before that period! This is the statement of NASADIYA SUKTA.

ऋतं च सत्यं चाभीद्धात्तपसोऽध्यजायत। ततो रात्र्यजायत ततः समुद्रो अर्णवः॥1II Rigveda 10-190-1.

ṛutaṁ ca satyaṁ cābhīddhāt tapaso dhy ajāyata | tato rātry ajāyata tataḥ samudro arṇavaḥ ॥1II Rigveda 10-190-1.

RITAM (ऋतम्) is that truth which is the root cause and the laws that govern the manifest universe and nature. The truth which self-manifests itself before the universe – VISHVA (विश्व). Proper presentation will be MULTIVERSE. Subsequently it annihilates and manifest again and again. The hard work or penance (तप) – action and interaction of basic elements in ABSOLITE TRUTH – PARAMAM SHIVAM (त्तपसोऽध्यजायत).

Anything which undergoes hard work needs TIME and TIME PERIOD or SAMAYA which is unit of time. To simplify this the self-manifest or SWAYAMBHU PARAM SHIV organizes the NATURE – SRISTI – सृष्टि, its laws, practical laws, day-night, and oceans in space (समुद्रो अर्णवः). All this needs time. Time originates at PARAM SHIV and dies too at PARAM SHIV. Sanskrit describes it as KAAL (death यम) of KAAL (Time). The MAYA (illusion of the appearance of manifest world) which is the product of incredible power (TEJODBHUT – तेजोद्भुत) of PARAM SHIV or absolute truth, is responsible for manifestation of the nature and the multiverses.

Next mantra clarifies it further (Rigveda 10-190-2and 3)

समुद्रादर्णवादधि संवत्सरो अजायत |अहोरात्राणिविदधद विश्वस्य मिषतो वशी II2II

samudrād arṇavād adhi saṁvatsaro ajāyata | ahorātrāṇi vidadhad viśvasya miṣato vaśī || Rigveda 10-190-2

सूर्याचन्द्रमसौ धाता यथापूर्वमकल्पयत |दिवं चपृथिवीं चान्तरिक्षमथो सवः II 3 II

sūryācandramasau dhātā yathāpūrvam akalpayat | divaṁ ca pṛthivīṁ cāntarikṣam atho svaḥ || Rigveda 10-190-3

After space ocean manifested (समुद्रादर्णवादधि). It is not the ocean of water on earth but sea of atomic particles in space. the SAMVASTRATMAK KAAL (संवत्सरात्मक काल) could manifest. As the world repeatedly manifests, the Sun, Moon, Swarga, Earth, and Aakash, the abodes in space get manifest from Param Shiva repeatedly in each KALPA (The length of a single cycle of the cosmos (or 'day of Brahma') from creation to dissolution. Period reckoned as 4,320 million human years).

SAMAYA is "time period" of KAAL. It is the unit of time. It is well explained in JAIN scriptures. TATTVARTH SUTRA, ADHYAYA 5, mantra 22-

वर्तना परिणाम क्रियाः परत्वापरत्वे च कालस्य II22 II TATTVARTH SUTRA Chapter 5, SUTRA 22.

Vartana parinam kriyah paratva paratve cha kaalasya II22 II TATTVARTH SUTRA Chapter 5, SUTRA 22.

Function of time is to help substances in their continuing to exist (वर्तना). To assist in their modifications (परिणाम). To support in their action and movements (क्रिया and in their priority or non-priority (परत्वापरत्व). Characteristic of time is to maintain the existing form of the substance. Any change in substance depends upon time. Jain philosophy considers the time of two types of Apparent time or VYAVAHARA KAAL and Real time or NISHCHAYA KAAL.

Time on earth is directly proportional to SUN. Or one can say the time on earth depends upon, revolving earth around the SUN, and revolving around its own AXIS (अक्ष). Day-night, days, months, years are all set as per the movement of earth around sun. In Rigveda 2-38-4.

पुनः समव्यद्विततं वयन्ती मध्या कर्तोर्न्यधाच्छक्म धीरः। उत्संहायास्थाद्व्यृ१-तूँरदर्धररमतिः सविता देव आगात्॥ ऋग्वेद - मण्डल» 2; सूक्त » 38; मन्त्र » 4

पुनरिति। सम्। अव्यत्। विऽततम्। वयन्ती। मध्या। कर्तोः। नि। अधात्। शक्म। धीरः। उत्। सम्ऽहाय। अस्थात्। वि। ऋतून् । अदर्धः। अरमतिः। सविता। देवः। आ। अगात्॥4॥

Punariti sam avyad vitataṁ vayantī madhyā kartoh ni adhāt s hakma dhīraḥ | ut saṁhāy āsthāt vy ṛutūm̐n adardhah aramatiḥ savitā devah aa āgāt ||

In summary, rotation of earth around Sun is responsible for the manifestation of Ritu or seasons in a year. The earth, rotating in space, revolves again and again in orbit in the solar region, using force and power to do the rounds, moving on, comes back to the same point and remains stable in the orbit. The Sun creates the seasons of the year.

Rigveda understands sun as AGNI (see details in 'AGNIMILE mantra' of Rigveda). At the same time Rigveda considers Sun as the fraction of main AGNI- the BRAHMA SHAKTI. It is not independent. It is in action due to the power from the Brahma-shakti. This categorically expressed in MUNDAKOPNISHAD – 2-5.

The sun has no independent existence but associated with Galaxy Milky way. It rotates around the centre of galaxy. Therefore, it has the "Time Cycle". Similarly, Everything, manifest in BRAHMANDA is rotating around the centre of its origin. Hence is bound with the time cycle. This time cycle is continuous with rotation around some centre or the other. But the time cycle meets its death at PARAM SHIVA level. Because the Param-Shiva is the centre for everything around it. Hence no rotation.

Therefore, all manifest elements in NATURE, have life span as per their rotational effect. Rudra has span of 11 manifestations, Vishnu has span of 14 Vishnu manifestations, While Brahma has 14 manifestations. What VEDA explains about it?

Therefore, Gita says that the: -

आब्रह्मभुवनाल्लोका पुनरावर्तिनोऽर्जुन :|मामुपेत्य तु कौन्तेय पुनर्जन्म न विद्यते ||16|| Gita 8-6

One day of Brahma (*kalp*) lasts a thousand cycles of the four ages (*mahā yug*) and his night also extends for the same span of time. The wise who know this understand the reality about day and night.

For clarity of the fact the following chart will be helpful: -**TIME PERIOD or SAMAYA (समय).**

(SAMAYA is Unit of Time)

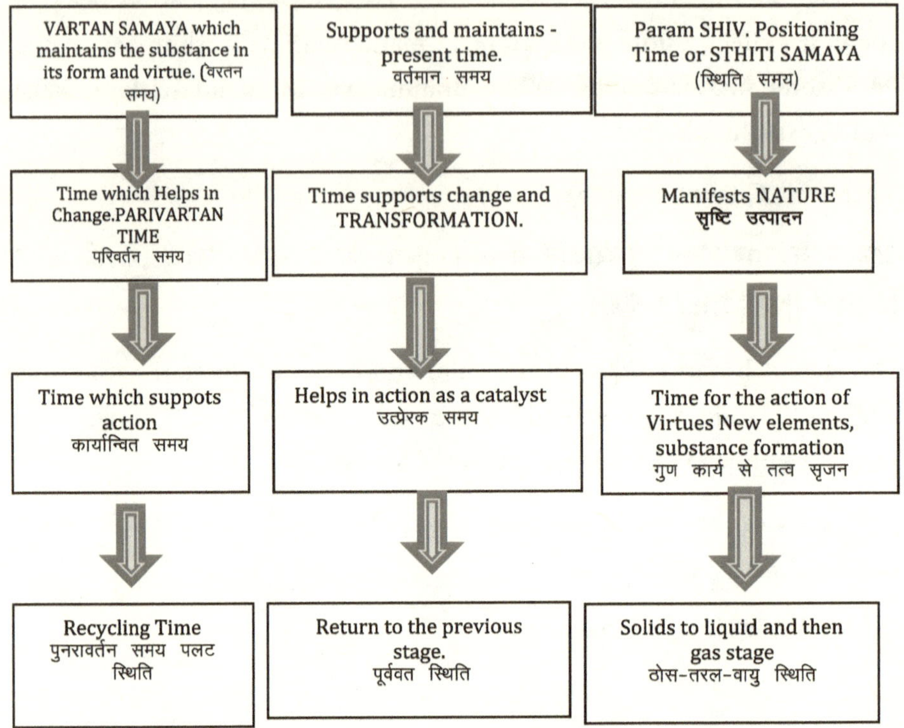

This SAMAYA CHAKRA – "time cycle period" is applicable to the beginning, behaviour and annihilation of the whole Verse (Uni and Multiverses) and the NATURE. See chart below: -

Cosmos undergoes iteration repeatedly.

Absolute truth and Time (Samaya) act like Catalyst

TIME CYCLE - SAMAYA CHAKRA

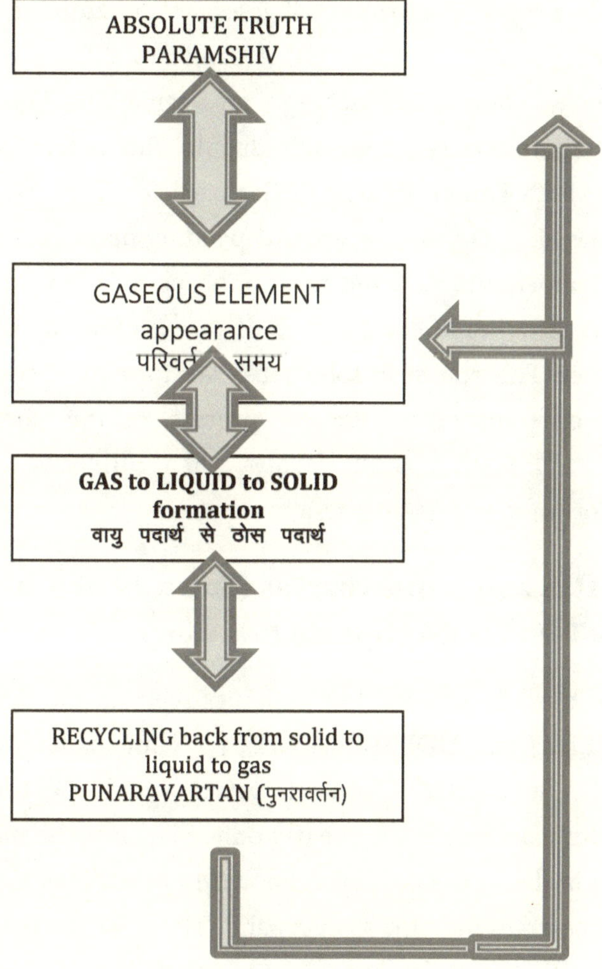

Cosmic drama can be explained Scientifically using knowledge available in Jain books in a better way. The matter is made up of SKANDHA (Molecule), Skandhadesh (Atom), Skandhapradesh (Ionized Atom), parmanu (elementary particles – e.g., Elctron, Proton), Such Parmanus are in a state of motion. State of the matter depends upon Division, Union, or both. In above chart the "Absolute truth" is hot and burning, it has all the ASHTADHA prakriti-(अष्टधा प्रकृति) in particle form or due to extreme heat it is in different form. When Gas evolves from absolute truth it circulates around Absolute truth. The primordial gases are a mixture of several types of gases. Science knows only few. Other gases are still un-recognized by modern science. These gases undergo amalgamation. The action and reaction are continuously happening due to the process of UNION, DIVISION or both Union division in Gas particles. This results in liquid formation (like $H_2 + O_2 = H_2O$= water depending upon environment and appropriate temperature and the time). The particles in liquid element undergo different types of combination of gases, union, division, or both actions together. This results in solid substance formation, which produce elements of different types. Reverse process in the same order or annihilation – PRALAYA (प्रलय) follows when conducive environment ceases (Punaravartan – पुनरावर्तन - iteration).

Other RISHIS and Jain Acharyas (Sutra 39 of 5th chapter of TATTVARTH SUTRA) uphold this view.

The living beings are grouped into 4 as per their origin e.g., JARAYUJ, ANDAJ, SWEDAJ and UDBEEJ. JARAYUJ – Humans live for 100 years approximately. But Swedaj – some insects live only for one day. This means total life span finishes in one day only. Similarly, the measurements of time given in the Vedas are beyond normal human imagination. As the celestial map enlarges the time span expand. The Vedas state that one year on the earth equals; one day and night of celestial gods. The calculation goes much further; 12,000 years of the celestial gods makes one *mahā yug* or all 4 YUG together (चतुर्युग). See the YUG span below: -

KaliYug:- 432,000years

DwāparYug:- 864,000years

TretāYug:- 1,296,000years

SatyaYug:- 1,728,000years

Total of 4 YUGAS is called MahāYug. It is equal to 4,320,000 years

Kalp: 4,320,000,000 years (1000 *Mahā Yug* = 1 day of Brahma). Similar time expands with BRAHMA.

One thousand m*ahā yug* make one day of Brahma, called a *kalp*, and then there is Brahma's night of equal duration. *Kalp* is the largest unit of time in the world; it equals 4.32 billion years.

As per the calculations of Vedas, the duration of the universe equals Brahma's lifespan, of 100 years. Brahma's one day and night put together make 8.64 billion earth years, and 36,000 such days of his lifespan would make 311 trillion 40 billion years. Hence, that will be one life cycle of our universe.

Brahma is a creator, performs his duty on behalf of PARAMSHIV. Brahma is also under the cycle of life and death. What is earth year and what is the Brahma year?

Calculation of a Divya Varsh or God year.

One day of Brahma = 1000 (one thousand) Chaturyuga (four yugas) and the same is the duration of the night.

One Chaturyug has 43,20,000 years of human beings.

One month =30 days and nights

One year = 12 months

Brahma's age is 100 years (Divya – God years).

{Note: - In one day of Brahma Ji, the term of rule of 14 Indra ends. The term of rule of one Indra is 72 Chaturyuga}.

Therefore, one day of Brahma is of 72 × 14 = 1008 Chaturyuga, and the same is the duration of the night, but for sake of simplicity it is taken as one thousand Chaturyuga only. Four Yugas are as follows.

Satyug, which is 1728000 years. 2. Treta Yug, which is of 1296000 years

3. Dwapar Yug, which is 864000 years. 4. Kalyug, which is of 432000 years. Total 4.32 million human years. Month = 30 × 2000 = 60000 (sixty thousand) chaturyuga. Year = 12 × 60000 = 720000 (seven lakh twenty thousand) chaturyuga. Age of Brahma – 720000 × 100 = 72000000 (seven crore twenty lakh) chaturyuga.

The Age of Vishnu: - Vishnu is dormant gaseous layer having full capacity to manifest Brahma. It exists due to the tremendous heat in RUDRA a fraction of absolute truth or TEJAHPUNJ or PARAM SNIV. But in a sleeping stage like seeds the life is dormant, a full memory of the vegetation exists. Vishnu is the preserver, who protects all manifestations in universe. Scientifically the heat, radiation, sound waves and other destructive elements present in the RUDRA prevented by this protective layer of gases. This primordial gaseous layer acts as barricade to all these harmful effects. Vishnu has been depicted in photos as sleeping human figure on serpent bed, is only to common population of human beings (Read details in SHRI VISHNU PURAN).

Age of Vishnu is seven times that of Brahma. 72000000 × 7 = 504000000 (fifty crore forty lakh) 4 yug together Chaturyuga. **The Age of Shiva: -** (For details please read Shiv Puran). **Age of Shiv is seven times that of Vishnu.:** - 504000000 × 7 = 3528000000 (three Arab 52 crore 80 lakh) 4 YUG or chaturyuga. The present Brahma as per VEDA, has attained the age of 50 years. He is running in his 51st year. Then these three together further continue creation, preservation, and destruction in Multi / universes. This cycle continues (पुनरावर्तिनोर्जुन).

What is the Age of "AKSHAR Purush" or PARAMSHIV. In Gita chapter 4 SHLOKA 5, Vyas Rishi narrates that, ARJUN and Shri Krishna 'had several births, Arjun had forgotten but Shri Krishna remembers everything.

सहस्रशीर्षा पुरुषः सहस्राक्षः सहस्रपात । सभूमिं विश्वतो वर्त्वात्यतिष्ठद दशाङ्गुलम ॥1॥ (Rigveda. 10 – 90 – 1).

sahasraśīrṣā puruṣaḥ sahasrākṣhaḥ sahasrapāt | sa bhūmiṁ viśhvato vaṛtvātya tiṣṭhad daśhāṅgulam || II1II (Rigveda. 10 – 90 – 1).

The AKSHAR Puruṣa, who has a thousand heads, a thousand AXIS or AKSHA (अक्ष), a thousand feet, investing the earth in all directions, exceeds measuring ten fingers. Even then this PURUSH must undergo life and death cycle. Some scholars consider AKSHA as eyes, can multiverses rotate around eyes, but certainly around multiple axis.

The age: Rudra Shiv is 70,000 (seventy thousand) years.

The details are in the main literature in BRAHM PURAN, MARKANDEYA PURAN, SHIV PURAN, JYOTISH TATVANK and MADBHAGWAT PURAN. For exploration of hidden science in stanzas of Gita, details from VED PURAN etc. are quoted. DR. B.G. MATAPURKAR Mahi Publication, Ahmedabad, 2020 ISBN 978-93-89339-47-5.

All the stages of Brahm undergo repetition but after merging with supreme soul this cycle stops. On scientific analysis of this stanza this indicates time cycle. Time is governed by speed. Speed is circular or space where time exists which is also circular. Theory of relativity (of A. Einstein) the light ray released from one point will return to same point again. Travel of light has speed. Therefore, speed is circular. In fact, the soul (-Jeevatma) after death released from material body (a physical form), circular speed related to time, will certainly bring back to physical form of material existence with time.

सर्वभूतानि कौन्तेय प्रकृतिं यान्ति मामिकाम् |कल्पक्षये पुनस्तानि कल्पादौ विसृजाम्यहम् ||7|| Gita 9-7.

sarva-bhūtāni kaunteya prakṛitiṁ yānti māmikām kalpa-kṣhaye punastāni kalpādau visṛijāmyaham Gita 9-7

All Char-Achar (सर्वभूतानि) i.e., living, and non-living beings, at the end of Kalp of Brahma, are unmanifested and get back into me. In the next Kalp, (कल्पक्षये पुनस्तानि कल्पादौ) 'I' manifest them again. This is within my power.

प्रकृतिं स्वामवष्टभ्य विसृजामि पुन :पुन :|भूतग्राममिमं कृत्स्नमवशं प्रकृतेर्वशात् || 8|| Gita 9-8.

prakṛitiṁ svām avaṣhṭabhya visṛijāmi punaḥ punaḥ bhūta-grāmam imaṁ kṛitsnam avaśhaṁ prakṛiter vaśhāt Gita 9-8.

The role of Prakriti or Nature is stressed again.' I 'unmanifest again and again. It is in the control of Prakriti- the Nature.

This is applicable to whole Brahm and material universe. Is it that the sages of Vedic time knew this theory of Einstein or the vice versa?

Let us understand more from next stanza: The nature has been described in two separate entities. One is manifest which is material world and the other is un-manifest. It is existing but nonmanifest form is eternal and is camouflaged. (GITA Chapter 8- Mantra 16, 17, 18, 19). There is another un-manifest element. The un-manifest form of nature is eternal and transcendental to this manifest and un-manifested matter. It is supreme and un-annihilable. Is it that the VEDA indicate here the DARK MATTER of modern science? It is never annihilated. While the manifest world is perishable (GITA chapter 8 stanza 20 given below).

परस्तस्मात्तु भावोऽन्योऽव्यक्तोऽव्यक्तात्सनातन यः स सर्वेषु भूतेषु नश्यत्सु न विनश्यति ॥20॥ Gita 8, 20).

paras tasmāt tu bhāvo 'nyo 'vyakto 'vyaktāt sanātanaḥ yaḥ sa sarveṣhu bhūteṣhu naśhyatsu na vinaśhyati II Gita 8-20

In addition to the manifest and unmanifest nature, there is another unmanifest nature element, which exist in nature, even if every other thing has annihilated. It does not cease to exist. It is SANATANA, inexhaustible, perpetual.

It is interesting to note that the universe is recurring type i.e., manifest and annihilates again and again (see above punaravarti). In other word, it undergoes cycles of repeated birth and death. To elaborate this, the original scientific explanation needs scrutinization. What is "yug" and "Brahm" mentioned in stanza 17 above? What is day and night of Brahma? During the days of BRAHMA all living beings of manifest nature come into being. During nights of BRAHMA all is annihilated. This is cyclical.

Sahastrayugpryantmaharyad brahmano vịduh I ratrim yugsahastrantam tehoratravido janah II 17 II (Gita 8, 17).

Day of Brahm is 1000 Yug so is night of Brahm.

It is repeatedly occurring during every day and night of BRAHMA. But when life of BRAHMA ends, they are all annihilated and remain un-manifest for millions of years. When BRAHMA is born again, they all manifest again after Brahm. How was this made knowledgeable? It is enigmatic. It is unbelievable. (See 7th stanza of Nasadiya sukta of Rigved above) These achievements are not possible in one's lifetime. Before understanding the life and time - period of Brahma. Understanding of the celestial movements in space - ANTARIKSHA. Vedic rishis understood celestial drama in space. The explanation is given in SHIV PURAN. To start with, assume that unmanifest element-SHIV self-manifest, as AGNI-LING, Having tremendous heat. Gasses are emitted which surround AGNI LING. Swirling balls of gasses are ejected out. The gas balls once thrown out of hot 'Agni ling', the balls, keep rotating and after some years of cooling get solidified and become celestial objects which become galaxies full of different stars (see diagram and charts above). These keep on rotating around central star of Galaxy. Some convert into solar systems with different planets. These also rotate around the Sun. (Sun like stars). In our solar system the planet earth rotates around the central Sun. This rotation decides time on earth i.e., Day, Night, month, and year etc. Similarly, the total mass of galaxies rotates, around Gas accumulation around AGNI LING. As explained in earlier sections of this book, that the Laws of universe are intricate and difficult to understand but have uniform applicability. The rotational celestial drama is seen in small atom also where electron and proton in atom rotate around the central neutron (explained earlier books, with diagrams, elsewhere). What is the measurement of time? Modern quantum theory of science understands that the electron is just a charged entity. It is not a matter. It exists because it is in motion, rotating in its orbit. The existence of electron is in its motion or speed. Existence of electron is because it moves around oppositely charged Proton. Hence attract each other. Mutual attraction of both, reduces, their charge. The time for spin of electron is RENU Sanskrit terminology, is its protection too is TRASRENU (TRAS = Protection and RENU is electron, (see – anoraniyan mahtomahiyan). The cosmos is filled with wavelengths of different types, depending upon expression of existence. Time required for electron wavelength is same as needed for energy to travel to infinity. When electron orbits around proton with opposite charge then why electron continues moving around in the orbit. Here the slip theory (of Neil Bohr. A Danish physicist, Nobel Laureate 1922.) is applicable. Electron can jump from one orbit to another by absorbing or releasing energy. Such electrons when unite in time, space, and relative number form compound, molecules, and the material world in universe. The number of electrons, in outer orbit determine the properties of element (Neil Bohr). (www.nobelprize.org>summary; www.britanica.com>physics; 1.m.wikiquote.org) As per Vedic knowledge the Cosmos expansion is limitless and unending. There are innumerable worlds beyond our limited world (Multiverse concept). There is no space, no time, no existence, and there is nothing. What we experience is all illusion (see Yog-vasishtha above). Let us understand all this celestial drama perceived by Rishis and sages of Sanskrit speaking civilization. What science is hidden in this statement? According to BRAHM PURAN SRISHTI KHAND, the age of BRAHM and time scale of YUG has been calculated and mentioned. BRAHM lives for 100 years. In other words, 100 years is life span of Brahma. This is known as PAR. Half of this i.e., Brahma's ½ life i.e., 50 years of Brahma is called PARARDH (half of par = par+ardh). The time scale of Sanskrit is as follows: (For details refer to "GITA Press Gorakhpur" publication - Shri Shivmahapuranank Uttarardh No. 1, Year 92 - Shri Shivmahapuran-Vayaviya Samhita Adhyaya 7 Shloka 1-25 and Adhyaya - 8, Shloka 1-31, page 450-58).

15 NIMESH = 1 KASHTHA (time needed for closing of upper eyelid = NIMESH)

30 KASHTHA = 1 KALA.

30 KALA = 1 MUHURT

30 MUHURT = 1 DIN-RAAT (day-night)

30 DIN-RAAT = 1 MAAS (month)

(like man month, "DEVTA month" also has 30 days, 12 months is 1 year but time-period is different than the earth).

1 MAAS = 2 PAKSHA - (SHUKLA PAKSH and KRISHN PAKSH).

6 MAAS = 1 AYAN (sun solstice, southern and northern - UTTARAYAN and DAKSHINAYAN).

2 AYAN = 1 VARSHA (year).

(“SHRI SHIV MAHAPURANANK Editorial note, page 26, “BRAHMA KI AAYU” (KAL KA PARIMAN & TRIDEV AAYUMAN”).

What is YUG and what are various YUG’s? What is the time span of each YUG? Time span on earth is grouped into four different YUG. These are named as SAT YUG, TRETA YUG, DWAPAR YUG and KALI YUG. 12000 years comprise 4 YUG (YUG CHATUSHK) i.e., SATYA YUG, TRETA YUG, DWAPAR YUG, KALI YUG, all 4 together. As per calculation the number of years in each YUG respectively is 4, 3, 2, 1 DIVYA years. At the end and beginning of every YUG there is joint time – a transition period (transition of one yug into next yug) which is 100 years. All 4 YUG together are called CHATUR YUG. One thousand CHATUR YUG is equal to one day of BRAHMA. Details are as follows: (As per BRAHMA PURAN Gita Press Gorakhpur, code 44, SRISHTIKHAND page 20-22.). Satya Yug time span is 4000 Divya years. In the beginning 400 years and at the end are 400 years. (800 years – Two joint periods of 400 years each, is the transition period between two Yug called Yug-sandhi). The period of duration of Satya Yug is 4800 Divya years. Like this Treta Yug is 3600 Divya years, Dwapr Yug 2400 years and Kali Yug is 1200 Divya years. (See Manusamhita stanzas scripted below). Manu a great sage – illumined Rishi – of Satya Yug, has written more clearly about four Yug in his Samhita: Years 4000 is Satya Yug, Twilight of morning and evening (Yug Sandhya) joint (Sandhi) period, 400 each, make 4800years. The thousands and hundreds decrease by one (3000 +300 and 300 =3600 Treta yug), 2000+200+200=2400 is Dwapar yug, 1000+100+100=1200 is Kaliyug) Total is 12000 years is Devyug. The 1000 years of Dev Yug is a Day and equal is Night of BRAHM. It is described in Manu Samhita:

चत्वार्याहुः सहस्त्राणि वर्षाणान्तु कृतं युगंम् ।

तास्य तावच्छती सन्ध्यां सन्ध्यांश्च तथाविधः ।।

इतरेषु ससन्ध्येषु ससन्ध्यांशेषु च त्रिषु ।

एकापायेन वर्तन्ते सहस्त्रणि शतानि च ।।

यदेतत् परिसंख्यातमादावेव चतुर्युगम् ।

एतद् व्दादशसाहस्त्रं देवानां युगमुच्यते ॥

दैविकानां युगानान्तु सहस्त्रं परिसंख्यया ।

ब्राम्हमेकमहर्ज्ञेयं तावती रात्रिरेव च ॥

Chatvaryahuh sahastrani varshanantu krutam yugam I tasya tavachchhati Sandhya sandhynshch tathavidhah II itareshu sasandhyeshu sasandhyansheshucha trishu I ekapayen vartante sahastrani shatani cha II yadetat parisam khyatmadavev chturyugam I etad dvadashasahastradevanam yugamuchchate II deivikanam yuganantu sahastram parisankhyaya I brahmamekamahardnyer yam tavati ratrirev cha II

(DIVYA year is 360 times more than the man years). (Quoted from "The holy Science" by Sri

Sri Swamy Sri Yukteshwar Giri, page 11, Yoganand Satsanga Society of India. Seventh Impression, 2013. Distributed by Jaico Publishing House). Accordingly, duration of Kali Yug is 4,32,000 years. Similarly, Dwapar Yug is 8,64,000 years, Treta Yug is 12,96,000 years and Satya Yug is 17,28,000 years. The sum of all these is 43,20,000 years. This is one Chatur Yug. Like this 1000 Chtur Yug is one day of BRAHMA. That is 4,32,00,00,000 man-years is one day of BRAHMA. In one day of BRAHMA there are 14 Manvantars. 71 Chatur Yug make 994 but one day of BRAHMA is of 1000 Chatur Yug. Hence 6 Chatur Yug are remaining. If 71 Chatur Yug day of BRAHM counted then it makes 4,29,40,80,000. Man years. If 14th part of six more Chtur Yug counted, it makes 4,32,00,00,000 years which is day of BRAHMA. After day of BRAHM night starts. The night is time of annihilation of life of living beings. Then again day starts, and life begins. This cycle goes on till 100 years (considered as life of BRAHMA). This is the meaning of GITA stanzas mentioned above. Scientific aspect, as per modern science is, the galaxies are rotating around centre of universe.

Solar system with all Planets rotates, around centre of the milky way galaxy. Similarly, earth and all planets of sun rotate around sun. Diagram to show EQUINOX movements "Piscean-Virgo" age (arrow.). Next equinox will be "Aquarion-Leo age. Transit of various yugas is in outer circle. Signs of zodiac in inner circle. Age is as per opposite signs of zodiac (Virgo-Pisces) "(Diagram: Virgo is the sign opposite Pisces. The autumnal equinox is falling in Virgo the opposite point, the Vernal Equinox, is perforce now falling in Pisces – Piscean Age (arrow marked). With retrograde movement will enter Aquarius-Leo. According to Shri GIRI's Theory, the world entered the Pisces – Virgo age in 499 AD and will enter Aquarius – Leo age in 2000 years later in the year 2499). Effect of such rotation is explained in text below YUG description is nicely encrypted in MANU SAMHITA. The illumined RISHI says in his shloka as mentioned above. 4000 years is TRETA yug, Joint period between two yug beginning and end i.e., 400+400, Total 4800 years. Similarly other three yug in 1000 and in 100 reduce by one i.e. 3000+ 300+300 total 3600 years and so on. Four yug together i.e. 4800+3600+2400+1200, Total 12000 years. This is the age of divine Gods. Sum of thousand divine ages constitute one Day of Brahma. Equal is night of Brahma. With reference to the diagram above, it can be summarized as follows (for details refer to original text):

According to Shri GIRI's Theory, the world entered the Pisces – Virgo age in 499 AD. And will enter Aquarius – Leo age in 2000 years later in the year 2499. 11501 B C when Autumnal equinox was on first point of Aries, the Sun began to move from nearest to centre, away towards point farthest from it. Autumnal equinox Aries – Libra the Sun moves away from the grand centre i.e. 4/20th portion – Satya Yug. Human Intellectual power began to reduce. During, 4800 years, the intellect of man lost power of grasping spiritual knowledge. During next 3600 years the Sun moves descending to next ¾th portion – Treta Yug. Divine magnetism reduces and in human minds. During, 2400 years next Sun passed through Dwapar-Yug, human mind lost the power of grasping electricity and its attributes.

During 1200 years of Kali Yug transit of Sun, which is farthest from the grand centre, at the first point of Libra, the intellectual power diminished to only material greed and sense gratification only or 500 A D considered the darkest part of Kali Yug in the whole cycle of 24000 years. Widespread ignorance, sufferings in all the nations of the world. From 499 A D onwards, Sun started to move towards centre, the human intellectual started to improve. During 1100 years of ascending Kali Yug, i.e., now 1599 A D. human intellect could comprehend fine matters of creation, Electricity. Next 100 years of joint period with Dwapar human intellect perceived attributes of electricity and fine matters of creation. The practical use of such knowledge like Magnetism, laws of astronomy, development of telescope, laws of gravitation etc. started advancing.

After 1899 on completion of 200 years of joint period of Kali - Dwapar yug, thorough understanding of attributes of electricity unfolds to human mind. History is the testimony to all these events of recent past. This happens in a cyclical manner. It keeps on repeating. This reiterates the fact that invention of Battery - the cell was invented by Rishi Vasishtha and used in generating Ozon gas using Basil leaves (TULSI) the same was later invented by Nikola Tesla. Is it not a repetition of invention? This certifies the truthfulness of the diagram (its interpretation) and its authenticity. Such is the influence of TIME-CYCLE (Samaya Chakra) which governs universe. Comprehending the kingdom of supreme soul. 'Man' year has 365 days as earth rotates around sun in 365 days. Sun rotation around centre of galaxy takes certain time (one rotation 360 days = one solar year). Solar seasons also change every 30 solar days which is month of sun). Seasons of sun also change, as on earth i.e., every 2-4 month. Galaxy takes its own time to rotate around centre of universe. BRAHM takes its own time for one rotation. That is how the day, night, and year of BRAHM was calculated. This knowledge was well known to Sanskrit speaking civilization, and it was common to all public. Therefore, this has been cited as example to Arjun by Lord Krishna, in Gita. BRAHM also takes its time to rotate around Vishnu. Time period for Vishnu is also mentioned. The Vishnu revolves around Shiv. Period of rotation of Vishnu is also set as Vishnu rotate around Rudra-Shiv. Details are narrated elsewhere. (Adopted from "The holy Science" a work by JNANAVTAR SWAMY SRI YUKTESWAR GIRI. 8th Indian edition 1990 (7th impression 2013), Published in India by YOGODA SATSANGA SOCIETY OF INDIA. ISBN 978-81-89535-19-3.)

As per Oriental Astronomy moons of a planet rotate around their planets. Planets along with moons rotate around their Sun. SUN with planets and moons rotate around some star. It takes 24000 earth years in one rotation. Sun also has another rotation around VISHNU NABHI – A seat of creative power – BRAHM. As per chart sun takes 12000 years up and down. The intellect of humans depends upon this rotational position. Changes take place both externally in material world and internally in intellectual world. Reader is referred to original work for details. Practical use of this in Sanskrit speaking civilization has also been established. While worshiping, honouring, reverencing "the GOD", Nature called SHODSHOPCHAR PUJA i.e., 16 rituals/types of reverencing, the place position period of all the planets, stars, signs of zodiac, position of moon and many other planetary details etc. (details are out of scope of this book) are clearly pronounced to start the PUJA CEREMONY – where on earth and at what place the puja is performed. This means the space science and earth geography is utilized in every walk of life. In modern days while on a flight during air travel at present the airhostess/pilot, mentions the position of aero plane. Air plane's height, altitude, temperature, speed, distance from departed airport and remaining distance to destination of arrival at the airport. Is it not a practical use of knowledge? Similarly, that civilization used their knowledge in every walk of life. Some details are given below about scientific use of knowledge of space, planetary positions of stars and nakshatra, earth's position in space, position of Sun and moon and in which sign of zodiac sun, moon are present. Apart from this the geographical position of site of reverencing to super soul (Paramatma). Site of place of worship in relation to River in the region, all are taken into consideration before taking oath and determination for reverencing along with prayer to GOD GANESH – to take care of all the obstacles and problems which may arise during reverencing. Instead of appreciating science in this it is propagated as orthodox and un-necessary repetitions. A question comes to mind why on flights the position of aircraft is repeated. Is it not orthodox? Probably the idea was to condemn whatever is BHARATIYA and make Bharatiya (Indians) feel inferior. So that the invaders are superior, and science oriented. The Reverencing is cited as for example: 16 types of reverencing, Primordial BRAHM, Second half of BRAHM, BRAHMA'S 2nd half-life of BRAHMA), After Brahma position of VISHNU i.e. KALP named SHWETVARAH KALP), MANU named VAIVASWAT MANVANTAR (one of 14 manvantaras), 28th out of 71 YUGCHATUSHK, group of four yugas (Ashtovinshatitame yug chatushke) First leg of YUG named KALI, JAMBU named continent Indian subcontinent, Deccon (Dakshin pathe) abode of RAM, Period of BUDDHA avatar and so on – DANDAK named jungle region AARANYA, south bank of river Godavary (SUN's particular sign of zodiac on the day of puja, moon's particular sign of zodiac on the day of puja, In fact position of earth in space and other planets, stars, NAKSHTRA (27 IN NUMBER. Details are in ephemeris – PANCHANG- celestial navigation calendar), PLACEMENT OF Sun, Moon, and their position in which sign of zodiac is explained. This narrates the position of earth on puja day in whole universe. Even to-day, this is in practice while performing PUJA CEREMONY. All sounds highly scientific. Condemning such scientific narration are we not condemning science itself!! This gives an understanding that every citizen of Sanskrit speaking civilization was aware of knowledge of space, astronomy and astrology and Ephemeris and geography of the place on earth). The scientific knowledge of the civilization cannot be ignored. It was very well advanced in many respects, in comparison to modern space age knowledge. The occurrence of ECLIPSES of moon and sun and that too accurately, was routinely calculated and scripted in advance for the whole year. It is going on year after year even now (in PANCHANG published every year). The names of HINDU months are according to the presence of moon in that NAKSHTRA viz. When moon in CHITRA NAKSHTRA the month is CHAITRA. When moon in VISHAKHA NAKSHTRA it is VAISHAKH and so on JAISHTHA- JESHTH NAKSHATRA, etc.

In summery all derivations are highly scientific. Not only this, but the effect of the celestial phenomenon in space affects all humans of the world, was also established by ancient RISHI's of Sanskrit speaking civilization. This is all available in ASTROLOGY and ASTROGNOMY developed by the Rishi, Muni, and saints. In fact, it is not an exaggeration to say that these highlighted words are synonyms of Scientists of Modern civilization. All astrological derivations are true even today. The calculations are scripted down and available even today. It is available in some centres in India. One such centre is in Hyderabad, Andhra Pradesh. Which is known to author of this book. It is called NAADI SHASTRA. (At this "centre" the organizers take thumb impression. Which is compared with the script available and if it matches your past and future is just read out for you.). It can be verified by any body by visiting the centre. How scientific, intellectual, and political scenario is influenced on earth due to celestial drama in space has been charted out by these RISHI and sages of Sanskrit speaking civilization. The intellectual development, scientific development, and political scenario of nations of the world, all in fact, due to the celestial phenomenon in space. The first 12000 years (see diagram,) are responsible for complete change in external material world and internal intellectual mental level of mankind. 12000 years are divided into 4 different stages. The first 1200 years, sun transit during $1/20^{th}$ portion of orbit is KALI YUG, during this period the mental virtues are $¼^{th}$ developed. Only gross material world is acceptable and understood. During next 2400 years, sun transits through 2/20th period of its orbit, known as DWAPAR YUG, mental values are in 2nd stage. Human mind perceives fine matters and electricity which form external world. The period of 3600 years sun transits through 3/20th orbit, is TRETA YUG. The mental values are in third stage. Human intellect can now comprehend divine magnetism, source of all electrical forces on which creation depends. The period of 4800 years sun transit is in remaining 4/20th orbit, is SATYA YUG, mental values are in 4th stage, when human mind and intellect now comprehend all even GOD - spirit, which is beyond material world. (For details reader is advised to consult original literature, as it is beyond the scope of this book). The un-manifest nature on the other hand is eternal and transcendental to manifest nature. It is supreme and is never annihilated. When all world is annihilated that part remains as it is. Interestingly after narrating all such knowledge Lord Krishna said all universe is perishable in cyclical manner (i.e.-rotation), then why ARJUN is worried for such a perishable being. Lord Krishna convincing ARJUN to follow his own KSHATRIYA DHARM and leave the outcome to super soul. During such conviction many scientific facts are mentioned as examples. Attempt is made to explain such hidden fact by original work found in various available and relevant Sanskrit literature on the subjects. The yug calculations are based on scientific calculation principles. These principles and calculations were prevalent in BHARATVARSHA till the reign of king VIKRAMADITYA. After this it was introduced as SAMVAT and named as VIKRAM SAMVAT.

The days of week are named after planets as Monday - SOMWAR = MOON, Tuesday - MANGALWAR = Mars, Wednesday Budhvaar - on planet Budh = Mercury-BUDH GRAHA and so on. Similarly, Months are as per NAKSHATRA movements as stated above. CHAITRA is as per the CHITRA NAKSHTRA, VAISHAKH as per VISHAKHA NAKSHTRA and so on. One more inference can be derived that the knowledge of ZERO is very old. Because of this zero, man could calculate accurately the calculation of stars and planets and it was made easy. The discovery of zero was a necessity. Pious literature or Shastra totally depends upon Mathematics. Without zero, calculation in maths is difficult. In Brahmotpatti the existence of manifest world came into being. Self-manifest SHIV is basically creator of all creation and creature in universe. Shiv is responsible for the Primordial Gasses in the form of Vishnu. Hot primordial Gaseous balls from the centre of Vishnu in the form of Brahma, which is responsible for different and innumerable Galaxies which came into existence. Manifestation of main elements like Earth, Air, Fire, Water, and Space as per Gita 7, stanza 4 and 5, (Chapter 7,) were possible by Brahma. In Prajotpatti with RAYI and Pranik energy living beings came into existence. Both conglomerate and responsible for galactic manifestations. The celestial drama is going on since time immemorial. To know the effect of "TIME CYCLE" on living beings the time was graduated by Sages, Rishis or contemporary in hours, Days, weeks, and months etc. and given names as per the Planets, Nakshatra etc mentioned above, also are under the influence of the cosmic manifestations. To study the influence of these cosmos was analysed and grouped and to study their influence on time and living beings. This is what Lord Krishn says in Gita Chapter 9 stanza 7, – "kalpkshaye punastani kalpadou visrujamyaham\", At the end of previous Kalp and beginning of next kalp, nature manifest the universe again. Chapter 10, Stanza 21, – "aadityanamham vishnurjyotisham ravviramshumana", Among 12 adityas 'I' am by the name 'Vishnu' and jyoti illumined one fraction is in Sun (Ravi). Chapter 10, Stanza 30 –"pralhadshchasmi deityanamkalah kalayatamaham\", 'I' am Prahlad (the devoted one) and death for demons, evil in the societies. Chapter 10 stanza 33 –"ahamevakshayah kalo dhatamaham vishvtomukha:", 'I' am unending time (time is the unending and ultimate killer) and creator of universe. Chapter10, stanza 35-"masanam margshirshoham rutunam kusumakara". 'I' am month Margshirsha (9th month or 'fall' season when tree leaves ripen and change colour, before shedding off). New spring season comes is "ritu kusumakar". These changes are natural manifestations due to supreme soul effect.

Life span of Brahma, life of Vishnu, and then life of Shiv has been explained in Markandeya Purana.

Ashtoyugsahastrani ahoratra prajapate aneinevatumanen shatambrahmasi jeevati pitamaha shateneiva Vishnorman vidhiyate nimishardhen-shambhostu sahastranichaturdash vinashyanti tatha vishnorsankhyatah-pitamaha.

8000 yug is Day and Night of Brahma, accordingly life of Brahma is 100 years. During span of ½ NIMESH of SHIV, 14000 VISHNU are 216. (SONG OF SCIENCE - SHRIMAD BHAGWADGITA by balkrishna Matapurkar, Notion Press, 2020).

In a day of Brahma there are 14 Manvantara. 71 ChaturYug is one Manvantara. 30,67,20,000 Man/earth years is one Manvantara or 8,52,000 Divya years is one Manvantara. Multiplied by 14 Manu is 1,19,28,000. This is a day of Brahma. In this manner 4,29,40,00,000 earth years is one day of Brahm. Like this, 100 years is life of Brahma. As said earlier everything manifests and continues during day of Brahma.

Chaturyuganam sankhyata sadhukahyeksaptatihi I manvantaram tasya sankhya manushabdeirnibodhame II 34 II Trinshat kotyastu sampurnah sankhyatah sankhyayadvij I Saptashashtistatha nyaniniyutani cha sankhyaya II 35 II Vinshatishcha sahastrani kaloyam sadhikamvina I etan manvantaram proktam deivyervarshernibodhame II 36 II Ashtouvarsha sahastrani divyaya sankhyaya yutam I dvipanchashattathanyani sahastranyadhikanitu II 37 II Chaturdash gunohyeshkalo brahmyamah smrutam I tasyante pralayah prokto brahmo neimittikobudhei II 38 II Markandeya Puran Ch. 43

(Markandeya Puran-chapter. 43 (brahmaji ke ayu ka pariman) stanza 8 Maarkandeya puran 145).

Rigveda. WAMIYA SUTRA 1 – 164 – 1-52.

It deals with the mystery of creation, an invisible source of initial manifestation in universe. What is the first cause of creation? Stimulates the study of cosmos to unfold the secrets of creator, creation, and the creature. Thought provoking analysis of working of cosmos, the laws on which the cosmos is governed and functioning. it is automatically governed. Delegation of work of cosmos to subsequent subordinate level comprising of different manifest modules of elements! It is astonishing to see the address of subject, before the creation, the Sky, Earth, Water, Fire, Air or (**भूमिरापोनलोनिलोनभ**). English words fail to connote the real meaning of Sanskrit word. i.e., 'Aap' is not the water only but a liquid matter, Air is element which is related with speed. Hence the Vedic literature becomes obscure and not easily understood. But there are enough opportunities in subsequent mantras to understand the real meaning of the words. An attempt is made in this book to unravel the obscurity.

अस्य वामस्य पलितस्य होतुस्तस्य भराता मध्यमो अस्त्यश्र्नःतर्तीयो भराता घृतपृष्ठो अस्यात्रापश्यम् विश्पतिम् सप्तपुत्रम् **II1II Rigveda. 1-164-1**

asya vāmasya palitasya hotus tasya bhrātā madhyamo asty aśnaḥ | tṛtīyo bhrātā ghṛtapṛṣṭho asyātrāpaśyaṃ viśpatiṃ saptaputram II1II Rigveda. 1-164-1

The meaning is obscure. For good health to all, middle part (**मध्यमो**) of sun is VAYU, 3rd part (**तृर्तीयो**) is AGNI, In the centre of these brothers there is in the form of RAYs is, 7 sons.

Before we analyse this mantra, let us ponder on the MANTRA 10 and 13 0f Sukta 88 of MANDALA 10. Below:

The three parts are clarified in Rigveda 10-88-10-

सतोमेन हि दिवि देवासो अग्निमजीजनञ्छक्तिभीरोदसिप्राम |तमू अक्रण्वन तरेधा भुवे कं स ओषधीःपचति विश्वरूपाः || Rigveda. 10-88-10 to 13.

stomena hi divi devāso agnim ajījanañ chaktibhī rodasiprām | tam ū akṛṇvan tredhā bhuve kaṃ sa oṣadhīḥ pacati viśvarūpāḥ || Rigveda 10-88-10-

At animal level the VISHVANARA is digestive AGNI which helps in digestion (अग्निमजीजनञ्छक्ति). God has provided SUN, in Aantariksha, and on earth, for happy living. Divided in 3 parts. It the AGNI in living beings' which digest food and manifests medicines (स ओषधीःपचति).

वैश्र्वानरम् कवयो यज्ञियासो अग्निम् देवा अजनयन्नजुर्यम् । नक्षत्रम् परत्नममिनच्चरिष्णु यक्षस्याध्यक्षन्तविषम् बर्हन्तम् II13II Rigveda 10-88-13.

vaiśvānaraṁ kavayo yajñiyāso gniṁ devā ajanayann ajuryam | nakṣatram pratnam aminac cariṣṇu yakṣasyādhyakṣaṁ taviṣam bṛhantam II13II Rigveda 10-88-13.

God has provided in the form of Vaishvanara - Agni, who has camouflaged and made lustreless, all the NAKSHATRA in space. Stars and Nakshtra visible in night-time only but in presence of Sunlight all disappear.

Now one can understand the 3 parts about the SUN. Analyse mantra 1 above and 2 below. The three parts can be Agni, Vayu, Aditya. Agni in 3 forms, creates nature, and help vegetation on earth (Growth, ripening, and seed development).

सप्त युञ्जन्ति रथमेकचक्रमेको अश्वो वहति सप्तनामा|तरिनाभि चक्रमजरमनर्वं यत्रेमा विश्वा भुवनाधितस्थुः ॥2॥

sapta yuñjanti ratham ekacakram eko aśvo vahati saptanāmā | trinābhi cakram ajaram anarvaṁ yatremā viśvā bhuvanādhi tasthuḥ || Rigved. 1-164-2.

What is single wheeled RATH-car? Pulled by one horse with seven names? Single wheel perfect and ageless having 3 hubs? This mantra is all obscure and enigmatic.

Sun as one wheeled car- RATH, Sun ray as one horse. 7 different names are the prism-spectrum forming 7 colours, VIBGYOR (Violet, Indigo, Blue, Green, Yellow, Orange, and Red). 3 NABHI as Agni, Vayu, Aditya. Agni and other two brothers, as energy of sun invigorating the three abodes – VISHVA. The Rucha appears obscure today, but the people of that civilization was learned and knowing all science.

इमं रथमधि ये सप्त तस्थुः ऽप्तचक्रं सप्त वहन्त्यश्वाः । सप्त सवसारो अभि सं नवन्ते यत्र गवां निहिता सप्त नाम ॥3॥ Rigveda 1- 164-3.

imaṁ ratham adhi ye sapta tasthuḥ saptacakraṁ sapta vahanty aśvāḥ | sapta svasāro abhi saṁ navante yatra gavāṁ nihitā sapta nāma II3II Rigveda 1- 164-3

The manner of presentation in Sanskrit literature is different. The obscure meaning must be explored, by reading in between the lines. It is possible that, it was the customary practice during the contemporary time of Vedic era.

अष्टौ पुत्रासो अदितेर्ये जातास्तन्वस परि । देवानुपप्रैत सप्तभिः परा मार्ताण्डमास्यत ||8||

aṣṭau putrāso aditer ye jātās tanvas pari | devām̐ upa prait saptabhiḥ parā mārtāṇḍam āsyat II 8 II Rigveda 10-72- 8.

सप्तभिः पुत्रैरदितिरुप परैत पूर्व्यं युगम । परजायै मर्त्यवे तवत पुनर्मार्ताण्डमाभरत ||9|| Rigveda 10-72- 9.

saptabhiḥ putrair aditir upa prait pūrvyaṁ yugam | prajāyai mṛtyave tvat punar mārtāṇḍam ābharat ||9|| Rigveda 10-72- 9.

ADITI -the Mother NATURE had eight sons. Eighth son is SUN. With seven sons mother Nature went to DEVA LOK or GOD'S Abode or source of Nature. Leaving SUN for mortals in their abode.

A scientific derivation and understanding can be.

सत्रियः सतीस्तानु मे पुंस आहुः पश्यदक्षण्वान नवि चेतदन्धः |कविर्यः पुत्रः स ईमा चिकेत यस्ता विजानात स पितुष पितासत II १६ II Rigved. 1-164-16.

striyaḥ satīstāmu me puṁsa āhuḥ paśyad akṣaṇvān na vi chetad andhaḥ | kaviryaḥ putraḥ sa īm ā chiketa yastā vijānāt sa pituṣh pitāsat II 16 II Rigved. 1-164-16.

Rays or radiation are female gender but are male too, this is appreciated by persons with vision, but blinds cannot. Son of poet knows it. But fathers father knows it too.

Considering the whole literature and the stanzas above and below mantra sixteen as above, the meaning is different. It can be the theory of ARDHANARINATESHWAR – **अर्धनारीनटेश्वर.** This is the thought propagated by Rigveda for the first time in the world. The whole cosmos is harbouring both elements. Male and female are present in heat and cold – AGNI+SOMA. Agni harbours heat and cold both so is soma.

In all living beings too, males have female element and females have male elements. This includes BRAHMA too – the creator. Biologically every living being has such male and female elements in both sexes. This is explainable by the example of hermaphrodites like Earthworms. The earthworm has male part and female part in one body. This is seen in some fishes – like Sharks (Belle Isle bamboo shark). This is more prominent in plant life. A flower has both elements – male and female-stamens and gynaecium.

The second line of the mantra sixteen, a person with eyes can appreciate but it cannot be appreciated by blind person. This means a person with VISION understands it. Blind means a person without the vision even if one has the eyes. Next is son of a poet knows at the same time his father or son's PITAMAH knows too. Pitamah can be BRAHMA himself.

यज्ञेन यज्ञमयजन्त देवास्तानि धर्माणि प्रथमान्यासन ते ह नाकम् महिमानः सचन्त यत्र पूर्वे साध्याः सन्तिदेवाः II50II 'गिवेदा ऋ-ऋघथ-त्रएं

yajñena yajñamayajanta devāstāni dharmāṇi prathamānyāsan | te ha nākam mahimānaḥ sachanta yatra pūrve sādhyāḥ santi devāḥ II50II Rigveda 1-164-50.

First essential duty of Yajaman (priest) is to please God with ignited Yadnya Agni. The Yadnya means research and investigation to achieve desired results by pleasing Gods – Supernatural basic elements (Details about Yadnya are explained in Song of science Shrimad Bhagwadgita, Notion Press, 2020 by Balkrishna Matapurkar. Reader is advised to refer to it). Mighty Devatas assembled in Heaven. Prayer is to extend the essential benefits to humans. And appropriately abide by rites. (५०(

समानमेतदुदकमुच्चैत्यव चाहभिः ।भूमिं पर्जन्या जिवन्ति दिवम् जिन्वन्त्यग्नयः II51II

samānam etad udakam uc caity ava cāhabhiḥ | bhūmim parjanyā jinvanti divaṁ jinvanty agnayaḥ II51II Rigveda 1-164-51.

Water (**उदक**) is same which goes to swarg due to heat and become clouds then fall back on earth as rains. This satisfies the earth and in turn the living beings on earth. II51II Rigveda 1-164-51.

दिव्यम् सुपर्णम् वायसम् बर्हन्तमपां गर्भम् दर्शतमोषधीनाम । अभीपतो वर्ष्टिस्तिर्पयन्तम् सरस्वन्तम्वसे जोहवीमि II52II Rigveda 1-164-52.

divyaṁ suparṇaṁ vāyasam bṛhantam apāṁ garbhaṁ darśatam oṣadhīnām| abhīpato vṛṣṭibhis tarpayantaṁ sarasvantam avase johavīmi II52II Rigveda 1-164-52.

The prayer is for celestial element - the Sun. We invoke for our protection the celestial, well-winged, swift-moving, majestic (Sun); who is in the centre (**गर्भम्**) of the waters; the manifester of medicinal herbs; the perpetuator of lakes and replenishes the ponds with rainwater. The root cause of rainwater is Sun, is well known.

Interestingly all above description seems highly scientific and analytical. If one gets out of mind-set of religious bend and find out the real hidden meaning in a scientific manner, the explanation gets revealed automatically without any bias.

CHAPTER 12 A

EARTH AXIS AND EARTH'S ORBIT AROUND SUN

Seasons on Earth (Fundamental Science)

In the context of Kaal Chakra Earth's Axis and earth's orbiting around Sun must be reviewed properly. The author has carried out research on this subject. Currently the modern science believes that the axis of Earth is tilted and remains tilted in a fixed direction. At the same time the earth rotates around the Sun in a horizontal and fixed orbit. Seasons on earth are due to the tilted axis. This has generated many doubts. This concept must be pondered, and correct basic concept must be re-established. Author is engaged in this research since childhood. The research is presented here .

Is the tilt of earth's axis absolute or do the earth shift? How truthful is Obliquity of the Earth Axis tilted to 23.50 and fixed, at the same time earth orbiting Sun is at horizontal plane and fixed. Is this responsible for seasons on Earth and shapes Ecosystem and behaviour of living beings?

Key words:

Tilted Axis, Earth Obliquity, Sun dial. Solar Solstices. Line of Cancer, Line of Capricorn, Equator, Hemispheres of earth, Polar Stars -North star and South star.

A simple experiment was attempted using Sundial or Solar watch. A staff in the center of a clean surface uniformly levelled. Shadow cast by staff is recorded till its maximum transit and starts traversing back to opposite direction. The solar solstices north and south are, to and fro movement of Sun limited up to the imaginary Tropic of Cancer on North hemisphere of earth and tropic of Capricorn on southern hemisphere of the earth. These are imaginary lines on earth. Accordingly, the shadow of staff in the center of the Sun Dial also changes on the dial surface. This forms an angle at the center of the dial. The shadow of staff noted, and angle measured at a fixed time and day at different places on earth. This angle is measured with the help of a 'D' of school compass box. This experiment was carried out at different places on earth, wherever the author visited for more than six months of the year. This experiment revealed that the angle was found to be 60^0 (+ and – 0.5^0 to 2.5^0) at different places of Northern hemisphere of earth and southern hemisphere. If the axis of earth is tilted or straight and fixed, at the same time the orbit of earth around the Sun is horizontal and fixed, the angle measurement is different at different places on earth. If earth moves upwards to 30^0 north and 30^0 south in relation to sun's horizon, the angle will remain constant. At the same time the sunshine will be for approximately for six months over the region of north pole and south poles of the earth, as in case of tilted axis. The earth's orbit is not fixed but gradually shifts towards north till line of Cancer and southward till the line of Capricorn. In conclusion the earth axis is not tilted but earth moves up and down accordingly the orbit of earth around the Sun, gradually changes due to the influence of electromagnetic, gravitational and radiation forces of stars (Sun) and constellations in space.

Introduction:

Time on earth is directly proportional to SUN. Or one can say the time on earth depends upon, rotation of earth on its own axis (अक्ष) and orbiting of earth around the SUN, Day-night, days, months, years are all set as per the movement of earth around sun. (Rigveda 2-38-4).

पुनः समव्यद्विततं वयन्ती मध्या कर्तोर्न्यधाच्छक्म धीरः।
उत्संहायास्थाद्व्यृ१तूँरदर्धररमतिः सविता देव आगात्॥ ऋग्वेद - 2; सूक्त » 38; 4

पुनरिति। सम्। अव्यत् (moving in space)। विऽततम् (Earth)। वयन्ती (rotates)। मध्या। कर्तोः। नि। अधात्। शक्म (As per its energy)। धीरः। उत्। सम्ऽहाय। अस्थात् (from place to place or different locations in space)। वि। ऋतून्। अदर्धः। अरमतिः (comparatively without rotation)। सविता (The Sun)। देवः। आ। अगात् (separates all seasons) ॥4॥

This Rigved statement is about earth which is free-floating round and other objects in space is by Rishi GRITSMAD SHONAK, and the statement is about the Sun - Savita. SUN is a Star. Sun and stars are powerful than Moon. Earth is much bigger than moon. These facts were known to Rishis of Vedic era. Sun moves but comparatively in galaxy, Nakshatra doesn't move (comparatively). Nakshatra is big but appear small due to the distance from the earth.

In summary, rotation of earth around Sun is responsible for the manifestation of Ritu or seasons in a year. The earth, rotating in space, revolves again and again in orbit in the solar region, using force and power to do the rounds, moving on, comes back to the same and remains stable in the orbit. The Sun creates and separates the seasons of the year.

Rigveda understands sun as AGNI (see details in 'AGNIMILE mantra' of Rigveda). At the same time Rigveda considers Sun as the fraction of main AGNI- the BRAHMA SHAKTI. It is not independent. It is in action due to the power from the Brahma-shakti. This categorically expressed in MUNDAKOPNISHAD – 2-5.

The sun has no independent existence but associated with Galaxy Milky way. The exploitation of nature for human benefits has been since time immemorial. Science is always exploring new truths over established truths. It is well- known that science is a never-ending process. New norms are always established over old established truth. Hence science is unfathomable.

Axis of Earth is an imaginary line passing through the earth poles. Time scale depends upon the rotation of celestial objects around some powerful center in space. Astrology and space science were highly advanced during the Ved and purana era. (Song of Science Shrimad Bhagavad-Gita Notion Press, India, Singapore, Malaysia, 2020.Hidden Science in Rigveda, G B D books, Delhi, 1st edition 2023)

As per the Vedic statement it is different for different objects in space. Accordingly, Vedic Rishis (Scientists) time scale is calculated as Yug, Manvantara, etc. Science can never claim the wholesome achievement. Because new inventions and discoveries always add new developmental knowledge to the existing knowledge. By using the word NA ITI meaning that this is not the end. Doors for new discoveries are kept open.

The present knowledge about the earth axis is that it is tilted to 23.5^0 in relation to the line joining the two earth poles North and South poles of the earth. This is termed as "Obliquity". In a fixed tilt it rotates around the Sun in an orbit which is horizontal in relation to solar equator. Rotation decides the time and seasons of the earth. Fixed axis tilt and fixed orbit of rotation of earth around Sun responsible for change of seasons on earth, creates doubt because of following reasons.

The tilt and rotation of earth as well as the solar solstices of sun were there during ice age also then why tilt is affecting seasons? Earth is like a free pendulum in space. The earth and the solar system are surrounded by electromagnetic rays and gravitational forces of space how the tilt remains fixed in one direction and rotates in a fixed orbit around sun. Earth in comparison to the Sun, North star, South star is a weak electromagnetic as well as weak gravitational energy in space. Even then the tilt and orbit are fixed and not influenced at all by such powerful forces around earth. The pole of earth rotates in circular manner due to influence of north star even then the imaginary axis tilt is fixed all the year.

Is it possible to verify all these doubts by Sun - dial shadows cast by solar solstices in one year? Can the doubts be cleared or prove the existing knowledge? Since childhood the author has been fascinated by the shadows of staff casting on Sun Dial or Solar watch surface. The shadows are related to the Solstices of the Sun. The casting of shadows is limited to a particular area. In one year, it casts shadow to and fro in a limited area of Sun- dial. Earth is divided by an imaginary line passing through the center of earth, the equator, into North and South hemispheres. On a particular day the SANKRANTI-day of north hemisphere the shadow starts returning till another SANKRANTI day of south hemisphere of earth, and so on. In summary the Sun rotates between the imaginary Line of Cancer and the line of Capricorn on the earth. This solar solstice is called UTTARAYAN and DKSHINAYAN in Vedic literature. An angle is cast between these two solar positions, shadows, with the central point of the staff. The angle between the two extremes is measured and kept in record.

Here again the doubt crops. Sun is rotating between the two lines Cancer and Capricorn for one year span. This has been going on for many years. The Sun is big, in size, having more powerful radiation and electromagnetic power compared to earth. The Sun being more powerful but moves up and down. This Sun movement is apparent or real?

The author measured the angle between the two extremes of cast shadows on Sundial, at various places on earth. Details are in Material and Method.

Material and Methods.

Sun dial is very easy to make. The Sun – dial or Solar watch was used to carry out the experiment. The central staff of the sundial casts shadow on the surface of the watch. The shadows show a common feature during Sankranti days i.e. summer and winter solstices of the Sun, longest day, and the shortest day of the year, when journey of Sun stops and returns to north or south hemisphere of earth. The earth is divided by an imaginary line called the equator. In other words, the solstices are limited by the lines of Capricorn and Cancer. The extreme sites of shadows marked on dial. The shadow of the staff on the dial surface was recorded. The angle between two shadows of the central staff was measured with the help of a "D" of School compass box. The author visited various places on earth. The details are as under:

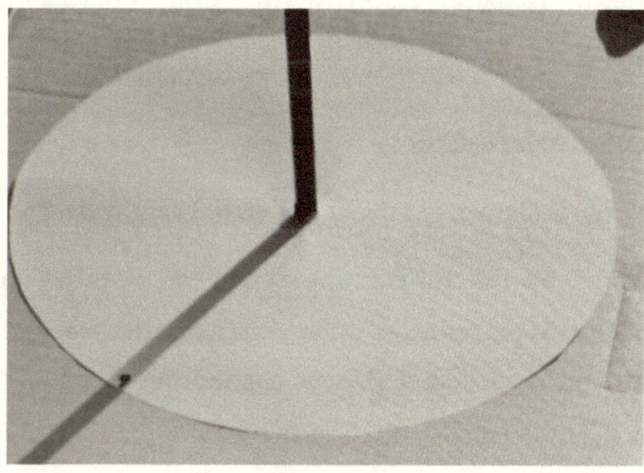

Sundial

Various places where Author carried out the experiment:

A. Northern Hemisphere,

1. At Morar, Lashkar, Gwalior, MP. Latitude 26.23N, Longitude 78.13E
2. Lashkar, Gwalior, M.P. Longitude and Latitude is approximately same as bove.
3. Delhi, Capital of India. Latitude 28.6 N and Longitude 77.2 E
4. Carnicobar, Andaman and Nicobar Islands, India Car Nicobar, A. & N Islands, India. Latitude 9.15 N and Longitude 92.8E.

5. Port Blair, Andaman and Nicobar Islands. Latitude 11.6N, Longitude 92.7E

6. Al Marj, Libya, (location Latitude 32.29N, Longitude 20^{0}E). Land separated by a range of Hills – Jebel Akhdar Mountains, from Mediterranean Sea.

7. Hibbing, Minneapolis, Minnesota, USA. Hibbing, MNS, Minnesota, USA. Latitude 47.25N Longitude 92.56W

8. Hopkins, Minnesota, USA. Hopkin, MN, USA. Latitude 44.5N. Longitude93.24W.

B. Southern Hemisphere,

The Ponds, Sydny, Australia, Latitude-33.86 S, Longitude-151.20 E

The angle formed by the staff at the centre on Sundial surface, by the shadows between two extremes of solar solstices, measured at all the above places on earth and recorded. This was carried out at a specific fixed local time of the day. The shadows recorded from one Sankranti day or end of Sun solstices in northern hemisphere i.e. end point of northern solstice of the Sun. The other side of shadow recorded at the end of southern solstice of the Sun. The angle at the central staff caused by the cast shadows on the sundial, was recorded.

Table: Measurement of angle at various places on earth.

Sr.No.	Names of places on earth	Measured angle
1	Morar, Gwalior, MP. India. Latitude 26.23N, Longitude 78.13E	60.25^0
2	Lashkar, Gwl. MP India. Latitude 26.23N, Longitude 78.13E	60^0
3	Delhi, India. Latitude 28.6 N and Longitude 77.2 E	60.3^0
4	Car Nicobar, A & N Islands, India. Latitude 9.15 N and Longitude 92.8E.	60.5^0
5	Port Blair, A & N Islands. India. Latitude 11.6N, Longitude 92.7E	60^0
6	Al Marj. Libya. Latitude 32.29N, Longitude 20^0E	60^0
7	Hibbing, MNS, Minnesota. USA Latitude 47.25N Longitude 92.56W	60.25^0
8	Hopkins, MNS, Minnesota. Latitude 44.5N. Longitude93.24W.	60^0
9	Southern hemisphere. Sydney, Australia. Latitude-33.86 S, Longitude-151.20 E	60^0

Results and Observations:

It is a common observation that in Solar solstice the Sun star moves up towards northern hemisphere and then moves towards the southern hemisphere. The distance of earth from Sun is constant. The shadows of staff on sundial surface remain constant and fixed. The distance of earth is increased then the shadows too will vary. Longer the distance shadows will form a small angle and vice-versa.

It is interesting to note that on average, the angle was constantly 60^0 at different places mentioned above. To analyze, let us understand the available existing knowledge about earth axis and space. Earth axis is 23.5^0 tilted in a fixed obliquity. Without any change in its obliquity earth rotates in a fixed orbit around the Sun. The Earth is divided by imaginary lines on Earth map called Longitude and Altitude. The earth is divided into North and South hemispheres by a central line Equator. The imaginary lines of Cancer (कर्क रेखा) and Capricorn (मकर रेखा) are on earth map North and South hemisphere respectively. The Sun solstices towards North and south hemispheres are limited to these imaginary lines of Cancer and Capricorn. In Sanskrit this celestial event is named Kirk Sankranti and Makar Sankranti. The Sun solstices are known as UTTARAYAN or dev-ayan and DAKSHINAYAN or Pitru Ayan. Thus, two AYANs of Sun make one year on earth.

Whether the earth axis is tilted or straight in relation to horizontal, the angle cast by staff at its extreme sites of Solar solstices, will measure different at different places on earth. This can be Understood by figures.

As Earth orbits the Sun, its tilted axis always points in the same direction. So, throughout the year, at different sites of the Earth get the Sun's direct rays. Sometimes it is the North Pole tilting toward the Sun (around June) and sometimes it is the South Pole tilting toward the Sun (around December). This decides the summer or winter season on earth.

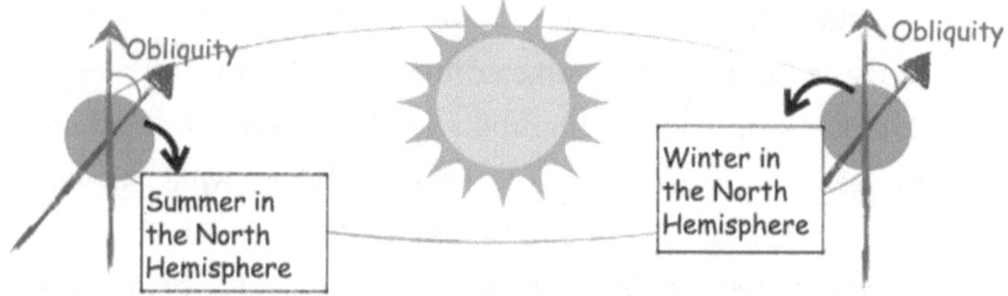

(From Wikipedia)

As per NASA observation and explanation the seasons change due to tilt of earth Axis. But Axis remains always unaltered and points towards the same direction.

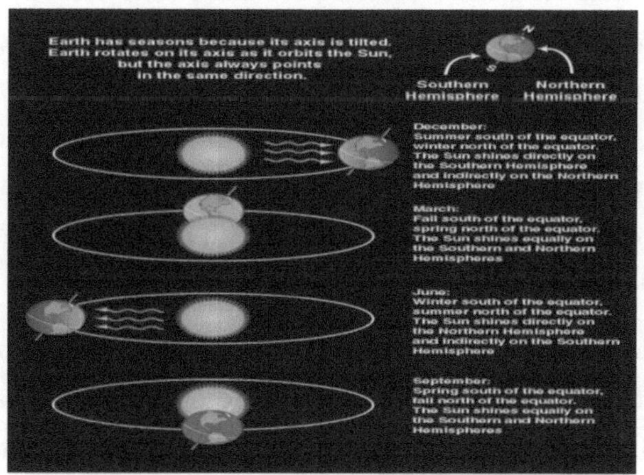

(The figure explains the current concept about obliquity of earth and season change on earth).

Any knowledge which is different than this knowledge is not easy to prove. But truth must become known. Author's fundamental research on "Adult stem cells" authenticated by international patent from USA, shows regeneration of smooth muscles. The results were contrary to medical textbook statement that "Smooth muscles do not regenerate, and Cardiac muscles never regenerate". But the author's research showed regeneration of smooth muscles. This statement was unacceptable to contemporary peers on the subject. At the same time in textbook the healthy healing granulation tissue has pulsatile character due to newly growing capillaries which have smooth muscles in the capillaries. These grow in the healing tissues. This provides nutrition to the healing and growing tissues of heling wounds. This means smooth muscles do grow. And textbook statement becomes questionable. The research paper could not get birth in any reputed journal.

The earth movement around sun and around its own axis is a highly complex and complicated. Earth's movement around its axis causes Sun rise and day and night on earth. But Sun is not rotating around earth. It is well known that the Earth's orbiting around Sun results in earth's year of 365 days. Year comprising of 12 months and two solar solstices, which are influenced by different twelve signs of zodiac (Rashis) and 27 different Nakshatras. The Sun and Nakshatra cause different seasons on earth. Sun shuttles between imaginary lines on earth named Lines of Cancer and line of Capricorn at 23.5 latitude North and South of imaginary central equator which divides earth into north and south hemispheres.

General observation is sun in summer solstice is on north hemisphere. Sun moves south after its maximum northern sojourn. This is gradual journey to south. Till it reaches line of Capricorn. It again travels towards north in a gradual manner till the line of Cancer.

Sun is a big star and is at a fixed position in relation to earth. Therefore, whatever the movement is of Earth and not Sun. This is established by the day and night on earth rotation on its own axis, and different months on earth due to earth rotating around sun and not the vice-versa.

If Sun moves up and down apparently during solstices, as seen on earth, then certainly the earth moves up and down in reality considering the other events like day and night and months on earth. The Sun being comparatively in a fixed position. How then the axis remains fixed, and the orbit is fixed and horizontal in relation to solar equator.

The following observations noted.

1. The experiments conducted to establish the truth. On earth surface at various places as given in the Material and Method section. The angle appeared due to shadows of central staff of Sun Dial at the centre, was measured which showed everywhere 60^0 angles. No change could be detected in the experiment conducted at all the places on earth. The line of Cancer and the line of Capricorn are important in the experiment.

2. If Earth axis is tilted at 23.5^0 obliquity all the time, then the angle will be different at various places on earth. On the contrary if Axis is not tilted and is at 90^0 with horizontal plane, even then the angle will not be constant 60^0 everywhere on earth. Angle made by shadows on sun dial at imaginary line of equator, Cancer and Capricorn will be different.

Then under what circumstances the angle will be constant and measure 60^0 at various places on earth. What will be the angle in following conditions:

Condition A. Earth Axis is straight and fixed, and solar orbiting of earth around the Sun is steady fixed in horizontal plane. The angles made by staff of sun dial, at different places on earth will vary and not constant. Earth poles will be deprived of sun light for six months during Uttar-Ayan phase of Solar solstice.

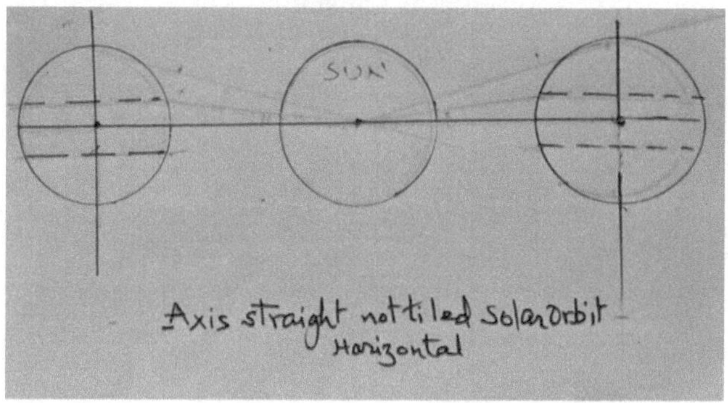

Condition B. Earth axis is tilted as is the current concept, and solar orbiting of earth is steady fixed in horizontal plane. The angles made by Sun dial staff will not be constant but varies. Sun light on earth poles will be as per existing norm for six months.

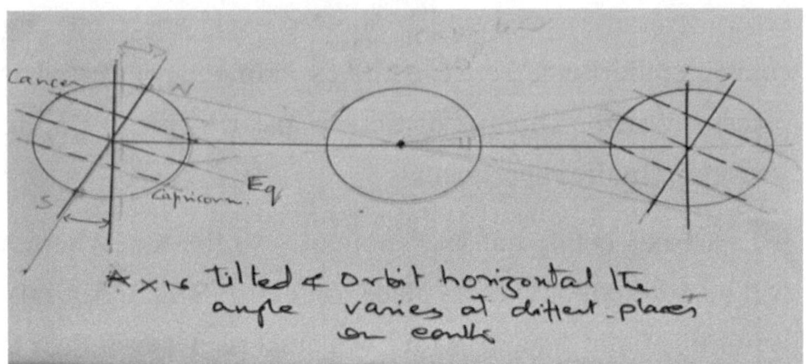

Condition C. Earth axis not tilted, and earth orbit is not constant instead the earth moves 30^0 up towards north during Uttar Ayan in relation to Sun's horizontal plane, and 30^0 down towards south during Dakshin Ayan phase of solar solstice. The total angle between the two shadows on sun dial, between two extreme points of north and south solar solstices, measures 60^0. At the same time sunshine and light will prevail for six months as usual. The orbit of earth is not steady but gradually moves to north and south direction while sun sojourns to south or north as per the solar solstices summer solstice and winter solstice (in Vedic language Uttar ayan and Dakshin ayan). In such imaginary calculations distance of earth from sun is important and remains constant.

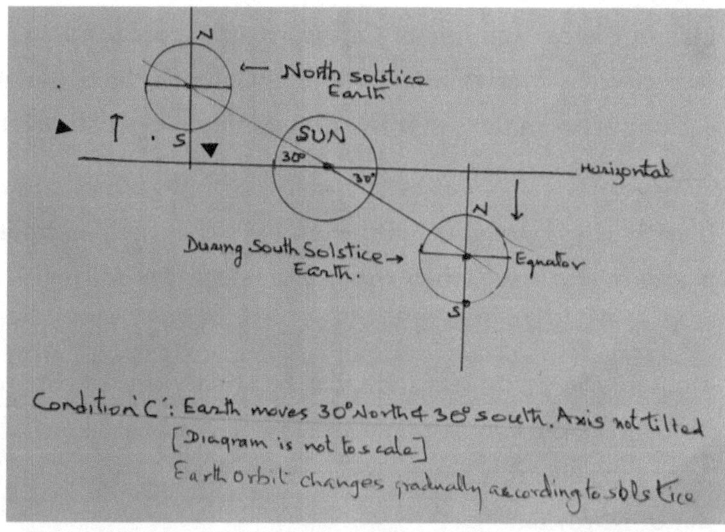

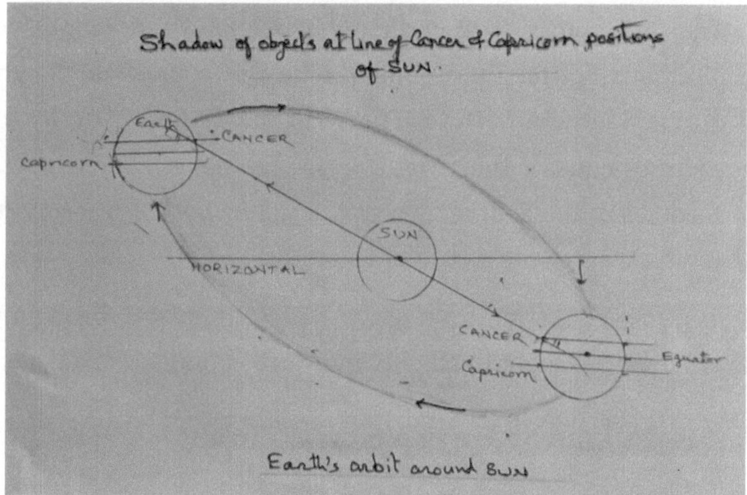

It is known that there is another movement of axis of earth, and that depends upon the electromagnetic and gravitational force of North Star. This disturbs the steady angle of obliquity of earth axis. How then the statement that axis is only in one direction all the time.

1. The constancy of 60^0 angle is only possible if Earth moves 30^0 up toward north and 30^0 south in relation to imaginary line of equator. Sun being steady and fixed. Understand by figure above.

2. Line of Cancer and line of Capricorn 23.5^0 north and 23.5^0 South respectively on earth. Similarly, if Equator is tilted the angle at equator between the two solar solstices shadows will be 47^0 ($23.5^0 + 23.5^0 = 47^0$aproximately).

3. If earth axis is straight, and the orbit is steady and horizontal, sun is steady and fixed, then the angle at equator will be 0^0 and at various places it will be different.

4. Modern science understands that Imaginary line of axis of earth which joins the two poles of earth is not steady but keep changing due to the electromagnetic and gravitational forces of North pole star or Dhruv tara.

5. The Sun shines over earth poles, for up to 6 months during Northern Solstice and similar time Sun shines on South pole during Southern Solstice. The earth moves up 30^0 north and 30^0 south of equator the angle will also remain 60^0 between the two shadows of the staff on Sun dial. The Sun will enlighten North and south poles for the period of 6 months.

This is open for verification from space. But truth must be brought to day light. Truth must be taught in schools after verification.

1. What is the knowledge in Ved and Puran?

Change of seasons:

Total number of Ritu is six in one year. The change of seasons is with months of the year. The names of the months are after the existing Nakshatras as per the Nakshatras position in space during those months. Summarily, names and the constellations influence the seasons.

No.नंबर	**Month** महिने	**Ritu** ऋतु	**Nakshtra** नक्षत्र
1.	**ChaitraVaishakh** चैत्र वैशाख	**Vasant Ritu** वसंत ऋतु	**Chitra Vishakha** चित्रा विशाखा
2.	**Jeshtha Aashadha** ज्येष्ठ आषाढ	**Summer season** ग्रीष्म ऋतु	**Jyestha Aashadha** ज्येष्ठा आषाढ
3.	**Shravan Bhadrapada** श्रावण भाद्रपद	**Rainy season** वर्षा ऋतु	**Bhadrapada Shravan** भाद्रपदश्रावण
4.	**Ashvin Kartik** अश्विन कार्तिक	**Winter season** शरद ऋतु	**Ashvin Kartik** अश्विनी कार्तिक
5.	**Margsheersh Paush** मार्गशीर्ष पौष	**Hemant Ritu** हेमंत ऋतु	**Mrigshirsha Pushya** मृगशीर्ष पुष्य
6.	**Maagh Phalgun** माघ फाल्गुन	**Shishir Ritu** शिशिर ऋतु	**Magha Phalguni** मघा फाल्गुनी
1.	**ChaitraVaishakh** चैत्र वैशाख	**Vasant Ritu** वसंत ऋतु	**Chitra Vishakha** चित्रा विशाखा

As per the Vedic space knowledge (**खगोल ज्ञान**) there are six Ritu's in a year. This is as per the influence of Nakshatra influence on earth when it passes through these Nakshtra and a pair of months.

Apart from this the effect of Rashi through which the sun passes every month, is also there which must be considered to understand the seasons on earth.

In summary, tilted Axis of earth is responsible for change of season is questionable. There are more reasons which must be addressed properly.

Discussion:

Since subject matter is related to the solar shadows of central staff of Sundial which is dependent upon the Sun's sojourn between imaginary lines on earth the line of Cancer and Capricorn, it becomes mandatory to understand the solar solstices. **Sun Solstices in Rigveda:** Sun solstices or Summer and Winter solstices were known to Vedic Rishis. (Rigved 10-18-1).

परं मृत्यो अनु परेहि पन्थां यस्ते स्व इतरो **देवयानात्** । चक्षुष्मते शृण्वते ते ब्रवीमि मा नः प्रजां रीरिषो मोत वीरान् ॥ Rigved 10-18-1.

Param mrutyo anu parahi pantha yaste sva itaro **devyanat** I chakshushmate shruvate te bravimi ma nah prajam ririsho mot viran II 1 II rigved. 10-18-1.

देवयानात् (dev+Ayan. देव + अयन) = Uttarayan = Summer Solstice. - Death God (yam यम) adopt different path and avoid killing of our brave soldiers and our progeny. 1.)

Manifestation of SUN. and its solstices. Stabilization of Sun in space is described in Rigveda Mantra Rigved 6- 67- 1. below: -

विश्वेषां वः सतां ज्येष्ठतमा गीर्भिर्मित्रां वरूणा वा वृषध्यै । सं या रश्मेव यमतुर्यमिष्ठा द्वा जनां असमा बाहुभिः स्वैः II1II Rigved. 6-67-1.

viśveṣāṁ vaḥ satāṁ jyeṣṭhatamā gīrbhir mitrāvaruṇā vāvṛdhadhyai I saṁ yā raśmeva yamatur yamiṣṭhā dvā janām̐ asamā bāhubhiḥ svaiḥ II 1 II Rigved. 6-67-1.

Mitra and Varun even though are different under control like reigns of horses, the two elements right and left reigns, responsible for Sun's solstices. These two elements + ive and – ive, concentrate to form Star, like SUN.

विद्युतो ज्योतिः परिसजिहान मित्रावरूणा विद्युत्सर्वे समाहिता (ऋगवेद. तैत्तरीय आरण्यक).

Vidyuto Jyotih parisajihan mitra Varuna vidyutsarve samahita Taittariya Aranyak

VARUN is responsible for stationing Sun in space - Antariksha (Rigved. Taittariya Aaranyak. Upanishad).

वनेषु व्यंतरिक्षं ततान वाजं मर्वत्सु पय उस्त्रियासु । हृत्सु ऋतं वरुणो अप्स्वग्निं दिवि सूर्य मदधात् सोमभद्रौ II 2 II Rigved 5-85-2.

Vneshu vyanta riksham tataan vajam marvatsu paya ustriyasu I hritsu rutam varuno apsvagni divi surya maddhat sombhadro II Rigved 5-85-2.

Varun manifests or establishes above trees of forest the Antariksha, intellect in humans, Fire – agni in water and Sun in antariksha, water in rivers, milk in cows, and strength in horses. Because of all this Varun is as Raja-SAMRAT in Rigved. 7-87-5.

तिस्त्रो द्यावो निहिता अन्तरस्मिन् तिस्त्रो भूमि रुपरा षडविधानाः । गुत्सो राजा वरुणश्चक्र एतं दिवि हिरण्यम् शुमेकम II5II

In other words, all actions in the universe or multiverse, are dependent upon VARUN i.e., Rigveda 8-41 – 6

यस्मिन विश्वानि काव्या चक्रे नाभिरिवश्रिता । त्रितं जूति सपर्यत व्रजे गावो न संयुजे युजे अश्रवाँ अयुक्षत नभन्ता मन्यके समें II 6 II Rigveda 8-41 – 6.

As per modern science, the Giant impact hypothesis says that the Moon collided with Earth and tilted the Axis of Earth. This giant impact had profound effects on Earth. It not only tilted the Earth Axis but established seasons on Earth and controlled ocean tides, slowed the speed of earth, and stabilized Earth from wobbling. If moon is responsible for ebb and tide of ocean, then tilt of earth axis or erect position of axis will have equal influence on ocean waters. How is the tilt cause of ebb and tide? How can tilt control it? Must be verified scientifically.

The net result and the current concepts are that the tilt of Earth Axis is responsible for seasons on Earth. This is the current fundamental knowledge.

To prove that the Earth rotates around the Sun, Sun light is considered important. Seasons change when the earth rotates around the Sun in a definite orbit. How correct is the present belief that the earth axis tilt is responsible for the seasons on the earth? There is doubt about this. The following doubts need be addressed:

An interesting statement exists in Rigved.

The description about AGNI is available in Rigveda, 4- 58- 3.

च॒त्वारि॒ शृङ्गा॒ त्रयौ अस्य॒ पादा॒ द्वे शी॒र्षे स॒प्त हस्ता॑सो अस्य । त्रिधा॑ ब॒द्धो वृ॑ष॒भो रौरवीति म॒हो दे॒वो मर्त्याँ॒ आ वि॑वेश ॥ Rigveda, 4- 58- 3.

Chatvari shringa trayo asya pada, dvei sheershe sapta hastaso asya I rorviti maho devo martya aa vivesh II 3 II Rigved, 4-58-3.

Meaning of mantra is Four horns (चत्वारी श्रृंगा), three legs (त्रयो अस्य पादा), two heads (व्दै शीर्षे), and seven hands (सप्त हस्तासो), the bull tied at three sites (त्रिधा बध्दो वृषभो), the great God enters from all around in mortal's abode and creates sound.

This is an enigmatic explanation about fire – the AGNI or Sun. It is an obscure picture. It is certainly symbolic. How it is so? The analysis is as follows:

It does not fit in the ordinary fire or flames of the fire, is obvious. If one considers AGNI (Flames or "Jwala") as SUN God, the meaning can be clear. The SUN showers energy or brilliance all around on earth. It energises all living beings when Sun rises in the morning. Sun is responsible for all types of seasons (three main Summer, Winter, and Rains, and spring make four horns.) on earth. Sun illuminates three abodes – BHUH, BHUVAH, SWAH. That is the area of three abodes up to which the sun rays and light exists. Modern science has established space station up to solar limit.

Sun Solstices are two – Summer and Winter or moves in two heads. Sun light beam, or Surya-Prakash, can be split into seven colours VIBGYOR is known to modern science.

Apparently, the Sun rotates up north and down south twice in one year. This rotation is called Summer and winter Solstices or in Vedic knowledge the solstices are called Uttar Ayan and Dakshin Ayan. This knowledge is since Rigved time. The oldest science treatise on earth. These Sun Solstices decide Summer and winter on earth's hemispheres.

एकचक्रं वर्तत एकनेमि सहस्राक्षरं प्र पुरो नि पश्चा। अर्धेन विश्वं भुवनं जजान यदस्यार्धं क्वS तद्बभूव ॥ अथर्ववेद - काण्ड » 10; सूक्त » 8; मन्त्र » 7.

Ek chakram vartat eknemi sahastraksharam pra puro ni pashcha I Ardhen vishvam bhuvanam jajan yadasyardham kva tadbabhuv II 7 II Atharv Ved. 10-8-7.

The absolute truth with its uniformly applicable and unbreakable laws of Nature is omnipresent and omniscient, in past, present, and future. With a fractional energy of this absolute truth, the boundless cosmos has been created.

To understand the cosmos Ved has cited example of wheel. One is the wheel of the universe, has the outer circumference - the transcendent Brahma, has the central axis, the immanent Brahma), yet thousands are the spokes and axes, **wheels within wheels, moving up and down, forward, and backward, east, and west.** With one part of his Shakti, Prakriti,

Brahma has formed the entire universe, where is the rest of it? What happened?

This mantra indicates the movements of celestial bodies in all directions. Why then the earth is moving in a fixed manner? Taking this hint the present analysis of experiment carried out.

During modern renaissance time of west, Louis Agassiz was the first person to hypothesize that the Earth was once subject to an ice age. He proposed this hypothesis to the Helvetic Society in 1837 and garnered attention, statement of A. Jutkiewicz Prof. D Muller in in Geology Magazine, from sediments in rocks claim the cause of ice age on earth. The solstices of Sun were also present at that time. And earth was also rotating around the Sun. The tilted axis of earth is responsible for change of seasons on earth creates doubt and is questionable. This needs to be explained in relation with the KHAGOL Vidya (KHA=Space and Gol =round), as per Vedic knowledge.

During ancient times, it was believed by western scientists, that the earth was a cube, flat disc to modern belief that the earth is a sphere. Sun rotating around earth to modern belief that earth rotates around the Sun. Nature of earth's orbit around the Sun determined to some accuracy. One pole of the earth is always tilted towards the Sun. Is it the absolute truth? This confirms the belief of Sanskrit Speaking Civilization scientists that science is unfathomable, or NA ITI, not the end.

Following considerations need be pondered:

1. All around the Earth as free pendulum, there is sphere of electromagnetic and gravitational forces. At the same time Powerful North Star and South star even then the earth rotates around the Sun without any change in its orbit or its Axis. It stimulates doubt when Earth is like a free pendulum in space. How it is possible?

2. The earth rotates whole year with tilted axis in one direction and in horizontal orbit around the sun. NASA statement in figure:

   As per NASA observation and explanation the seasons change due to tilt of earth Axis. But Axis remains steady and always points the same direction. See diagram.

Is it the ultimate truth? How is it possible when powerful stars are around the Solar system? Doesn't it need verification?

Apart from this the Vedic statement is:

Month of Chaitra is named due to the influence of the constellation – The Nakshatra CHITRA. Similarly, Vishakh month is due to the influence of nakshatra Vaishakha and so on. Accordingly, there are six seasons in Vedic Bharat Varsha. One season covers two months. Like Chaitra-Vishakh = Vasant Ritu, Jyeshtha- Aashaadha = Grishma Ritu, Shravan- Bhadrapada = Varsha Ritu, and so on. This clearly explains the possibility of change of Seasons are due to the influence of Nakshatra - the star constellations. Jyeshtha - Aashaadha nakshatra cause summer season – Grishma Ritu. All seasons are due to changed Nakshtra influence. See chart on page 244.

3. When earth passes under an influence of powerful star or constellation the Axis will not be influenced by it or remain in one direction only? Needs verification.

   Hugh Leyton Engineer (1960–2023) believes that the Earth's axis is not steady. (From: Axial tilt - Wikipedia). He assumes Earth's obliquity may have been reasonably accurately measured as early as 1100 BC in India and China. The ancient Greeks had measured the obliquity since about 350 BC,

4. Modern science understands that Axis of earth changes due to the influence of North star, and it rotates at steady tilted axis of earth. How is it possible?

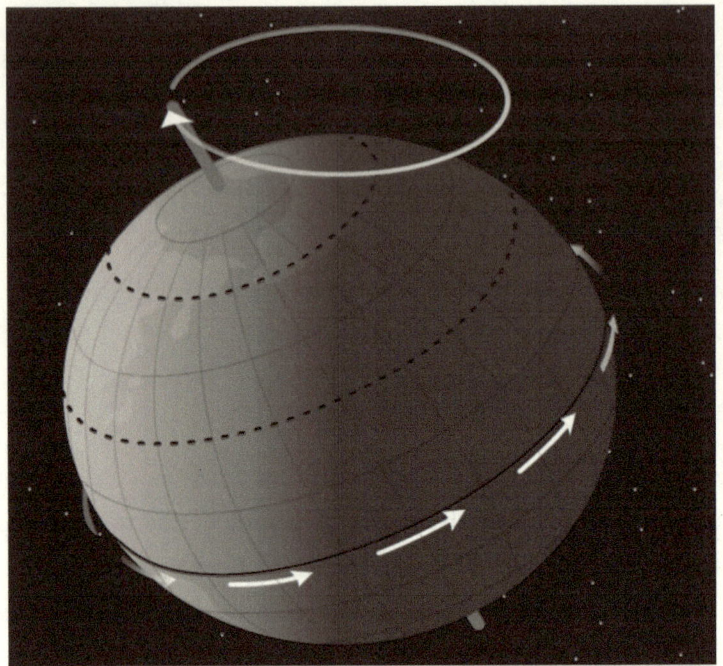

Earth rotation and its orbiting around Sun is not simple. Scientific revolution of west is recent, with due to efforts of Copernicus, Galileo etc. but the Rishis of Vedic period have researched out and toiled hard to understand the space and KHAGOL shastra was highly developed. Rishis not only understood the stars and constellations of space, but they established the effect of stars, Rashis (signs of zodiac) and constellations on life human beings. The calculation of YUG, MANVANTAR etc were established. Life span of Brahma, Vishnu and Rudra-shiv was calculated. Zero was invented for massive calculations.

5. Summer and Winter seasons alter with Sun's solstices. Is there any alternative to this which will be in line with scientific facts.?

6. As compared to the Sun earth is a weaker planet. The Sun is extremely powerful star even then the earth is rotating around in a

steady tilted axis and in an orbit which is not disturbed by Sun's power?

7. Tilt is related to its orbit around the Sun which is horizontal. That is, it is related to the equator as well if earth is in erect position that is north and south poles of earth are tilted accordingly. Subsequently the tilt is of equator also by 23.5^0. Does It need verification?

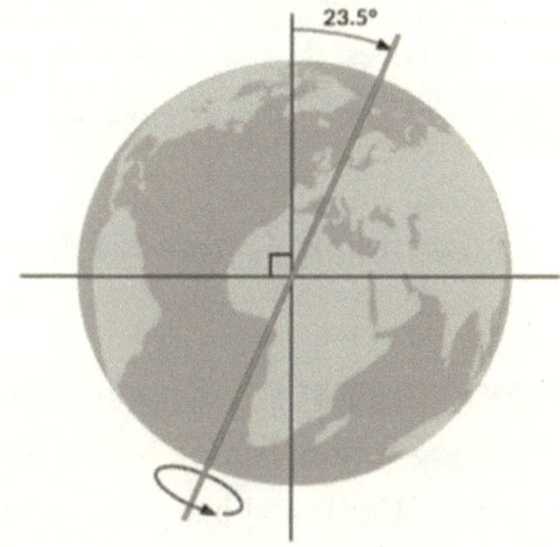

8. Sun rays falling on earth causing shadows of objects, can justify and verify the scientific truth about all this?

9. The powerful gravitational force of North star has no influence on Axis of earth. If it influences, then still it remains tilted? Similarly, the south Star has any influence on the axis.

10. Earth rotates around the Sun at the same time it comes across various constellations. **The Sun also while rotating around the centre of the Galaxy passes through various groups of stars in space, then does it influence the seasons of Solar system and the earth.** The ice age and heat age on earth can be due to the sun's rotation in space around the centre of galaxy. Does this rotation

not influence the imaginary Axis and the orbit circumference of earth around the Sun?

11. A powerful magnet when comes near another smaller magnet then it influences the smaller magnet and even turns it 180^0 and its poles so that North pole attracts south pole or vice a versa. Then how Earth maintains its steady axis and the uniformly steady orbit. How it is possible?

12. The change of seasons also takes place on other planets as well. Modern science believes that it does not, and the reasons are unknown. Then why only the change exists on earth? Doubt deepens.

बृहत्साम तथा साम्नां गायत्री छन्दसामहम् । मासानां मार्गशीर्षोऽहमृतूनां कुसुमाकरः ॥
Gita. १०-३५॥

Ritu Kusumakar (ऋतु कुसुमाकर = Kusum means flower) is an indication of arrival of spring season. (spring season November- December month), In ved it is month of Kartic and margasheersha, (कार्तिक-मार्गशीर्ष का महीना) Among hymns also I am the BRIHAT-SAM; among mantras I am GAYATRI; among months I am parts of December-January (MARGA-SHIRSHA month); among seasons I am the flowery-spring.

13. Earth moves around Sun and solar system along with earth rotate around the centre of Galaxy Milky way, it passes through many stars and groups of stars like Signs of zodiac and many constellations. Then how the earth maintains tilt without getting influenced?

14. Seasons change because of heat and light of Sun which alters with the rotation. Axis which is imaginary line, remaining uniformly tilted, and the orbit of earth rotation around Sun, all the time imaginary horizontal, is doubtful and subject to verification.

15. If earth axis remains aligned and unchanged, then how and why seasons alter?
16. The heat and light of Sun will be more effective on earth if Earth moves up and down in relation to Sun while orbiting around Sun rather than steady orbit which is steady and not changed.

Some solutions are possible from Milankovitch cycle theory.

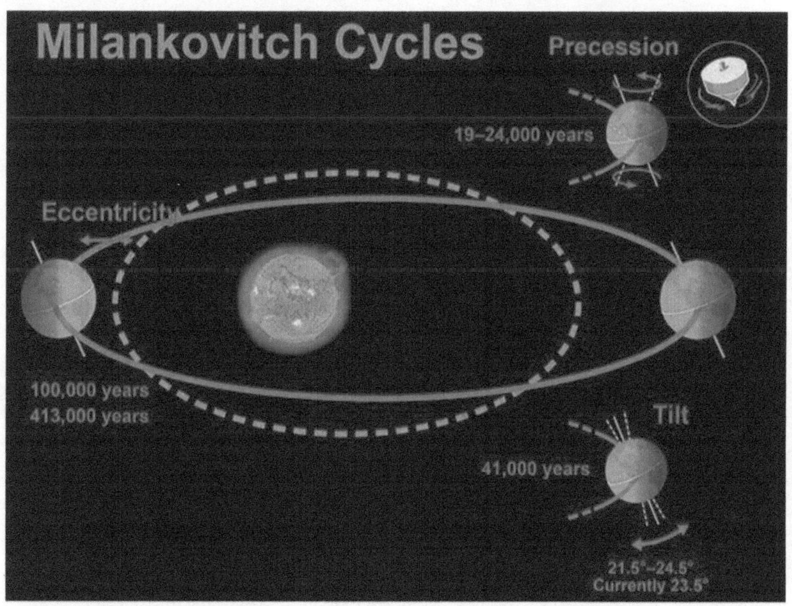

Milankovitch cycle is on the cyclical rotation of earth around Sun in a fixed orbit. It deals with the obliquity theory. Earth rotates on its axis causing Day and Night on earth. It deals with power of North Star responsible for rotation of poles of earth and not steady. Do this rotatory movements of poles of earth influence heat pattern on earth? This polar movement change tilt of earth axis. Then obliquity of earth and orbit around the sun in a steady fixed manner, becomes questionable.

Earth axis under the influence of North Star and South Star keeps on changing and has circular movements, like rotating top. Thus, axis tilt is not constant. This statement creates doubt on the current space knowledge. Such a knowledge is taught in the schools also. Humans are always on the move for the correct knowledge about universe. Interestingly Sanskrit Speaking civilization had coined the statement that thus so far we know verification and progress is the duty of the younger generation. The word used is NA ITI means not the end. Thus, the obliquity needs to be verified.

Figure below is to depict the current knowledge:

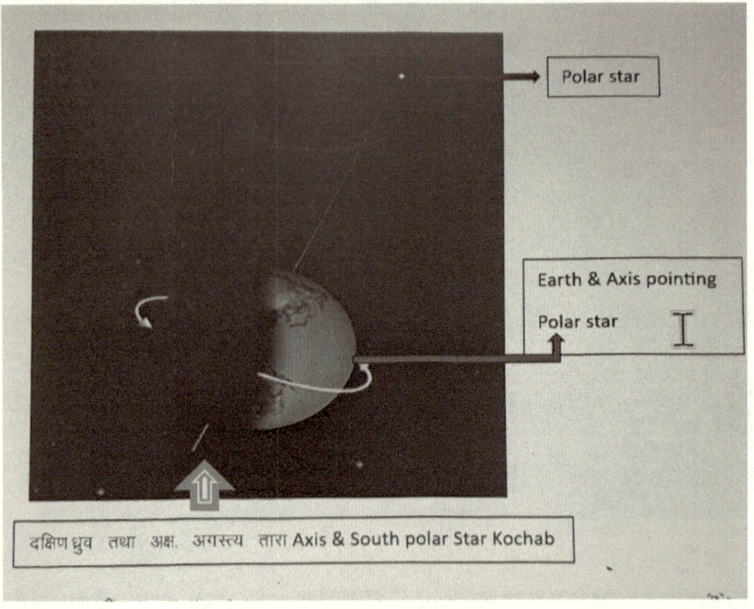

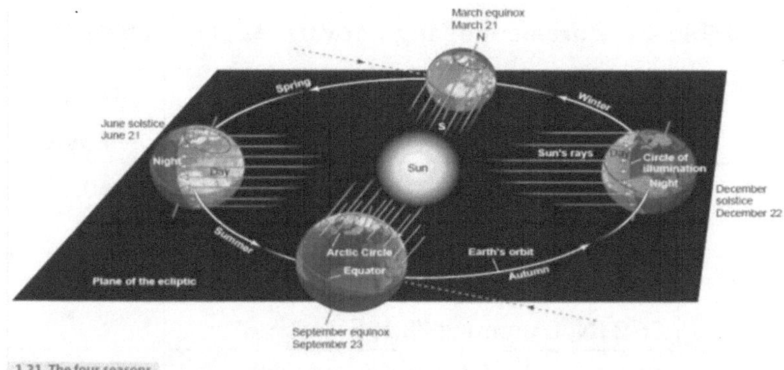

1.21 The four seasons

The Earth revolves once around the Sun in a year, passing through each of its four seasons. The four seasons occur because the Earth's tilted axis is always pointed toward the same point in space, very close to the North Star. That is, a line through the Earth's axis of rotation at each season is parallel to a line through the axis at any of the other seasons. Because of this fixed direction of rotation, the northern hemisphere is tipped toward the Sun for the June solstice and away from the Sun for the December solstice. Both hemispheres are illuminated equally at the equinoxes.

The Sun – dial or Solar watch used to carry out the experiment. The central staff of the sundial casts shadow on the surface of the watch. The shadows show a common feature during Sankranti days i.e. summer and winter solstices of the Sun, longest day, and the shortest day of the year, when journey of Sun stops and returns to north and south hemisphere of earth divided by the imaginary line of equator. In other words, the solstices are limited by the lines of Capricorn and Cancer. The extreme sites of shadows marked on dial. The shadow of the staff on the dial surface was recorded. The angle between two shadows of the central staff was measured with the help of a divider from School compass box. To study the angle at the center of the dial, the author visited various places on earth. See chart on page 5, above.

Table: Measurement of angle at various places on earth.

Sr.No,	Names of places on earth	Measured angle
1	Morar, Gwalior, MP. India. Latitude 26.23N, Longitude 78.13E	60.25^0
2	Lashkar, Gwl. MP India. Latitude 26.23N, Longitude 78.13E	60^0
3	Delhi, India. Latitude 28.6 N and Longitude 77.2 E	60.3^0
4	Car Nicobar, A & N Islands, India. Latitude 9.15 N and Longitude 92.8E.	60.5^0
5	Port Blair, A & N Islands. India. Latitude 11.6N, Longitude 92.7E	60^0
6	Al Marj. Libya. Latitude 32.29N, Longitude 20^0E	60^0
7	Hibbing, MNS, Minnesota. USA Latitude 47.25N Longitude 92.56W	60.25^0
8	Hopkins, MNS, Minnesota. Latitude 44.5N. Longitude93.24W.	60^0
9	Southern hemisphere. Sydney, Australia. Latitude-33.86 S, Longitude-151.20 E	60^0

The constancy of angle cast by staff of sundial i.e. 60^0 indicate that the earth axis is straight and not tilted and the orbit of rotation of earth around Sun in one year too moves accordingly.

When earth moves to north the sunshine is on south pole up to six months and when earth moves down towards south the sun illuminates north pole for up to six months. The seasons change is not due to the tilted axis of earth but due to sunshine and heat of Sun as well as the influence of constellations and Signs of Zodiacs (or Rashis - Vedic statement) and their electromagnetic and gravitational influences on earth.

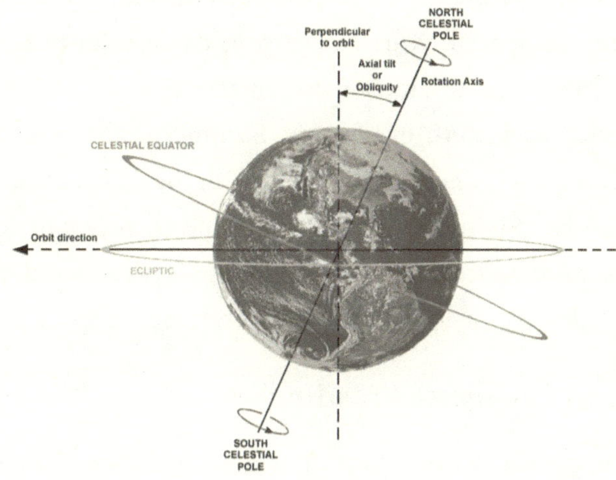

Earth's axial tilt (or obliquity) and its relation to the rotation axis and plane of orbit. Credit: Wikipedia Commons

Conclusion:

The constancy of obliquity of earth axis and rotation of earth around the Sun in a fixed orbit is questionable. The movement of the Sun southward and northward every six months in one year observed by earthlings seems apparent. Because the Sun is more powerful than earth in many respects. Then why does the Sun move? At the same time day and night occur due to earth rotation around its axis and not the other way round. Year on earth is due to earth orbiting around the Sun and not vice versa. Why then does the Sun sojourns in solstices?

With experimental verification it can possibly be concluded that the Earth axis is not tilted but straight. Tilted or straight axis in relation to horizontal, will result in different degrees of angle as per experiment. Instead, earth moves up towards north and down to south of the equator and the Sun is relatively fixed powerful pendulum object in space. Instead of the Sun movement, the earth's movement is 30^0 up north and 30^0 down south . This is responsible for the constant measurement 60^0 of the angle on sundial. The movement is as per the solar solstices or Uttar Ayan and Dakshin Ayan in one earth year. The seasons change due to the movement of earth around the Sun in an orbit which also changes as per the upward north to equator and south of equator. Summer and winter are effective due to the sun's influence on earth, along with the influence of Nakshatras every two months. Six months sunshine on north pole and south pole of earth depends on the direct sun rays on poles North or south respectively, during up and down movements of earth pendulum in space.

References and suggested reading:

1. B. G. Matapurkar, Exploration of science in Shrimad Bhagavad-Gita, Analytical study, Mahi Publication, 1st edition, 2020, Ahmadabad, Gujrat, India.

2. B. G. Matapurkar, Hidden science in Rigveda, Pigeon books Delhi, India, G B D books, 1st edition, 2023.

   Courtney Seligm an, How does the atmosphere change the effects of the Earth's rotation? Question Log, Quora, google. https://www.quora.com › Is-the-tilt-of-earth-s-axis-abso.

   Wikipedia.

3. Buis, Alan (27 February 2020). "Why Milankovitch (Orbital) Cycles Can't Explain Earth's Current Warming". NASA. Retrieved 29 July 2022.

4. Buis, Alan (27 February 2020). "Milankovitch (Orbital) Cycles and Their Role in Earth's Climate". NASA's Jet Propulsion Laboratory. Retrieved 8 January 2024.

5. Edvardsson S, Karlsson KG, Engholm M (2002). "Accurate spin axes and solar system dynamics: Climatic variations for the Earth and

Mars". Astronomy and Astrophysics. 384 (2): 689–701. Bibcode:2002A&A...384..689E. doi:10.1051/0004-6361:20020029. This is the first work that investigated the derivative of the ice volume in relation to insolation (page 698).

6. Roe G (2006). "In defense of Milankovitch". Geophysical Research Letters. 33 (24): L24703. Bibcode:2006GeoRL..3324703R. doi:10.1029/2006GL027817. S2CID 13230658. This shows that Milankovitch theory fits the data extremely well, over the past million years, if we consider derivatives.

7. Hidden science in Rigved. Analytical thought by B.G.Matapurkar. 1st Ed. 2023. GBD books Pigeon books India.

CHAPTER 13

SCIENCE OF PRONUNCIATION AND SCRIPT WRITING

This chapter deals with what Rigveda acknowledge about pronunciation and writing. Author could not find details about pronunciation and script writing in Rigveda. It may be due to improper scholarship. Therefore, other Sanskrit literature was scanned to elaborate the subject. But it is based on Rigvedic statement. Appropriate "Richas" from Rigved are incorporated.

Spoken Sanskrit Language was existing even before Vedic era. Sanskrit is mother of all languages. Why is it called as "SANSKRIT"? Because it is influenced by Sanskaar-संन्स्कार in English it is Sacrament, ordination. To affect power on anything by sacrament, it must exist. Therefore, some sort of language must be there before the Sanskrit Language. First the spoken language must have existed. Then only language in the form or in script format could be developed. According to western scholars Rigveda was carried forward through spoken and memorized form from generation to generations by word of mouth. Exactly this was given to understand the generation of Bharatiya during recent past. This has been taught in schools. The following script is worth the reading.

The Brahmanas are particularly noted for their instructions on the proper performance of rituals, as well as explanations on the symbolic importance of sacred words and rituals. {Encyclopædia Britannica (2013) }. Academicians, such as P. Alper, K. Klostermaier and F.M, Muller, state that these instructions insist on exact pronunciation (accent), {see Harvey P. Alper (2012), Understanding Mantras, Motilal Banarsidass, ISBN 978-8120807464, pages 104-105}. *chhandas* (छन्दः, meters), precise pitch, with coordinated movement of hand and fingers – that is, perfect delivery. [Klaus Klostermaier (1994), A Survey of Hinduism, Second Edition, State University of New York Press, ISBN 978-0791421093, pages 67-69]. Klostermaier adds that the Satapatha Brahamana, for example, states that verbal perfection made a mantra infallible, while one mistake made it powerless. Scholars suggest that this orthological perfection preserved Vedas in an age when writing technology was not in vogue, and the voluminous collection of Vedic knowledge were taught to and memorized by dedicated students through Svādhyāya, then remembered and verbally transmitted from one generation to the next. It seems breaking silence too early in at least one ritual is permissible in the Satapatha (1.1.4.9), where 'in that case mutter some Rik [RigVeda] or Yajus-text [YajurVeda] addressed to Vishnu; for Vishnu is the sacrifice, so that he thereby regains obtains a hold on the sacrifice, and penance is done by him'. [*www.sacred-texts.com.* Retrieved 28 January 2020].

The following description will convince the reader Contrary to this interpretation, based on analysing the Rigveda.

Word AKSHAR – **अक्षर,** which means permanent script word, has appeared in Rigveda Mantra. Rigveda, 1-164-39: -

ऋचो अक्षरे परमे व्योमन्यस्मिन्देवा अधि विश्वे निषेदु । यस्तन्न वेद किम ऋचा करिष्यति य इत्तव्दिदुस्त इमे समासते II 39 II Rigveda 1- 164-39.

ṛicho akṣare parame vyoman yasmin devā adhi viśhve niṣeduḥ | yas tan na veda kim ṛichā kariṣhyati ya ittadvidusta ime saāsate II 39 II Rigveda 1-164-39.

The gods exist in heaven and in the permanent, imperishable (text) knowledge (**ऋचो अक्षरे**) of the Veda. Spoken Richa can-not be Akshar (**अक्षर- अ + क्षर** = not perishable). It is likely to be distorted or lost. Script can only be Akshar and permanent (**अक्षर**). Reasonably or one can say that the Gods exist in the RUCHAS of Veda. If someone does not know the RUCHA, then what Rucha can do (किम ऋचा करिष्यति)? In summary, one who does not know this what he will do with the Veda? but others who do know it, they understand all and are perfect.

These statements clearly indicate that he script and writing skill was present in Vedic civilization.

As stated earlier that the spoken language must be there before written words. There is scientific study on sound in Rigveda. Based on the sound, the script words developed by sages of Sanskrit civilization. For this UCCHAR SHASTRA or phonetics of language was developed.

It is interesting that Rigveda has classified forms of sounds (Rigveda. 1-164-45), one can deduce the fact that this knowledge must have been there before that Rigveda scripted down the statement.

चत्वारि । वाक् । परिमिता । पदानि । तानि । विदुः । ब्राह्मणाः । ये । मनीषिणः । गुहा । त्रीणि । निहिता । न । इङ्गयन्ति । तुरीयम् । वाचः । मनुष्याः । वदन्ति ॥45॥ Rigveda, 1-164.

catvāri vāk parimitā padāni tāni vidur brāhmaṇā ye manīṣiṇaḥ | guhā trīṇi nihitā neṅgayanti turīyaṃ vāco manuṣyā vadanti ॥45॥ Rigveda, 1-164.

Chatvāri = Four (4). Vāk = speech; voice; conversation; sound. Parimitā = "weigh; measure." Padāni = "word; पद = pada, Manuṣyā = man; people. vadanti < vad = "describe; teach; speak.

Rigveda maintains that the sound called UDGEET OM, is cause for the manifest world in entire cosmos. This fact cannot be ignored at the same time it confirms that sound and pronunciation was known to Sanskrit Speaking Civilization since time immemorial. Pantanjal Yog Sutra considers Ohm (ॐ) as Nada Brahma or Primordial sound. This is responsible for all manifest world. Pantajal Yoga Sutra

तस्य वाचकः प्रणवः ॥२७॥

(Tasya Vachakah Pranavah-1.27).

Similar quotation is observed in Mandukya-upnishad – माण्डुक्य उपनिषद्. It has only 12 Mantras. It is different from Mandukopnishad – मंण्डुक उपनिषद.

हरिः ओम् । ओमित्येतदक्षरमिदं सर्वं तस्योपव्याख्यानं भूतं भवद्भविष्यदिति सर्वमोङ्कार एव | यच्चान्यत्त्रिकालातीतं तदप्योङ्कार एव ॥ १ ॥

hariḥ om | omityetadakṣaramidaṃ sarvaṃ tasyopavyākhyānaṃ bhūtaṃ bhavadbhaviṣyaditi sarvamoṅkāra eva | yaccānyattrikālātītaṃ tadapyoṅkāra eva || 1 ||

Ohm is past, present, and future. It is Aum. That which is beyond Kal Chakra or time cycle, is Aum.

The eighth anuvaka of Taittiriya Upanishad's first chapter discusses what is Aum? Yajurvedic ATHARVASHEERSHA goes further to state the Om Naad word can be expressed in words or 'in figure SWAROOP or Roop' and has been described in the mantra. How the script is framed in words, or one can say the sound is figured out in the words of script in "Ganapati Atharva sheersha" of Yajurveda, see below. This is clear indication that the language, script and the spoken words were prevalent during Vedic era.

The origin of sound and the forms of sound were perceived by sages and Rishis of that era.

गणादिं पूर्वमुच्चार्य वर्णादींस्तदनन्तरम् । अनुस्वारः परतरः । अर्धेन्दुलसितम्।तारेण ऋद्धम्।एतत्तवमनुस्वरूपम्॥७॥

ganaadim poorvamuchchaarya varnaadim tadanantaram ||anusvaarah' paratarah'|| ardhendulasitam || taarena ri'ddham ||etattava manusvaroopam ||7II

saishaa ganeshavidyaa ||ganakari'shih' || nichri'dgaayatreechchhandah ||ganapatirdevataa || om gam ganapataye namah' || 7 ||

The mantra addresses GANPATI in form (or roop), or Ganpati Swaroop is presented in words. It shows writing skill. 7.1: (The Mantra Swarupa of Ganapati is as follows) The first syllable of the word Gana (g`) is to be pronounced first; then the first syllabus varna – var (var-mala) (i.e. "A") should immediately follow (thus making "Ga" - g), 7.2: The Anuswara should follow next (thus making "Gam" g.), 7.3: Then it should be made to shine with the Half-Moon (i.e. the Nasal Sound of Chandrabindu – (चंद्रबिंदु), thus making "Gang"), 7.4: This should be Augmented by Tara (a Note signifying Om) (thus making "Om Gang"), 7.5: This is Your Mantra Swarupa (O Ganapati). In the same context the next mantra says:

गकारः पूर्वरूपम् । अकारो मध्यरूपम् । अनुस्वारश्चान्त्यरूपम् । बिन्दुरुत्तररूपम् । नादस्संधानम् । सगंहिता संधिः ॥८॥

gakaarah' poorvaroopam ॥ akaaro madhyamaroopam ॥ anusvaarashchaantya roopam ॥ binduruttararoopam ॥ naadah' sandhaanam ॥ samhitaasandhih' ॥8II

8.1: In Mantra, the Swarupa G-kara (g-kar) is the first form or पूर्व रूपम, 8.2: A-kara (A kar) is the middle form, + मध्यम p 8.3: And Anuswara is the last form अन्त्य रूपम\. Gam"), 8.4: Bindu is the form on the top (giving the nasal sound of chandra-Bindu, thus forming "Gang"), 8.5: This is joined with Nada, 8.6: All the combine (and when it finally ends with Nada, it gives the mantra a transcendental form).

Vaani or Vak or Sound is described in a voluminous literature in Vedas. As described above, in Rigveda the description is: -

चत्वारि वाक्परिमिता पदानि तानि विदुर्ब्राह्मणा ये मनीषिणाहा त्रीणि निहिता । गु : नेङ्गयन्ति रीयं वाचो मनुष्या वदन्तिII45II Rigveda. 1-164-45.

chatvāri vāk parimitā padāni tāni vidur brāhmaṇā ye manīṣiṇaḥ | guhā trīṇi nihitā neṅgayanti turīyaṃ vāco manuṣyā vadanti ॥45II Rigveda, 1-164.

Pronunciation has 4 forms. Wise Brahmans know this. Out of these four, three are hidden in caves (GUHA - guha). These are difficult to be heard. Or one can say 3 are latent. Only one can be heard. One which can be heard or experienced is in the form of speech. The speech is utilised by humans. Sound is a physical reaction. **It has light and heat**. Sound is a useful in the life of animal kingdom. Sound exists in whole cosmos - Brahmanda. Sound is a powerful element. According to the Vedas, there are four degrees of human speech. The following description is from different Sanskrit literature: -

Vaikhari (वैखरी), which is ordinary verbal speech, the kind we all hear and use daily, is an expression of *kriya shakti*, the power of action.

Madhyama (मध्यमा) is mental speech, verbalized but unspoken, the internal monologue and dialogue; it expresses Dn̈yana shakti (ज्ञान शक्ति), the power of knowledge and wisdom

Pashyanti (पश्यन्ति), single-minded speech, is perceptible but not particularized. It is the vehicle for *iccha shakti*, the power of desire. When you speak at the pashyanti level, you are sure of your message; your intentions are always clear.

Para-Vak is the highest form of sound. It issues forth from the Supernatural Ether (परम व्योमन param vyomam) where all the sound vibrations that build the various worlds **pre-exist in an undifferentiated state.** It is a cosmic manifestation. Para as the form of speech that displays no thought.

This Vak is further explained in Jaiminiya Upanishad (जैमिनि) - Brahmana, 1-40-1. It is similar to above Rigveda

श्रोत्रम् पदो वाग इका चतुर्ताह पदः Thought of mind is spoken. What is seen Richa (1-164- 45). Division of four is clear in this:

तस्य एत्स्ये वाको मनः पाद चक्षुः पादस is spoken. What is heard is spoken.

Speech has 4 sections of ¼th each. Mind is 1/4th, Sight 1/4th, Listening 1/4th, Speech.

In a question answer form the description in 4th question of Kenopnishad (केनोपनिषद) it is: -

यद्वाचानभ्युदितं येन वागभ्युद्यते । तदेव ब्रह्म त्वं विद्धि नेदं यदिदमुपासते ॥४॥ Kenopnishad. 1-4.

Yadvāchān abhyuditaṃ yena vāgabhyudyate | tadeva brahma tvaṃ viddhi nedaṃ yadidamupāsate || 4 ||

Conscious cosmos is without element of word sound, or one can say it is which cannot be described by words.

यदर्चिमद्यदणुभ्योणु च यस्मिन्ल्लोकाऽनिहिता लोकिनश्च । तदेतदक्षरं ब्रह्म स प्राणस्तदु वाङ्मनः । तदेतत्सत्यं तदमृतं तद्वेद्धव्यं सोम्य विद्धि ॥ २ ॥

yadarcimadyadaṇubhyoṇu ca yasmiṃllokā'nihitā lokinaśca tadetadakṣaraṃ brahma sa prāṇastadu vāṅmanaḥ tadetatsatyaṃ tadamṛtaṃ tadveddhavyaṃ somya viddhi ~ Verse 2.2.2

The immortal Brahman on which depend are prana, speech, mind, and all. According to the Sruti 'It is the *prana* of *prana*. This immortal Brahman which is the internal intelligence of *prana*. The meaning is that the mind should be concentrated upon the *Brahman or* concentrate mind upon that Brahman.

On analysis one recognizes that The Rig Veda 1.164.45 says that the speech - Vak (वाक्) that exists in four forms. Three are hidden and the fourth is revealed., Raja Bhartruhari, states in Vakyapadiya 1.112: "*vageva viswa bhuvanani jajne*" वागेव विश्व भुवनानी जज्ञे - means Vak which has created all the worlds). Cosmos is set in motion by the primordial vibration or throb (*Adi-spanda*) and that all objects of the Universe are created by sound. In other words, sound precedes the formation of objects.

Even the Bible in verse, says "In the beginning was the Word, and the Word was with God, and the Word was God" [John 1:1], says word was God before the manifestation of cosmos. Abstract from Bible: -

John 1. Berean Standard Bible. The beginning. Genesis 1:1 1-2. Hebrews 11:1-3. In the beginning was the Word, and the Word was with God, and the Word was God. He was with God in the beginning. Through Him all things were made, and without Him nothing was made that has been made. In Him was life, and that life was the light of men. The Light shines in the darkness, and the darkness has not overcome it.

The Witness of John. There came a man who was sent from God. His name was John. He came as a witness to testify about the Light, so that through him everyone might believe. He himself was not the Light, but he came to testify about the Light.

The true Light who gives light to every man was coming into the world. He was in the world, and though the world was made through Him, the world did not recognize Him [https:// biblehub.com/john/1-11.htm]. He came to His own, and His own did not receive Him. But to all who did receive Him, to those who believed in His name, He gave the right to become children of God— children born not of blood, nor of the desire or will of man, but born of God.

वागेवर्क् प्राणः सामोमित्येतदक्षरमुद्गीथ । तव्दा एतन्मिथुनं यव्दाक्व प्राणश्चर्क च साम II5II Chhandogyopnishad 1-1-5.

vāgevarkprāṇaḥ sāmomityetadakṣaramudgīthaḥ | tadvā etanmithunaṃ yadvākca prāṇaścarkca sāma ca || Chhandogyopnishad 1.1.5 ||

According to this Upaniṣad, the evolution of the gross world is in this order: earth, water, plants, human beings, speech, Ṛk, Sāma, and udgītha (Om). Udgītha is rasatamā, the essence of all essences, the cause of all causes. It occupies the eighth position—that is, it is the ultimate in the evolution of things. It is the Paramātman, the Self of all selves.

Markandeya Puran, Durga Saptashati Chapter 4 – The Devi Stuti, Mantra 10, mentions the energy or Shakti is word. All veda derived from word.

शब्दात्मिका सुविमलर्ग्यजुषां निधान-मुद्गीथरम्यपदपाठवतां च साम्नाम्। देवी त्रयी भगवती भव भावनायवार्ता च सर्वजगतां परमार्तिहन्त्री॥१०॥ Markandeya puran, Chapter 4, durga Saptashati, Mantra 10.

Shabdaatmikaa suvimalargyajushhaa nidhaanan mudgeetharamya padapaa cha vataan cha saamnaam |devee trayee bhagavatee bhava bhaavanaayavaarta cha sarva jagataam paramaartihantree ||10||

Cosmic energy or Shakti is Shabdarupa or ROOP like word. All vedas are having source from word. World manifestation is due to word naad - sound. Shabda Brahma meaning is absolute reality as primordial and immanent sound or speech principle. Shakti is the destroyer of all problems of the world.

Rigveda appreciate the support of VAYU and help in speech using lip and voice. See mantra below: -

वायो॒ इति॑ । तव॑ । प्र॒ऽपृ॒ञ्च॒ती । धेना॑ । जि॒गा॒ति॒ । दा॒शुषे॑ । उ॒रू॒ची । सोम॑ऽपीतये ॥3II Rigveda. 1-2-3.

vāyo tava prapṛñchatī dhenā jigāti dāśuṣe | urūcī somapītaye II3II Rigveda. 1-2-3.

(prapṛuñchatī = nominative. Dhenā = lip; voice).

ऋ॒तेन॒ यावृ॑ता॒वृधा॑वृ॒तस्य॒ ज्योति॑ष॒स्पती॑ । ता मि॒त्रावरु॑णा हुवे ॥5II Rig Veda 1.23.5.

ṛtena yāv ṛtāvṛdhāv ṛtasya jyotiṣas patī | tā mitrāvaruṇā huve II5II Rig Veda 1.23.5.

Mitra and Varuṇa, who with true speech (ṛutena < ṛuta. = ṛuta which means word), are invited who are the encouragers of pious acts, and are lords of true light".

In this context it will be worth elaborating regarding speech. In Taittariya Upanishad, Shkshavalli, Anuwak 2.

शीक्षां व्याख्यास्यामः । वर्ण स्वरः । मात्रा बलम् । साम संन्तानः । इत्युक्त शीक्षाध्यायः II1II Shikshavalli, Anuvak 2, Taittariya Upanishad.

aum shixam vyakhyasyamah. varnah svarah. matra balam.h. sama santanah. ityuktah shixadhyayah.. 1.. iti dvitiyo.anuvakah..

In education lectures regarding pronunciation of word, the importance is on Vovels -Varna, Speech-Swar, Vovel signs-Matra, bal (stress on word), Sam (Samatva – **समत्व** -Balance), and Santan-**संतान**-extension, are termed as education -**शिक्षाध्याय.**

Wamiya Sutra of Rugved:- Science of sound- SHABDA BRAHM – **शब्द ब्रम्हः**:- Vedik knowledge developed, by deep study of Nature- PRAKRITI - **प्रकृति** The origin of nature and the universe as a whole and the manifestation of sound studied. This developed philosophy on such concepts. This led to evolution of existence of matter and the source of matter as sound. Ved found link between material and spiritual reality. All forms of speech are from SHABDA BRAHM. Referrence:-Vision in long darkness by V.S. Agrawala, Prof. B.H.U., 110 SCIENTIFIC PERSPECTIVE OF UNIVERSAL ETERNAL DHARM & RELIGION 1963. Prithvi Prakashan India.

चत्वारि वाक्परिमिता पदानि तानि विदुर्ब्राह्मणा ये मनीषिणः। गुहा त्रीणि : निहिता नेङ्गयन्ति तुरीयं वाचो मनुष्या वदन्ति ॥45 II R.V. 1.164.45.

chatvāri vāk parimitā padāni tāni vidur brāhmaṇā ye manīṣiṇaḥ | guhā trīṇi nihitā neṅgayanti turīyaṃ vāco manuṣyā vadanti ||45 II R.V. 1.164.45.

The successive phases of Vaak Para, Pashyanti, Madhyama and Vaikhari are explained in Shrimad Bhagavata Purana as follows: -

श्रीभगवानुवाच | स एष जीवो विवरप्रसूतिः प्राणेन घोषेण गुहां प्रविष्ट :। मनोमयं सूक्ष्ममुपेत्य रूपं मात्रा स्वरो वर्ण इति स्थविष्ठ :॥ १७ ॥ Shrimad Bhagwat Puran 11.12.17.

śrī-bhagavān uvācha I sa eṣha jīvo vivara-prasūtiḥ prāṇena ghoṣeṇa guhāṁ praviṣṭaḥ I mano-mayaṁ sūkṣmam upetya rūpaṁmātrā svaro varṇa iti sthaviṣṭhaḥ II 17 II **Shrimad Bhagwat Puran** 11.12.17.

This is that perceptible Supreme Lord who infuses life in all and who manifests himself within the nerve -centres or plexuses (chakras) known as MULADHAR and others (existing in the nternal parts of the human body). With the prana impregnated with nada (called para speech), he enters the cave (known as adhara chakra, located near the anus). He proceeds (ahead) assuming the subtle mental form (known as pashyanti and Madhyama forms of speech in the spiritual plexuses called Manipura and Vishuddhi located at naval and at the throat respectively. He reveals Himself in the mouth in the form of short and long notes, accents (such as udatta, anudatta and svarita) and articulate sounds (like the velars, palatals, dentals etc.) This is the grossest speech-form (called Vaikhari) of the Vedas and branches. Speech is divided into four categories; this is known to intelligent brāhmaṇs. Three of them are hidden and the fourth category is spoken by ordinary people. Rishi DIrghatmas- thinker who represents grappling with the long darkness of the mystery of creation. The ignorance about cosmos in its pre manifest conditions before creation when ignorance was widespread darkness or TAMAS – ignorance. The dark matter prevalent in times before creation. Retrieval of lost meaning at the same time reorientate and resolve the stalemate of VEDIC interpretation. This Eternal Dharm (Religion) and Universal Management 111 means the religious think tanks needs reorientation according to modern scientific interpretation. The rhythms of cosmic vibrations issue forth from four levels which correspond to the various levels in manifestation: Para-Vak is the highest form of sound. It issues forth from the Supernal Ether (paramam vyomam) where all the sound vibrations that build the various worlds pre-exist in an undifferentiated state. Pashyanti is the sound vibration heard in the Causal worlds. Pashyanti in Sanskrit means "seeing speech". A sage whose consciousness is concentrated in the causal body is able, to "glimpse" a Truth in a vision or a revelation. Knowledge is perceived, in the inner mind by sight without the use of the reasoning faculty or sensory data. Madhyama (Middle) is the sound as perceived in the subtle or the Pranic world. A good example of this would be the thought-forms held in our mind. Vaikhari is the lowest form of sound, and it signifies outward expression. This is the spoken word emerging from throat. The formulation that the whole world of Time Space relation is governed by the wheel principle or a rhythmic, cyclic motion about which science and philosophy, agree with respect to their explanations of cosmic dynamism. 1 Mantras 2, 3, 11, 12,13,14 and 8. Asya vamiya sukta, has been described as paroksha (परोक्ष).

The Vamiya Sukta of Rigveda has 52 Mantra in Mandal/Chapter 1- Sukta 164. It is by Rishi Dirghatamas (nick name Long Darkness). Revelation is vision and concealment is mystery. Example is creation which is a mystery. An insoluble riddle.

Script Writing:

Script is a writing method which inscribes the spoken sound in the visual form as word. While both writing and speech are useful in conveying messages, writing differs in also being a reliable form of information storage and transfer.

Rigvedic statement in 10-71-4 indicates the script writing existed even before Rigvedic era. It is a statement saying with example about the written language.

उत त्व :पश्यन्न ददर्श वाचमुत त्व :शृण्वन्न शृणोत्येनाम् । उतो त्वस्मै तन्वं१ वि सस्रे जायेव पत्य उशती सुवासा :॥ Rigvedic statement in 10-71-4

uta tvaḥ paśyan na dadarśa vācam uta tvaḥ śṛṇvan na śṛṇoty enām | uto tvasmai tanvaṃ vi sasre jāyeva patya uśatī suvāsāḥ || Rigvedic statement in 10-71-4

This mantra in split details is:

"उत । त्वः । पश्यन् । न । ददर्श । वाचम् । उत । त्वः । शृण्वन् । न । शृणोति । एनाम् । उतो इति । त्वस्मै । तन्वम् । वि । सस्रे । जायाऽइव । पत्ये । उशती । सुऽवासाः ॥ १०.७१.४".

uta tvaḥ paśyan na dadarśa vācam uta tvaḥ śṛṇvan na śṛṇoty enām | uto tvasmai tanvaṃ vi sasre jāyeva patya uśatī suvāsāḥ ||Rigved. 1-71-4

Explanation: One who sees the script but unable to see, or spoken sentence heard but unable to understand, (पश्यन्न ददर्श वाचमुत त्व :शृण्वन्न शृणोत्येनाम्) because the person has no knowledge about the written or spoken language. It is just like a wife; she will not expose and bare herself to any other person except her husband (तन्वं१ वि सस्रे जायेव पत्य उशती सुवासा:). So is the written or spoken language, to a knowledgeable person it exposes fearlessly.

Another revelation in this Mantra is there was dress material in use in Rigveda era. Hence quoted in Poetry.

Without knowledge about language, script or spoken one cannot understand it. This with example quoted above, clearly indicates the script was in existence even before the Rigveda era. It is unfortunate that existing generation of the same civilization thinks that the language writing, dress material, clothes (*suvāsāḥ* = clothing; fabric; garment; feather; dress; envelope) etc are from western civilization! The above mantra clearly indicates the use of clothes by females to explain and emphasize the language script if not legible or not understandable is not the fault of script. Example is explained above.

Western knowledge of script writing during Vedic era is not proper and full of vested interest. The illusion was spread by invaders that Sages and Rishis of Vedic era were ignorant about script writing. But Max Mueller opined that the script writing was known to India since 400 BC. The above statements in Rigveda and its analysis, clearly indicate that the script was existing even before the Vedic era. There is clear indication that the spoken words disappear due to the sound waves decipher. To establish quality to words form must be provided and hence the word written called as AKSHAR – **अक्षर** i.e., or which does not KSHAR or **क्षर** or disappear. The written words provide permanency to spoken words or language. Great example is in Ganapatya Atherva sheersha Shloka 7, 8 of Yajurveda: It is in three distinct scientific narration.

गणपति अथर्वशीर्ष श्लोक 7.

1. गणादिम् पूर्वमुच्चार्य, वर्णादिन् तदनन्तरम् । अनुस्वारः परतरः । अर्धेन्दुलसितम् । तारेण ऋद्धम् । एतत्तव मनुस्वरूपम् ।

   ganaadim poorvamuchchaarya varnaadim tadanantaram ||anusvaarah' paratarah' || ardhendulasitam || taarena ri'ddham ||etattava manusvaroopam ||

   First is pronouncing, next is effective recognition with -vovel or **वर्ण**, nasal sound by dotting or Anuswar-**अनुस्वार**, half word for expressing more effectively or with pressure on sound, effectively balancing the sound. That is how script gets form or Roop- **रुपं**.

2. गकारः पूर्वरूपम्। अकारो मध्यमरूपम् ।अनुस्वारश्चान्त्यरूपम् । बिन्दुरुत्तररूपम् । नादः सन्धानम् । संहिता सन्धिः ।

gakaarah' poorvaroopam ||akaaro madhyamaroopam || anusvaarashchaantyaroopam ||binduruttararoopam || naadah' sandhaanam ||samhitaasandhih' ||

G or 'g' is before or in the beginning, Aa or 'A' is extension in the middle, at the end is nasal sound form or expression.

If it is expressed scientifically, as per Umasamhita of Shiva puran, G or गकार- is close being first, A or अ is extension of sound in between, next is nasal sound expressed by dot at the end hence dot or बिंदु which is away in the word formed, Uttar roop-उत्तर रुप. The sound or Naad – नाद is source of the word, is Sandhan-संन्धान, and the Samhita or Mantra in group of words, is uniting the all or Sandhi-संन्धि.

3. सैषा गणेशविद्या । गणक ऋषिः । निचृद्गायत्री छन्दः । गणपतिर्देवता । ॐ गँ गणपतये नमः।।

saishaa ganeshavidyaa ||g anakari'shih' || nichri'dgaayatree-chchhandah' || ganapatirdevataa || om gam ganapataye namah' || 7 ||

This is Ganesh knowledge- गणेश विद्या. expressed by 'Ganak Rishi' in Chhanda छन्द or poetically expressed lord Ganesh. Bow to Gam ganapati.

The Ganapati Atharva sheersha (in red colour) from a page of original work?

The script was developed after the scientific analysis of sound word. Script writing based on science of sound and phonation of words. The art of writing and that the origin of the Brahmi script developed in India 300-400 years before Christ. But foreign scholars spread the concept that the script writing came to India from Greece. Sanskrit civilization was ignorant about script writing. This misconception is prevailing since the study Western researchers of the 18th-19th centuries. But, while writing the history of Sanskrit literature, Max Muller expressed his opinion in the context of the development of script that the art of writing came into existence in India 400 years before Christ. Different studies by archaeologist and calligrapher A.B. Walawalkar and scribe Laxman Sridhar Wakankar proved that the Indian script originated in India itself and the tradition of writing on **phonetic basis** has existed since the Vedic period, which is also confirmed by much archaeological evidence. Apart from this the Shiv script or MAHESHWARI script it is, "Lord Shiva played his "Damru" (musical instrument used by Shiva in his cosmic celestial dance) nine and five times, that is, fourteen times, in the interval of his heavenly dance. From that came 14 sound sutras, which are called Maheshwar sutras. It is described as-Nrittavasane Nataraja Rajo (The details can be found in Panini, who mentions the fourteen Maheshwar Sutras).

Clip from Mahabharat, Adiparva 1-1-112 to 115.

स्मृतमात्रो गणेशानो भक्तचिन्तितपूरकः । तत्राजगाम विघ्नेशो वेदव्यासो यतः स्थितः ॥ **112** ॥

smrutamatro ganeshano bhaktachintitapurakah। tatrajgam vignesho vedvyaso yatah sthitah॥ 1-1-112 (112

पूजितश्र्चोपविष्टश्र्च व्यासेनोक्तस्तदानघ । लेखको भारतस्यास्य भव त्वं गणनायक। मयैव प्रोच्यमानस्य मनसा कल्पितस्य च II113 II Aadiparva Mahabharat. 1-1 113.

lekhako bharatasyasya bhav tvam gananayak॥ mayaiv prochyamanasya manasa kalpitasya ch॥ 1-1-113 (113)

श्रुत्वैतप्राह घ्निशो यदि मे लेखनी क्षणम् । लिखतो नावतिष्ठेत तदा स्यां लेखको ह्यहम् II 114 II Aadiparva Mahabharat. 1-1 114.

shrutvaitatprah vignesho yadi me lekhani kshanam। likhato navatishthet tada syam lekhako hyaham॥ 1-1-114 (114) vya...

व्यासोऽS प्युवाच तं देवम्बुध्वा मा लिख क्वचित् । ओमित्युक्त्वा गणेशोपि बभूव किल लेखकः II 115 II Aadiparva Mahabharat. 1-1-115

omityuktva ganeshopi babhuv kil lekhakah॥ 1-1-115 (115) granthagranthim tada chakre munirgudham kutuhalaat।

During Mahabharat era the above mantras clearly indicate the writing skill of "Lord Ganesh". Not only the skill but the dictation by Veda Vyas must be uninterrupted, otherwise the Ganesh will stop writing. It is almost like the modern-day computer writing the spoken words get printed on the screen. Gana-Isha is Ganesh. SANGANAK is computer. Is it some device or actual human in the form of Ganesh? Is a point for research.

There is a deep study on how a sound is produced. Based on that the vowels are framed. By Rishis of Sanskrit Speaking Civilization. The Chatvari vak padani mantra of Rigveda (1-164-45) discussed above has 4 types of speeches.

The three i.e., **Para** is transcendental, is from Atma, **Pashyanti** is pictures is visible. **Madhyama** is intermediary, what one can say muttering, are latent speech while the fourth is **Vaikhary** which is an articulate speech which humans, Animals, birds speak. It is a communication link between the two individuals.

The sound which comes out of mouth in the form of speech has been very deeply studied by the Sages of Sanskrit era. Accordingly, the vowels were framed. This is as per the pictorial forms of Devanagari script or Lipi, A pre-Ashoka Brahmi lipi – ब्राम्ही लिपी.

Sound from throat: It is **Kanthastha**- like Ka, Kha, Ga, gha, Nga- (अ, क, ख, ग, घ, ङ., ह,ळ, क्ष).

Sound from palate: **Talustha or Talavya**. It is produced by touching tongue with front of hard palate- like Cha, Chha, ja, jha, yan – च, छ, ज, झ, ञं, य, श, ज्ञ.

Sound produced by touching tongue to teeth. **Dantavya or dantastha**. Ta, Tha, Da, Dha, Na – त, थ, द, ध, न, ल, स, त्र.

Sound produced when the tongue touches the upper pert of hard palate. **Murdhanya**. Ta, tha, D, Dha, na – ट, ठ, ड, ढ, ण, ऋ, र, ष, श्र

Sound produced when lips touch each other. **Othastha or Othavya**. Pa, Pha, Ba, Bha, Ma - प, फ, ब, भ, म, उ, वं (For detailed study original work may be consulted by A. E. Walavalkar).

It will be of interest to know that the Sanskrit or Devanagari script is so scientific that the words from all the languages of the world can be written using Sanskrit script and not the vice varsa, without disturbing original phonetics of that language. Everything is without any mistake. For example a Marathi SIRNAME – last name or family name is हरवळकर-HAR WALKER in English it is pronounced as "HER WALKER". A name is DAGDOO-दगडू- in Maharashtra state of India. In UK English it is pronounced as DAG- DOO -डेग डू. In Sanskrit the words are specifically used and pronounced, and scientifically developed that pronunciation will not change. The scientific basis was developed to create word and script. HRASVA and DEERGHA means short and long pronunciation. It is only in Sanskrit and Devanagari script or Lipi.

CHAPTER 14

RIGVEDA AND MANAGEMENT

Understanding of the constitution of the 'absolute truth and its creation' – the nature, is only possible by exploiting it. Humans have been exploiting the nature since time immemorable. Exploitation of nature by man for the benefit of humanity, is since the presence of man in nature. In recent years, the VEDIC concept of "The world is one family" - VASUDHEV KUTUMBAKAM is shattered, due to the religious sectarian practices in human societies. Self-interest of family incumbents can destroy the family. The humanity is fractioned by region, colour of skin and eyes. The peoples of every sovereign country are trying to prove their supremacy, power, by their destructive power of weapons of mass destruction. Without understanding that the only absolute power of superiority will be responsible for the annihilation of humanity and their existence. In this chapter the discussion is on Nature's constitution and its laws of management.

Vedic literature in understanding the origin of absolute truth has developed NASADIYA SUKTA in 10th Mandal of Rigveda. The ultimate source of the order in the universe – and - multiverses is unfolded in a scientific manner. The discussion is symbolic, obscure, and enigmatic. It can only be understood by Meditating on the subject in silent dynamism. It can unfold the secrets of the Nasa Diya Sukta Mantras. Wonderful time for this is "BRAHMA MUHURTA" i.e., between 3 AM and 6 PM during morning hours (Song of science Shrimad Bhagavad-Gita, Notion Press, 2020 ed. ISBN 978-1-63714-582-1 By Dr. B. G. Matapurkar).

Constitution of "absolute truth" is self-governing, self-interacting and dynamically applicable in the multiverses. This can clarify the facts of nature. Rigveda wonders on space or sky as STUPA or dome without any supportive pillar. Galaxies, Stars, and constellations – a group of celestial bodies, hanging like pendulum without string. Body of foetus grows in mother's womb from a single celled fertilised ovum. Not only this if the fertilised ovum if inserted in the uterus of a female who has crossed the age of childbearing capacity, converts the body of that female to the natures' advantage and aim. It develops the milk in breasts for the nourishment of the future aim of nature – the healthy next generation. Who governs? What laws are responsible to carry such missions? Are these unconstitutional? What a wonderful management is this? Should we not understand this? Such is the attempt of RIGVEDA in VEDIC literature. Understand this, one needs to understand the creator, creation, and its by-product the creature.

In reality, "Absolute Truth" has an un-written constitution, and laws to govern and manage. This is eternal, non-changing, ultimate source of order and harmony, which is prevailing in the whole creation of "ABSOLUTE TRUTH." Interestingly the laws of nature are uniformly applicable, equal in enforcing within the constitution. The ancient Vedic wisdom understood the science of the constitution of the nature. Testimony to this is Vedic scientists never accepted the ultimate success in any scientific derivation. They called at the end that it is NA-ITI or 'Neti' which means not complete, more explorations are essential. To illustrate, the earth was flat later round as now. Is it end? Sun rotating around stationary earth, and now the earth is rotating around Sun. Future explorations may alter this opinion. Science is never complete. It is always open for more investigations and correction of past achievements.

Fundamental laws govern Nature or "PRAKRITI" by its own. Unearthing of such laws is essential for human benefits. The self-interacting dynamics of laws and thus form constitution of multiverses of cosmos. These laws are for the order and harmony in cosmos. What Rigveda says about it: -

रथः। न। यातः। शिक्वऽभिः। कृतः। द्याम्। अङ्गेभिः। अरुषेभिः। ईयते। आत्। अस्य। ते। कृष्णासः। धक्षि। सूरयः। शूरस्यऽइव। त्वेषथात्। ईषते। वयः ॥ १.१४१.८. Rigved. 1-141-8.

ratho na yātaḥ śikvabhiḥ kṛto dyām aṅgebhir aruṣebhir īyate | ād asya te kṛṣṇāso dakṣi sūrayaḥ śūrasyeva tveṣathād īṣate vayaḥ || Rigved. 1-141-8.

The chariot once made ready, deft hands and actions (शिक्वऽभिः कृतः) of driver fly it in sky (द्याम्) using the parts of Chariot (अङ्गेभिः। अरुषेभिः।). Similarly, Sun – Agni-अग्नि, rises in sky and removes darkness and ignorance. In this the example of chariot is full of science and space travel. Next mantra talks about the Sun, Varun, Mitra, and Aryama giving an example of wheel and spokes, concurrent just like the rim of a wheel, holding the spokes together running and working together. Like the wheel of chariot, the work of cosmos is supported and functions.

त्वया॒ ह्य॑ग्ने॒ वरु॑णो धृ॒तव्र॑तो मि॒त्रः शा॑श॒द्रे अ॑र्य॒मा सु॒दान॑वः। यत्सी॒मनु॒ क्रतु॑ना वि॒श्वथा॑ वि॒भुर॒रान्न ने॒मिः प॑रि॒भूरजा॑यथाः ॥ Rigved. 1-141-9.

tvayā hy agne varuṇo dhṛtavrato mitraḥ śāśadre aryamā sudānavaḥ | yat sīm anu kratunā viśvathā vibhur arān na nemiḥ paribhūr ajāyathāḥ II 9 II Rigved. 1-141-9.

Agni, with light, life, power, regulate Varun, and Mitra, who abide by the laws of Nature, remove darkness, while Aryama, with abundant and dynamic nature staying in between the two, keep them separate. In summary, their functions and encompassing them all, like the circumference encompasses the spokes of a wheel. Wheel has an iron circumference and spokes unite at the hub similarly the soul or Aatma manifests elements-tattva which is surrounded by the Pran – life energy, like iron circumference of a wheel. Thus, protects and controls as well.

This indicates the existing knowledge in Sanskrit civilization about wheel, spokes, and their function. The manifestation of super soul / the absolute truth, regulated by the laws of nature and governed by those laws efficiently.

These laws are uniformly applicable in the whole cosmos. This can be explained by the following: -

The source of the order and harmony exist in the Creators creation everywhere in cosmos. Vision and wisdom of scientists can visualize such laws and utilised for the human benefits. In Rigveda hymns symbolically invite Devatas – supernatural elements who govern and are beneficial for humans, in Yajnas (fundamental research and developments) for the help. This is in the form of prayers. They have offered SOMARASA (सोमरस) for such help. This is obscure and enigmatic. But are not these autosuggestions? Because they never depended on their help but put KARMAYOGA to achieve success and benefits. Meditative practices developed for peace and tranquillity. This is for the real achievements in silent dynamism. Using power of brain and thus intellect, to its maximum for the ultimate success. The access to the constitution and the laws to enforce nature, is by transcendental Meditation and exploitation of human body, mind, and intellect to its full potential. In the thoughtlessness of meditational practices person – scientist receives all help and support of unified laws and the constitution of cosmos. Hence the VEDAs are not by human or are Apourusheya (अपौरुषेय). How it can be true?

Understand the constitution and the laws one must first understand the manifestation of the Cosmos in totality. In earlier chapters of this book, it is discussed.

To start with think about self-manifest absolute truth. If laws of nature are uniformly applicable, then how can anything manifest without any cause what's so ever? Absolute truth is composed of all the elements for future manifest cosmos and the nature. Gita and Veda indicate that the Cosmos and nature are the manifestation from already existing cause. It is the deformed nature, exhibit as manifest world, or VIKRITI (विकृति) of

PRAKRITI (प्रकृति). The particles of future manifest elements came together and conglomerated to form the absolute truth. The heat generated to mixing of different existing particles, resulted into one uniform absolute truth. This later resulted into gaseous layer. Mixing of different gas particles solidified and cosmos got manifested. At the time of annihilation when the time cycle is over, the same manifest nature and cosmos undergoes the reverse order, and everything gets back to the origin of Absolute truth. (See figure).

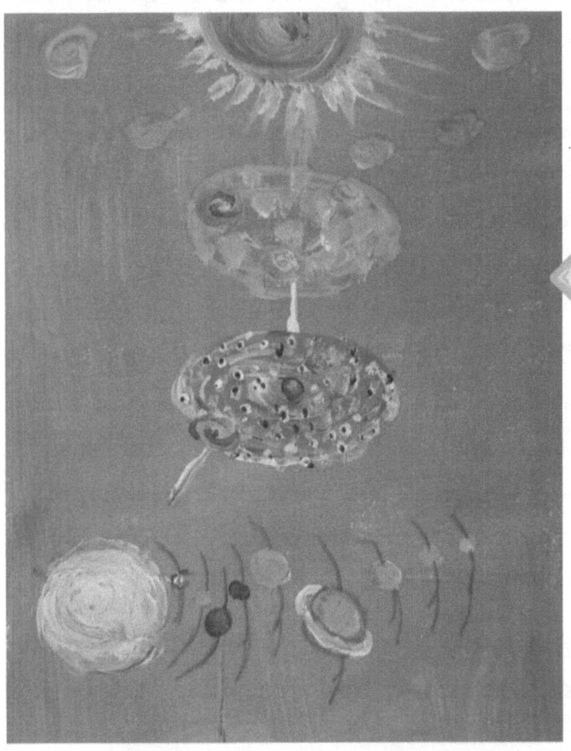

After primordial gas layer is Manidveep where energy exists which supports manifestation of nature. It prevents harmful effect of intense radiation, waves, heat, on manifest nature - Brahma. See text

Above diagram depicts the evolution of cosmos -the Brahmanda. Multiverses of the cosmos rotate around the original source. Rudra-shiv rotate around Param-shiv. Primordial gasses -the Vishnu rotate around the Rudra-shiv, Galaxies rotate around the centre of the Brahma. All stars and constellations of galaxy, rotate around the centre of the Galaxy. Our Solar system-a part of galaxy of the Milky Way rotates around the centre of the galaxy. In solar system all the planets rotate around the central Sun. On earth in the smallest particle the Atom has Electron and proton rotating around central nucleus the neutron.

Sun and the solar planets. Planets rotate around Sun

Smallest particle Atom has electron, proton, rotating around nucleus

Not only this the earth has $3/4^{th}$ water and $1/4^{th}$ land. All living beings have same composition as earth. The living animals have the same $3/4^{th}$ and $1/4^{th}$ water, and $1/4^{th}$ solid material. The smallest cell of living beings is cell, which has the same composition of water.

Earth has $3/4^{th}$ water and$1/4^{th}$ solid and so is living body

Interesting enough is that the stars of cosmos take birth and die, and universe continues. The innumerable cells of our body take birth and die but body perpetuates. What a wonderful applicability of the laws of the unified constitution of nature and the cosmos!!! What an intelligent, infinite power of organization? This is applicable to the smallest of the small and the biggest of the big – "**अणोरणियान् महतोमहियन्**."

Veda literature is the outcome of the Observation by Veda Kaleen enlightened Rishis. This involves Observer, process of observation, and the observed. Process is DEVATA. Observer is Rishi. The known is Chhanda. Rishi, Devata, and Chhanda makes Rigveda. It is a pure knowledge.

As a medical professional the author is convinced about the constitution of cosmos and its laws are explainable through Human physiology, its functioning, and overall administrative effect.

Cosmic constitution and laws are percolating from Absolute truth to our earth. The laws descend through galactic constituent of cosmos to structure and function of Solar system. From here descend to our Earth. From earth to individual living and non-living beings on earth. This cosmic administrative discipline is also administering physiology of living beings. This is the unified constitution and laws control the body, its structure and function. The Rigvedic statement approves this by a statement "Brahma Bhavati Sarathi" (ब्रम्ह भवति सारथी) which means cosmos is charioteer.

दीर्घतमा मामतेयो जुजुर्वान्दशमे युगे। अपामर्थं यतीनां ब्रह्मा भवति सारथिः ॥6॥ Rigveda. 1-158-6.

Like a driver of the chariot, controls, guides, and orderly execute its laws of its constitution. The execution is by the process of automation. Physiology of heartbeat, propulsion of intestines, pushing of urine to urinary bladder are few automatic processes. In embryological development of foetus in womb is other automation process. No one has ever seen fully developed brain in pelvic cavity or sex organs in the cavity of skull. Fully functioning normal Kidneys grow in lumbar regions. Ovum developed in ovary gets to fallopian tube who guides it. What guides is laws of constitution descending to individual corpus and guide function of different tissues and organs. Humans can only admire the perfect administration. Rigvedic statement is as follows:

ऋचो अक्षरे परमे व्योमन्यस्मिन्देवा अधि विश्वे निषेदुः। यस्तन्न वेद किमृचा करिष्यति य इत्तदविदुस्त इमे समासते ॥ 39॥ Rigveda. 1-164-39.

The Mantras are as extensive as unending Aakash (परमे *व्योम*), where the Devatas are as director, controller, and executioner (*अधि*) reside (Nishedu – निषेदुः). Knower of this fact enjoys life and is a spectator and enjoys. The absolute truth acts via these sub authorities.

This is the fundamental and needful ingredient of physiology in living beings on earth. This is the scientific way of thinking in Rigveda, a fact no one can deny, if proper analysis of mantras is carried.

It would not be out of the way to mention here that the ancient SANSKRIT speaking civilization developed expertise in ASTROLOGY, PALMISTRY and ASTRONOMY etc,. The art and science of planetary positions, planetary rotation in space, different constellations (NAKSHTRA - 27 in number) their effects on different endocrine glands, tissues, and organs (already described) the reasons of diseases presented in hospitals in groups and crops majority of times and not alone or sporadic cases. 27 NAKSHTRA influence nuclei of brain and efficiently run the whole body. Nature or super soul is present everywhere and pervades each particle of nature smaller than smallest or bigger than biggest (“**अणोरणियान महातोमाहियान**”). The Laws of nature are within the constitution of universe. The laws govern the manifest and un-manifest world. The law, structured in the DNA of every cell is in totality, the same natural law and law of automation. **The whole physiology is by the automation principle of expanding universe and the living body in the material world**. The relation of individual with cosmos, or one can say that influence of cosmos is on every grain of creation in this universe. In fact, the supreme soul organizes the whole universe by its natural laws. In Gita stanza seven it is clearly emphasized that:

ममैवांशो जीव लोके जीव भूतः सनातनः I मनःषष्ठानिन्द्रियाणि प्रकृतितस्थानि कर्षति II 7 II Gita 15. 7.

All living beings are fraction of eternal super soul. Life lives in physical existence, with the help of mind and Senses. How are mind and sense governed? The automation governance of super soul following explanation is important. Maharishi Mahesh Yogi’s Vedic Science and technology is especially useful to elaborate this. There is direct relation, direct action, and influence of SOLAR SYSTEM on brain. There are nine planets in solar system. These nine planets influence the 9 elements of brain:

SURYA – Sun has influence on Thalamus.

CHANDRA – moon has influence on Hypothalamus,

MANGAL – Mars has influence on Red Nucleus, Amygdala.

BUDH –mercury has influence on Sub-thalamus.

GURU – Jupiter has influence on Globus Pallidus.

SHUKRA – Venus has influence on Substantia Nigra (mid brain)

SHANI – Saturn has influence on Putamen – (Regulate movement and learning)

RAHU – SHEWET – Uranus? Has influence on head of Nucleus caudates

KETU – Neptune? – Has influence on tail of Nucleus Caudates –

(Uranus and Neptune names of Rahu and Ketu are shadow planets (छाया ग्रह) debatable in English, and hence the question mark)

Similarly, Solar system influences DNA constituents – Guanine (GURU, Sign of zodiac, Capricorn or MAKARA Rashi), Adenine (SHANI – KARK Rashi, Cancer), Cytosine (MANGAL, - TULA rashi- Libra), Thymine (SHUKRA Sign of Zodiac –MESH Rashi / ARIES), Sugar (Planet BUDH बुध ग्रह), Phosphate (CHANDRA or planet moon), Enzymes (RAHU, KETU). 12 parts of Nucleotides of DNA have their counter parts in 12 signs of zodiac (RASHIS). Through - Planets (GRAHA) Super soul organizes, directs and controls (through solar system).

universe influences human brain through twelve signs of zodiac - the RASHIS, and cortical areas of brain have one to one relationship. As per Horoscope chart or RASHI KUNDALI have twelve houses (BHAV as per Sanskrit astrology). Each house has its own influence on the individual person. These BHAV (house in the astrology chart - a “Kundali”) influenced by the 12 RASHIS which in turn influence the cortical areas of brain.

1st - TANU BHAV – Generally is about birth or "Janma Bhava". Gives idea about what a person gets at birth. In brain it is **Right and Left Occipito-temporal area – self-image memory, Identification - Aries.**

2nd – DHAN BHAV – It forecasts persons Prestige and wealth. In Brain it is Right Occipital area – Vision, face identification, appreciation of objects - Taurus.

3rd – SAHAJ BHAV – It identifies courage, travel, research, art etc. of the person. Right Parietal area sensory representation of hand, arms, Skill, perception of space– Gemini.

4th – BANDHU BHAV – It foretells Feeling and desire of the person. Right Limbic area – Emotional, instinctive function, Gustatory and Olfactory association - Cancer

5th – PUTRA BHAV – Persons Learning, knowledge, progeny is predicted. Right Frontal area – Memory, learning - LEO

6th - ARI BHAV – About enmity is indicated in this house. Right Prefrontal area – mood regulation, motivation, Mental diseases - Virgo

7th – YUVATI BHAV – Life partner, partnership, heroism etc. is indicated in this house. Right-Left Temporal area –Sensorial function - Libra

8th – RANDHRA BHAV – Age, is dealt in this bhava. **left pre-frontal area - Scorpio**

9th – DHARM BHAV -- Spiritualism, long life is considered in this bhava. **Left Frontal area – Reasoning, prognostication, interest in Occult - Sagittarius**

10th – KARMA BHAV – indicates Karm and karma field. Left Limbic area elaboration of personality, Vocation – MAKAR – Capricorn.

11th – LABH BHAV – Opportunities predicted from this bhava. Left Parietal area – Sensory integration, Physical comfort - Aquarius

12th – VYAY BHAV – indicate Family pleasures. Left Occipital area – Visual discrimination, Temptation - Pisces

Through this arrangements celestial and planetary relations, super soul regulates and controls with automation. That is how Vedic statement which becomes self-explanatory ब्रम्ह भवति सारथि: (RIGVED, 1. 158. 6).

गामाविश्य च भूतानि धारयाम्यहमोजसा |पुष्णामि चौषधी :सर्वा :सोमो भूत्वा रसात्मक :|| 13||Gita Chapter 15- stanza13.

This explains the form of energy- Shakti or soul contained in all living beings, the protection, nourishment and sustain life with the help of MOON by providing juice of vegetation and medicinal plants taking help from inexhaustible Nitrogen cycle (PUSHNA CHAKRA, Rigveda 6-54-3), which is also under control of super soul.

पूष्णश्चक्रं न रिष्यति न कोशोऽवं पद्यते। नो अस्य व्यथते पविः ॥३॥ Rigveda. 6-54-3.

pūṣṇaś cakraṁ na riṣyati na kośo va padyate | no asya vyathate paviḥ II 3II Rigveda. 6-54-3.

Brahma Bhavati Sarathi a Rigvedic statement though an exceedingly small but has a very vide spread meaning. Super soul controls Primordial gasses-zone of VISHNU. The primordial gaseous layer protects BRAHMA from harmful effects of radiation, light (TEJ), heat and unknown rays emitting from super soul-SHIV, which are still unknown. Modern science needs more research in that direction. In other words, supreme authority of universe is in fact a charioteer for all living beings. This Brahma under protection of Vishnu becomes charioteer. SARATHI means driver of chariot- a horse driven cart. The cart is under control of driver with reigns to control horses and guide the chariot. Super soul after creation of universe and galaxies, stars, different constellations, groups of stars and planets like solar system, with the help of automation reigns over living beings. Cosmic rays from celestial elements of cosmic manifestations, using as reigns control the living beings of whole universe. The controlling mode has been explained above, with the help of Constellations, Nakshatra, Sun, and Planets of solar system. Indirectly the super soul becomes Charioteer. This is the meaning of RIGVED stanza and Gita that super soul controls the whole universe.

Gita says here that super soul fractionalized enters the planets and with that energy they stay in orbit. Fractionalized super soul in moon controls activity, there by produce Sap- the juice of life in all plants and vegetables, in turn to energize all living beings of material world. Thus, they depend upon super soul and so "BRAHM BHAVATI SARATHI" or BRAHM

CHAPTER 15

SPACE TRAVEL

Why must one consider that the space travel was prevalent during and before the Vedic era? Below mentioned queries if answered scholarly the possibility of space travel during Vedic era, can be affirmatively acceptable.

1. Why the invention of zero was essential? What was the necessity to use zero in calculations?
2. Why calculate the inter planetary or inter galactic distances?
3. Why mapping of space was essential?
4. Was it essential to discover the "Abodes" in space?
5. Why was the discovery of different abodes in space was gradual in different time scales, and not in one go?
6. What was the reason to decide the age of Brahma, Vishnu, and Rudra Mahesh?
7. Why it was essential to map the different constellations and groups of stars in space?
8. Why name the stars and constellations in space after the eminent scientists of Vedic Sages and Rishis?
9. Why the RATH and flying machines discovered?
10. Why Rishi Bharadwaj wrote about VIMAN Shastra?
11. Why was the Vedic science more developed in many respects when modern science is inching slowly towards the similar goal?
12. Why the origin of Moon and mercury is not from Sun. Now it is believed that the planets of Solar system are born from Sun.

13. Why in Vedas and Upanishads the statement about Rishi NARAD is as "Space traveller? With profound Astrological and Astronomical knowledge of Vedic era can it be only fiction and mythological stories?

14. Why calculate speed of light and speed of Vehicles during Rigvedic era, as more than speed of mind?

15. Why the space traveller does not age?

16. What was the method used for calculating the time scale of earth and other celestial objects? Why the years of Sun, Planets, movement of Galaxies and their years are different and in multiples of earth years?

17. Why there are stories mentioned repeatedly, about time travel and speed of travel which is different. Earth time is different, and the time is different in different abodes of space.

Before one think about space travel in Rigveda, it will be of interest to consider a story of "King Kukudmi" narrated in Mahabharat purana (Read Sanskrit version below). Even if one considers the story as fiction, the statement is at par with the modern scientific understanding. It also is like the theory of relativity of A. Einstein. Einstein, the founder of modern theory of relativity, himself has written in his book that the **"We owe a lot to Indians, who taught us how to count without which no worthwhile scientific discovery could have been made".** He might have read or heard the fact from Indian science before his path breaking discovery. When Kakudmi went to Brahma Loka to meet Lord Brahma possible by the means of an Interstellar spacecraft or any other superior technology, yet unknown to us.

The story is as under: -

The reason for the travel to Brahma loka:

In Satya yuga, a king named Kakudmi, went in space to see BRAHMA in BRAHMA Lok along with his beautiful daughter named Revathi, having mystical and auspicious qualities. The king was Unable to find a suitable match for his lovely, talented daughter on earth. Hence king Kakudmi decided to travel to Brahma Lok (that exist millions of light years away from earth) to get advice from lord brahma.

On arriving brahma Lok, both were told to wait as Lord Brahma was listening to a musical performance by celestial Dancers. After the musical performance, Lord Brahma asked Kakudmi for the reason behind his visit.

Brahma laughed and said "My dear Kakudmi, since the time you have travelled here in Brahma Lok, millions of years have passed (27 Maha-yugas) and no one of them you have left on earth and their descendants are alive now. Go back and marry off your daughter to Balarama, the elder brother of Krishna".

ŚB 9.3.29. ककुद्मी रेवतीं कन्यां स्वामादाय विभुं गत। : पुत्र्यावरं परिप्रष्टुं ब्रह्मलोकमपावृतम् ॥ २९ ॥

ŚB 9.3.30. आवर्तमाने गान्धर्वे स्थितोऽलब्धक्षणक्षणम् । : तदन्त आद्यमानम्य स्वाभिप्रायं न्यवेदयत् ॥ ३० ॥

ŚB 9.3.31. तच्छ्रुत्वा भगवान् ब्रह्मा प्रहस्य तमुवाच ह । अहो राजन् निरुद्धास्ते कालेन हृदि ये कृता॥ ३१॥ :

ŚB 9.3.32. तत्पुत्रपौत्रनप्तृणां गोत्राणि च न शृण्महे । कालोऽभियातस्त्रिणवचतुर्युगविकल्पित॥ ३२॥ :

ŚB 9.3.33. तद् गच्छ देवदेवांशो बलदेवो महाबल। : कन्यारत्नमिदं राजन् नररत्नाय देहि भो॥ ३३॥ :

ŚB 9.3.34. भुवो भारावताराय भगवान् भूतभावन। : अवतीर्णो निजांशेन पुण्यश्रवणकीर्तन : ॥ ३४॥

ŚB 9.3.35. इत्यादिष्टोऽभिवन्द्याजं नृप। :स्वपुरमागत : त्यक्तं पुण्यजनत्रासाद् भ्रातृभिर्दिक्ष्ववस्थितै॥ ३५॥ :

(The story is narrated below for the interested reader: -

In the 9 chapter of Shrimad Bhagvat, one incident is narrated, which states that king Sharyati had a son named Anart. He had a son named Revat who constructed a town upon the island of the sea and stayed at that place and ruled the Anart kingdom from there. His son named Kukudmi had a daughter named Revati. She was good looking, well versed, well-mannered, and having merits. As this girl attained an age of marriage, number of kings, princes, etc. asked for her hand in marriage. As king Kukudami, who was one of the deities of Devkoti, could not decide whom to choose and so he took his daughter to Brhamalok (heavens) to consult Bhramaji. At that time the celebration and singing program of Gandharva was going on in Brahmalok. Therefore, he did not get the time to ask Brahmaji. He also sat in the singing program and upon completion of the singing program, king Kukudmi greeted Bhramaji and asked his opinion for a good husband for his gem-like daughter Revati. At that time Brahmaji laughed a lot and told him that the husbands that he had considered for your daughter are not alive. This is because in your country twenty-seven chokdis (chokdi of four Yuga) have lapsed. This is because one second of Mrityulok and Brahmalok is as much as one century. However, at present Sankarshan Avatar Balramji, the elder brother of Purshottam Shri Krushna, is proper match for marriage and he would accept your daughter. With these words of Bhramaji, Kukudami the son of Raivatraja returned to his native place (Okha island). At that time, his entire family had been destroyed and therefore he prayed to Balaram to perform marriage of his daughter at Dwarka to which Baldevji gave permission happily. In fact, Bhagwan Shri Krishna was in hurry than Balramji, as the younger brother shall get a chance only after the elder brother's marriage is fixed. Upon pondering as to the venue for marriage it was important to select a safe place. There was danger of Krishna and Balaram would have been burnt in the fire at Praharshan mountain caused by the king Jarasandh of Magadh. Therefore, if he would come to know about it, he may cause great hindrance. Hence marriage arranged hurriedly. Meanwhile Naradji came. When Kukudami inquired about the place of marriage, Devarshi Naradji informed about the place of Devsagar situated on the bank of Sabarmati River where great Rishis had performed Tapa for lacs of years. The power of the enemies is lost immediately at this place. So, the king Kukudami arranged the venue of marriage of his daughter Revati at the bank of Devsagar. Bhagwan Shri Krishna Dwarkadhis arrived with Chhapan koti Yadavs as the relatives of the bridegroom Balramji. Naradji informed the deities about the marriage of Bhagwan Sankarshan Balramji and thirty-three crore deities came with their families to participate in the marriage ceremony. Deity Vishwakarma had planned for the stay and meals of the guests. Deity Kuberji had decided for the money. Gandharvas played beautiful music. The Brahmins recited all four Vedas also remained at the ritual of marriage. Rishis, Munis, Digpals, Basus, Adhistatas of Grahmandal, four Vedas and Puranas in the form of deities also remained present. The place was beautifully decorated. First, Charan-Prakshalan of Balramji performed, with the water of Dev-sagar. Pithi and essence of the herbal plants applied upon the body of Baldevji. The Brahmins performed and completed the ritual of marriage amidst the hails by the deities. In this way, king Kukudami got his daughter married with Baldevji and offered Dakshina of golden pearls and cows with golden horns to the Brahmins. Thereafter, the king went to Badrikashram to perform Tapa in the pious company of Bhagwan Shree Narnarayan. With the time passed, Dev Sagar shrinked to Dev Sarovar at whose western bank Indrapur village developed. This is the importance of Dev Sarovar a place of pilgrimage which is also 'Shangaar of Jetalpurdham'. So Shreeji Maharaj stated that, this place was very dear to Balramji's, idol installed in the temple. Now the question came as to from where the idol be brought. Shreeji Maharaj looked at Gangama who in turn stated that, there are idol images of Baldev, Revti and Laxmanji at the place of her father. Maharaj asked to bring those idols.)

Scientific aspect of story and moral is even if one considers the story as fiction or not real, but the time travel and events in the story are as per the modern scientific facts.

Another story is when, in the of battle of DEVAS and ASURAS King MUCHKUNDA helped devas to fight and win the battle. Indra in gratitude says to King Muchkunda " Then Indra said to the king Muchukunda, "O king, we, the deities are indebted to you for the help and protection which you have given us, by sacrificing your own family life. **Here in the heaven, one-year equals three hundred and sixty years of the earth.** Since, it has been a long time, there is no sign of your kingdom and family because it is destroyed, with the passage of time. You came here in Treta Yuga and now its Dwapara Yuga on earth. We are happy and pleased with you, so ask for any boon except Moksha (liberation) because it is beyond our capacities".

The above story again mentions about time travel and speed of travel is different. Earth time is different in different abodes.

Modern science with flying in space has detected four abodes. Atmosphere surrounding earth is three hundred miles. Beyond that altitude the atmosphere merges imperceptibly into the near vacuum of outer space. The four distinct layers are: -

The lowest – atmosphere is 10 miles deep. Storms are born here. The great wind system keeps the clouds in motion.

Next layer is stratosphere. It lies between 10-30 miles above earth. It is calm and without turbulence as in like troposphere. Jet planes fly here to avoid turbulence.

Third layer is mesosphere. It is chilly layer. It is 30-50 miles above earth. Meteors exist here.

4 Beyond the mesosphere lies electrically charged thin air particles. It is thermosphere. The northern and southern lights exist here. 'Mah' layer appears the luminous, colourful visible. flares of the Aurora Borealis and in the lower layer of 'Mah' the meteoric strikes and showers. (Family guide to NATURE, published by Reader's digest, first edition, 1983).

More research and space travel reveals atmosphere as: -

Earth's atmosphere stretches from the surface of the planet Earth, up to as far as 10,000 kilometers (6,214 miles) troposphere, stratosphere, mesosphere, thermosphere, and exosphere.02-Oct-2019. The Edge of Outer Space. While there's no clear boundary between where Earth's atmosphere ends and outer space begins, most scientists use a delineation known as the Karman line, located 100 kilometres (62 miles) above Earth's surface, to denote the transition point, since 99.99997 percent of Earth's atmosphere lies beneath this point. A February 2019 study using data from the NASA / European Space Agency Solar and Heliosphere Observatory (SOHO) spacecraft suggests, however, that the farthest reaches of Earth's atmosphere — a cloud of hydrogen atoms called the Geocorona — may extend nearly 391,000 miles (629,300 kilometres) into space, far beyond the orbit of the Moon. (Alan Buis / NASA's Global Climate Change website). Diagram for better understanding:

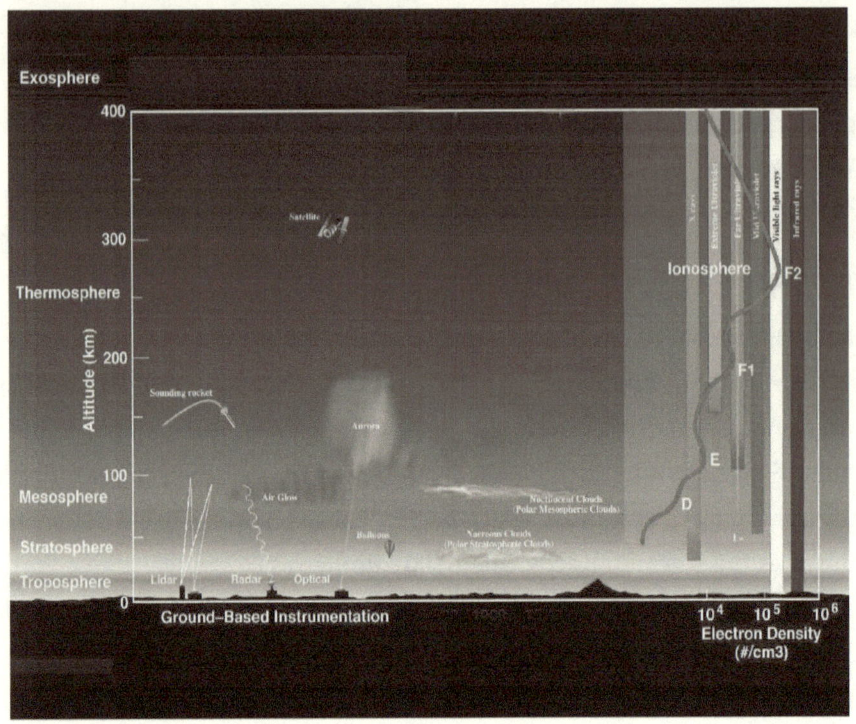

Diagram of the layers within Earth's atmosphere. Credit: NASA

Interestingly, in Vedic literature initially there were three abodes BHUH, BHUVAH, SWAH. Later Rishi MAHACHAMAS detected fourth called as MAHA abode. (Taittariya Upanishad, Anuvak-5, Mantra 1-5) With more space travel three more abodes discovered (Total 7). Scientists from Sanskrit era, - the RISHIs of Sanskrit Speaking Civilization detected seven abodes above earth surface. These are BHUH, BHUVAH, SWAH, MAH, JANAH, TAPAH, and SATYAH. As per the story of King Kukudmi travelled much beyond modern space traveller. Obviously, they had noticed these layers which are beyond the understanding of modern science and debating. Of course, modern science is inching towards that goal. Interesting description is in Umasamhita of Shiv puran which explains that the JANA loka there is no burning: -

Sixty-three hundred thousand Yojanas from JANA LOK is stationed the LOK where the gods called VAIRAJAS (वैराज) stay. They are free from burning sensation. DAH VIVARJITA or free from burning (DAHAN). (All the Vedic concept of universal abodes are found mentioned in 19, 1-39, of UMA SAMHITA of Shri Shiv Mahapuranank, Year 92, Number 1, 2018. Page 303).

If it is true, then the Rishi must have visited the abode (in physical form or subtle form)!! It is a subject of further research.

Beyond Satya-Loka or Brahma Loka there is Energy centre – Shakti Kendra. It is considered as the abode of Maha-Devi or Bhuvaneshvari - Goddess of all abodes. The energy here is soft and tender energy and is responsible to manifestation of Nature. It has been discussed earlier chapters.

"The purpose of above comparison, is to stimulate the young Indian scientist community to take a scientific look at our Vedic heritage, read, and look to Vedas from purely scientific point of view. It has no relation to modern religion".

The Sanskrit literature mentions TAPAH and SATYAM Lok or abodes. Discovery of these two abodes need be discovered by modern science. Russian astronauts were the first to travel and place "Space station" in space orbit. Exosphere and discovery of atmospheric layers above earth surface, is after that. Total five layers known to modern science. Is not this an indication that the space travel was very much prevalent in that era? Therefore, the seven abodes were known to them. These all seven abodes are above our planet earth.

भूर्भुवस्सुवरिति वा एतास्तिस्त्रो व्याहृतयः । तासामुह स्मैतां चतुर्थीम् । माहाचमस्यः प्रवेदयते । मह इति । तद्ब्रम्ह । स आत्मा । अंगान्यन्या देवताः ॥1॥

भूरिति वा अयं लोकः । भुव इत्यंन्तरिक्षंम् । सुवरित्यसौ लोकः । मह इत्यादित्यः। आदित्येन वाव सर्वे लोका महीयन्ते ॥2॥

First three, the Bhuh – the earth, Antariksha, Swarga, are "VYAHRITAYAH (व्याहृतयः). According to Dr. P. V. Vartak, VYAHRITI means VYA = special efforts, + HRIH = to receive = +TI = total, which means place to gain in total. That time or era the TRAILOKYA or 3 abodes were known. All the TRAILOKYA must be utilized by earthlings, was an internal desire. (Upanishadaanche Vidnyan nishtha Nirupan. By P.V.Vartak, 7th Ed. 2018,).

In summary, more abodes will be discovered when the space travel will advance further. This is what happened during Sanskrit era.

In Rigveda there is mention of flying chariots or Machines for air travel. Some of the Mantras indicate the essential requirement for the construction of air vehicles. Some of the mantras from Rigveda are quoted below: -

प्रातर्युजा विबोधयाश्विनावेह गच्छताम्। अस्य सोमस्य पीतये ॥ 1 II Rigveda. 1-22-1.

prātaryujā vi bodhayāśvināv eha gacchatām | asya somasya pītaye || 1 II Rigveda. 1-22-1.

Persons interested in construction must first indulge in knowledge on earth and Agni for the vehicle to travel in sky.

For the successful construction of vehicle to fly in sky, must understand and study the conditions of earth and Agni – the Sun, without such wisdom vehicles to fly in sky is impossible. I।१ ।।

या सुरथा रथीतमोभा देवा दिविस्प्रशा |अश्विना ता हवामहे II2II Rigveda 1-22-2.

yā surathā rathītamobhā devā divispṛśā | aśvinā tā havāmahe II2II Rigveda 1-22-2.

Speedy Rath which can traverse the Akash or Space (दिविस्पृशा) which are made possible by men ॥२॥

surathā = "chariot; ratha. *divispraśā* = "heavenward."DYU heaven or Antariksha. Asvini kumar are two persons having RATH for travelling in Aakash, to DYU LOK.

य इ॑न्द्राग्नी चि॒त्रत॑मो॒ रथो॑ वाम॒भि विश्वा॑नि॒ भुव॑नानि॒ चष्टे॑ । तेना या॑तं स॒रथं॑ तस्थि॒वांसाथा॒ सोम॑स्य पिबतं सु॒तस्य॑ ॥ 1 II 1-108-1 Rigveda.

ya indrāgnī citratamo ratho vām abhi viśvāni bhuvanāni caṣṭe | tenā yātaṃ sarathaṃ tasthivāṃsāthā somasya pibataṃ sutasya || 1 II 1-108-1 Rigveda

Word meaning: viśvāni = viśva, "whole; complete; viśva - world." bhuvanāni = "Earth; being; world; bhuvana caṣṭe (c*3e) = "watch; look." tenā = "towards. yātaṃ [verb], dual, Present imperative, "go and travel; disappear; reach; come; campaign; elapse; arrive; drive; reach; leave; run; depart; ride." sarathaṃ = together. sarathaṃ = ratham = atha, "chariot; warrior; ratha

The wonderful CHITRATAMA Chariot (चि॒त्रत॑मो॒ रथो॑) travelling all BHUVANS – (Bhuh, Bhuvah, Swah) and "Indra and Agni, sitting together in the RATH, that wonderful car which illuminates all beings, approach and drink of the effused Soma."

Not only space travel as mentioned in above mantras, the ASHVINI Kumar used vehicle the chariot or RATH which could fly and float on the water surface. The vehicle speed, seats in vehicle, number of wheels in the rath, it's capacity and capability has been described in Rigveda Richas. All this does not leave doubt about possibility of air and space travel during Rigveda era. The flight described was for three days continuously for saving person called BHUJJYU. See Rigveda Richas below. Reader can decide himself.

तुग्रः॑ । ह॒ । भु॒ज्युम् । अ॒श्वि॒ना॒ । उ॒द॒ऽमे॒घे । र॒यिम् । न । कः । चि॒त् । म॒मृ॒ऽवान् । अव॑ । अ॒हाः॒ । तम् । ऊ॒ह॒थुः॒ । नौ॒भिः । आ॒त्म॒न्ऽवती॑भिः । अ॒न्त॒रि॒क्ष॒प्रुत्ऽभिः॑ । अप॑ऽउदकाभिः ॥ 3 ॥ Rigveda 1-116-3 tugro ha bhujyum aśvinodameghe rayiṁ na kaś cin mamṛvām̐ avāhāḥ | tam ūhathur naubhir ātmanvatībhir antarikṣaprudbhir apodakābhiḥ II 3 II Rigveda 1-116-3

There was fight between TUGRA and BHUJJYU (तुग्रः । ह । भुज्युम्.). TUGRA drowned BHUJJYU in the sea. Ashvini Kumars could save BHUJJYU by using such a KITE (पतंगैः). In Sanskrit it is as follows: -

तिस्रः क्षपस्त्रिरहातिव्रजद्भिर्नासत्या भुज्युमूहथुः पतंगैः । समुद्रस्य धन्वन्नार्द्रस्य पारे त्रिभी रथैः शतपद्भिः षळश्वैः ॥4II Rigveda. 1-116-4.

tisraḥ kṣapas trir ahātivrajadbhir nāsatyā bhujyum ūhathuḥ pataṃgaiḥ | samudrasya dhanvann ārdrasya pāre tribhī rathaiḥ śatapadbhiḥ ṣaḻaśvaiḥ || ॥4II Rigveda. 1-116-4.

"Three nights, and three days, plane (PATANG) could fly. Nāsatyas, have you conveyed Bhujyu in three rapid, revolving cars, having a hundred wheels, and drawn by six horses, along the ocean and the sea.".

RISHI (sage) Kakṣīvān, Devatā (deity) aśvinau, Chandas (meter) triṣṭup, Svara (tone) Swar.

अनारम्भणे । तत् । अवीरयेथाम् । अनास्थाने । अग्रभणे । समुद्रे । यत् । अश्विना । ऊहथुः । भुज्युम् । अस्तंम् । शतऽअरित्रान् । नावंम् । आतस्थिवांसम् ॥ 5 ॥ Rigveda 1-116-5

anārambhaṇe tad avīrayethām anāsthāne agrabhaṇe samudre | yad aśvinā ūhathur bhujyum astaṃ śatāritrāṃ nāvam ātasthivāṃsam II 5 II Rigveda 1-116-5.

"Ashvini Kumars saved BHUJJYU, drowning in the ocean, where there is nothing to give support, nothing to rest upon and nothing to cling to, and brought-picked up (ऊहथुः) Bhujyu, using a hundred-oared ship (नावंम्), to hand over BHUJYU to his father.

The following description of RATH chariot or vehicle clearly indicate the type of rath, its composition, and its wheels etc: -

तं युञ्जाथां मनसो यो जवीयान तरिवन्धुरो वर्षण यस्त्रिचक्रः |येनोपयाथः सुक्र्तो दुरोणं तरिधातुन पतथोविर्न पर्णैः ॥ 1 ॥ Rigveda 1-183-1.

taṁ yuñjāthām manaso yo javīyān trivandhuro vṛṣaṇā yas tricakraḥ | yenopayāthaḥ sukṛto duroṇaṁ tridhātunā patatho vir na parṇaiḥ

II 1 II Rigveda 1-183-1.

A car which has three seats to sit, three wheels, and has speed of mind, with which, embellished with three metals, and in which you travel like a bird with wings, please come to the pious Yajna site."

सुऽवृत् । रथः । वर्तते । यन् । अभि । क्षाम् । यत् । तिष्ठथः । क्रतुऽमन्ता । अनु । पृक्षे । वपुः । वपुष्या । सचताम् । इयम् । गीः । दिवः । दुहित्रा । उषसा । सचेथे इति ॥ 2 II

suvṛd ratho vartate yann abhi kṣāṁ yat tiṣṭhathaḥ kratumantānu pṛkṣe | vapur vapuṣyā sacatām iyaṁ gīr divo duhitroṣasā sacethe II 1 II Rigveda 1-183-1.

"The vehicle lands upon the earth, at the sacred place of Yajnya, you stop for the sake of the (sacrificial) food; may this hymn, promotive of your personal welfare, be associated with your forms, and meet the dawn, the daughter of heaven i.e., USHA or dawn."

आ तिष्ठतं सुवृतं यो रथो वामनु व्रतानि वर्तते हविष्मान्।येन नरा नासत्येषयध्यै वर्तिर्याथस्तनयाय त्मने च॥3II Rigveda 1-183-3

āa tiṣṭhataṁ suvṛtaṁ yo ratho vāmanu vratāni vartate haviṣhmān | yena narā nāsatyeṣhayadhyai vartir yāthastanayāya tmane cha || II 1 II Rigveda 1-183-3.

"Vehicle in which you are travelling reaches to the site of YAJNYA, Car or the Ratha, in which the ASHVNIS, (*nāsatyeṣayadhyai* "Asvins; nāsatya leaders, you purpose to come to the sacrifice, and proceed to the dwelling (of the worshipper), for (bestowing upon him) offspring, and for his own (good)."

Another evidence about the space travel is in Mandal 2 Sukta 18, What substance to be used so that the speed of transport vehicle be faster. Travel on Prithvi, Water and Antariksha is indicated.

Rig Veda Book 2 Hymn 18

पराता रथो नवो योजि सस्निश्चतुर्युगस्त्रिकशः सप्तरश्मिः |

दशारित्रो मनुष्यः सवर्षाः स इष्टिभिर्मतिभीरंह्यो भूत ||1

सास्मा॒ अरं॑ प्रथ॒मं स द्वि॒तीयं॑मु॒तो तृ॒तीयं॒ मनुं॑ष॒ :स होता॑ । अ॒न्यस्या॒ गर्भं॑म॒न्य ऊं॑ जनन्त॒
सो अ॒न्येभिः॑ सचते॒जेन्यो॒वृषा॑॥2II

हरी नु कं रथ इन्द्रस्य योजमायै सूक्तेन वचसा नवेन |

मो षु तवामत्र बहवो हि विप्रा नि रीरमन यजमानासो अन्ये ||3

आ दवाभ्यां हरिभ्यामिन्द्र याह्या चतुर्भिरा षड्भिर्हूयमानः |

आष्टाभिर्दशभिः सोमपेयम यं सुतःसुमख मा मर्धस कः ||4

आ विंशत्या तरिंशता याह्यर्वां आ चत्वारिंशता हरिभिर्यजानः |

आ पञ्चाशता सुरथेभिरिन्द्रा षष्ट्या सप्तत्या सोमपेयम ||5

आशीत्या नवत्या याह्यर्वां आ शतेन हरिभिरुह्यमानः |

अयं हि ते शुनहोत्रेषु सोम इन्द्र तवाया परिषिक्तो मदाय ||6

मम बरह्मेन्द्र याह्यछा विश्वा हरी धुरि धिष्वा रथस्य |

पुरुत्रा हि विहव्यो बभूथास्मिञ्छूर सवने मादयस्व ||7

न म इन्द्रेण सख्यं वि योषदस्मभ्यमस्य दक्षिणा दुहीत |

उप जयेष्ठे वरूथे गभस्तौ पराये-पराये जिगीवांसः सयाम ||8

नूनं सा ...|

In above Richas the 2nd is important.

सः। अस्मै। अरम्। प्रथमम्। सः। द्वितीयम्। उतो इति। तृतीयम्। मनुषः। सः। होता। अन्यस्याः। गर्भम्। अन्ये। ऊँ इति। जनन्त। सः। अन्येभिः। सचते। जेन्यः। वृषा॥2 II Rigveda 2-18-2.

Sa āsmā aram prathamaṁ sa dvitīyam uto tṛtīyam manuṣaḥ sa hotā | anyasyā garbham anya ū jananta so anyebhiḥ sacate jenyo vṛṣā II 2 II Rigved. 2-18-2.

A powerful)वृषा (vehicle, a means for travel (अस्मै) is constructed which can travel first on Earth, second in Water, and third in Antariksha. Man Made elements and substances)सः मनुषः (used to empower the vehicle. Other substance used can be power from Agni or Sun (**अन्यस्याः। गर्भम्। ऊँ इति। जनन्त। सः।**). Learned can utilise other energy source. The same is reiterated in next richa of Rigved.

हरी इति। नु। कम्। रथे। इन्द्रस्य। योजम्। आऽयै। सूक्तेन। वचसा। नवेन। मो इति। सु। त्वाम्। अत्र। बहवः। हि। विप्राः। नि। रीरमन्। यजमानासः। अन्ये॥ Rigved. 2-18-3

harī nu kaṁ ratha indrasya yojam āyai sūktena vacasā navena | mo ṣu tvām atra bahavo hi viprā ni rīraman yajamānāso anye II 3 II Rigved. 2-18-3

Still more interesting evidence about the Vehicle is in Richa of Rigveda, Mandal 10-Sukta 135- Mantra 3, wherein the vehicle without wheels and can travel anywhere. The Richa has expressed surprize that such vehicle was not seen before (अपश्यन् अधि)!!

यम् । कुमार । नवम् । रथम् । अचक्रम् । मनसा । अकृणोः । एकऽईषम् । विश्वतः । प्राञ्चम् । अपश्यन् अधि । तिष्ठसि II3II Rigveda 10-135-3

yaṁ kumāra navaṁ ratham achakram manasākṛṇoḥ | ekeṣaṁ viśvataḥ prāñcham apaśyann adhi tiṣṭhasi II3II Rigveda 10-135-3

"The new vehicle - chariot, is wheelless (achakram), single-poled, can go everywhere, which you, my child, mentally formed-- you stand thereon though you see it not."

Ashvini Kumaras had a vehicle which can touch the DYU LOK. (दि॒वि॒ऽस्पृशा॑ - *divispṛśā* "heavenward." Heaven).

या । सु॒ऽरथा॑ । र॒थिऽत॑मा

। उ॒भा । दे॒वा । दि॒वि॒ऽस्पृशा॑ । अ॒श्विना॑ । ता । ह॒वा॒म॒हे ॥2॥ Rigveda. 1-22-2.

yā surathā rathītamobhā devā divispṛśā | aśvinā tā havāmahe ॥2॥ Rigveda. 1-22-2

"We invoke the two Aśvins, who are both divine, the best of charioteers, riding in an excellent car and attaining heaven."

य इन्द्राग्नी चित्रतमो रथो वामभि विश्वानि भुवनानि चष्टे। तेना यातं सरथं तस्थिवांसाथा सोमस्य पिबतं सुतस्य II 1 II Rigveda 1-108-1.

ya indrāgnī citratamo ratho vām abhi viśvāni bhuvanāni caṣṭe | tenā yātaṁ sarathaṁ tasthivāṁsāthā somasya pibataṁ sutasya II 1 II Rigveda 1-108-1.

Rath capable of moving to all the Abodes (Earth, Antariksha, Swarga lok) of the world (विश्वानि भुवनानि चष्टे।). Water and energy (Indra and Agni), sitting together in Vehicle, which is a wonderful Rath which travels (*yātaṃ* "go; enter travel)in all the abodes of the cosmos., approach and drink the Soma rasa.

अ॒श्विनो॑रसनं॒ रथ॑मन॒श्वं वा॒जिनी॑वतोः। तेना॒हं भूरि॑ चाकन II 10 II Rigveda 1-120-10.

aśhvinorasanaṁ ratham anaśvaṁ vājinīvatoḥ | tenāham bhūri cākana II 10 II Rigveda 1-120-10.

"I have obtained, the car without horses. The vehicle of food-bestowing Aśvins, and expect (to gain) by it much (wealth)."

Created a vehicle, which can float and roam on the ocean waters for the son of Tugra, with mind devoted to the gods, and son was rescued, the vehicle descended from sky.

ज॒म्भय॑तम॒भितो॒ राय॑त॒ :शुनो॑ ह॒तं मृधो॑ वि॒दथु॒स्तान्य॑श्विना। वाच॑वाचं जरि॒तू र॒त्निनी॑ कृतमु॒भा शंस॑ नासत्यावतं॒ मम॑ ॥4॥ Rigveda. 1-182-4.

jambhayatam abhito rāyataḥ śuno hatam mṛdho vidathus tāny aśvinā | vācaṁ-vācaṁ jaritū ratninīṁ kṛtam ubhā śaṁsaṁ nāsatyāvatam mama ||॥4II Rigveda. 1-182-4.

Saviours are those who have the capacity to control evil minded people, who win over the enemies, and courage to listen to scholars and learned. ॥ ४ ॥

युवम् । एतम् । चक्रतुः । सिन्धुंषु । प्लवम् । आत्मन्ऽवन्तम् । पक्षिणम् । तौग्र्याय । कम् । येन । देवऽत्रा । मनसा । निःऽऊहथुः । सुऽपप्तनि । पेतथुः । क्षोदसः । महः ॥ Rigveda 1-182-5.

yuvam etaṁ cakrathuḥ sindhuṣhu plavam ātmanvantam pakṣhiṇaṁ taugryāya kam | yena devatrā manasā nih ūhathuḥ supaptanī petathuḥ kṣhodaso mahaḥ II 5 II Rigveda 1-182-5.

The people with above mentioned qualities (Stanza 4), and travel to and fro, through rivers and sea, in their own vehicles. Saved Son of Togra. Such persons travel in big vehicles. They are satisfied and satisfy others. ॥ ५ ॥

तं वां रथं वयमद्या हुवेम स्तोमैरश्विना सुविताय नव्यम् । अरिष्टनेमिं परि द्यामियानं विद्यामेषं वृजनं जीरदानुम् II 10 II Rigveda. 1-180-10.

taṁ vāṁ rathaṁ vayam adyā huvema stomair aśvinā suvitāya navyam | ariṣṭanemim pari dyām iyānaṁ vidyāmeṣaṁ vṛjanaṁ jīradānum II 10 II Rigveda. 1-180-10.

Aśvini Kumars, are invoked with hymns., The praiseworthy chariot of undamaged wheels, travelling the sky. Prayer to provide new fresh food, strength, and long life.

आ वां रथोऽवनिर्न प्रवत्वान्त्सृप्रवन्धुरः सुवितायं गम्याः । वृष्णं :स्थातारा मनसो जवीयानहम्पूर्वो यजतो धिष्ण्या यः II 3 II Rigveda. 1-181-3.

ā vāṁ ratho vanir na pravatvān sṛpravandhuraḥ suvitāya gamyāḥ | vṛṣṇaḥ sthātārā manaso javīyān ahampūrvo yajato dhiṣṇyā yaḥ II 3 II Rigveda. 1-181-3.

Rath of Aśvins, (chariot), vast, with broad front, having speed of mind, rapid as thought, cumulative and adorable, come at Yajna site. Apart from his the RIBHUS (Three brothers) have constructed a RATH which has three wheels, horse not needed to drive, and can fly in Aakash.

अनश्वो जातो अंनभीशुरुक्थ्योइ रथस्त्रिचक्रः परि वर्तते रजं :। महत्तदवौ देव्यस्य प्रवाचनं द्यामृंभवः पृथिवीं यच्च पुष्यथ ॥4॥ Rigveda. 4-36-1.

anaśvo jāto anabhīśur ukthyo rathas tricakraḥ pari vartate rajaḥ | mahat tad vo devyasya pravācanaṁ dyām ṛbhavaḥ pṛthivīṁ yac ca puṣyatha ||4|| Rigveda. 4-36-1.

The three-wheeled RATH for the use of Aśvins, made by Ṛbhus. which travels without horses, without reins. It's a great divine power, of Ṛibhus, therefore Ribhus can enjoy the offerings of Yajnya.

उरु वां रथ :परि नक्षति द्यामा यत्संमुद्रादभि वर्तते वाम् । मध्वां माध्वी मधुं वां प्रुषायन्यत्सीं वां पृक्षो रजन्त पक्वाः ॥5॥ Rigveda 4-43-5.

uru vāṁ rathaḥ pari nakṣati dyām ā yat samudrād abhi vartate vām | madhvā mādhvī madhu vām pruṣāyan yat sīṁ vām pṛkṣo bhurajanta pakvāḥ || ||5|| Rigveda 4-43-5.

The chariot can reach heaven and can be on ocean, Ashvini Kumars come on such a RATH. Mix milk and SOMA is offered to them.

आ नो यातं दिवो अच्छा पृथिव्या हिरण्ययेन सुवृता रथेन । मा वांमन्ये नि यंमन्देवयन्त : सं यद्दे नाभि :पूर्व्या वाम् ॥ 5 ॥ Rigveda. 4-44-5.

ā no yātaṁ divo acchā pṛthivyā hiraṇyayena suvṛtā rathena | mā vām anye ni yaman devayantaḥ saṁ yad dade nābhiḥ pūrvyā vām II 5 II Rigveda. 4-44-5.

In golden chariot from heaven come to earth, at YAJNYA site. Give importance to first request. There is likely to be confusion about the RICHA indicates Sun -the Agni or Vehicle, which is clarified in stanza below. The Sun and the chariot are separate. See Rigveda. 5-63-7. Below: -

धर्मणा मित्रावरुणा विपश्चिता व्रता रक्षेथे असुरस्य मायया । ऋतेन विश्वं भुवनं वि राजथ : सूर्यमा धत्थो दिवि चित्र्यं रथम् ॥5 ॥ Rigveda 5-63-7.

dharmaṇā mitrāvaruṇā vipaścitā vratā rakṣethe asurasya māyayā | ṛtena viśvam bhuvanaṁ vi rājathaḥ sūryam ā dhattho divi citryaṁ ratham || ॥5 II Rigveda 5-63-7.

Mitra and Varuṇa, protector of pious acts like Yajnya Karmas, you illumine the whole world and; you sustain the sun, and the chariot in the sky.

अनेनो वो मरुतो यामो अस्त्वनश्वश्चिद्यमजत्यरथीः । अनवसो अनभीशू रजस्तूर्वि रोदसी पथ्या याति साधन् ॥7II Rigveda. 6-66-7.

aneno vo maruto yāmo astv anaśvaś cid yam ajaty arathīḥ | anavaso anabhīśū rajastūr vi rodasī pathyā yāti sādhan ॥7II Rigveda. 6-66-7.

Split words for understanding the meaning: -

अनेनः । वः । मरुतः । यामः । अस्तु । अनश्वः । चित् । यम् । अजति । अरथीः । अनवसः । अनभीशुः । रजःऽतूः । वि । रोदसी इति । पथ्याः । याति । साधन् ॥7II

(*rodasī* = "heaven and earth; Earth.")

"Chariot of, Maruts,, which is without driver, without horses, without provender, without traces, traverses heaven and earth and the paths.

One meaning of marut is wind or VAYU. But the meaning of MARUT here is MEN. Who are MARUT is clarified in Rigveda Richa 5-53-3 and 1-85-4.

ते म आहुर्य आययुरूप द्युभिर्विभिर्मदे नरो मर्या अरेपस इमान्पश्यन्निति ष्टुहि II3II Rigveda. 5-53-3.

te ma āhur ya āyayur upa dyubhir vibhir made | naro maryā arepasa imān paśyann iti ṣṭuhi II3II Rigveda. 5-53-3.

(Marudgana - m=d\g`) riding on horses came to enjoy the Somarasa, must be praised.

रुद्रादित्या वसवो ये च साध्या विश्वेऽश्विनौ मरुतश्चोष्मपाश्च ।गन्धर्वयक्षासुरसिद्धसङ्घावीक्षन्ते त्वां विस्मिताश्चैव सर्वे ॥ ११-२२॥ Bhagwadgita 11-22.

RudraadityaH, vasavH, ye, ch, saadhyaH, vishwe, ashvinau, marutH, ch, ooshmpaH, Ch, gandharvyakshaasursiddhsanghaH, veekshante, tvaam', vismitaH, ch, ev, sarve ||22|| Bhagwadgita 11- 22.

In Gita, Chapter 11 mantra 22, Arjun after seeing VISHVAROOP of Shri Krishna says, 11 RUDRA, 12 Aditya, 8 VASU, Sadhyagana, vishvedev, Ashvini kumars, and **Marudgana,** as well as group of pitar-fathers, Gandharva, yaksha, Rakshasa, group of Sidha persons are all amazed to see your this Vishvaroop. 49 sons of RUDRA DEV from VRISHNI, are MARUDGANA. GANA is group of counted soldiers. They are soldiers of Devatas. Rigvedd. 1-85-4.

वि । ये । भ्राजन्ते । सुमखासः । ऋष्टिभिः । प्रच्यवयन्तः । अच्युता । चित् । ओजसा । मनःजुवः । यत् । मरुतः । रथेषु । आ । वृषव्रातासः । पृषतीः । अयुग्ध्वम् ॥4II Rigveda 1-85-4.

vi ye bhrājante sumakhāsa ṛṣṭibhiḥ pracyāvayanto acyutā cid ojasā | manojuvo yan maruto ratheṣv ā vṛṣavrātāsaḥ pṛṣatīr ayugdhvam ‖4II Rigveda 1-85-4

Marudgana are laced with weapons and are invincible, Maruts, swift as thought, entrusted with the duty of sending rain, yoke the spotted deer to your Rath.

गोमातरो यच्छुभयन्ते अञ्जिभिस्तनूषु शुभ्रा दधिरे विरुक्मतः । बाधन्ते विश्वमभिमातिनमप वर्त्मान्येषामनु रीयते घृतम् II 3 II Rigveda. 1-85-3.

gomātaro yac chubhayante añjibhis tanūṣu śubhrā dadhire virukmataḥ | bādhante viśvam abhimātinam apa vartmāny eṣām anu rīyate ghṛtam ||II 3 II Rigveda. 1-85-3.

Symbolically the Maruts are persons, (MARUTA is also used for Wind God). But the MARUDGANA word used here is soldiers of DEVATAS. In this stanza indicates that the persons only decorate themselves with ornaments, they shine in their decorations; they keep aloof every adversary; the waters follow their path. Obviously, the word is used for humans. The following stanza strongly indicates the presence of Aeroplanes and in multiple numbers: -

वयो॒ न ये श्रेणीः॑ पप्तुरोज॒सान्ता॑न्दि॒वो बृ॑ह॒तः सानु॑न॒स्परि॑ । अश्वा॑स एषामु॒भये॒ यथा॑ वि॒दुः प्र पर्व॑तस्य नभ॒नूँर॑चुच्यवुः ॥ 7 ॥ Rigveda. 5-59-7.

vayo na ye śreṇīḥ paptur ojasāntān divo bṛhataḥ sānunas pari | aśvāsa eṣām ubhaye yathā viduḥ pra parvatasya nabhanūm̐r acucyavuḥ II 7 II Rigveda. 5-59-7.

vayo = bird; na = "not; like; no; ye, "who; which; śreṇīḥ = club; line. paptur = fall down, limit; region; outskirt; divo = "sky; Svarga;

The flying Rathas fly in rows (श्रेणी॑) like birds in rows and in clubs, over the mountains, up in the sky, till its end. (The ends of the firmament). aśvāsa = "horse, *eṣām* = idam-This, ubhaye = both, this is known to both equally. (Gods and mortals), *yathā* = equally; their horses have caused the waters of the cloud to descend, as both know. Commentary by Sāyaṇa: Ṛgveda-bhāṣya: Both gods and mortals: (ubhaye yathā viduḥ) as both know; men of course know by perception the setting in of the rains; the gods know it by the agrayāna and other sacrifices which are offered at that season. The following description of Ashvini's Rath explains the flying vehicle, its speed, capable of moving on water,

आ वां॒ रथो॑ अश्विना श्ये॒नप॑त्वा सुमृळी॒कः स्ववाँ॑ यात्व॒र्वाङ् । यो मर्त्य॑स्य॒ मन॑सो॒ जवी॑यान्त्रिवन्धु॒रो वृ॑षणा॒ वात॑रंहाः ॥1॥ Rig Veda 1.118.1.

ā vāṁ ratho aśvinā śyenapatvā sumṛḻīkaḥ svavām̐ yātv arvāṅ | yo martyasya manaso javīyān trivandhuro vṛṣaṇā vātaraṁhāḥ ॥1II Rig Veda 1.118.1

Oh Ashvin your Rath, swift as a hawk (श्येनपत्वा - Syenapatvā = hawk, bird of prey, falcon, Śyena, eagle), having speed of mind, descend down to Yajnya site, for showering benefits, by three columns, and rapid as the wind.

त्रिवंधुरेणं त्रिवृता रथेन त्रिचक्रेणं सुवृता यांतमर्वाक् ।पिन्वंतं गा जिन्वंतमर्वतो नो वर्धयंतमश्विना वीरमस्मे II 2 II Rigveda 1-118-2.

trivandhureṇa trivṛtā rathena tricakreṇa suvṛtā yātam arvāk | pinvataṁ gā jinvatam arvato no vardhayatam aśvinā vīram asme II 2 II Rigveda 1-118-2.

Come to us with your chariot having three seats, three-wheeled, nourish our cows, horses, and let each of us grow strong.

आ वां श्येनासो अश्विना वहंतु रथे युक्तासं आशवः पतंगाः ।ये अप्तुरो दिव्यासो न गृध्रां अभि प्रयो नासत्या वहंति II Rigveda 1-118-4.

ā vāṁ śyenāso aśvinā vahantu rathe yuktāsa āśavaḥ pataṁgāḥ | ye apturo dāso na gṛdhrā abhi prayo nāsatyā vahanti II Rigveda 1-118-4.

O Asvins, come in your swift flying like kite (पतंगाः), the Rath - chariot, O Nasatyas, be at the Yajnya site. Persons well versed with all present knowledges) नासत्या (roaming like swift) दिव्यासः (Hawks) गृध्दाः, गिध्द (in Antariksha) अप्तुरः (and reach) अभि, वहन्ति(the site like kites)श्येनासः (and shining like Sun) आशवः (riding in flying Rath which take Ashvins to the desired site. II ४ II

Even though there is no material evidence about air travel, but the above narrations make one believe the fact about space travel in vehicles capable of flying and reaching Antariksha and higher planes in space.

CHAPTER 16

SCIENCE BEHIND DIFFERENT BUSINESSES OF VEDIC CIVILIZATION

Different types of works were prevalent in the society of Sanskrit Speaking civilization. Like Stitching, Knitting of cloths etc. Tanning of animal skin, Carpentry, Metallurgy, Jewellery, Architecture, Shipping, Boating and travel on water- sea and river, Pottery, Agriculture, etc did not only exist but were highly developed. To assist agriculture Astronomy, Astrology and Jyotish shastra was researched so that the rain and adverse atmospheric changes can be predicted. Even though there is no direct evidence written in Rigveda, but multiple indications exist in Veda that there was fully active "Garment Industry". The terminologies used indicate this antiquity of Indian textiles. the term 'guna' -गुण, is about a single thread; the term 'tantra' तंत्र, in the Veda, 'tan' refers to the weaving and stretching of textiles). At the same time, other terms like sutra-सूत्र, prabandha-प्रबंध, etc., all belong to textile terminology.

It is not surprising that we find ancient Indians using many terminologies associated with the textiles for defining philosophical theories and expressing general view on life. As for example, an ancient industry; the cotton, silk, and natural dyes along with the patterning and designing have been the backbone of our textiles. It is now imperative that all Indians start taking a more informed interest and play an active role in preservation and continuation of this ancient art of handloom industry that started from the pre-historic era and continues to this day. After reading Rigveda Richas (ऋचा, मंत्र), one must accept that the Sanskrit Speaking Civilization was highly developed, and it will not be out of the way to say even more advanced than the modern civilizations.

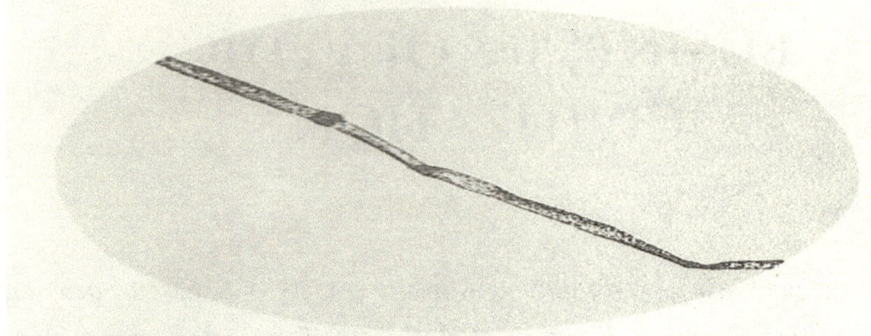

Number of businesses were prevalent. The ancient Indus Civilization (3500-1700 BCE).. Exploration of the sites, seals, jewellery, figurines, and other artifacts from that era. It is obvious that the use of cotton, weaving etc was not unknown and was prevalent even before that time. See the stanza from Rigveda Rigveda 2-32-4, quoted Below.

राकामहं सुहवां सुष्टुती हुवे शृणोतु नःसुभगा बोधतु त्मना । सीव्यत्वपः सूच्याच्छिद्यमानया ददातु वीरं शत दाय मुक्थ्यम् ॥ २.०३२.०४.

rākāmahaṁ suhavāṁ suṣṭutī huve śṛṇotu naḥ subhagā bodhatu tmanā | sīvyatv apaḥ sūcyācchidyamānayā dadātu vīraṁ śatadāyam ukthyam ||Rigveda 2-32-4,

A suitable female must listen to us This above mantra indicates use of needles in the society. Needle word has been used to indicate prevalent stitching. Knitting the work as the cloth is knitted with the help of needle. It is a symbolic comparison; the stitching is only possible when the knitting is already present (सूच्याच्छिद्यमानया = Needle without hole. It must be for knitting or a modern-day Crochet).

Like Male, if female is also wise and intelligent and produce progeny, the next generation will be wise and intelligent. Here the example is cited. This is just like a cloth is knitted or repaired with the help of needle. The loving couple is accepted and adored by all. ॥४॥

आ॒ध्रेण॑ । चि॒त् । तत् । ऊँ इति॑ । एक॑म् । च॒का॒र॒ । सिं॒ह्य॑म् । चि॒त् । पे॒त्वेन॑ । ज॒घा॒न॒ । अव॑ । स्र॒क्तीः । वे॒श्या॑ । अ॒वृ॒श्च॒त् । इन्द्रः॑ । प्र । अ॒य॒च्छ॒त् । विश्वा॑ । भोज॑ना । सु॒ऽदासे॑ ॥ Rig Veda 7.18.17.

ādhreṇa cit tad v ekaṁ cakāra siṁhyaṁ cit petvenā jaghāna | ava sraktīr veśyāvṛścad indraḥ prāyacchad viśvā bhojanā sudāse Rig Veda 7.18.17

"Indra, has slain an old lion (enemy) by a goat (Sudas), a pauper; he has cut the angles of the sacrificial post with a needle; he has given all the donations (property of the enemy) to Sudāsa.". Indra once got the work done and slain the Lion like enemy by poor Sudasa, weak like goat and weapon like needle. He gave all the enemy wealth to Sudasa. In Rigveda mantra, use of needle is mentioned which was used for stitching and knitting purpose.

The Rigveda mantra 10-85-35 mentions different types of clothes used: -

आ॒शस॑नं वि॒शस॑न॒मथो॑ अधिवि॒कर्त॑नम् । सू॒र्याया॑ :पश्य रू॒पाणि॒ तानि॑ ब्र॒ह्मा तु शु॑न्धति ॥ 35॥ Rigveda 10-85-35.

āśhasanaṁ viśhasanamatho adhivikartanam | sūryāyāḥ paśya rūpāṇi tāni brahmā tu śundhati II 35॥ Rigveda 10-85-35

Clothes used by Sūrya, the āśasana (border cloth) the viśasana (headcloth), the adhivikartana (divided skirt); Aśasana = Border of cloth, the fringe, is of different colour; Viśasana = Clothe used on the head, Adhivikartanam = the garment which is cut into three pieces.

One thing is clear from above revelations, that the cotton was in use and at the same time weaving and knitting was practiced by Sanskrit Speaking civilization. Peoples were using cotton clothes. Leather and Wool was also in use which is clear from the following Richas of Rigveda.

अस्येदु मातुः सवनेषु सद्यो महः पितुं पपिवाञ्चार्वन्ना । मुषायद्विष्णुः पचतं सहीयान्विध्यद्वराहं तिरो अद्रिमस्ता ॥7 II Rig Veda 1.61.7.

asyed u mātuḥ savaneṣu sadyo mahaḥ pitum papivāñ cārv annā | muṣāyad viṣṇuḥ pacataṁ sahīyān vidhyad varāhaṁ tiro adrim astā ॥7 II Rig Veda 1.61.7.

"Quickly quaffing the libations, and devouring the grateful viands (presented) at the three (daily) sacrifices which are dedicated to the creator (of the world), he, the pervade of the universe, stole the ripe (treasures of the asuras); the vanquisher (of his foes), the hurler of the thunderbolt, encountering pierced the cloud."

Commentary by Sāyaṇa: Ṛgveda-bhāṣya

Viṣṇu = 378 ervade, an epithet applied to Indra, sarvasya jagato vyāpakaḥ. Cloud = varāha. Viṣṇu is the person nified yajña; he attracted the accusative ulated wealth of the asuras; then, he remained concealed behind seven difficult passes, or the days of initiatory preparation for the rite. Indra crossed the seven defiles or went through the seven days of initiation and pierced the sacrifice. Taittirīya expands this further: Varāha, the stealer of what is beautiful, cherishes beyond the seven hills, the wealth of the asuras; Indra, having taken up the tufts of grass, and pierced the seven hills, slew him: varāhoyam vamamoṣaḥ saptānam giriṇām parastād vittam vedyam asurāṇām bibharti; sa darbhapiñjulam uddhṛtya, sapta girin bhitvā, tam ahanniti

This is further clarified in Taittariya Upanishad from Shukla Yajurveda by Rishi YAGYAVALKYA. Shikshavalli-Anu 4, Mantra 2, 3.

आवहन्ती वितन्वाना । कुर्वाणाऽचीरमात्मनः । वासा• सि मम गावश्च ।अन्नपाने च सर्वदा । ततो मे श्रियमावह । लोमशां पशुभिः सह स्वाहा ॥ 3 ॥ आमायन्तु ब्रह्मचारिणः स्वाहा।विमाऽऽयन्तु ब्रह्मचारिणः स्वाहा ।

प्रमाऽऽयन्तु ब्रह्मचारिणः स्वाहा ।दमायन्तु ब्रह्मचारिणः स्वाहा ।शमायन्तु ब्रह्मचारिणः स्वाहा ॥4॥

Next bring me, without delay, fortune accompanied by **wool and cattle**—fortune which always provides me **with clothes and cattle, food, and drink**. Increase them when they have been acquired and preserve them long when increased. Svaha! May brahmacharins come to me variously! Svaha! May brahmacharins come to me!. Svaha! May brahmacharins practise self—control! Svaha! May brahmacharins enjoy peace! Svaha!

Indirect evidence about the thread and weaving is from the Vamiya Sukta of Rigveda 1- 164- 5

पाकं :पृच्छामि मनसाविजानन्देवानामेना निहिता पदानि। वत्से बष्कयेऽधि सप्त तन्तून्वि तत्रिरे कवय ओतवा उ ॥ 5 ॥ Rigveda. 1-164-5.

pākaḥ pṛcchāmi manasāvijānan devānām enā nihitā padāni | vatse baṣkaye dhi sapta tantūn vi tatnire kavaya otavā u II 5 II Rigveda. 1-164-5.

"Immature understanding undiscerning in mind, must inquire about things which are hidden and the seven threads (सप्त तन्तून्वि) which the sages have spread to envelop the sun, in whom all abide?"

In India the fine cotton muslin textile export to different parts of the world. In ancient and medieval times, Mulmal or Muslin cloth is mentioned in old travel accounts of the Chinese, Italian, and Arabic traders and in the Arthashastra- **अर्थशास्त्र**, where it is mentioned as fine cloth from Pundra and Bangal, at present west Bengal and Bangal Desh.

Question arises that why such a developed cotton industry lost its lustre from India? One must learn the history of cotton since the Sanskrit speaking civilization. It is recorded that In Veda Sage "Gritsa-mad" started growing cotton. Who is rishi Gritsamada? Gritsamada (Sanskrit: गृत्समद, IAST: Gṛtsamada/Gṛtsamāda) was **a Rigvedic sage**. Most of Mandala II of the Rigveda is attributed to him. He was the son of Śunahotra Āṅgirasa and the adopted son of Śunaka Bhārgava.

Before the Gritsmada sage use of cotton one must understand the scientific rituals and Puja practiced by Hindus of Sanskrit Speaking Civilization. It is interesting to know that the religious practices forced the population to observe the rituals set by wise men. It is human psychology which was well known to sages and Rishis. Author remembers a story. During modern times or recent past due to non-availability of Urinals in cities and villages, people started urinating anywhere it is possible. A wise man put the photos of Hindu Gods on the walls where the people wanted to urinate. If anyone tries urinating and sees the God-photo the person avoided to pass urine. This example is to impress the effect of human psychology.

During Ramayana era, it was a advisory, not to cover the woman, her character is her protection. This indicates that the clothes ere in use: -

न गृहाणि न वस्त्राणि न प्राकारास्तिरस्क्रियाः | नेदृशा राजसत्कारा वृत्तमावरणं स्त्रियः ||-
- Valmiki Ramayana, Yudha Kaanda, Ch114.

Neither house, nor clothes, nor compound-wall, nor doors, nor any types of Royal honours cover a woman. Her character is her shield which protects her.

अ॒धः प॑श्यस्व॒ मोपरि॑ सं॒त॒रां पा॑दु॒कौ ह॑र । मा ते॑ कशप्ल॒कौ दृ॑श॒न्त्स्त्री हि ब्र॒ह्मा ब॒भूवि॑थ
॥19॥ 8.33.19 Rigveda

“O men and women, keep your eyes down on earth and not sky let your lower legs be covered and not exposed; walk on both feet together(as two wheels and two horse draw chariots together, let women be high priest of Home Yajna”…

Above is verse 8.33.17 of Rigveda. It is in context of yajna. The following verses are also in the same context and as you can see both men and women are asked to follow the same guidelines, there is no discrimination between men and women.

Sages were aware of the effect of deforestation on environment and nature. Not only this they were aware of the importance of certain trees and shrubs like Peeple - **पीपल**, Banyon-**बड, बरगद**, Bael – **बिल्व, बेल**, Tamarind Amla – **चिंच, ईमली**, Basils – **तुलसी** etc. Some of these plants have the property to produce Oxygen during day as well as night and take away the Carbon -di-Oxide from the atmosphere. the Vedic sages implemented forest conservation in the society as a religious ritual. The plants like Basil, Pipal, Banyan trees are considered as sacred, so that these plants will not be cut or destroyed. Obviously for preservation. The rishis mastered the science of weather forecasting, identified, and classified different types of land and prevented exploitation. In Rigveda Nitrogen cycle has been categorically explained Rigveda. 6-54-3, Pushna or Nitrogen Chakra is so important that the stock never gets depleted, nor its effective sharpness gets exhausted.

पूष्ण चक्रं न रिष्यति न कोशोऽवपद्यते । नो अस्य व्ययते पविः **II 3 II (Previously explained).**

What a scientific expression of the Nitrogen cycle, which is as per the modern science also is true!!

Maintenance of soil capacity was a major concern for them, they knew that the lost nitrogen could be restored by crop rotation, they grew legumes to return the depleted nitrogen from grain-crop farming back to the field. Sages discovered natural root promoters. Hence treatment of seeds with honey before sowing. Mantras were chanted while sowing seeds, it is an example that the music and soothing sound waves have a great effect on the crops and seedlings. The ploughing, reaping, and harvesting, was considered as worship and the yield was considered a blessing of good deeds done. This is done specially on an auspicious day. Farmers were taught to perform "Chaturmasya yagya" in which offerings of herbs, grains, ghee and fragrant raisins etc. Yagyas (**यज्ञ**) not only purify the air, but also create clouds that bring good rain (for details see Song of Science -Shrimad Bhagvadgita, Notion Press, India Singapour, Malaysia, 2020 ed. By the Author). The Sages and Rishis were aware of the Panch Maha Bhutas – five basic elements and their role in manifestation of nature-Prakriti- प्रकृति. Since Vayu is one of the five elements that bind and influence everything in the universe, the Rigvedic sages made certain yagyas mandatory for every person, or for all the humanity. Agriculture itself was passed down from generation to generation to people as a religious activity by their forefathers. What a practical way of spreading science to people who do not understand it, but practice it as a ritual. Prayer mantra for vanaspati is:-

मम इष्ट पूजनार्थाय प्रार्थयामि वनस्पतें

Mam Ishta Pujanarthay Prarthyami Vanaspate.

The five essential basic elements or Panch maha Bhutas are worshiped by Sanskrit civilization and their descendants and without any exploitation. Because everything manifest in cosmos is from these five basic elements. The humans are also manifested from the same principles of cosmic nature. Earth is the most fundamental element in the formation of our physical self.

Population believed that using leaves, cow dung and other such materials for manure and using Arjuna plant wood chips, barley husk and sesame flowers to remove impurities and fix nitrogen in the soil. This old wisdom was made to believe that it is unscientific and out of date. They were made to believe that ancient knowledge passed down through generations was unscientific and unproductive. In the name of faster agricultural production, the Green Revolution, funded by the Rockefeller Foundation and the Ford Foundation, changed agricultural practices forever, relying on chemical fertilizers. Thanks for the awareness as it is being reversed. With ancient Vedic scientific knowledge finest cloth could be produced in land of Bharatvarsha-India. In fact, India was the top producer and exporter of cloth made from cotton fibre. Mulmul or Muslin being finely woven cotton that first originated in Dhakeshwari or Dhaka now in Bangladesh, which was then a part of India.

Apart from the above the growing of cotton and using it for making thread and weaving etc. was developed since the time of Rigveda. Rishi Gritsmada made thread from the cotton wool, and then to make cloth from thread he made wooden bobbins. The raw thread called TANTTU in Sanskrit, using tantu, Gritsmada made cloth.

साध्वपांसि सनता न उक्षिते उषासानक्ता वय्येव रण्विते। तन्तुं ततं संवयन्ती समीची यज्ञस्य पेशः सुदुघे पयस्वती॥ Rigveda. 2-3-6.

sādhv apāṁsi sanatā na ukṣite uṣāsānaktā vayyeva raṇvite | tantuṁ tataṁ saṁvayantī samīcī yajñasya peśaḥ sudughe payasvatī Rigveda. 2-3-6.

The threads) तन्तुम्(made from cotton wool) वय्येव (used to weave cloth using pipe)रण्विते (similarly help in Yagya Karma to be carried out. ॥६॥

The European traveller Marco Polo visited India in 13th Century commented that coastal areas Coromandel produced all types of clothes, which were finest in the world.

With such evidence of use of cloth, where the scientific knowledge disappeared. With conspiracy the invaders destroyed the cottage industry and even the thumbs of weavers were severed so that they cannot weave fine cloths. This was to promote the clothe prepared by west is used and consumed and their industry thrives. The cotton produced in India taken away in ship loads for this purpose.

Agriculture: - Study of soil, Rains, animal use, fencing of fields agricultural fields were studied and developed. Even genetics and grafting of plants practiced during Vedic era.

The detailed study about plants in India dates to a few thousand years. The ancient science of botany was quite developed in its understanding of the plant kingdom, as also in taxonomy (Naming and classifying animals and plants). The classification of plants according to their properties exists.

There are sufficient indications to show that Agriculture, Medicine, Horticulture, developed to a great extent during the Vedic Period. In the Vedic literature we find many terms used in the description of plants a definite attempt at classification of plants and evidence that use of manure and rotation of crops were practiced for the improvement of fertility of soil and nourishment of plants. Rigveda mentions that Vedic Indians had knowledge about the food manufacture, the action of light on the process and storage of energy in the body of plants. In later period in literature there is enough evidence to show that botany developed as an independent science on which was based the science of medicine (the Charaka and Susruta Samhitas), Agriculture (Krsi-Parasara) and Arbori-Horticulture (as Upavana-vinoda a branch of Botany). The Rgveda mentions Soma plant. The Veda describes Soma as the Lord of the forest. The botanical identity of Soma remains obscure even today. The other plant described in Rgveda is peepal or the Asvattha (Ficus religiosa) during the Vedic period. Even in Shrimad Bhagwadgita reverse Ashwath tree has been described.

The Vedic civilization knew about flowering and fruit-bearing plants. (Palasa, varieties of lotus – white (pundarika) and blue (puskara), lily (kaumudi), cucumber – urvaruka (MahaMrityunjaya Mantra), jujuba, audumbara, kharjura, bilva etc are few to name)

Architecture:

अश्विना यज्वरीरिषो द्रवत्पाणी शुभस्पती। पुरुभुजा चनस्यतम्॥ (Rigved, 1-3-1).

aśvinā yajvarīr iṣo dravatpāṇī śubhas patī | purubhujā canasyatam Rigved, 1-3-1.

How to be expert in Architecture यज्वरीः (शिल्पविद्या) is mentioned here. Give importance to Architecture as if you love food (चनस्यतम्). The word used Ashvina) अश्विना (for water and Agni -heat. A must Knowledge about elements) द्रवत्पाणी - पदार्थविद्या) ॥१॥

अश्विना पुरुदंससा नरा शवीरया धिया। धिष्ण्या वनतं गिरः॥Rigveda 1-3-2

Workers involved in Architecture must understand the importance of Agni and Water. With expertise perform the attempts. Perfection in work and actions ()पुरुदंससा() for architecture work and get better results. Take help from Light, Heat, sound, and Water॥२॥.

The use of light in architecture creates doubt in mind but to set the material in place light is used in Dentistry. This is called "Light curing", which is in practice in Dentistry.

(As per the understanding of the Author. It is as per the description given in the Mantras in different Chapters of the Rigvedas.)

Agni. A source of heat and light. Sun and other Celestial components of the Universe, Multiverse in Galaxies and. Agni Devta.

Indra. A layer of electromagnetic waves, Radiation zone, ultrasonic sound waves. Indra Devta – Rain God.

Varun. A product from Indra and Mitra. Varun Devta. व=णो निरपः सृजत (10- 124-7). Varun responsible for the raining down water from clouds

Mitra. Sun – a friend for the whole living beings-Char and Achar-Moving and non-moving.

Mitra-Varun. Both together provide energy and help in YADNYA-KARMA or work. They support the welfare of the intellectuals. They safeguard the energy needed for the work.

Vayu. Vayu is a speedy element in Nature. It is one of the 5 basic elements of nature. It is one of the components of the manifest Nature and it manifests nature along with other basic elements.

Indra-Vayu. Together in collaboration provide Food and juice – som-ras, in vegetation. Responsible for rain on earth. Along with SUN destroy the harmful elements in surroundings in nature.

Ashwini Kumar (Twins). Healers of Devatas.

DIVYASTRA (दिव्यास्त्र) DYU (or द्यु+अस्त्र) means missile capable of going to Aakash. A missile which can fly in Antariksha.

Āgrāyaṇa (आग्रायण—.(The fourth son of the Agni, Bhānu. (Śloka 13, Chapter 221, Vana Parva, Mahābhārata). Āgrayaṇa (आग्रयण—.(A Pitṛ ritual; offering of *śyāmāka* and sugar;[1] the first *soma* libation at the agniṣṭoma sacrifice. (Source: Cologne Digital Sanskrit Dictionaries: The Purana Index)

APPENDIX 1

Tarkshya – Garuda is a celestial element – in English it is a star - AQUILA), It looks like Garuda (see figure below). Related to summer and winter solstice of Sun. It decides Spring and Rainy seasons. Southern Solstice of Sun invites rain on the earth hemisphere.

(Aquila is a constellation on the celestial equator. Its name is Latin for 'eagle' and it represents the bird that carried Zeus/Jupiter's thunderbolts in Greek-Roman mythology.

Its brightest star, Altair, is one vertex of the Summer Triangle asterism. The constellation is best seen in the northern hemisphere during summer, as it is located along the Milky Way. Because of this location, many clusters and nebulae are found within its borders, but they are dim). The following figure is adopted from Google search. Above description is from Wikipedia. Figure below simulates Garuda – eagle. This indicates how deep was the research and knowledge acquired by Sanskrit Speaking Civilization?

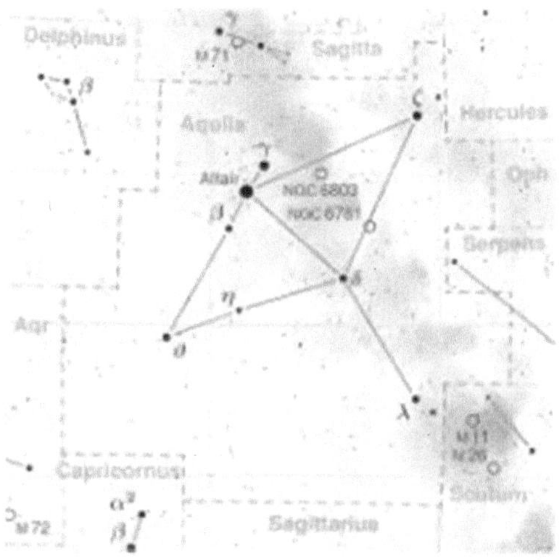

Tarksha is Garuda and in English is Eagle. Rigveda description is exactly matches Greek assumption. Rigveda is considered the oldest ever written document. It is unfortunate that the Rishi culture is ignored, and due credit is missing to the Vedic knowledge.

APPENDIX 2

The Vedas speak of thirty-three different deities.

According to the Shatapatha Brahmana, these thirty-three deities include eight Vasus, eleven Rudras, twelve Adityas, Dyaus, and Prithvi.

Yajnavalkya at one stage says, 'The eight Vasus, eleven Rudras, twelve Adityas, Indra and Prajapati are the thirty-three gods".

According to Yaska, the original thirty-three gods (eight Vasus, eleven Rudras, twelve Adityas and two Asvinis) are divided equally in three different planes of existence namely the celestial plane (dyuloka) the intermediate region (antarikshaloka) and the terrestrial plane (bhurloka) each plane having eleven gods.

The dyuloka (celestial plane) is presided over by Savitri or Surya; while antarikshaloka (intermediary space) is presided over by Indra or Vayu; and the bhurloka (terrestrial plane) is presided over by Agni.

2. Agni has a special position among the Vedic gods. Agni is the symbol of Paramatman and all the other gods are different aspects or manifestations of Agni. According to many scholars, the appropriate Vedic symbol of the Supreme is Agni. Agni is the fire principle that shines in the sun and is the one who carries our offerings to other gods. Agni is the fire of inner awakening. He is the friend of man and mediates on our behalf. He is the symbol of wisdom, knowledge, compassion and lordship.

3. It would be safer to make a distinction between The God the Supreme principle the substratum of all existence; and the gods who represent different aspects, powers and glory of the God. While the God is One, the gods are many. All the gods lead to One God. And, one should make a distinction between a path and the goal.The goal is consciousness of the Supreme in all its manifestations.

4. All gods mentioned in the Rig-Veda have human features such as the face, limbs etc, their forms are shadowy but they have a distinct power and personality.

For instance; Indra is endowed with strength and vigor; Pushan with ability to protect; so is Vishnu. The sun stands for many forms of brilliance; while Rudra represents the anger.

The physical features represent a specific form of nature.

APPENDIX 3

CLEVE BACKSTERb. 1924. He talked to plants. And they talked back. In human subjects, a polygraph measures three things: pulse, respiration rate and galvanic skin response, otherwise known as perspiration. If you're worried about being caught in a lie, your levels will spike or dip. Backster wanted to induce a similar anxiety in the plant, so he decided to set one of its leaves on fire. But before he could even get a match, the polygraph registered an intense reaction on the part of the Dracaena. To Backster, the implication was as indisputable as it was unbelievable. Not only had the plant demonstrated fear — it had also read his mind. y had the plant demonstrated fear — it had also read his mind. Backster concluded that plants had some heretofore undiscovered sense (he called it "primary perception") that could detect and respond to human thoughts and emotions. When he publicized his findings, the so-called Backster effect became a pop-culture hit. There was a TV program hosted by Leonard Nimoy and a best-selling book, "The Secret Life of Plants," inspired by Backster's research. Backster was interviewed by Johnny Carson, Art Linkletter, Merv Griffin and David Frost. Even Backster's old employers at the C.I.A. investigated the possibility of human-plant communication. Not only had the plant demonstrated fear — it had also read his mind.Scientists, however, were less convinced. No one could reproduce Backster's results — a problem Backster explained away with a variety of post-hoc qualifiers. (A lettuce leaf didn't respond to harmful stimuli? It probably shut down to protect itself.) As a result, Backster mainly worked outside the establishment, publishing his findings in outlets like The International Journal of Parapsychology, Volume X. And yet — publicly, at least — his faith never wavered. Backster went on experimenting until the end, expanding his theory of nonhuman consciousness to encompass chicken eggs and even sperm, forever finding more proof of what he called the "fundamental attunement between living things." He never married, preferring the company of his Siamese cats, and he never again performed experiments that burned plants. If the pseudoscience of his second act retroactively called into question the science of his first — after all, what is lie detection but mind-reading by another name? — Backster remained unbowed. "Such high resistance to new ideas does not concern me," he once said. "I have a truly wonderful ally: Mother Nature."

APPENDIX 4

SKANDA PURAN

Verse 4.2.21.5. parent: Chapter 21

स्वयमिंद्रः स्वयं वायुः स्वयं चंद्रः स्वयं यमः ।स्वयमग्निः स्वयं पाशी धनदोभूत्स्वयं बली ॥ ५ ॥

svayamiṃdraḥ svayaṃ vāyuḥ svayaṃ caṃdraḥ svayaṃ yamaḥ |svayamagniḥ svayaṃ pāśī dhanadobhūtsvayaṃ balī || 5 ||

The English translation of Skandapurana Verse 4.2.21.5 is contained in the book The Skanda-Purana by G. V. Tagare. This book is available online or you could buy the latest edition:

1) Indra (इन्द्र—:(m. (for [etymology] as given by native authorities See, [Nirukta, by Yāska x, 8; Sāyaṇa on Ṛg-veda i, 3, 4; Uṇādi-sūtra ii, 28]; according to, [Boehtlingk & Roth's Sanskrit-Woerterbuch] [from] *in* = √*inv* with [suffix] *ra* preceded by inserted *d*, meaning 'to subdue, conquer'; according to Muir, S. T, [v, 119], for *sindra* [from] √*syand*, 'to drop'; more probably from √*ind*, 'to drop' q.v., and connected with *indu* above), the god of the atmosphere and sky

2) the Indian Jupiter Pluvius or lord of rain (who in Vedic mythology reigns over the deities of the intermediate region or atmosphere; he fights against and conquers with his thunder-bolt [*vajra*] the demons of darkness, and is in general a symbol of generous heroism; *indra* was not originally lord of the gods of the sky, but his deeds were most useful to mankind, and he was therefore addressed in prayers and hymns more than any other deity, and ultimately superseded the more lofty and spiritual Varuṇa; in the later mythology *indra* is subordinated to the triad Brahman, Viṣṇu, and Śiva, but remained the chief of all other deities in the popular

mind), [Ṛg-veda; Atharva-veda; Śatapatha-brāhmaṇa; Manu-smṛti; Mahābhārata; Rāmāyaṇa] etc. etc.

3) (he is also regent of the east quarter, and considered one of the twelve Ādityas), [Manu-smṛti; Rāmāyaṇa; Suśruta] etc.

4) in the Vedānta he is identified with the supreme being

5) a prince

6) ifc. best, excellent, the first, the chief (of any class of objects; cf. *surendra*, *rājendra*, *parvatendra*, etc.), [Manu-smṛti; Hitopadeśa]

7) the pupil of the right eye (that of the left being called Indrāṇī or Indra's wife), [Śatapatha-brāhmaṇa; Bṛhad-āraṇyaka-upaniṣad]

8) the number fourteen, [Sūryasiddhānta]

9) Name of a grammarian

10) of a physician

11) the plant Wrightia Antidysenterica (See *kuṭaja*), [cf. Lexicographers, esp. such as amarasiṃha, halāyudha, hemacandra, etc.]

12) a vegetable poison, [cf. Lexicographers, esp. such as amarasiṃha, halāyudha, hemacandra, etc.]

13) the twenty-sixth Yoga or division of a circle on the plane of the ecliptic

14) the Yoga star in the twenty-sixth Nakṣatra, γ Pegasi

15) the human soul, the portion of spirit residing in the body

16) night, [cf. Lexicographers, esp. such as amarasiṃha, halāyudha, hemacandra, etc.]

17) one of the nine divisions of Jambu-dvīpa or the known continent, [cf. Lexicographers, esp. such as amarasiṃha, halāyudha, hemacandra, etc.]

18) Indrā (इन्द्रा]—:(from indra] f. the wife of Indra See indrāṇī

19) [v.s....] Name of a plant, [cf. Lexicographers, esp. such as amarasiṃha, halāyudha, hemacandra, etc.]

Source: Cologne Digital Sanskrit Dictionaries: Yates Sanskrit-English Dictionary

Indra (इन्द्र—:((ndraḥ) 1. m. The deity presiding over the Hindu paradise; the supreme Being; an organ of sense. (In comp.) Best. (ndrā) f. Wife of Indra; a plant.

Source: DDSA: Paia-sadda-mahannavo; a comprehensive Prakrit Hindi dictionary (S)

Indra (इन्द्र (in the Sanskrit language is related to the Prakrit words: Iṃda, Iṃdā.

[Sanskrit to German]

Indra in German

context information

Sanskrit, also spelled संस्कृतम्)*saṃskṛtam*), is an ancient language of India commonly seen as the grandmother of the Indo-European language family (even English!). Closely allied with Prakrit and Pali, Sanskrit is more exhaustive in both grammar and terms and has the most extensive collection of literature in the world, greatly surpassing its sister-languages Greek and Latin.

Discover the meaning of *indra* in the context of Sanskrit from relevant books on Exotic India

APPENDIX 5

Translations available

Title	Commentary/Translation	Year	Language	Notes
Ṛig-Veda-Sanhitā: A Collection of Ancient Hindu Hymns	H. H. Wilson[148]	1850–88	English	Published as 6 volumes, by N. Trübner & Co., London.
Rigved Bhashyam	Dayananda Saraswati	1877–9	Hindi	Incomplete translation. Later translated into English by Dharma Deva Vidya Martanda (1974).
The Hymns of the Rig Veda	Ralph T.H. Griffith[148]	1889–92	English	Revised as *The Rig Veda* in 1896. Revised by J. L. Shastri in 1973. Griffith's philology was outdated even in the 19th-century and questioned by scholars.[148]
Der Rigveda in Auswahl	Karl Friedrich Geldner[148]	1907	German	Published by Kohlhammer Verlag, Stuttgart. Geldner's 1907 work was a partial translation; he completed a full translation in the 1920s, which was published after his death, in 1951.[148] This translation was titled *Der Rig-Veda: aus dem Sanskrit ins Deutsche Übersetzt*. Harvard Oriental

Title	Commentary/Translation	Year	Language	Notes
				Studies, vols. 33–37 (Cambridge, Massachusetts: 1951–7). Reprinted by Harvard University Press (2003) ISBN 0-674-01226-7.
Hymns from the Rigveda	A. A. Macdonell	1917	English	Partial translation (30 hymns). Published by Clarendon Press, Oxford.
Series of articles in Journal of the University of Bombay	Hari Damodar Velankar[148]	1940s–1960s	English	Partial translation (Mandala 2, 5, 7 and 8). Later published as independent volumes.
Rig Veda – Hymns to the Mystic Fire Archived 8 September 2014 at the Wayback Machine	Sri Aurobindo	1946	English	Partial translation published by N. K. Gupta, Pondicherry. Later republished several times (ISBN 978-0-914955-22-1)
Rig Veda	Ramgovind Trivedi	1954	Hindi	
ऋग्वेद संहिता	Shriram Sharma	1950s	Hindi	
Rigveda Parichaya	Nag Sharan Singh	1977	English / Hindi	Extension of Wilson's translation. Republished by Nag, Delhi in 1990 (ISBN 978-81-7081-217-3).
The Rig Veda	Wendy Doniger O'Flaherty	1981	English	Partial translation (108 hymns), along with critical apparatus. Published by Penguin (ISBN 0-14-044989-2). A bibliography of

Title	Commentary/Translation	Year	Language	Notes
				translations of the Rig Veda appears as an Appendix.
Pinnacles of India's Past: Selections from the Rgveda	Walter H. Maurer	1986	English	Partial translation published by John Benjamins.
The Rig Veda	Bibek Debroy, Dipavali Debroy	1992	English	Partial translation published by B. R. Publishing (ISBN 978-0-8364-2778-3). The work is in verse form, without reference to the original hymns or mandalas. Part of *Great Epics of India: Veda* series, also published as *The Holy Vedas.*
The Holy Vedas: A Golden Treasury	Pandit Satyakam Vidyalankar	1983	English	
Ṛgveda Saṃhitā	H. H. Wilson, Ravi Prakash Arya and K. L. Joshi	2001	English	4-volume set published by Parimal (ISBN 978-81-7110-138-2). Revised edition of Wilson's translation. Replaces obsolete English forms with more modern equivalents (e.g. "thou" with "you"). Includes the original Sanskrit text in Devanagari script, along with a critical apparatus.
Ṛgveda for the Layman	Shyam Ghosh	2002	English	Partial translation (100 hymns).

Title	Commentary/Translation	Year	Language	Notes
				Munshiram Manoharlal, New Delhi.
ऋग्वेद	Govind Chandra Pande	2008	Hindi	Partial translation (Mandala 3 and 5). Published by Lokbharti, Allahabad
The Hymns of Rig Veda	Tulsi Ram	2013	English	Published by Vijaykumar Govindram Hasanand, Delhi
The Rigveda	Stephanie W. Jamison and Joel P. Brereton	2014	English	3-volume set published by Oxford University Press (ISBN 978-0-19-937018-4). Funded by the United States' National Endowment for the Humanities in 2004.[154]

APPENDIX 6

Mantrapushpanjali.

As per puja ceremony, at the end certain mantras are recited. Ts are from different these mantras are from different sources of the Sanskrit literature. Detailed account is given below:

ॐ यज्ञेन यज्ञमयजन्त देवास्तानि धर्माणि प्रथमान्यासन् | ते ह नाकं महिमानः सचन्त यत्र पूर्वे साध्याः सन्ति देवाः || 1 || Ṛgveda, 1, 1 smann वयं वैश्रवणाय कुर्महे | स मे कामान्कामकामाय मह्यम् कामेश्वरो वैश्रवणो ददातु | कुबेराय वैश्रवणाय महाराजाय नमः || 2 || Taittiriya Aranyaka, Prapāṭhaka 1, Anuvāka 31, Mantra 6.

ॐ स्वस्ति| साम्राज्यं भौज्यं स्वाराज्यं वैराज्यं पारमेष्ठ्यं राज्यं माहाराज्यमाधिपत्यमयं समंतपर्यायी स्यात्सार्वभौमः सार्वायुष आंतादापरार्धात्पृथिव्यै समुद्रपर्यंताया एकराळिति || 3 || Hymn 3 (sāmrājyam... ekarāḷiti) is from Aitareya Brahmana, Pañcikā VIII, Khaṇḍa 15.

तदप्येषः श्लोको ऽभिगीतो |मरुतः परिवेष्टारो मरुत्तस्यावसन् गृहे | आविक्षितस्य कामप्रेर्विश्वे देवाः सभासद इति || 4 ||. Hymn 4 (tadapyeṣa... iti) is also from Aitareya Brahmana, Pañcikā VIII, Khaṇḍa 21.

वि॒श्वत॑श्चक्षुरु॒त वि॒श्वतो॑मुखो वि॒श्वतो॑बाहुरु॒त वि॒श्वत॑स्पात् । सं बा॒हुभ्यां॒ धम॑ति॒ सं पत॑त्रै॒र्द्यावा॒भूमी॑ ज॒नय॑न्दे॒व एकः॑ :॥ 5 ॥ Rigveda (10.81.3).

Hymn 1

यज्ञेन यज्ञमयजन्त देवास्तानि धर्माणि प्रथमान्यासन् | ते ह नाकं महिमानः सचन्त यत्र पूर्वे साध्याः सन्ति देवाः || 1 ||

By means of sacrifice the Gods accomplished their sacrifice: these were the earliest ordinances. These Mighty Ones attained the height of heaven, there where the Sādhyas, Gods of old, are dwelling.[4]

Origin: Hymn 1 (yajñena... devāḥ) is from Ṛgveda, Mandala 1, Sūkta 164, Ṛc 50.[5] This hymn also occurs in Ṛgveda, Mandala 10, Sūkta 90, Ṛc 16 and in Atharvaveda, Kāṇḍa 7, Sūkta 5, Mantra 1.

Hymn 2

ॐ राजाधिराजाय प्रसह्यसाहिने नमो वयं वैश्रवणाय कुर्महे | स मे कामान्कामकामाय मह्यम् कामेश्वरो वैश्रवणो ददातु | कुबेराय वैश्रवणाय महाराजाय नमः || 2 ||

We bow to Rājādhirāja Prasahyasāhī Vaiśravaṇa. May he, Kāmeshvara Vaiśravaṇa, grant me my desires for enjoyment of pleasures. [We] bow to Mahārāja Vaiśravaṇa Kubera.[6]

Hymn 2 honours Vaiśravaṇa Kubera, a Vedic deity. Vaiśravaṇa (descendant of Viśravas), Rājādhirāja (king of kings), Prasahyasāhī (victorious conqueror), Kāmeshvara (god of wishes or desires), and Mahārāja (a great king) are all epithets of Kubera.

Origin: Hymn 2 (rājādhirājāya... namaḥ) is from Taittiriya Aranyaka, Prapāṭhaka 1, Anuvāka 31, Mantra 6.

Hymn 3

साम्राज्यं भौज्यं स्वाराज्यं वैराज्यं पारमेष्ठ्यं राज्यं माहाराज्यमाधिपत्यमयं समंतपर्यायी स्यात्सार्वभौमः सार्वायुष आंतादापरार्धात्पृथिव्यै समुद्रपर्यंताया एकराळिति || 3 ||

... Universal sovereignty, enjoyment (of pleasures), independence, distinguished distinction as a king, the fulfilment of the highest desires, the position of a king, of a great king, and supreme mastership, that he might cross (with his arms) the universe, and become the ruler of the whole earth during all his life, which may last for an infinitely long time, that he might be the sole king of the earth up to its shores bordering on the ocean.[7]

Hymn 3 is a wish-list of a priest for his Kśattriya host of the Mahābhiśeka ("great inauguration") ceremony. Context for Hymn 3 is provided by the portion [...] below from the translation by Haug.

[Fourth chapter (The Mahābhisheka ceremony performed on a King. What Rishis performed it, and for what Kings they performed it.) 15. (The consequences of Mahābhisheka. The oath which the King must take before the priest performs the ceremony.) The priest who, with this knowledge (about the Mahābhisheka ceremony) wishes that a Kshattriya should conquer in all the various ways of conquest, to subjugate all people, and that he should attain to leadership, precedence, and supremacy over all kings, and attain everywhere and at all times to] universal sovereignty, enjoyment (of pleasures), independence, distinguished distinction as a king, the fulfilment of the highest desires, the position of a king, of a great king, and supreme mastership, that he might cross (with his arms) the universe, and become the ruler of the whole earth during all his life, which may last for an infinitely long time, that he might be the sole king of the earth up to its shores bordering on the ocean; [such a priest should inaugurate the Kshattriya with Indra's great inauguration ceremony. But before doing so, the priest must make the king take the following oath: "Whatever pious works thou mightest have done during the time which may elapse from the day of thy birth to the day of thy death, all together with thy position, thy good deeds, thy life, thy children, I would wrest from thee, shouldest thou do me any harm." The Kshattriya then who wishes to attain to all this, should well consider and say in good faith all that is above mentioned (thou mayest wrest from me, &c. &c.)]

Monier Williams provides different translations of some words.[8] For example, Monier Williams translates bhuaujya as "the rank of a king with the title of bhoja", vairājya as "extended sovereignty", māhārajya as "the rank of a reigning prince or sovereign", pārameṣṭhya as "highest position, supremacy", samantaparyāyin as "all-embracing", and sārvāyuṣa as "possessing full vitality or vigour".

Origin: Hymn 3 (sāmrājyam... ekarāḷiti) is from Aitareya Brahmana, Pañcikā VIII, Khaṇḍa 15.

Hymn 4

तदप्येषः श्लोको ऽभिगीतो | मरुतः परिवेष्टारो मरुत्तस्यावसन् गृहे | आविक्षितस्य कामप्रेर्विश्वे देवाः सभासद इति || 4 ||

Regarding this event there is the following Stotra chanted: "The Maruts resided as the distributors of food in the house of Marutta, the son of Avikshit, who had fulfilled all his desires; all the gods were present at the gathering."[9]

Hymn 4 describes an episode about Marutta, a king inaugurated with the Mahabhiśeka ceremony, who went on to conquer the whole earth and performed the horse offering. Context for Hymn 4 is provided by the portion [...] below from the translation by Haug.

[21. (What kings had the Mahābhisheka ceremony performed; their conquest of the whole earth, and the horse sacrifices. Stanzas on Janamejaya, Vishvakarma and Marutta.) ... With this inauguration ceremony Samparta, the son of Angiras, inaugurated Marutta, son of Avikshit. Thence Marutta went conquering everywhere over the whole earth up to its ends, and offered the ceremonial horse.)] Regarding this event there is the following Stotra chanted: "The Maruts resided as the distributors of food in the house of Marutta, the son of Avikshit, who had fulfilled all his desires; all the gods were present at the gathering."

Monier Williams translates Āvikśita as a descendant of Avikśit, and Kāmapri as son of Kāmapra, name of Marutta. Monier Williams also translates viśve devāḥ as "all the gods collectively" or the "All-gods" (a particular class of gods, plural of viśva deva, forming one of the nine gaṇas enumerated under gaṇadevatā).

Origin: Hymn 4 (tadapyeṣa... iti) is also from Aitareya Brahmana, Pañcikā VIII, Khaṇḍa 21.

The auspicious salutations ॐ) om) and ॐ स्वस्ति) om svasti) are later additions to the original Vedic text.

Hymn 5

वि॒श्वत॑श्चक्षुरु॒त वि॒श्वतो॑मुखो वि॒श्वतो॑बाहुरु॒त वि॒श्वत॑स्पात् । सं बा॒हुभ्यां॒ धम॑ति॒ सं पत॑त्रै॒र्द्यावा॒भूमी॑ ज॒नय॑न्दे॒व एक॑ :॥ 5 ||

Hymn 5 is often skipped is in currently prevalent recitals of Mantra Pushpanjali performed after Arati. But the original scriptures of Deve have this chanted in a slow rhythm.[10][3][11] The mantra comes originally from Rigveda (10.081.003). It describes the only ultimate supreme truth (एकःदेवः (that created and encapsulates the entire universe and how with its metaphorical strong arms and legs manages the lifecycle of celestial bodies such as stars and earth.

SUGGESTED READING

1. The essentials of Hinduism by Swami Bhaskarananda. 2nd edition, 2002. Reprinted 2005, 2009, 2012. Viveka Press, Seattle.ISBN-10 1884852041.

2. Niramaya. Ved ek paripeksha me. Pratham pushpa. By Dr. Govinda Hari Marathe. 1986. Gwalior. Jaihind. Swadesh Parisar. Jayandra ganj, Gwalior-474009.

3. Veidik vidnyan va Vedkal Nirnaya.By Dr P. V. Vartak Publishar-Vartak Prakashan, and Pushkar P. Vartak, VartakAashram 497, Shanivar Peth, Pune, 411030. 2nd edition, 2012.

4. Yog Vasishtha Ramayana ed by Shriram Acharya Sanskrit Sansthan, Baraily U.P.

5. "Apourusheya Bhashya" by Maharishi Mahesh Yogi Commentary on Rigveda.

6. Bhagwadgita (Vyas meaning), 2nd ed. Publisher ShriT M Harkare, Nagpur, Maharashtra).

7. India's Glorious Scientific Tradition by S. Soni. Ocean Books Pvt. Ltd. Ed. 2010.

8. Cosmology Old and New. By prof. G. R. Jain. Bharatiya Jnanpith publication. 2nd ed. 1991.

9. Rigveda

10. Sayna bhashya on Rigveda

11. RIG-VEDA- SANHITA.THE SACRED HYMNS OF THE BRAHMANSTRANSLATED AND EXPLAINED BY F. MAX MULLER, M.A., LL.D. FELLOW OF ALL SOULS COLLEGE;

PROFESSOR OF COMPARATIVE PHILOLOGY AT OXFORD; FOREIGN MEMBER OF THE INSTITUTE OF FRANCE, ETC., ETC, VOL. I. HYMNS TO THE MAHUTS OR THE STORM-

12. Taittiriya Upanishad Transliterated Sanskrit Text Free Translation & Brief Explanation By T.N. Sethumadhavan Published In Esamskriti.com 27th October, 2011 Kartika Shukla Pratipada (Bali Pratipada) Nagpur tnsethumadhavan@gmail.co

13. Exploration of science in Shrimadbhagwadgita. Analytical study by Dr. B. G. Matapurkar. Mahi Publication, ISBN: 978-93-89339-47-5. !st edition 2020. Ahmedabad.India.

14. Song of Science. Shri Madbhagwadgita. Dr. B.G.Matapurkar. Notion Press. 1st ed. 2020. India, Singapor, Malaysia. ISBN 978-1-63714-582-1

15. Exploration of Science in Shri Madbhagwadgita. Analytical study by Dr. B. G. Matapurkar. Mahi Publication. Ahemdabad2020. ISBN 978-93-89339-47-5

16. Scientific perspective of Universal Eternal Dharm and Religion. Analytical thought by Dr. b. g. Matapurkar. First ed 2022. Pigion Books India. Imprint by GBD Books. Printed at Repro books Ltd.

17. RIG-VED-SAMHITA. Sacred hymns of the Brahmins.by F. MAX MULLER 1869

18. Astronomy and its Role in Vedic Culture Subhash Kak Louisiana State University Baton Rouge, LA 70803-5901, USA Chapter 23 in Science and Civilization in India, Vol. 1, The Dawn of Indian Civilization, Part 1, edited by G.C. Pande, ICPR/Munshiram Manoharlal, Delhi, 2000, pp. 507-524.

19. Hidden science in Rigved. Pigeon books. By B. G. Matapurkar 1st ed. 2022.

ABOUT AUTHOR

Dr. B. G. Matapurkar

Dr. B. G. Matapurkar is a Surgeon retired from CHS, Govt. of India. He is a renowned scientist and has international patents to his credit (International patent Office USA 1995, 2002, and 2003). His innovative research is on Adult Stem Cells. He has used body tissue cells for the regeneration of tissues and organs in the body. With this technique, a few new operative techniques have been developed which are published in Medical Textbooks. He has a new physiological phenomenon of "Desired Metaplasia" to his credit. The use of stem cells is useful for future "space travel" by providing food production in Spacecraft and Space labs – a lightweight cargo.

Received National and International awards including elected active membership in the New York Academy of Sciences (a 200-year-old science organization). Limca Book of World Records, G. R. Medical College Ratna, etc. His Biography has been published in various National and International Biography books of repute.

He has scientifically analyzed the birth of 101 children (Kauravas) from the Adi Parva of Mahabharat. He has mentioned this event at many national and international conferences. It became PTI news in 2002 and was broadcasted on many National and International TV channels. He has delivered lectures on hidden Science in GITA and Purana on International and National invitations.

During his posting at Andaman and Nicobar Islands, he developed Intra Venous use of (local resource) tender coconut water and published his research in medical journals. He was forced to carry out such research due to short supply, scarcity, or nonavailability of Intravenous fluids in the remotest territory of A. N. Islands in 1974 to 1976, and proved aphorism that Necessity is the mother of invention.

www.ingramcontent.com/pod-product-compliance
Lightning Source LLC
LaVergne TN
LVHW041009150826
845672LV00001B/25

* 9 7 9 8 8 9 4 9 8 8 5 9 7 *